ARCHAIC FEATURES OF CANAANITE PERSONAL NAMES IN THE HEBREW BIBLE

HARVARD SEMITIC MUSEUM

HARVARD SEMITIC MONOGRAPHS

edited by
Frank Moore Cross

Number 47
Archaic Features
of Canaanite Personal Names
in the Hebrew Bible

by
Scott C. Layton

Scott C. Layton

ARCHAIC FEATURES OF CANAANITE PERSONAL NAMES IN THE HEBREW BIBLE

Scholars Press
Atlanta, Georgia

Archaic Features of Canaanite Personal Names in the Hebrew Bible

by
Scott C. Layton

Library of Congress Cataloging in Publication Data

Layton, Scott C. 1953-
Archaic features of Canaanite personal names in the Hebrew Bible /
Scott C. Layton.
p. cm. -- (Harvard Semitic monographs ; no. 47)
Originally presented as the author's thesis (Ph.D.--University of Chicago, 1987).
Includes bibliographical references and indexes.
ISBN 1-55540-513-4 (alk. paper)
1. Names in the Bible. 2. Names, Personal--Canaanite.
3. Canaanite language--Inflection. I. Title. II. Series.
BS1199.N2L38 1990
492'..6--dc20

90-41663
CIP

Acknowledgments

This study is a thorough revision of a dissertation submitted to the Department of Near Eastern Languages and Civilizations at the University of Chicago in October 1987. I would like to take this opportunity to thank those who assisted me in the preparation of this study. I am deeply indebted to Dennis Pardee, who introduced me to the study of Northwest Semitic and directed the course of this dissertation. Not only did he give unstintingly of his time, but he also provided encouragement for a topic that lay outside the beaten path. I would also like to thank the other members of my committee, Walter Farber, and Gene Gragg, each of whom made valuable suggestions in their fields of specialization, namely, in Akkadian and South Semitic respectively, as well as in general linguistics. Special thanks are also tendered to Jan Johnson, who read the portions of this study that touch upon the field of Egyptology. Gary Greig and Michael Wise contributed as a result of discussions on certain points.

While researching a related topic in Israel, I received encouragement and constructive criticism from Ran Zadok, Jonas Greenfield, and Avi Hurwitz. John Huehnergard's criticisms and suggestions improved this study considerably. Many thanks to Professor Frank M. Cross, Jr, who accepted this study for publication in the Harvard Semitic Series. I am grateful to Southwestern University, where I was provided unlimited access to the Apple LaserWriter. Finally, I wish to acknowledge the support and encouragement of my wife, Jane Ann, without whom this study could not have been completed, and who had to endure both the composition and revision of this study.

Contents

Acknowledgments iii

Abbreviations viii

Chapter

1. INTRODUCTION 1

I. Language, Proper Names, and Archaic Features 1
A. Language and Proper Names 1
B. Proper Names and Archaic Features 4
C. Archaic Features and Semitic Proper Names 8
II. Methodology 12
A. Scope and Format of Study 12
B. On the Separation of Canaanite PNN from Other PNN 15
C. On the Nature of Linguistic Evidence in the Text of the Hebrew Bible 18
D. On the Detection of Archaic Morphological Features.. 21
E. On the Interpretation of Canaanite PNN 22
III. Sources for the Study of West Semitic PNN 25
A. Alphabetic, Syllabic Cuneiform, and Hieroglyphic Scripts 26
B. Early West Semitic PNN (second millennium B.C. and earlier) 28
C. Late West Semitic PNN (first millennium B.C. and later) 32

2. THE NOMINATIVE CASE ENDING *-U* 37

I. Early West Semitic 38
II. Canaanite 46
III. Canaanite PNN in the Hebrew Bible 49
A. Probable Examples 50
B. Dubious Examples 87
1. Medial *û* 87

2. Final *û* 94
3. Final *ô* 98
C. Non-Canaanite Example 100
IV. Late West Semitic PNN (extrabiblical) 101
V. Summary 103

3. THE *ḤIREQ COMPAGINIS* 107

I. Early West Semitic 109
II. Canaanite 115
III. Canaanite PNN in the Hebrew Bible 118
A. On the Detection of the h.c. in Canaanite PNN 118
B. Probable Examples 122
C. Ambiguous Examples 129
D. Dubious Examples 131
E. Non-Canaanite Examples 142
1. Probable Example 142
2. Ambiguous Example 145
F. Compound PNN Formed with Kinship Terms 145
IV. Late West Semitic PNN (extrabiblical) 150
V. Summary 153

4. MIMATION AND ENCLITIC *-M* 155

I. Early West Semitic 156
II. Canaanite 166
III. Canaanite PNN in the Hebrew Bible 167
A. Probable Examples 168
B. Dubious Examples 181
C. Non-Canaanite Examples 189
1. Probable Examples 190
2. Dubious Example 192
IV. Late West Semitic PNN (extrabiblical) 193
V. Summary 196

5. THE FEMININE MORPHEME *-AT* 199

I. Early West Semitic 199
II. Canaanite 201
III. Canaanite PNN in the Hebrew Bible 204
A. Probable Examples 205
B. Dubious Examples 223

IV. Late West Semitic PNN (extrabiblical) 228
V. Summary 230

6. **CONCLUSIONS** 233

I. The Nominative Case Vowel *-u* 234
II. *The Ḥireq Compaginis* 236
III. Enclitic *-m* 236
IV. The Feminine Morpheme *-at* 238
V. Synthesis 239

Appendix: The Feminine Morpheme *-(a)y* 241

I. Early West Semitic 241
II. Canaanite 246
III. Canaanite PNN in the Hebrew Bible 246
1. Probable Example 246
IV. Late West Semitic PNN (extrabiblical) 248
V. Summary 249

Bibliography 251

Indices 293

Abbreviations

1. *General*

A	Arad
ABH	Archaic Biblical Hebrew
Akk.	Akkadian
Amm.	Ammonite
Amor.	Amorite
Arab.	Arabian
Aram.	Aramaic
BH	Biblical Hebrew
C	consonant
Can.	Canaanite
CN(N)	Common noun(s)
c.s.	common singular
EA	El-Amarna
Edom.	Edomite
Eg.	Egyptian
EH	Epigraphic Hebrew
GA(A)	Gentilic adjective(s)
GN(N)	Geographical name(s)
Grk	Greek
Ḥaḍ.	Ḥaḍrami
Hat.	Hatran
h.c.	*ḥireq compaginis*
IAram.	Imperial Aramaic
JAram.	Jewish Aramaic
K	Kethiv
L	Lachish
LB	Late Babylonian
LBH	Late Biblical Hebrew
Liḥ.	Liḥyanite
LXX A	Septuagint, Codex Alexandrinus
LXX B	Septuagint, Codex Vaticanus
MB	Middle Babylonian
Min.	Minaean
MLArab.	Modern Literary Arabic
Moab.	Moabite

m.s.	masculine singular
MT	Masoretic Text
NA	Neo-Assyrian
Nab.	Nabatean
NB	Neo-Babylonian
OAram.	Old Aramaic
Palm.	Palmyrene
Ph.	Phoenician
Ph-P.	Phoenician-Punic
PN(N)	Personal name(s)
Pun.	Punic
Q	Qere
Qat.	Qatabanian
S	Samaria
Sab.	Sabaean
Saf.	Safaitic
SamP	Samaritan Pentateuch
SArab.	South Arabian
SBH	Standard Biblical Hebrew
s.v.	sub voce, under the word in question
Syr.	Syriac
SyrP	Syriac Peshiṭta
Tham.	Thamudic
Ug.	Ugaritic
v	vowel
WS	West Semitic
*	original, reconstructed, or unattested form
=	two forms have same referent
>	becomes
<	derives from
[ ]	marks break and restoration
⌜ ⌝	marks partially damaged signs
?	marks uncertainty
!	indicates the preceding letter, word, or statement is not a slip of the pen

Abbreviations of the Names of Biblical Books are in accordance with the guidelines established by the Society of Biblical Literature.

The masculine determinative is omitted in the transliteration of the masculine PNN discussed throughout this study.

2. *Literature*

AB	Anchor Bible
AcOr	*Acta Orientalia* (Copenhagen)
AfO	*Archiv für Orientforschung*
AION	*Annali dell'istituto orientali di Napoli*
AJSL	*American Journal of Semitic Languages and Literatures*
ALIA	Kent P. Jackson, *The Ammonite Language of the Iron Age*
AmPN	Richard S. Hess, *Amarna Proper Names*
ANG	Johann Jakob Stamm, *Die Akkadische Namengebung*
APN	Knut L. Tallqvist, *Assyrian Personal Names*
AOAT	Alter Orient und Altes Testament
APNMT	Herbert B. Huffmon, *Amorite Personal Names in the Mari Texts*
ARET	Archivi reali di Ebla testi
ArOr	*Archiv orientální*
AT	D. J. Wiseman, *The Alalakh Tablets*
ATTM	Klaus Beyer, *Die aramäischen Texte vom Toten Meer*
AURIII	Giorgio Buccellati, *The Amorites of the Ur III Period*
AUSS	*Andrews University Seminary Studies*
BA	*Biblical Archaeologist*
BASOR	*Bulletin of the American Schools of Oriental Research*
BDB	Francis Brown, S. R. Driver, and Charles A. Briggs, *A Hebrew and English Lexicon of the Old Testament*
BHAN	Johann Jakob Stamm, *Beiträge zur hebräischen und altorientalischen Namenkunde*
BHS	*Biblia Hebraica Stuttgartensia*
Bib	*Biblica*
BJPES	*Bulletin of the Jewish Palestine Exploration Society*
BJRL	*Bulletin of the John Rylands University Library of Manchester*
BL	Hans Bauer and Pontus Leander, *Historische Grammatik der hebräischen Sprache des Alten Testament*
BM	*Beth Mikra*
BN	*Biblische Notizen*
BO	*Bibliotheca orientalis*
BSOAS	*Bulletin of the School of Oriental and African Studies*
BZ	*Biblische Zeitschrift*
BZAW	Beiheft zur Zeitschrift für die alttestamentliche Wissenschaft
CAAA	Ignace J. Gelb, *Computer-Aided Analysis of Amorite*

CAD	*The Assyrian Dictionary of the Oriental Institute of the University of Chicago*
CBQ	*Catholic Biblical Quarterly*
CGSL	Sabatino Moscati, ed., *An Introduction to the Comparative Grammar of the Semitic Languages: Phonology and Morphology*
DBS	*Dictionnaire de la Bible, Supplément*
EB	*Encyclopaedia Biblica*
EI	*Eretz-Israel*
EncJud	C. Roth et al., eds., *Encyclopaedia Judaica*
EM	E. L. Sukenik et al., eds., *Enṣîqlôpedyâ Miqrāʾît*
ETL	*Ephemerides theologicae lovanienses*
ExpTim	*Expository Times*
GAG	Wolfram von Soden, *Grundriss der akkadischen Grammatik*
GAGNWS	Daniel Sivan, *Grammatical Analysis and Glossary of the Northwest Semitic Vocables in Akkadian Texts of the 15th-13th C.B.C. from Canaan and Syria*
GKC	W. Gesenius, *Gesenius' Hebrew Grammar*, ed. E. Kautzsch and A. E. Cowley, 28th ed.
GM	*Göttinger Miszellen*
GVG	Carl Brockelmann, *Grundriss der vergleichenden Grammatik der semitischen Sprachen*
HSM	Harvard Semitic Monographs
HSS	Harvard Semitic Series
HUCA	*Hebrew Union College Annual*
ICC	International Critical Commentary
IEJ	*Israel Exploration Journal*
IOS	*Israel Oriental Studies*
IPN	Martin Noth, *Die israelitischen Personennamen im Rahmen der gemeinsemitischen Namengebung*
JANES	*Journal of the Ancient Near Eastern Society*
JAOS	*Journal of the American Oriental Society*
JBL	*Journal of Biblical Literature*
JBR	*Journal of Bible and Religion*
JCS	*Journal of Cuneiform Studies*
JJS	*Journal of Jewish Studies*
JNES	*Journal of Near Eastern Studies*
JNSL	*Journal of the Northwest Semitic Languages*
JPOS	*Journal of the Palestine Oriental Society*
JQR	*Jewish Quarterly Review*
JSJ	*Journal for the Study of Judaism*
JSS	*Journal of Semitic Studies*

JTS	*Journal of Theological Studies*
KAI	H. Donner and W. Röllig, *Kanaanäische und aramäische Inschriften*
KAT	Kommentar zum Alten Testament
KB2	Ludwig Koehler and Walter Baumgartner, *Lexicon in Veteris Testamenti Libros*, 2d ed.
KB3	Ludwig Koehler and Walter Baumgartner, *Hebräisches und aramäische Lexikon zum Alten Testament*, 3d ed.
KTU	M. Dietrich, O. Loretz, and J. Sanmartín, *Die keil-alphabetischen Texte aus Ugarit, Teil I: Transkription*
MVAG	Mitteilungen der vorderasiatisch-ägyptischen Gesellschaft
NFJ	Abraham Shalit, *Namenwörterbuch zu Flavius Josephus*
OAA	Walter Kornfeld, *Onomastica Aramaica aus Äypten*
OBO	Orbis biblicus et orientalis
OLP	*Orientalia lovaniensia periodica*
OLZ	*Orientalistische Literaturzeitung*
Or	*Orientalia*
OrAnt	*Oriens antiquus*
PEFQS	*Palestine Exploration Fund, Quarterly Statement*
PEQ	*Palestine Exploration Quarterly*
PIAN	G. Lankester Harding, *An Index and Concordance of Pre-Islamic Arabian Names and Inscriptions*
PIH	Sabri Abbadi, *Die Personennamen der Inschriften aus Hatra*
PNPI	Jürgen K. Stark, *Personal Names in Palmyrene Inscriptions*
PNPP	Frank L. Benz, *Personal Names in the Phoenician and Punic Inscriptions*
PSBA	*Proceedings of the Society of Biblical Archaeology*
PTU	Frauke Gröndahl, *Die Personennamen der Texte aus Ugarit*
PRU	*Le palais royal d'Ugarit*
QDAP	*Quarterly of the Department of Antiquities in Palestine*
RA	*Revue d'assyriologie et d'archéologie orientale*
RANL	*Rendiconti della classe di scienze morali, storiche e filologiche della Accademia Nazionale dei Lincei*
RB	*Revue biblique*
RHR	*Revue de l'histoire des religions*
RivB	*Rivista biblica*
RSO	*Rivista degli studi orientali*
RVJPNE	Michael H. Silverman, *Religious Values in the Jewish Proper Names at Elephantine*
SBLDS	SBL Dissertation Series
Sem	*Semitica*

SPARI	Mohammed Maraqten, *Die semitischen Personennamen in den alt- und reicharamäischen Inschriften aus Vorderasien*
TA	*Tel Aviv*
TDOT	*Theological Dictionary of the Old Testament*
TZ	*Theologische Zeitschrift*
UF	*Ugarit-Forschungen*
Ug V	*Ugaritica V*
UT	Cyrus H. Gordon, *Ugaritic Textbook*
VSE	F. Vattioni, "I sigilli ebraici," *Bib* 50 (1969) 357-88; idem, "I sigilli ebraici," *Augustinianum* 11 (1971) 447-54; idem, "Sigilli ebraici III," *AION* 38 (1978) 227-54.
VSP	F. Vattioni, "I sigilli fenici," *AION* 41 (1981) 177-93.
VT	*Vetus Testamentum*
VTSup	Vetus Testamentum, Supplements
WO	*Die Welt des Orients*
WSB	Ran Zadok, *On West Semites in Babylonia during the Chaldean and Achaemenian Periods: An Onomastic Study*
WUS	Joseph Aistleitner, *Wörterbuch der ugaritischen Sprache*
WZKM	*Wiener Zeitschrift für die Kunde des Morgenlandes*
ZA	*Zeitschrift für Assyriologie*
ZAW	*Zeitschrift für die alttestamentliche Wissenschaft*
ZDMG	*Zeitschrift der deutschen morgenländischen Gesellschaft*
ZDPV	*Zeitschrift des deutschen Palästina-Vereins*
ZKT	*Zeitschrift für katholische Theologie*
ZNW	*Zeitschrift für die neutestamentliche Wissenschaft*
ZS	*Zeitschrift für Semitistik und verwandte Gebiete*

CHAPTER 1

INTRODUCTION

I. Language, Proper Names, and Archaic Features

The study of proper names is relevant to many fields of inquiry. Among these may be included literature, sociology, settlement history, prosopography, and the history of religion, to name a few.[1] For our purposes it is the contribution of onomastics to the study of language that claims attention.

A. *Language and Proper Names*

There is a consensus among onomatologists that proper names can be derived, both semantically and morphologically, from an appellative (= common noun) or some other "pre-individualizing" ground form.[2] Initially the proper name and the ground form from which it is derived are homophones. The range of their use, however, is markedly different. Kurylowicz has pointed out that any appellative has both a content and a zone of employment, and the latter is related inversely to the former: the more specific the semantic content, the more restrained the employment of a given word.[3] Since the proper name has an exceedingly rich content, its range of applicability is reduced to the minimum. Originally it referred to a class composed of a single

---

[1]Elsdon C. Smith, "The Significance of Name Study," in *Proceedings of the Eighth International Congress of Onomastic Sciences*, ed. D. P. Blok, Janua Linguarum, Studia memoriae Nicolai van Wijk dedicata, Series Maior, vol. 17 (Paris: Mouton & Co., 1966), pp. 492-99; Francis L. Utley, "The Linguistic Component of Onomastics," *Names* 11 (1963) 146-48. Other applications of onomastic studies may be found in the following periodicals: *Beiträge zur Namenforschung, Names, Onoma, Onomastica* (Wroclaw), and *Revue internationale d'onomastique.*

[2]O. Leys, "Der Eigenname in seinem formalen Verhältnis zum Appellativ," *Beiträge zur Namenforschung*, n.s., 1 (1966) 113-23; Herbert Penzl, "Personal Names and German Noun Inflection," *Names* 30 (1982) 69.

[3]Jerzy Kurylowicz, "La position linguistique du nom propre," *Onomastica* (Wroclaw) 2 (1956) 1-2; reprinted in *Esquisses linguistiques*, ed. Eugenio Coseriu, International Library of General Linguistics, vols. 16/1 & 37 (Munich: Wilhelm Fink, 1973), 16/1:182-83.

individual, and therefore in principle is not transmissible. Whereas common nouns 'designate', proper nouns 'name'.[4]

Since proper nouns do not follow the same currents of change that common nouns do, eventually the homophony that existed between the proper name and its ground form is resolved. While the proper name goes its own way, the appellative develops separately in time. To cite two examples, the German proper names *Witte* and *Grote* are archaic fossilized forms of the current adjectives *weiß* and *groß*, meaning "white" and "great."[5] This divergence can best be understood against the backdrop of one of the most fundamental principles of linguistics--language change. The two aspects of this change are addition and subtraction. Concomitant with creating new forms by internal development and borrowing, old forms fall into disuse, either disappearing entirely or continuing in limited use as archaisms. Weinreich and others have constructed a theory of language change that recognizes the coexistence of an archaic and an innovating form within a grammar.[6] An opposition exists between these forms, and when the social and linguistic issues attached to them are resolved and the opposition is no longer maintained, the receding variant disappears, unless, as we may add, it is retained as an archaism.

Although the appellative or ground form undergoes changes involving many different linguistic levels and many different mechanisms, the proper name is not liable to some of these mechanisms, and in turn undergoes mechanisms of its own (e.g., "Jacob" becomes "Jim"). Indeed to some extent change would be contrary to its very function. As Pulgram states: ". . . once a proper name has become attached to an individual entity, . . . a change would run counter to the aim of its func-

---

[4]For similar remarks, see Benjamin Kedar-Kopfstein, "The Interpretative Element in Transliteration," *Textus* 8 (1973) 57-58; and Wolfgang Fleischer, "Zum Verhältnis von Name und Appellativum im Deutschen," *Wissenschaftliche Zeitschrift der Karl-Marx-Universität Leipzig, Gesellschafts- und Sprachwissenschaftliche Reihe* 13 (1964) 377, who states "Zwischen Namen und Appellativum besteht ein grundsätzlicher Funktionsunterschied, nicht nur ein Gradunterschied. Das Appellativum *charakterisiert*, der Name *identifiziert*."

[5]These examples are cited by Georg Kampffmeyer, "Südarabisches," *ZDMG* 54 (1900) 633-34. To be sure, the difference between the two sets of forms is of a regional and dialectal nature as well. Note also the German names *Otto*, *Berta*, and *Minna*, which preserve the masculine and feminine endings of Old High German, which were elsewhere reduced to ĕ (so F. W. Geers, "Das endschwache Zeitwort in hebräischen Eigennamen," *AJSL* 27 [1910-11] 302).

[6]Uriel Weinreich, William Labov, and Marvin I. Herzog, "Empirical Foundations for a Theory of Language Change," in *Directions for Historical Linguistics: A Symposium*, ed. W. P. Lehmann and Yakov Malkiel (Austin: University of Texas Press, 1968), pp. 97-188, esp. pp. 149-50.

tion, which is unambiguous identification."[7] Proper names therefore may represent an arrested stage in the development of language. They are immune from much of the intractable development and change that attends the growth of any language. Names are, in fact, "linguistic isolates; they are singular terms; . . . [they] do not share the developmental properties of 'normal' grammatical items."[8] Because of their marginal position with respect to the growth of a language, names often show special developments in phonology, morphology, syntax, and lexicon.[9]

Because of these special developments proper names have often been excluded from grammars and lexicons. Such an exclusion, however, arises from a misunderstanding. Though proper names occupy a marginal position with respect to the *growth* of a language, they are nonetheless important constituents of language itself. Algeo has defended their inclusion in the lexicon alongside other vocables,[10] while Utley has argued that ". . . a grammar that does not include proper names is no grammar at all."[11] Moreover, in considering the linguistic position of the proper name in the system of language, Kurylowicz concluded that concrete appellatives and proper names constitute the core of the category of substantive.[12] Therefore the uniqueness of proper names among other elements of a language does not justify their exclusion from normal linguistic pursuits.[13]

---

[7]Ernst Pulgram, "Theory of Names," *Beiträge zur Namenforschung* 5 (1964) 172.

[8]T. L. Markey, "Crisis and Cognition in Onomastics," *Names* 30 (1982) 131, 141.

[9]Some examples will be discussed on pp. 8-12.

[10]John Algeo, *On Defining the Proper Name*, University of Florida Humanities Monograph, no. 41 (Gainesville: University of Florida Press, 1973), pp. 75-76.

[11]Utley, *Names* 11 (1963) 165. See also Ralph B. Long, "The Grammar of English Proper Names," *Names* 17 (1969) 107-26.

[12]Kurylowicz, *Onomastica* (Wroclaw) 2 (1956) 1-3.

[13]John Huehnergard has urged caution in the use of linguistic data derived from the study of proper names and excluded all such data from his description of Ugaritic. See his *Ugaritic Vocabulary in Syllabic Transcription*, HSS 32 (Atlanta: Scholars Press, 1987), pp. 8-10; idem, "Northwest Semitic Vocabulary in Akkadian Texts," *JAOS* 107 (1987) 714-15. Some of the issues he has raised are discussed elsewhere in this chapter. It suffices to say here that many Ug. PNN could have been included in his study as supplementary data without distorting his description of Ugaritic. He has well recognized that names tend to retain archaic features, and with proper methodological controls, this study intends to isolate some of these archaic features. In studying poorly preserved ancient languages (e.g., Amorite!), we can ill afford to ignore the data of proper names.

B. *Proper Names and Archaic Features*

Because of their resistance to some kinds of linguistic change, proper names retain archaic features. According to *The Compact Edition of the Oxford English Dictionary*, archaic can be defined as follows:

> a) marked by the characteristics of an earlier period; old-fashioned, primitive, antiquated. b) especially of language: belonging to an earlier period, no longer in common use, though still retained either by some individuals, or generally, for special purposes, poetical, liturgical, etc.[14]

Within the category of proper names one may note certain distinctions that are relevant for the study of archaism. The two main categories of proper names are personal and geographical.[15] The distinction between GNN and PNN is valid, even though one must admit a degree of overlap between the two categories.[16]

It is widely recognized that GNN are 'super-archaic' in comparison to PNN. They evidence an extreme resistance to change, and the original GN is frequently maintained even when the population changes and the language spoken in the area is itself replaced.[17] Modern examples include the persistence of Polynesian place names in Hawaii and the large number of states in the United States that bear Indian names. Among GNN further distinctions are possible. The names of rivers and mountains usually represent the oldest layers of a language; on the other hand, the names of various inhabited sites may change, as a result of renaming after the conquest, abandonment, or destruction of

---

[14] *The Compact Edition of the Oxford English Dictionary*, 2 vols. (Oxford: Oxford University Press, 1971), 1:108.

[15] In Near Eastern studies, divine names and tribal names are often mentioned as additional categories. The second category appears to be derivative, insofar as tribal names derive from GNN (e.g. Cushites < Cush) or PNN.

[16] A. F. Rainey, "The Toponymics of Eretz-Israel," *BASOR* 231 (1978) 4, is of the opinion that a few sentence names, attested as GNN, are most probably PNN that have become attached to geographical features. See also similar remarks by W. F. Albright, "An Ostracon from Calah and the North-Israelite Diaspora," *BASOR* 149 (1958) 33 n. 4. Modern examples of GNN derived from PNN are plentiful (Bolivia < Simón Bolívar). In general, see Iorgu Iordan, "Les rapports entre la toponymie et l'anthroponymie," *Onoma* 14 (1969) 14-22. Any proper name attested as a PN in the Hebrew Bible comes under consideration in this study.

[17] Theodora Bynon, *Historical Linguistics* (Cambridge: Cambridge University Press, 1977), pp. 273-78; Pelio Fronzaroli, "West Semitic Toponymy in Northern Syria in the Third Millennium B.C.," *JSS* 22 (1977) 146.

a settlement.[18] PNN, in contrast, are also archaic, but not to the same degree as GNN. To follow up on the above-mentioned example, Polynesian PNN have not been retained in Hawaii. Markey has formulated a rule to explain the complementarity between indigenous place names and non-indigenous personal names:

> . . . an indigenous population regularly gives up its personal names (and personal naming system) in favor of those introduced by newcomers, while newcomers regularly adopt indigenous place names, but not indigenous personal names. Therefore, toponyms from non-indigenous sources are characteristically younger than anthroponyms from non-indigenous sources.[19]

The difference between GNN and PNN as regards archaism is largely a function of a difference in accessibility: place is permanently accessible, person is not. While GNN often persist for millennia, the continued existence of PNN is dependent upon their recycling.

This fundamental difference between GNN and PNN has been noted in ancient Near Eastern studies. In several articles concerned with ethnic reconstruction in ancient Syria and Mesopotamia, Gelb has made careful use of both GNN and PNN.[20] Almost all of the geographical names known in the earliest historical periods of Babylonia are non-Sumerian and non-Semitic, while the PNN are Sumerian and Semitic. This lack of correlation illustrates Markey's rule and highlights the difference between GNN and PNN. The GNN are 'super-archaic,' supporting the assumption that Babylonia was first settled by a non-Sumerian population of unknown ethno-linguistic affiliation. The PNN, on the other hand, reflect the new ethnic situation consisting of Sumerian and Semitic populations. Hence the GNN reflect an older layer of language than the PNN.

---

[18] I. J. Gelb, "Ethnic Reconstruction and Onomastic Evidence," *Names* 10 (1962) 48, makes the same point by stating that the names pertaining to natural features are generally more difficult (if not impossible) to understand than are the names pertaining to man-made features. In the Hebrew Bible, the Israelites generally accepted the old names inherited from their Canaanite predecessors. Instances of changing the former name are rare. For a brief discussion, see Rainey, *BASOR* 231 (1978) 3. In *La toponymie antique. Actes du Colloque de Strasbourg 12-14 juin 1975* (Leiden: E. J. Brill, 1977), several articles deal with the topic of continuity and change in ancient toponymy.

[19] Markey, *Names* 30 (1982) 135.

[20] I. J. Gelb, "Sumerians and Akkadians in Their Ethno-Linguistic Relationship," *Genava*, n.s., 8 (1960) 258-71. See also idem, *Names* 10 (1962) 48-50; idem, "The Early History of the West Semitic Peoples," *JCS* 15 (1961) 41.

In his discussion, Gelb characterized the GNN as conservative and the PNN as innovative.[21] It is clear from the context that his contrast is relative and not absolute; he is emphasizing the greater degree of archaism that attends GNN in comparison to PNN. While the GNN are conservative and tend to preserve the old ethnic picture, the innovative character of the PNN tends to reflect more quickly the new ethnic situation. Therefore, PNN have a two-fold character; on the one hand, they are conservative, preserving archaic features; on the other, they are innovative, reflecting linguistic change.[22] Huffmon well summarizes the character of PNN when he states that ". . . they usually reflect an ambivalence between the older, more archaic, and younger stages of a language."[23]

The innovative character of PNN may be explained by the fact that PNN may reflect current speech patterns. Gelb supported this notion by consideration of the Semitic naming practice:

> . . . they [personal names] are generally easy to understand. The reason for this comprehensibility is that they were usually couched in the language of the person or persons giving the name. The reason for their being couched in the current language of the name-givers was that the latter customarily formed names for their children in order to express a sentiment, a wish, or gratitude, revolving around their progeny or themselves. . . . the conclusion that the ancient Near Eastern names reproduced the current language of the name-givers and were consequently easily understood holds true.[24]

Silverman has reached the same conclusion in his study of Jewish proper names at Elephantine. Most of the names are of the Hebrew-Aramaic type, thus corresponding to the spoken language. As such

---

[21]Gelb, *Names* 10 (1962) 50; idem, *Genava*, n.s., 8 (1960) 265.

[22]For a study of the conservative and innovative traits of Icelandic naming patterns, see Richard F. Tomasson, "The Continuity of Icelandic Names and Naming Patterns," *Names* 23 (1975) 281-89.

[23]Huffmon, *APNMT*, p. 107. Witold Mańczak, "Une tendance générale dans le développement de la flexion des noms de personnes," *Revue internationale d'onomastique* 12 (1960) 125-36, discusses innovations in the inflection of PNN. One of his examples is the diptotic declension of Arabic PNN. This phenomenon has been isolated and discussed as regards Ugaritic PNN by Mario Liverani, "Antecedenti del diptotismo arabo nei testi accadici di Ugarit," *RSO* 38 (1963) 131-60.

[24]Gelb, *Names* 10 (1962) 47.

they were immediately comprehensible to the name-givers.[25] That biblical PNN of the imperfect verb type conform to the Barth-Ginsberg law would also indicate that PNN may reflect the spoken language.[26] On other occasions as well scholars have appealed to the effect of speech to explain the orthography, morphology, or phonology of names.[27] At any rate, Huffmon's observation that personal names do not always conform to the grammar of the language as it was actually spoken[28] is a moot point, given the ambivalent character of personal names and our often lacunary knowledge of the spoken languages in question.

Proper names, be they geographical or personal, are not the only areas where the archaic features of a language can be found. In the introduction to his grammar, Gesenius noted that an earlier stage in the development of the "Canaanitish-Hebrew" language can be discerned from archaisms preserved in two sources: 1) the names of persons and

---

25 Michael H. Silverman, *Religious Values in the Jewish Proper Names at Elephantine*, AOAT 217 (Kevelaer: Butzon & Bercker; Neukirchen-Vluyn: Neukirchener, 1985), pp. 16-17, 198-99. For similar remarks on the transparent meaning of Hebrew names, see Jeffrey H. Tigay, *You Shall Have No Other Gods: Israelite Religion in the Light of Hebrew Inscriptions*, HSS 31 (Atlanta: Scholars Press, 1986), pp. 5-6.

26 See C. Rabin, "Archaic Vocalisation in Some Biblical Hebrew Names," *JJS* 1 (1948-49) 22-26, and the discussion at p. 11 below.

27 E.g., 1) William W. Hallo and Hayim Tadmor, "A Lawsuit from Hazor," *IEJ* 27 (1977) 4-5, have noted the earliest evidence for the sound shift **ā* > **ō* in the PN *DUMU-ḫa-nu-ta*, understanding the element *ḫa-nu-ta* (= **ʿanōt*) as a biform of *ʿanāt*; 2) Martin Noth, *Die israelitischen Personennamen im Rahmen der gemeinsemitischen Namengebung* (Stuttgart: W. Kohlhammer, 1928; reprint ed., Hildesheim: Georg Olms, 1980), p. 107 n. 3, was of the opinion that the BH PN *hôšāmāʿ* (< **yĕhôšāmāʿ*) reflects the occasional loss of the initial syllable in speech (compare the N/LB PN *^{d}ḫu-ú-na-tan^{an}-na* [Ran Zadok, *On West Semites in Babylonia During the Chaldean and Achaemenian Periods: An Onomastic Study* (Jerusalem: H. J. & Z. Wanaarta and Tel-Aviv University, 1977), p. 244]. Matthew W. Stolper, "A Note on Yahwistic Personal Names in the Murašû Texts," *BASOR* 222 (1976) 25, remarks that the spelling of this N/LB PN cannot be attributed to simple scribal lapse, since it occurs in precisely the same form three times in the text); 3) Michael D. Coogan, "Patterns in Jewish Personal Names in the Babylonian Diaspora," *JSJ* 4 (1973) 187 n. 11, proposed that the EH PN *ywkn* reflects a haplography in popular speech of the full form of the name (**yahûyākīn/-*yawyākīn > yawkīn*); 4) Gary A. Rendsburg, "The Ammonite Phoneme /Ṯ/," *BASOR* 269 (1988) 73-79, esp. p. 74, has argued that the spelling of the Amm. PN *baʿălîs* (Jer 40:14), with *samek* instead of *shin*, reflects the way the Judean writer pronounced the Ammonite name; 5) Nahman Avigad, "A Bulla of Jonathan the High Priest," *IEJ* 25 (1975) 10 n. 9, has suggested that the spelling *yntn* "Yonatan" on a bulla may perhaps reflect a colloquial pronunciation of the name.

28 Huffmon, *APNMT*, p. 89.

places; and 2) isolated forms chiefly occurring in poetic style.[29] In addition to proper names, poetry tends to preserve ancient forms of the language.[30] In particular, certain ancient poems preserved in the Pentateuch and Former Prophets have been rigorously studied in an effort to identify archaic features.[31] The most important study of archaisms in poetic language is David A. Robertson's *Linguistic Evidence in Dating Early Hebrew Poetry*.[32] Although early poetry has been the object of intense study in order to identify archaic features, proper names for the most part have suffered neglect.[33]

In summary, since there are two primary sources of archaic features in the Hebrew Bible, it makes sense to compare data from and conclusions regarding the two sources. In the concluding chapter of this study, I will seek to correlate archaic features preserved in proper names with their counterparts retained in early Hebrew poetry.

C. *Archaic Features and Semitic Proper Names*

It is a generally accepted tenet of ancient Near Eastern studies that proper names tend to preserve archaic features of a language. As such they constitute an important source for reconstructing the older stages of any language. This statement holds true for PNN as well as for GNN, though these two sources may not complement one another in some instances. Previous studies regarding the subject of archaic features and Semitic proper names are scarcely to be found. In fact, most of the examples cited below are merely incidental remarks gleaned from a wide variety of sources. I will first cite examples of archaic features in Semitic proper names in general, and then turn to the treatment of Canaanite proper names in particular.

In contrast to other Semitic languages, Babylonian forms the feminine of the third person singular of the verb in most cases with the masculine prefix **y*, and much less often with feminine prefix **t*. The

---

[29] Wilhelm Gesenius, *Gesenius' Hebrew Grammar*, 28th ed., ed. E. Kautzsch and A. E. Cowley (Oxford: Oxford University Press, 1910), §2k.

[30] On archaic vocabulary in poetry, see G. R. Driver, "Hebrew Poetic Diction," VTSup 1 (1953) 26-39.

[31] W. F. Albright and his disciples, Cross and Freedman, produced a series of pioneering studies on early Hebrew poetry. In general, see David N. Freedman, "Archaic Forms in Early Hebrew Poetry," *ZAW* 72 (1960) 101-7, with further bibliography in n. 1. Many of Freedman's articles on poetry have been collected and are now available in *Pottery, Poetry, and Prophecy: Studies in Early Hebrew Poetry* (Winona Lake: Eisenbrauns, 1980).

[32] SBLDS 3 (Missoula: Society of Biblical Literature, 1972).

[33] What little has been done will be briefly surveyed in the following section.

original prefix of the feminine, however, is preserved in certain phases of the Akkadian language: in Old Akkadian, usually in Assyrian, and under Aramaic influence, in Neo-Babylonian.[34] The distribution of the third person morphemes is distinctive in Old Assyrian, with the prefixes **t* and **y* used for verbs with a personal and an impersonal feminine subject respectively. On the other hand, the feminine prefix **t* is archaic in Old Babylonian, and it is sometimes still retained in names and in the hymnic-epic dialect. Further, it occurs next to **y* occasionally in later poetic texts. The occurrence of feminine **t* in Old Akkadian PNN is to be expected. For our purposes, we should note the frequent occurrence of this archaic feature in Old Babylonian PNN (e.g., *tab-ni-Ištar*). What is even more striking is that this morpheme is still found occasionally in Middle Babylonian PNN.[35]

From Old Babylonian onward, the determinative pronoun *ša* occurs as a fossilized form of the accusative singular and thus serves for all genders. Only in the oldest stage of the language, Old Akkadian, is the full declension of this pronoun preserved: nominative *šu*, genitive *ši*, and accusative *ša*. The nominative form *šu* has been retained as an archaism in the hymnic-epic dialect and in Old Assyrian and Old Babylonian PNN.[36]

A final example from the Semitic languages concerns Amharic GNN. In her study of the internal grammar of these names, Little has noted two archaic features of construct-type names.[37] First, the word *däbr*, "mountain," which occurs as the *nomen regens* in construct phrase names (e.g., *däbrä zäyt* "mountain of olive"), is a lexical archaism restricted to proper names. The form *tärara* has replaced *däbr* as the

[34]Wolfram von Soden, *Grundriss der akkadischen Grammatik*, Analecta Orientalia, vols. 33/47 (Rome: Pontifical Biblical Institute, 1969), §75h. See also I. J. Gelb, *Inscriptions from Alishar and Vicinity*, Oriental Institute Publications, vol. 27; Researches in Anatolia, vol. 6 (Chicago: University of Chicago Press, 1935), pp. 41-42.

[35]Wolfram von Soden, "Der hymnisch-epische Dialekt des Akkadischen," *ZA* 41 (1933) 149. For a list of examples, see Albert T. Clay, *Personal Names from Cuneiform Inscriptions of the Cassite Period*, Yale Oriental Series, vol. 1 (New Haven: Yale University Press, 1912), p. 137. D. O. Edzard, "^{m}*Ningal-gāmil*, ^{f}*Ištar-damqat.* Die Genuskongruenz im akkadischen theophoren Personennamen," *ZA* 55 (1962) 116, denies that the verbal forms with feminine prefix **t* are archaisms, since these feminine verbal forms are the result of gender congruence with the sex of the name bearer. But these verbal forms with prefix **t* in theophoric PNN are still archaic, regardless of the matter of gender congruence.

[36]Von Soden, *GAG* §46b; Carl G. Rasmussen, "A Study of Akkadian Personal Names from Mari" (Ph.D. dissertation, The Dropsie University, 1981), pp. 365, 387. Note the PN *šu-baʿlu*(^{d}*IM*) at Ugaritic (Gröndahl, *PTU*, p. 191).

[37]Greta D. Little, "Internal Grammar in Amharic Place-Names," *Names* 26 (1978) 3-8, esp. pp. 4-5.

common noun "mountain." Second, the head noun is marked by *-ä*, which indicates the construct state. This *-ä* is the old accusative and construct (?) case marker. It is no longer productive in modern Amharic, appearing only in compounds or archaic expressions. The construct state marker *-ä*, therefore, is a morphological archaism. This construct state marker is very common in PNN as well.

Several articles, or portions thereof, have treated archaic features in Canaanite proper names. In addition to those studies which are cited here, incidental remarks may be found in grammars, lexicons, commentaries, and other sources. Those remarks that we have found and that are relevant to the archaic features to be discussed herein will be mentioned at the appropriate place in the body of the study.

There is no doubt that the Hebrew language was not the same in every location in which it was spoken. On the contrary, several different dialects must have existed. Because of the leveling of the written literary language, the Hebrew Bible contains very scant testimony to this dialectal variation. Furthermore, the vocabulary of ancient Hebrew must have been greater than what can be known from the Hebrew Bible.[38] Bauer attempted to remedy these shortcomings by turning to Hebrew PNN as an alternative source of linguistic knowledge.[39] He made a synthetic study of Hebrew PNN with respect to phonology, morphology, and vocabulary. Unfortunately, the results of this study are uneven; the study was carried out without proper controls[40] and tainted by Bauer's idiosyncratic notion of Hebrew as a *Mischsprache*.

In a wide-ranging article Eshel has studied the distinctive morphological and phonological features which are found in GNN and PNN of the Hebrew Bible.[41] Most of his study is concerned with the variation of vocalization of certain Canaanite PNN (e.g., *kālēb* versus *kĕlūb*). Eshel claims that such variations are indicative of genuine

---

[38]See especially Edward Ullendorff, "Is Biblical Hebrew a Language?" *BSOAS* 34 (1971) 241-55; reprinted in *Is Biblical Hebrew a Language?* (Wiesbaden: Otto Harrassowitz, 1977), pp. 3-17.

[39]H. Bauer, "Die hebräischen Eigennamen als sprachliche Erkenntnisquelle," *ZAW* 48 (1930) 73-80. For the contribution of Ugaritic PNN to the Ugaritic lexicon, see Anton Jirku, "Ugaritische Eigennamen als Quelle des ugaritischen Lexikons," *ArOr* 37 (1969) 8-11.

[40]E.g, Bauer, *ZAW* 48 (1930) 74, emended the PN *qmwʾl* to **qwmʾl* in order to fit in a series of PNN of the form $*C_1wC_2$ + DN, interpreting the initial element as a Qal perfect verbal form, with the phonological development **ā > *ō*. Disregarding the matter of the putative vowel shift, the PN *qmwʾl* already belongs to a series of PNN of the form $*C_1\breve{e}C_2\hat{u}$*ʾēl*. See discussion s.v. "qĕmûʾēl," pp. 76-78.

[41]Ben-Zion Eshel, "lhgym whgywt lpy šmwt šbmqrʾ," in *mwgš lkbwd hprwpʾ n. h. ṭwr-syny lmlʾt lw šbʿym šnh*, ed. Menahem Haran and B. Z. Luria, Publications of the Society for the Study of the Bible in Israel, vol. 8. (Jerusalem: Society for the Study of the Bible in Israel, 1960), pp. 243-78.

dialectal features. His treatment of PNN is relevant for our study because some of the morphological features he treats qualify as archaisms, viz. enclitic *-m* and the feminine suffix *-at*.[42]

Rabin's study of the vocalization of the imperfect verbal forms in Hebrew names is a most important contribution on the topic of archaic features retained in proper names.[43] His study demonstrates that biblical names that contain imperfect verbal forms conform to the Barth-Ginsberg law. Omitting I-guttural roots, which invariably have an *a* prefix vowel, and the conflicting picture presented by III-h roots, the following pattern emerges: 1) all names beginning with *ya-* have an *i* or *u* class vowel in the following syllable; 2) all names beginning with *yi-* have an *a* class vowel in the following syllable. Stated another way, no biblical names with an *o* or *i* stem vowel have the expected Biblical Hebrew form of the third person masculine singular (i.e., the post-Barth-Ginsberg form with **ya- > yi-*). Rabin concludes that since these names in *y-* were originally ordinary verbal forms, then the Barth-Ginsberg law must have been observed in the normal speech patterns when and where these names were coined. In short, their adherence to the Barth-Ginsberg law is striking evidence of their archaic phonology, as compared with standard BH phonology.

In an important study on mimation and nunation in the Semitic languages, Gelb adduced numerous examples of Hebrew, Phoenician, and Punic PNN that preserve remnants of mimation.[44] We will forego further discussion for now, since this archaic morphological feature will be treated in Chapter 4.

It was mentioned above that almost all of the GNN known in the earliest sources in Mesopotamia were non-Sumerian and non-Semitic. As such, linguistic information gleaned from GNN cannot complement that which is obtained from a study of PNN. This discrepancy between the language spheres of GNN and PNN also predominates in North Syria, though to a lesser extent. The situation in Palestine differs sharply; the great majority of these GNN are Semitic. Therefore, Canaanite GNN may supplement Canaanite PNN as an additional source for reconstructing the earlier stages of the language in that area. In his survey of the toponymics of Palestine, Rainey devotes a section to the grammatical analysis of ancient Semitic toponyms.[45] He dis-

---

42For his remarks on enclitic *-m* and the feminine suffix *-at*, see pp. 258-59 and 265-66, and the discussions in the relevant chapters of this study.

43Rabin, *JJS* 1 (1948-49) 22-26.

44I. J. Gelb, "La mimazione e la nunazione nelle lingue semitiche," *RSO* 12 (1930) 229-43. He cited further instances of mimation in Aramaic, North Arabian, and Ethiopic PNN (pp. 241-43, 254-59).

45Rainey, *BASOR* 231 (1978) 4-5.

cusses two morphological features that qualify as archaisms. First, some GNN terminate in the *-at* suffix, which became *-â* in Masoretic Hebrew.[46] Second, the infinitive of the Gt stem is attested in the GN *ʾeštĕmōaʿ* (Josh 21:14 and elsewhere), with the variant *ʾeštĕmōh* (Josh 15:50), which in turn can be compared to the Ug. GN *ʾilštmʿ*, vocalized as *URUilu(DINGIR)-iš-tam-i*.[47] This verb stem was still productive in Ugaritic, Old Aramaic, Phoenician, and Moabite, but not in classical Biblical Hebrew.[48]

II. Methodology

A. *Scope and Format of Study*

As indicated by the preceding discussion, the phenomenon of archaism in PNN has long been recognized but seldom subjected to intense scrutiny. The study of archaisms in PNN deserves a systematic treatment; hitherto impressionistic statements stand in need of replacement by detailed examination of all the evidence. The purpose of the present study is to fill this need. It is primarily a collection and interpretation of certain Canaanite PNN that have preserved archaic features. In contrast to GNN, the category of PNN appears most promising, because 1) the greater variety of construction increases the likelihood of the retention of archaic linguistic elements;[49] and 2) on the whole, PNN are easier to interpret than GNN.

Two main areas of linguistic inquiry may be considered: 1) grammar, consisting of phonology, morphology, and syntax; and 2) lexicon. From a preliminary study of Canaanite PNN in the Hebrew Bible, the subset of morphology appears to be the most profitable for

---

[46]These will be cited in Chapter 5, where this phenomenon with Canaanite PNN is treated.

[47]*PRU* VI 131.1'; *PRU* III, pp. 109 (16.251,6), 188 (10.044,8'). Note also *URUilu(DINGIR)-iš-[t]am-i* (*Ug V* 95.17), the Ug. gentilic *ʾilštmʿy* (*KTU* 4.68.29 and elsewhere), and the Gt imperative *ʾištmʿ* (*KTU* 1.16:VI:42).

[48]A few petrified survivals of the Gt stem may be found in weak verbs. See H. L. Ginsberg, "The Northwest Semitic Languages," in *The World History of Jewish People, Vol II: Patriarchs*, ed. Benjamin Mazar (Tel Aviv: Jewish History Publications, 1967; Rutgers University, 1970), p. 113.

[49]Note Gelb's comment, *CAAA*, p. viii: ". . . it is possible that the grammar of Amorite, reconstructed almost entirely from names, may become better known than that of several Semitic languages attested in thousands of inscriptions, for example, Nabatean, Palmyrenian, or South Arabian. The reason may be not so much the amount of documentation as *the structural richness* [emphasis added] of Amorite names (as opposed to the linguistic poverty of the preserved inscriptions of some Semitic languages)."

investigation.[50] Although all parts of language change, some of the changes, especially the morphological ones that affect common nouns, do not affect proper nouns and, to the extent that the parts spared by morphological and other change are not subject to other kinds of changes proper to PNN, PNN can be a repository of archaic morphological features.

I propose to treat the following set of morphological features: 1) the nominative case vowel *u* (Chapter 2); 2) the *ḥireq compaginis* (Chapter 3); 3) mimation and enclitic *-m* (Chapter 4); and 4) feminine *-at* in the absolute state (Chapter 5). This set of archaic features has been selected for two reasons. First, each of these features is allegedly attested in a number of Canaanite PNN in the Hebrew Bible. This circumstance contrasts with most other putative archaic morphological features, which are attested only once.[51] Second, none of these morphological features are solely dependent upon the Masoretic vocalization. This statement is obviously true for the feminine morpheme *-at*, as well as mimation and enclitic *-m*, which are consonantal morphemes. But to a lesser extent, it is also true of the nominative case vowel *u* and the *ḥireq compaginis*. These archaic features are always written *plene*, with *matres lectionis*; hence, their presence in Canaanite PNN in the Hebrew Bible is noted in the consonantal script.

The format for each chapter will vary, depending on the particular archaic feature that is being considered. Each chapter will begin with a summary of the morpheme in early West Semitic textual and onomastic material, and in the Canaanite languages. The above-mentioned archaic morphological features will be collected in the corpora of Canaanite PNN in the Hebrew Bible by analyzing and interpreting each name that appears to contain one of these features. An important step in the interpretive process is the comparison of these names with similar or identical older, West Semitic names. Principally, this includes Amorite and Ugaritic, as well as West Semitic names found in the Akkadian texts from Ugarit, the Alalakh tablets, Bronze

[50]Each of the other topics that might be studied has its own drawbacks. With the exception of the imperfect verbal forms studied by Rabin, instances of archaic phonology are rare (and this is, of course, an example of morphophonology). Since the syntactic constructions of Canaanite PNN are sharply curtailed, the topic of archaic syntax leads to meager results. The lexicon is an area that warrants study, because of the many concrete items; yet the meaning of individual lexemes is often inaccessible. We will note any phonological, syntactic, or lexical archaisms that occur in the Canaanite PNN containing the relevant archaic morphological features.

[51]The feminine morpheme *-ay* is attested only in the feminine PN Saray. As the most celebrated instance of a morphological archaism among Canaanite PNN in the Hebrew Bible, I have decided to discuss it in an appendix (pp. 241-49).

Age texts from Palestine, the El-Amarna letters, the Egyptian execration texts, and the Hayes list. Akkadian and Eblaite names[52] will occasionally be cited, especially when these languages present a parallel name (full or partial) to the West Semitic name being discussed.

The absence or rarity of these features among the Canaanite languages will be noted. GNN and DNN from the Hebrew Bible or extrabiblical sources will also be cited if they contain the archaic feature under consideration. Furthermore, an effort will be made to trace these morphological features in first millennium B.C. and later West Semitic onomastic materials, namely West Semitic names in cuneiform texts, epigraphic Hebrew, the Transjordanian dialects, Phoenician-Punic, Neo-Punic, Old and Imperial Aramaic, Palmyrene, Ḥatran, North Arabian, South Arabian, and West Semitic names in Greek inscriptions and papyri.

In sum, this investigation aims to isolate these archaic morphological features in Canaanite PNN by comparison with older West Semitic PNN. This comparative study will in turn shed light on the older stages of Northwest Semitic and provide an analysis and interpretation of an important class of Canaanite PNN. A "mini-grammar" of these archaic morphological features will be constructed. Lastly, the distribution of these names containing morphological archaisms will be studied to see whether any patterns (geographical, chronological, linguistic, or literary) emerge. Now that the scope, intent, and format of the study have been outlined, it is necessary to discuss methodology and to define some of the terms mentioned above.

---

[52]Eblaite PNN will be cited from the name indices contained in the series Archivi reali di Ebla. Six volumes have been published to date: A. Archi, *Testi amministrativi: assegnazioni di tessuti*, ARET I (Rome: Missione archeologica italiana in Siria, 1985); D. O. Edzard, *Verwaltungstexte verschiedenen Inhalts*, ARET II (Rome: Missione archeologica italiana in Siria, 1981); A. Archi and M. G. Biga, *Testi amministrativi di vario contenuto*, ARET III (Rome: Missione archeologica italiana in Siria, 1982); M. G. Biga and L. Milano, *Testi amministrativi: assegnazioni di tessuti*, ARET IV (Rome: Missione archeologica italiana in Siria, 1984); D. O. Edzard, *Hymnen, Beschwörungen und Verwandtes aus dem Archiv L. 2769*, ARET V (Rome: Missione archeologica italiana in Siria, 1984); Edmond Sollberger, *Administrative Texts Chiefly Concerning Textiles*, ARET VIII (Rome: Missione archeologica italiana in Siria, 1986). For studies on the Eblaite onomasticon, see Manfred Krebernik, *Die Personennamen der Eblatexte: Eine Zwischenbilanz*. Berliner Beiträge zum Vorderen Orient, Band 7 (Berlin: Dietrich Reimer, 1987); A. Archi, ed., *Eblaite Personal Names and Semitic Name-giving. Papers of the symposium held in Rome, July 15-17, 1985*, Archivi reali di Ebla, Studi 1 (Rome: Missione archeologica italiana in Siria, 1988).

B. *On the Separation of Canaanite PNN from Other PNN*

The use of the term Canaanite, to describe the onomastic corpus under investigation, needs justification. The Northwest Semitic group of languages is generally divided into two branches: Canaanite and Aramaic. Since the earliest extant Aramaic epigraphs date to the beginning of the first millennium B.C., this two-fold classification, strictly speaking, is valid only from that time onward. In this classificatory scheme, Canaanite has a purely negative meaning: whatever is not Aramaic is, by default, Canaanite.[53] While Canaanite in the strict sense of the term is confined to the non-Aramaic Northwest Semitic languages of the first millennium B.C., it is no less true that Canaanite did not spring forth in full bloom at the turn of the millennium without earlier antecedents. Rather Canaanite is simply a stage of development from earlier West Semitic language, and where the latter left off and the former begins is to a large extent an arbitrary decision that reflects the scarcity of linguistic data, our lacunary knowledge, and the inadequacy of classificatory schemes.

Canaanite appears to be the most suitable term to describe the non-Aramaic West Semitic PNN found in the Hebrew Bible.[54] While this term embraces those Canaanite dialects--Phoenician, the Transjordanian dialects, epigraphic Hebrew, and Biblical Hebrew--that make their historically and epigraphically attested appearance in the first millennium B.C., it also reaches back into the last half of the second millennium B.C. Both temporally and linguistically, the term Canaanite represents roughly the corpus of names that constitute the subject of this study. Aramaic PNN in the Hebrew Bible have been excluded from this study because they are few in number and attested mostly during the later periods (sixth century B.C. and afterwards).[55]

---

[53]Sabatino Moscati, "Israel's Predecessors: A Re-Examination of Certain Current Theories," *JBR* 24 (1956) 254; idem, *The Semites in Ancient History* (Cardiff: University of Wales Press, 1959), pp. 98-100; idem, ed., *An Introduction to the Comparative Grammar of the Semitic Languages*, Porta Linguarum Orientalium, New Series, vol. 6 (Wiesbaden: Otto Harrassowitz, 1969), §3.2.

[54]Such terms as Northwest Semitic or West Semitic are simply too broad to describe this corpus.

[55]For a list of the Aramaic PNN in the Hebrew Bible, see Max Wagner, *Die lexikalischen und grammatikalischen Aramaismen im alttestamentlichen Hebräischen*, BZAW 96 (Berlin: Alfred Töpelmann, 1966), p. 151; Ran Zadok, "Die nichthebräischen Namen der Israeliten vor dem hellenistichen Zeitalter," *UF* 17 (1985) 388-90. The two Aramaic PNN that constitute probable examples have been discussed under the subsection "Non-Canaanite examples." See s.v. "ʾăḥûmay," pp. 100-101; and "zabdîʾēl," pp. 142-45.

The criteria by which Canaanite PNN are separated from other PNN in general, and from Aramaic PNN in particular, are of two types, linguistic and topical.[56] The linguistic criterion can be subdivided into phonological, morphological, and lexical subjects. The topical criterion consists of theological, genealogical, historical, geographical, and ethnic subjects. Although these criteria can be used in conjunction to separate Canaanite PNN from other PNN, priority must be given to the linguistic side of the matter. After all, it is the names themselves and not the name bearers that are primarily being studied. The linguistic criterion is by far the most reliable means of identifying Canaanite PNN.[57] It is hoped that the topical criterion will confirm the analyses based on the linguistic criterion. To sum up, Canaanite names are those of which the language is Canaanite.

The distinction between Canaanite PNN and other non-West Semitic PNN[58] in the Hebrew Bible is transparent. As for Aramaic, Silverman utilizes the linguistic criterion to distinguish Hebrew and Aramaic name-types in the Elephantine texts.[59] His use of the criterion can be imitated, *mutatis mutandis*, to separate the Canaanite PNN from the small corpus of Aramaic PNN in the Hebrew Bible. For our purposes, it is a desideratum to make further distinctions within the Canaanite group of languages. The linguistic criterion may not be fully adequate in this regard. Some of the languages, such as the Transjordanian dialects, are so poorly attested that a distinct linguistic profile can hardly be constructed. And even in those cases where distinctions obtain, a given PNN may not manifest its linguistic affiliation.

Under these circumstances, topical criteria may be of help. An ethnicon, such as Edomite or Moabite, may indicate the linguistic affiliation of a name. But some ethnica, especially in the stereotypic list of pre-Israelite nations, may be used rhetorically.[60] Nonetheless, each ethnicon must be evaluated on its own merit.[61] Theophoric elements

---

[56]This is adapted, with some changes, from Zadok, *WSB*, pp. 21-28.

[57]On Amor. PNN, Huffmon, *APNMT*, p. 17, states "the ultimate basis for including a name in a list of probable Amorite names is formal and linguistic." For similar remarks on Aramaic PNN, see n. 59 below.

[58]Egyptian, Akkadian, Hurrian, Hittite, and Persian.

[59]Michael H. Silverman, "Aramean Name-Types in the Elephantine Documents," *JAOS* 89 (1969) 691-98; idem, "Hebrew Name-Types in the Elephantine Documents," *Or* 39 (1970) 465-85; idem, *RVJPNE*, pp. 48-51.

[60]John Van Seters, "The Terms 'Amorite'and 'Hittite' in the Old Testament," *VT* 22 (1971) 64-81. See also John C. L. Gibson, "Observations on Some Important Ethnic Terms in the Pentateuch," *JNES* 20 (1961) 217-38; Tomoo Ishida, "The Structure and Historical Implications of the Lists of Pre-Israelite Nations," *Bib* 60 (1979) 461-90; Robert North, "The Hivites," *Bib* 54 (1973) 43-62.

[61]An outstanding example of a PN which, in my estimation, would never have been correctly interpreted save for its accompanying ethnicon, is that of Uriyah, the

can be peculiar to a language. Theophoric PNN containing the DNN Eshmun, Kemosh, Qaus, and Milkom may be classified as Phoenician, Moabite, Edomite, and Ammonite respectively. Likewise, the occurrence of a shortened form of the DN Yahweh signals either a Hebrew or Aramaic name. The linguistic criterion may decide between the two. When utilizing this topical criterion, one must not be misled by a *Mischname*[62] or a non-theophoric homograph.[63]

The Hebrew Bible contains a wealth of genealogical, historical, and geographical information that may aid in identifying the linguistic affiliation of a name. This material must be used with discrimination, however. On the basis of this material, further distinctions among Hebrew PNN may be drawn. It may be possible to trace Hebrew PNN to a particular tribe[64] or geographical area. For extrabiblical PNN attested in inscriptions, palaeography plays a role in determining the lan-guage of the names. This method is based on the analysis of the script in which a PN is written.[65] Sometimes, however, the script in which a language is traditionally written does not accord with the language of the PN.

Hittite. See Yoël L. Arbeitman, "Luwio-Semitic and Hurrio-Mitannio-Semitic Mischname-Theophores in the Bible, on Crete, and at Troy," *Scripta Mediterranea* 3 (1982) 5-53.

62Another example of a *Mischname* is the IAram. PN *ʾtrly* (< Iranian **ātar* + Aram. **ʾilī*) "Atar is my god," discussed by Pierre Swiggers, "A Syncretistic Anthroponym in the Aramaic Documents from Egypt," *Beiträge zur Namenforschung*, n.s., 16 (1981) 348-50. For additional examples of *Mischnamen*, see F. M. Fales, "A List of Assyrian and West Semitic Women's Names," *Iraq* 41 (1979) 70; R. Zadok, "Notes on the Early History of the Israelites and Judeans in Mesopotamia," *Or* 51 (1982) 393 and n. 24.

63Noth, *IPN*, p. 105; Gad B. Sarfatti, "Hebrew Inscriptions of the First Temple Period--A Survey and Some Linguistic Comments," *Maarav* 3 (1982) 82 and n. 120.

64Note, for example, the study of Ariella D. Goldberg, "Northern-Type-Names in the Post-Exilic Jewish Onomasticon" (Ph.D. dissertation, Brandeis University, 1973), p. 101, who claims that Canaanite divine elements are most prevalent in PNN traceable to the tribe of Benjamin.

65Palaeography is the principal criterion used by what we might call the "Paris" school (P. Bordreuil, A. Lemaire, J. Teixidor, E. Puech, and F. Israel) in articles scattered throughout various journals, especially *Syria* and *Sem*. For representative articles, see Pierre Bordreuil and André Lemaire, "Nouveaux sceaux hébreux, araméens et ammonites," *Sem* 26 (1976) 45-63; idem, "Nouveau groupe de sceaux hébreux, araméens et ammonites," *Sem* 29 (1979) 71-84, Plates III-IV. See also Pierre Swiggers, "Proper names, Languages and Scripts," *Beiträge zur Namenforschung*, n.s., 19 (1984) 381-84; Joseph Naveh, "The Scripts in Palestine and Transjordan in the Iron Age," in *Essays in Honor of Nelson Glueck: Near Eastern Archaeology in the Twentieth Century*, ed. James A. Sanders (Garden City: Doubleday & Co.), pp. 277-83; and the much criticized work of Larry G. Herr, *The Scripts of Ancient Northwest Semitic Seals*, HSM 18 (Missoula: Scholars Press, 1978).

The use of linguistic and topical criteria outlined above is theoretically sound; the procedure adopted in this study is to classify Canaanite PNN as specifically as possible on the basis of the linguistic criterion, and supplementing this with the topical or palaeographical criterion whenever possible. In practice, however, it is often difficult if not impossible to specify the precise dialect from which a name derives.[66] Therefore, it is expedient to classify most names as Canaanite without further specification. In a few instances, on the basis of a careful weighing of linguistic and topical criteria, names may be classified more specifically.[67]

C. *On the Nature of Linguistic Evidence in the Text of the Hebrew Bible*

Since the Hebrew Bible is the primary source for the Canaanite PNN which are to be studied, it is necessary to consider the nature of the linguistic evidence of the text. The Masoretic text is comprised of three historically distinct elements, viz. the consonants, the use of certain consonants as *matres lectionis*, and the system of diacritical marks for the vowels and cantillation. Considering that West Semitic scripts were originally purely consonantal, it follows that the consonants are the oldest of the three elements. *Matres lectionis* were introduced gradually at first and they occur with increasing frequency as one moves forward in time. The third element of the text, commonly known as the pointing, was added by the Masoretes during the period A.D. 600-1000. It is important to note that the Masoretic activity consisted on the whole in creating a system of graphic markings that represented the traditional vocalization, a vocalization which heretofore existed in oral form. Therefore, the apparent time gap between the consonantal text and the Masoretic vocalization is decreased to the extent that the reading tradition represented by the pointing is ancient.[68]

---

[66]Huehnergard, *Ugaritic Vocabulary*, p. 9; idem, *JAOS* 107 (1987) 714.

[67]Names with Yahwistic theophores may be classified as Hebrew (see s.v. "yĕhôšabʿat," pp. 211-13; and "ḥizqîyāh," pp. 122-25); the PN Huram is Phoenician (s.v. "ḥûrām," pp. 59-60). Throughout this study (e.g., in the parallels section), the proper names from the Hebrew Bible are referred to as either biblical or Canaanite, unless specific isoglosses justify a more precise classification.

[68]James Barr, "The Nature of Linguistic Evidence in the Text of the Bible," in *Languages & Texts: The Nature of Linguistic Evidence*, ed. Herbert H. Paper (Ann Arbor: University of Michigan, 1975), pp. 35-57, esp. pp. 35-40. On p. 40, Barr states that the Masoretes were phonetic conservators rather than interpretive innovators; still he allows for the possibility that in certain cases, their decisions may have been based on semantic-exegetical or other grounds. See further his

The language of the Hebrew Bible exhibits a surprising degree of uniformity; this despite the multi-layered character of the text, emanating from different parts of Palestine over a period of several centuries.[69] This uniformity is mainly because much of the Hebrew Bible was written and edited in a standardized literary language. Thus the text underwent a great deal of levelling and revision--grammatical as well as orthographic--in the course of its transmission. Such levelling would, of course, favor intelligibility in later times. Consequently, the end product is a unified language that tends to mask or eliminate altogether genuine dialectal differences of temporal and/or local origin. Furthermore, some of the features of Masoretic Hebrew are demonstrably late; the anaptyxis of **qvtl* nouns and the extension of **yi-* prefixes to all strong roots in the imperfect are two cases in point.

In this study, it is important to try to determine the extent to which Canaanite PNN are affected by the processes of revision that produced Masoretic Hebrew. As a general rule, PNN lie outside the mainstream of language change and thus are immune to the editorial and linguistic revision to which the surrounding text is subject.[70] There are, however, some exceptions to this general rule. One may cite at least two instances in the Hebrew Bible in which Aramaic PNN are partially altered. The Aramaic PN *br hdd* occurs in the Bible under the Canaanite form *ben-hădad*, and the Aramaic PN **Hadad-ʿidrī* appears in Hebrew guise as *hădadʿezer*.[71] Occasionally a pagan theophoric element is deleted and replaced by an opprobrious term. The outstanding example of this religiously motivated deformation is a series of PNN in which the DN Baal is replaced by the Hebrew word *bōšet* "shame."[72] In light of the stability and antiquity of the consonants, these changes probably took place in ancient times and are, at any rate, exceptional.

There remains to consider the Masoretic pointing of Canaanite PNN. As noted above, none of the archaic features under consideration depend on the pointing. Nevertheless, the interpretation of any

---

Comparative Philology and the Text of the Old Testament (Oxford: Clarendon Press, 1968), pp. 188-222.

[69]Gotthelf Bergsträsser, *Hebräische Grammatik*, 2 vols. (Leipzig: F. C. W. Vogel, 1918-29), 1:11-14; BL §2q-s; Ullendorff, *BSOAS* 34 (1971) 245; Joshua Blau, in *EncJud*, s.v. "Hebrew Language. Biblical," 16:1571-72; Barr, "Linguistic Evidence," pp. 47-48.

[70]Tigay, p. 7, made the same point by stating that the names of characters were not invented by the authors but supplied by historical tradition. It seems reasonable to assume that names would be immune to archaizing tendencies.

[71]On the latter name, see the discussion of Ran Zadok, "Remarks on the Inscription of Hdysʿy from Tall Fakhariya," *TA* 9 (1982) 120.

[72]For further discussion with additional examples, see Tigay, p. 8 and n. 10, 18 and n. 58.

given PN is based in part upon the traditional vocalization of the name. And semantic considerations do play an important role in the detection of some archaic features (e.g., the *ḥireq compaginis*). It is noteworthy that Canaanite PNN of the nominal pattern **qvtl* do appear as segholates. In other names the Masoretic pointing stands in need of correction.[73] Nevertheless, the Masoretic pointing is an important witness to the interpretation of PNN in the Hebrew Bible. The certain cases of deformation, uncommon as they may be, show only that every name must be evaluated in the light of recent advances in the study of Hebrew phonetics and morphology. Additional sources are available that can serve as controls on the Masoretic readings. The LXX transliterations of PNN have the advantage of being chronologically nearer to the early, pre-Masoretic Hebrew Bible.[74] Of special value is Joshua Blau's *On Polyphony in Biblical Hebrew*,[75] in which it is demonstrated that with the exception of the late biblical books of Ezra and Nehemiah, the LXX transliterations of proper names consistently distinguish between the phonemes *ḫ/ḥ* (χ versus zero/vowel mutation) and *ǵ/ʿ* (γ versus zero/vowel mutation). The writings of Flavius Josephus[76] and the Vulgate[77] also contain transliterations of PNN from the Hebrew Bible. Another control is provided by cuneiform transliterations of PNN. These transliterations are especially valuable because of the antiquity of the cuneiform sources and the ability of the script to indicate vowels. A final control is provided by non-Masoretic Hebrew texts. In the texts discovered at Qumran, the use of vowel letters

---

[73]The initial syllable of the biblical PN *mĕpîbōšet* must be vocalized as **mipp-*.

[74]Loring W. Batten, "The Septuagint Transliteration of Hebrew Proper Names" (Ph.D. dissertation, University of Pennsylvania, 1893); Clemens Könnecke, *Die Behandlung der hebräischen Namen in der Septuaginta*, Programm des koeniglichen und groening'schen Gymnasiums zu Stargard in Pommern, no. 124 (Stargard, 1885); G. Lisowsky, "Die Transkription der hebraeischen Eigennamen des Pentateuch in der Septuaginta" (Inaugural-Dissertation, Basel, 1940); A. Murtonen, *Hebrew in Its West Semitic Setting, Part One: Comparative Lexicon; Section A: Proper Names*, Studies in Semitic Languages and Linguistics, Vol. XIII (Leiden: E. J. Brill, 1986); Einar Brønno, "Einige Namentypen der Septuaginta: Zur historischen Grammatik des Hebräischen," *AcOr* (Copenhagen) 19 (1943) 33-64; in English translation, "Some Nominal Types in the Septuagint: Contributions to Pre-Masoretic Hebrew Grammar," *Classica et Mediaevalia* 3 (1940) 180-213.

[75]Proceedings of the Israel Academy of Sciences and Humanities, vol. 6/2 (Jerusalem: Israel Academy of Sciences and Humanities, 1982).

[76]Abraham Schalit, *Namenwörterbuch zu Flavius Josephus* (Leiden: E. J. Brill, 1968).

[77]R. Weber, ed., *Biblia sacra iuxta Vulgatam versionem*, 3d, rev. ed., 2 vols. (Stuttgart: Deutsche Bibelgesellschaft, 1983).

provides some clues to the vocalization of names and sometimes reveals reinterpretations of the names.[78]

D. *On the Detection of Archaic Morphological Features*

While many Semitic scholars mention in passing that proper names tend to retain archaic features, the question of methodology on the detection of these features is rarely discussed. The primary exception is Robertson's *Linguistic Evidence in the Dating Early Hebrew Poetry.*[79] With some minor changes his methodology can be adapted and applied to the study of archaic features in Canaanite PNN. His study and the one undertaken here differ in at least one major respect. Robertson's goal was two-fold: to reconstruct early poetic Hebrew by isolating archaic features, and then to use this as a means of dating early Hebrew poetry. In the present study, no attempt is made to date Canaanite PNN on the basis of archaic features. About all that can be said is that if a Canaanite PN preserves an archaic feature, then it is probably an old name, and its creation predated the time when the given archaic feature was no longer productive in the living language.

Any methodology for detecting archaisms entails comparison in two directions. On the one hand, the corpus of Canaanite PNN must be compared with the grammatical profile of the Canaanite languages. In those instances in which the Canaanite PN can be defined as, e.g., Hebrew or Phoenician, it would be apposite to compare that particular name with the grammatical profile of Hebrew or Phoenician. On the other hand, the corpus of Canaanite PNN must be compared with the older, West Semitic epigraphic materials, which are predominantly onomastic in nature. In order to qualify as an archaism, a feature must be attested in older West Semitic but be either absent or rare in Canaanite. Sound methodology necessitates that the comparison be made in both directions. While it is true that many rare linguistic features of Canaanite PNN are probably archaic, a rare feature is not necessarily an archaic one.[80] Contrarily, a rare feature could be an

---

[78]See Dewey M. Beegle, "Proper Names in the Dead Sea Isaiah Scroll (DSIa), With a Detailed Examination of the Use of the Vowel Letters Waw and Yod" (Ph.D. Dissertation, The Johns Hopkins University, 1952), pp. 81-105; idem, "Proper Names in the New Isaiah Scroll," *BASOR* 123 (1951) 26-30; Eduard Y. Kutscher, *The Language and Linguistic Background of the Isaiah Scroll (1 Q Isa*[a]*)*, Studies on the Texts of the Desert of Judah, vol. 6 (Leiden: E. J. Brill, 1974), pp. 96-125.

[79]Pp. 1-6.

[80]Neither is a feature attested predominantly in late Hebrew necessarily late. See Blau, *Polyphony*, p. 4, on the presumably Proto-Semitic particle *š*.

innovation that was not fully incorporated into the literary language of SBH.[81] Or it could have been in common use throughout the biblical period but occur only a few times in the sample of SBH preserved in the Hebrew Bible. But if a rare feature of Canaanite PNN is attested in earlier West Semitic materials, one can be reasonably assured that the feature is actually archaic. It should be added that occasionally it is necessary to reconstruct Proto-West Semitic to determine that a linguistic feature is archaic.

E. *On the Interpretation of Canaanite PNN*

The interpretation of PNN, be they Canaanite or otherwise, presents a unique challenge. The surrounding context provides no clues to the meaning of the name elements. In Chapters 2-5, the principles discussed in this section will be applied to determine the most probable interpretation of a name. The importance of these interpretive guidelines should be obvious. Too often names have been approached in an unsystematic and haphazard manner. The results are predictable: when proper controls are ignored, scholars generate a plethora of possible meanings for each name. This approach, of course, obscures the primary and fundamental task of the scholar: "to produce studies in the probable, not the possible."[82] For example, in his commentary on Genesis Cassuto listed seven possible explanations for the WS PN Abram.[83] Cassuto has compiled a list of possible meanings, without paying sufficient attention to the structure and language of the name itself. The Akkadian (!) PN "Abamrama" that he cited is unrelated to the WS PN Abram. In contrast, Thompson's lucid treatment of the PN Abram is a model of onomastic analysis. He carefully distinguishes West and East Semitic PNN and, taking into account the structure and

---

[81]The term SBH assumes Kutscher's tripartite division of Biblical Hebrew. SBH represents Biblical prose, and it is to be distinguished from ABH, the poetry of the Pentateuch and the Early Prophets, and LBH, as it appears in the Chronicles and other books. See Eduard Y. Kutscher, *A History of the Hebrew Language* (Jerusalem: Magnes Press; Leiden: E. J. Brill, 1982), p. 12, and similarly Joshua Blau, "The Historical Periods of the Hebrew Language," in *Jewish Languages: Themes and Variations*, ed. Herbert H. Paper (Cambridge, MA: Association for Jewish Studies, 1978), pp. 1-2. It must be admitted that there are portions or books (e.g., Job) of the Hebrew Bible that do not fit comfortably into this threefold division.

[82]David A. Robertson, Review of *Psalms I, 1-50*, by Mitchell Dahood, *JBL* 85 (1966) 484.

[83]Umberto Cassuto, *A Commentary on the Book of Genesis, Part II: From Noah to Abraham*, transl. Israel Abrahams (Jerusalem: Magnes Press, 1964), p. 267.

language of the name, he arrives at the most probable interpretation, "Father is exalted."[84] The use of the comparative method in onomastics sheds much light on the structure and meaning of PNN. This comparative enterprise must be carried out with due respect to cultural, linguistic, and chronological differences between names. Priority should be given to comparisons within the corpora of Canaanite PNN.

To be sure, it may not be possible to arrive at one interpretation for each name, especially when a PN contains an obscure lexeme, the meaning of which is unknown or susceptible to several different interpretations. The interpretation of most names, however, can be reduced to two, or at the most, three options. Often the difference between these options is minimal. For example, the difference between "the Father" versus "my Father" is both structural and semantic, but it should not be exaggerated.[85] Likewise, distinguishing between subject and predicate in some nominal-sentence names is impossible[86] and does not significantly advance our understanding of the names. In most cases, the overall interpretation of the name remains unaffected. In compound PNN containing two nominal elements, it is far more important to attempt to distinguish between construct phrase names and nominal-sentence names. To summarize, names should be interpreted as far as possible. What is to be avoided is the unnecessary multiplication of explanations. The principles enumerated below are intended to reduce the number of interpretive options. These principles can be applied to the interpretation of Canaanite PNN with varying degrees of success and failure, depending on the difficulty of any given name. As already acknowledged, some PNN resist our best efforts at interpretation. Because of lack of context and insufficient knowledge of the language of the PN, the meaning of individual lexical elements is often only approximate.[87] Thus the interpretations of the Canaanite PNN proffered below can be described as provisional. One is upon much safer ground with respect to grammatical structure, since structure can

[84]Thomas L. Thompson, *The Historicity of the Patriarchal Narratives,* BZAW 133 (Berlin: Walter de Gruyter, 1974), pp. 22-36, esp. p. 23. The only flaw in Thompson's otherwise exemplary treatment is that he too easily brushes aside the *y* in the name *ʾăbîrām* as having no significance whatever. See the discussion at pp. 145-50.

[85]The same applies to kinship terms, which may or may not be theophoric. Admittedly, whether the referent of the kinship term is human or divine is a significant difference. But the overall structure of the name, as well as the meaning of the predicate, remain the same, i.e., the difference is of cultural or religious significance, rather than of specifically linguistic significance.

[86]Noth, *IPN,* pp. 15-20; Benz, *PNPP,* p. 217-22.

[87]Both Buccellati, *AURIII,* p. 126, and Huffmon, *APNMT,* p. 153, note the tentative nature of lexical discussions with regard to PNN.

be determined by comparing one name with another. To detect archaic features, it should be noted that it is not always necessary to interpret a name fully. Even if a lexeme remains unknown, the overall structure of the PN may betray an archaic feature.

Semantic considerations play a important role in the interpretation of PNN.[88] This is based on the likely assumption that names were generally couched in the language of the name-giver(s) and expressed a sentiment, a wish, or gratitude that was intelligible to ancient man.[89] Different cultures have different attitudes about the intelligibility of names.[90] Semitic naming practice has little or no parallel with its counterpart in the modern world. Admittedly, some trends in the naming of children, such as papponymy, prestige and vogue names, diverge from this general practice. Nevertheless, these divergent trends are isolated exceptions to an otherwise valid principle. As Gelb noted:

> Since names based on these trends are relatively rare, the conclusion that the ancient Near Eastern names reproduced the current language of the name-givers and were consequently easily understood holds true. By contrast, we may note in our modern world such first names as John, Henry, George, Mary, Helene, Frances, or, to a lesser degree, such family names as Walker, Webster, Kennedy, Breasted, which are not couched in the current language of the name-givers and therefore are generally not understood by the public.[91]

Though most Hebrew names are intelligible, some are difficult if not impossible for the modern reader to understand. Problems in interpretation arise due to the incomplete knowledge of the languages in which the names were cast. Nevertheless the transparency in meaning of names allows semantic considerations to be taken into account in their interpretation.

Structural considerations also play an important role in the interpretation of PNN. By structure is meant the laws according to

---

[88]Huffmon, *APNMT*, pp. 61, 66, 118; Gröndahl, *PTU*, p. 32; Benz, *PNPP*, pp. 217-22, 225-32.

[89]See also p. 6. Similar remarks may be found in James Barr, "The Symbolism of Names in the Old Testament," *BJRL* 52 (1969-70) 11, 14-15, 17.

[90]Barr, *BJRL* 52 (1969-70) 11-15, highlights some of the differences between the ancient Hebrew attitude toward names and that of our modern (English-speaking) society.

[91]Gelb, *Names* 10 (1962) 47. See also Silverman, *RVJPNE*, pp. 16-17, 195-201.

which nominal elements, verbal elements, prepositions, and suffixes enter into combination with each other. It is often possible to predict whether an element is nominal or verbal, theophoric or profane, by observing the structure of compound PNN. For example, in construct phrase names of the form "servant + X," X is invariably a DN or an appellative of a deity.[92] Semantic and structural considerations often work in tandem to point to the proper interpretation of a name. There are instances, however, in which structural considerations alone suggest which of two or more semantically viable interpretations is to be preferred. The importance of structure in the interpretation of PNN is recognized by all practitioners in the field of onomastics. In particular, Noth made many important observations on the structure of Amorite PNN in a series of studies.[93]

III. Sources for the Study of West Semitic PNN

West Semitic PNN are widely scattered throughout the ancient Near East in a variety of epigraphic sources. To cite extremes, they occur in papyri and on vases in ancient Egypt and in the cuneiform tablets of ancient Mesopotamia. In Syria and Palestine West Semitic PNN appear in various kinds of inscriptions, graffiti, letters, and on seals, bullae, vases, and jars, to name the primary forms. In a comparative study of the kind undertaken here, it is not feasible to cite the names from the primary sources. In fact, this study could not have been carried out without reliance upon numerous secondary sources that have collected and analyzed West Semitic PNN.

It is fortunate that within the last twenty years or so, a number of full-scale treatments of various West Semitic onomastica have been produced. Whenever possible, names will be cited from these basic onomastic studies, according to the following system: (author +) abbreviated title of book + page number. An exception to this is in the event that the reading of a name is disputed. In such case, the primary source will be consulted and cited. If a West Semitic PN is not included in a

---

[92]For a brief study of names with this structure, see Walter Kornfeld, "Onomastica aramaica und das Alte Testament," *ZAW* 88 (1976) 109-12.

[93]Noth, *IPN*, pp. 11-41; idem, "Die syrisch-palästinische Bevölkerung des zweiten Jahrtausends v. Chr. im Lichte neuer Quellen," *ZDPV* 65 (1942) 9-67; idem, "Mari und Israel: Eine Personennamenstudie," in *Geschichte und Altes Testament: Albrecht Alt zum siebzigsten Geburtstag dargebracht*, Beiträge zur historischen Theologie, Band 16 (Tübingen, 1953), pp. 127-52; reprinted in *Aufsätze zur biblischen Landes- und Altertumskunde*, 2 vols., ed. Hans W. Wolff, vol. 2: *Beiträge altorientalischer Texte zur Geschichte Israels* (Neukirchener-Vluyn: Neukirchener, 1971), pp. 213-33.

full-scale treatment, I will endeavor to cite the name from the initial publication, insofar as this is reliable and easily accessible. In some instances, it is preferable to cite from a subsequent study or republication of the text.

Before surveying the sources for the study of West Semitic PNN, it is fitting to make some general remarks on the suitability of the scripts for adequately recording West Semitic PNN. Three basic scripts or systems of writing will be considered: alphabetic, syllabic cuneiform, and hieroglyphic.

A. *Alphabetic, Syllabic Cuneiform, and Hieroglyphic Scripts*

The West Semitic family of languages is characterized by the alphabetic system of writing.[94] Originally these languages were written in an alphabet that consisted only of consonants. In time some of these consonants also served to mark vowels. Still the West Semitic script is deficient in providing information on vocalization. The number of consonants in the alphabet varies, depending on the particular language. The Ugaritic alphabet consists of thirty characters (twenty-seven basic phonemes, plus three additional graphs). Although Ugaritic rarely makes use of vowel letters, some information concerning vocalization can be gleaned from the use of the three *ʾalephs* (*ʾa*, *ʾi*, *ʾu*). The Phoenician alphabet consists of twenty-two characters. The difference between the two alphabets lies in five Proto-Semitic phonemes (*ḫ*, *ṯ*, *ḏ*, *ǵ*, *ẓ*); their merger is reflected in the Phoenician alphabet, which has aptly been termed a reduced alphabet. Hebrew, Aramaic, and the Transjordanian dialects are written in this reduced alphabet.

The East Semitic family of languages is represented by the various dialects of Akkadian. Akkadian is written in a cuneiform script that consists of several hundred signs of differing value (logographic[95] and syllabic). Many West Semitic PNN are recorded in cuneiform texts. The primary disadvantage of the script is that it was not conceived for the purpose of representing Semitic phonemes. Because of its Sumerian origin, it was not designed to represent gutturals except for *ḫ*,[96] or many other Akkadian phonological distinctions. Even more

---

[94]I. J. Gelb, *A Study of Writing*, rev. ed. (Chicago: University of Chicago Press, 1963), pp. 149, 204, disputes the use of the term "alphabetic" to describe the West Semitic system of writing. For a defense of the use of the term, see Sandra L. Gogel, "A Grammar of Old Hebrew," 2 vols. (Ph.D. dissertation, University of Chicago, 1985), 1:29-33, with further bibliography.

[95]Under logographic are subsumed determinatives.

[96]This statement is valid for post-Old Akkadian cuneiform script.

serious problems are caused by the polyphonous nature of the script, whereby a sign can have more than one value. Furthermore, various consonant groups, such as bilabial plosives, dentals, velars, and sibilants, are not precisely distinguished in most periods. Some controls are provided by West Semitic scripts, especially at Ugarit, where West Semitic PNN are written in both Ugaritic and Akkadian scripts. The primary advantage of this system of writing as compared with the alphabetic scripts is that it represents vowels. Thus, as mentioned above, Akkadian transliterations of PNN can act as a check on the Masoretic vocalization of Canaanite PNN.

The Egyptian system of writing is complex. Some signs represented individual consonants, while others stood for words. The hieroglyphic script also includes polyphonous signs as well as determinatives. As regards West Semitic PNN, two points should be made. First, early Egyptian material preserves the distinction between the following pairs of Proto-Semitic phonemes: *ṯ/š*, *ḫ/ḥ*, and *ʿ/ġ*.[97] Later texts witness their coalescence. Second, the Egyptians employed a special system, known as 'group writing' or 'syllabic orthography', for recording foreign words and names.[98] Egyptologists disagree over the nature of this special system; in particular, whether the Egyptian weak consonants (*3*, *ʾi*, *y*, *w*) may denote specific vowels.[99] The West Semitic PNN included in our study are found in early material--the execration texts and the Hayes list. For the study of the selected archaic features, all we need to know is whether the consonant *w* represents the (nominative case) vowel *u*. In contrast to certain sign-groups that appear to have been *vieldeutig*, having all three vocalic values (e.g., *ba*, *bi*, *bu*), the representation of the vowel *u* by the Egyptian consonant *w* is one of the least controversial aspects of group writing.[100] Therefore, chapter 2 includes a list of West Semitic proper

---

97Chaim Brovender, in *EncJud*, s.v. "Hebrew Language. Pre-Biblical," 16:1563-64.

98Wolfgang Helck, *Die Beziehungen Ägyptens zu Vorderasien im 3. und 2. Jahrtausend v. Chr.*, 2d rev. ed. (Wiesbaden: Otto Harrassowitz, 1971), pp. 505-75.

99The fundamental work in favor of syllabic orthography is William F. Albright, *The Vocalization of the Egyptian Syllabic Orthography*, American Oriental Series, vol. 5 (New Haven: American Oriental Society, 1934). In addition, see William F. Albright and Thomas O. Lambdin, "New Material for the Egyptian Syllabic Orthography," *JSS* 2 (1957) 113-27; Kenneth A. Kitchen, Review of *Die Ortsnamenlisten aus dem Totentempel Amenophis III*, by Elmar Edel, *BO* 26 (1969) 198-202; Donatella Lippi, "New Considerations about 'Egyptian Syllabic Orthography'," *OrAnt* 23 (1984) 93-95. For an opposing view, see W. F. Edgerton, "Egyptian Phonetic Writing, from its Invention to the Close of the Nineteenth Dynasty," *JAOS* 60 (1940) 473-506.

100In his review of Edel, Kitchen, *BO* 26 (1969) 198, states "within words, Edel has no difficulty in illustrating the validity of *w* = *u* in his texts as in others."

nouns, in which the Egyptian consonant *w* appears to represent the (nominative case) vowel *u*.

The sources for the study of West Semitic PNN are presented in the next two sections. In the first section the West Semitic onomastic sources predate the writing of the Hebrew Bible. The order of presentation is roughly from east to west--Mesopotamia, Syria, Palestine, and Egypt. In the second section the West Semitic onomastic sources are contemporary with or later than the Hebrew Bible. These sources are presented according to the following language groups: Canaanite, Aramaic, and Arabian. In these two sections, I have cited the bibliographic sources in an unabbreviated form so that the reader will not have to refer constantly to the list of abbreviations.

B. *Early West Semitic PNN (second millennium B.C. and earlier)*

The Amorite language is known almost exclusively from PNN occurring in Akkadian and Sumerian texts. The largest number of Amorite PNN are documented for the Old Babylonian period; a smaller quantity of names stems from the Ur III period. The geographical distribution of Amorite PNN extends from Upper Mesopotamia (Mari and Chagar Bazar) and Syria (Alalakh) through Babylonia, and the areas east and south of the latter. The Amorite language shares many isoglosses with Ugaritic and Canaanite.[101]

The most important source for the study of Amorite PNN is I. J. Gelb, *Computer-Aided Analysis of Amorite.*[102] This study supplants all previous lists, containing an estimated 5,922 different names.[103] A promised second volume, which was to include the grammar, glossary, and general discussion, has not yet appeared, and may be inordinately delayed, due to the untimely passing of the author. The absence of the second volume is, however, palliated by certain features of the first, namely the glossary and the presentation of names based on structural analysis of constituent parts. Two additional studies provide grammatical and structural analysis of Amorite PNN. Giorgio Buccellati has

[101]Jonas C. Greenfield, "Amurrite, Ugaritic and Canaanite," in *Proceedings of the International Conference on Semitic Studies, held in Jerusalem, 19-23 July 1965* (Jerusalem: Israel Academy of Sciences and Humanities, 1969), pp. 92-101.

[102]Assyriological Studies, no. 21 (Chicago: Oriental Institute of the University of Chicago, 1980).

[103]For an earlier study of Amor. PNN, see Theo Bauer, *Die Ostkanaanäer: Eine philologische-historische Untersuchung über die Wanderschicht der sogenannten "Amoriter" in Babylonien* (Leipzig: Asia Major, 1926). It contained 786 names, excluding variants.

studied the Ur III Amorite PNN,[104] and Herbert B. Huffmon has analyzed Amorite PNN in the Mari texts.[105]

The excavations at Alalakh in North Syria yielded West Semitic PNN in levels IV and VII. The principle publication of the texts is that of D. J. Wiseman.[106] This work is incomplete in that it does not include handcopies and transliterations of all the texts. This weakness has been remedied in part by subsequent publications.[107] Unfortunately, Wiseman made no attempt to sort the names according to language (Hurrian, West Semitic, etc.). Furthermore, it is difficult to determine which of the levels (IV or VII) the West Semitic PNN come from. Despite these shortcomings, it is necessary to cite West Semitic PNN from Wiseman's publication of the Alalakh tablets.

The excavations at ancient Ugarit (= Ras Shamra) uncovered numerous tablets written in alphabetic cuneiform script.[108] Many Ugaritic PNN bear striking resemblance to later Canaanite PNN. The most important study of PNN is that of Frauke Gröndahl, *Die Personennamen der Texte aus Ugarit.*[109] This work also includes the West Semitic PNN that occur in the Akkadian texts from Ugarit. For the most part, these Akkadian texts were originally published in the series *Mission de Ras Shamra*. At Ugarit, it is sometimes possible to correlate alphabetic and syllabic forms of West Semitic PNN, the latter supplying the vocalization lacking in the former.

The number of Bronze Age texts from Palestine is very meager, and their contribution to West Semitic onomastics is accordingly small.[110] The most important group of texts were unearthed at Tell

---

[104] *The Amorites of the Ur III Period*, Pubblicazioni del seminario di semitistica, Ricerche 1 (Naples: Istituto orientale di Napoli, 1966).

[105] *Amorite Personal Names in the Mari Texts: A Structural and Lexical Study* (Baltimore: Johns Hopkins Press, 1965).

[106] *The Alalakh Tablets*, Occasional Publications of the British Institute of Archaeology at Ankara, no. 2 (London: British Institute of Archaeology, 1953). The index of PNN is found on pp. 125-53.

[107] Donald J. Wiseman, "Supplementary Copies of the Alalakh Tablets," *JCS* 8 (1954) 1-30; idem, "Abban and Alalaḫ," *JCS* 12 (1958) 124-29; idem, "Ration Lists from Alalakh VII," *JCS* 13 (1959) 19-32; idem, "Ration Lists from Alalakh IV," *JCS* 13 (1959) 50-62.

[108] For the most recent edition of the Ugaritic texts, presented in transliteration, see M. Dietrich, O. Loretz, and J. Sanmartín, *Die keilalphabetischen Texte aus Ugarit. Einschließlich der keilalphabetischen Texte außerhalb Ugarits. Teil 1: Transkription*, AOAT 24/1 (Kevelaer: Butzon & Bercker; Neukirchen-Vluyn: Neukirchener, 1976).

[109] Studia Pohl, no. 1 (Rome: Pontificium Institutum Biblicum, 1967).

[110] According to Albert E. Glock, "Texts and Archaeology at Tell Taʿannek," *Berytus* 31 (1983) 58, the latest count is thirty-five Akkadian texts.

Taanach and published by F. Hrozný.[111] The total epigraphic yield consists of seven tablets and five fragments, with an onomasticon of approximately eighty names. According to Gustavs' study, only twenty-one PNN can be classified as "Canaanite."[112] Another Akkadian cuneiform tablet was recovered in excavations at the site in 1968.[113] It contains eleven names, seven of which are West Semitic. Finally a short alphabetic cuneiform tablet from Taanach was initially published by Hillers[114] and republished by Cross with a different reading.[115] According to Cross' readings, it contains two names that may be West Semitic.

Another group of Akkadian texts was discovered in the excavations of Ras el ʿAin (Tel Aphek). Out of a total of eight tablet fragments, only the best preserved of the lot--a letter from Takuḫlina of Ugarit--contains PNN; of the four names in this letter, only one (e.g., *Adduya*) appears to be West Semitic.[116] No other site in Palestine has produced a significant cache of tablets. A few West Semitic PNN can be gleaned from the cuneiform tablets discovered at Shechem, Tell El-Ḥesi, and Hazor.[117]

The most important source for the language spoken in Canaan in the pre-biblical period is the El-Amarna tablets. They were discovered at Tell el-Amarna in Egypt in 1887 and consist of letters between the Egyptian court and their vassal rulers in Canaan. All the proper names--personal, geographical, and divine--have been collected and

---

[111]In Ernst Sellin, *Tell Taʿannek*, Denkschriften der kaiserlichen Akademie der Wissenschaften in Wien, Philosophisch-historische Klasse, vol. 50 (Vienna, 1904), pp. 113-22, Plates X-XI; idem, *Eine Nachlese auf dem Tell Taʿannek in Palästina*, Denkschriften der kaiserlichen Akademie der Wissenschaften in Wien, Philosophisch-historische Klasse, vol. 52/3 (Vienna, 1905), pp. 36-41, Plates I-III.

[112]A. Gustavs, "Die Personennamen in den Tontafeln von Tell Taʿannek," *ZDPV* 50 (1927) 1-18 and 51 (1928) 169-218, esp. pp. 185-97. The names have also been studied by B. Maisler (Mazar), "lwḥwt tʿnk," in *Sēper Qĕlôzner: mʾsp lmdʿ wlsprwt yph mwgš lprwpswr ywsp qlwznr lywbl hššym*, ed. N. H. Torczyner (Tel Aviv, 1937), pp. 44-66.

[113]A. E. Glock, "A New Taʿannek Tablet," *BASOR* 204 (1971) 17-31.

[114]D. R. Hillers, "An Alphabetic Cuneiform Tablet from Taanach (TT 433)," *BASOR* 173 (1964) 45-50.

[115]F. M. Cross, Jr., "The Canaanite Cuneiform Tablet from Taanach," *BASOR* 190 (1968) 41-46.

[116]Anson F. Rainey, "Two Cuneiform Fragments from Tel Aphek," *TA* 2 (1975) 125-29; idem, "A Tri-Lingual Cuneiform Fragment from Tel Aphek," *TA* 3 (1976) 137-40; William W. Hallo, "A Letter from Tel Aphek," *TA* 8 (1981) 18-24; David I. Owen, "An Akkadian Letter from Ugarit at Tel Aphek," *TA* 8 (1981) 1-17.

[117]See respectively W. F. Albright, "A Teacher to a Man of Shechem about 1400 B.C.," *BASOR* 86 (1942) 28-31; idem, "A Case of Lèse-Majesté in Pre-Israelite Lachish, with Some Remarks on the Israelite Conquest," *BASOR* 87 (1942) 32-38; Hallo and Tadmor, *IEJ* 27 (1977) 1-11.

analyzed by Richard S. Hess.[118] The standard edition of the texts remains that of J. A. Knudtzon;[119] the additional twenty-one texts that appeared after Knudtzon's work have been collected into one volume by Anson F. Rainey.[120]

The Egyptian execration texts are a rich source for West Semitic PNN and GNN. The texts are inscribed on vases and figurines, and record the names of potential enemies. In a magical rite portraying the destruction of the enemy, the vase or figurine was broken. The two groups of texts date to the Twelfth Dynasty (circa twentieth-nineteenth centuries B.C.); the earlier group was published by Sethe,[121] the later by Posener.[122] West Semitic PNN and GNN from these texts will be cited according to the standard conventions: e + number (Sethe), and E + number (Posener). The Egyptian transliterations have been updated according to Helck's treatment.[123] Slightly later is the Hayes list, a papyrus dating to the Thirteenth Dynasty (eighteenth century B.C.) that contains roughly thirty West Semitic PNN (cited as Hayes + number).[124] An important study of these West Semitic PNN was published by W. F. Albright.[125] Finally mention should be made of Burchardt's collection of West Semitic loanwords and PNN in Egyptian texts, which

[118] "Amarna Proper Names" (Ph.D. dissertation, Hebrew Union College-Jewish Institute of Religion [Cincinnati], 1984). All the PNN, West Semitic and otherwise, are treated in alphabetical order in Chapter 2 (pp. 38-318). Note also the glossary of West Semitic elements (pp. 325-33).

[119] *Die El-Amarna-Tafeln*, 2 vols. (Leipzig, 1915; reprint, Aalen, 1964).

[120] *El Amarna Tablets 359-79, Supplement to J. A. Knudtzon Die El-Amarna-Tafeln*, 2d rev. ed., AOAT 8 (Kevelaer: Butzon & Bercker; Neukirchen-Vluyn: Neukirchener, 1978).

[121] Kurt Sethe, *Die Ächtung feindlicher Fürsten, Völker und Dinge auf altägyptischen Tongefäßscherben des mittleren Reiches*, Abhandlungen der preussischen Akademie der Wissenschaften, Philosophisch-historische Klasse, no. 5 (Berlin: Akademie der Wissenschaften, 1926), pp. 43-58 for the "Asiatic" (West Semitic) PNN.

[122] G. Posener, *Princes et pays d'Asie et de Nubie. Textes hiératiques sur des figurine d'envoûtement du moyen empire* (Bruxelles: Fondation égyptologique reine élisabeth, 1940), pp. 62-96 for the "Asiatic" (West Semitic) PNN.

[123] Helck, *Beziehungen Ägyptens*, pp. 44-67.

[124] William C. Hayes, *A Papyrus of The Late Middle Kingdom in the Brooklyn Museum (Papyrus Brooklyn 35.1446)* (n.p.: The Brooklyn Museum, 1955), pp. 87-89, 92-99 for the "Asiatic" (West Semitic) PNN.

[125] W. F. Albright, "Northwest-Semitic Names in a List of Egyptian Slaves from the Eighteenth Century B.C.," *JAOS* 74 (1954) 222-33. As acknowledged by Hayes, p. 94, the interpretation of the Asiatic names in his publication is a condensation, prepared by Thomas O. Lambdin, of Albright's article. For a recent treatment of the PNN, see Th. Schneider, "Die semitischen and ägyptischen Namen der syrischen Sklaven des Papyrus Brooklyn 35.1446 verso," *UF* 19 (1987) 255-82.

was published before any of the above-mentioned texts were known.[126]

C. *Late West Semitic PNN (first millennium B.C. and later)*

The West Semitic PNN in cuneiform texts may be Canaanite, Aramaic, or Arabian. The most comprehensive study of West Semitic PNN in first millennium B.C. cuneiform sources is that of Ran Zadok.[127] He analyzes the West Semitic onomasticon of first millennium Babylonia, which is recorded in Neo- and Late-Babylonian and Neo-Assyrian texts. The book consists of two large sections, treating Aramaic and Arabian PNN, followed by an appendix on orthography and phonology, synoptic lists, and indices. An older work that treats the West Semitic PNN in Neo-Assyrian sources is that of Knut L. Tallqvist.[128] Coogan has studied the West Semitic PNN recorded in the Neo-Babylonian Murašû archive, which was discovered at Nippur and dates to the fifth century B.C.[129]

Within Canaanite, one may distinguish between Hebrew (biblical and epigraphic), the Transjordanian dialects (Ammonite, Moabite, and Edomite), Phoenician-Punic, and Neo-Punic. The older collections of Hebrew inscriptional remains are clearly out of date.[130] Lawton has compiled a list of Hebrew PNN found in preexilic epigraphic sources.[131] The most comprehensive list of Hebrew seals (and seal-impressions), with PNN indexed, is presented in a series of articles by

---

[126]M. Burchardt, *Die altkanaanäischen Fremdwörter und Eigennamen im Ägyptischen*, 2 vols. (Leipzig: J. C. Hinrichs, 1909-10).

[127]*On West Semites in Babylonia during the Chaldean and Achaemenian Periods: An Onomastic Study* (Jerusalem: H. J. & Z. Wanaarta and Tel Aviv University, 1977). Zadok has published supplementary notes to this major study in *The Jews in Babylonia during the Chaldean and Achaemenian Periods according to the Babylonian Sources*, Studies in the History of the Jewish People and the Land of Israel, Monograph Series, vol. 3 (n.p.: University of Haifa, 1979), pp. 90-95, and *Sources for the History of the Jews in Babylonia during the Chaldean and Achaemenian Periods, with an Appendix on West Semitic Names in 1st-Millennium Mesopotamia* (Jerusalem, 1980), pp. 1-44.

[128]*Assyrian Personal Names*, Acta Societatis Scientiarum Fennicae, vol. 48/1 (Helsinki, 1914). Tallqvist marks non-Assyrian PNN with an asterisk.

[129]Michael D. Coogan, *West Semitic Personal Names in the Murašû Documents*, HSM 7 (Missoula: Scholars Press, 1976).

[130]David Diringer, *Le iscrizioni antico-ebraiche palestinesi* (Florence: Felice Le Monnier, 1934); Sabatino Moscati, *L'epigrafia ebraica antica* (Rome: Pontifico Instituto Biblico, 1951).

[131]Robert Lawton, "Israelite Personal Names on Pre-Exilic Hebrew Inscriptions," *Bib* 65 (1984) 330-46.

Francesco Vattioni.[132] Each article has gradually expanded the corpus; at the end of the third one, the total is 452 items. With the refining of palaeographic analysis, so that national script traditions can now be discerned, it has become apparent that many of Vattioni's so-called Hebrew seals actually belong to other Canaanite languages. To the best of my knowledge, I have sought to cite only Hebrew seals from his list, unless otherwise noted. Names recorded on these seals will be cited as VSE (= Vattioni, "Sigilli ebraici") + number. For PNN on bullae, an most important work is Nahman Avigad's *Hebrew Bullae from the Time of Jeremiah: Remnants of a Burnt Archive.*[133] Yigal Shiloh has also published a group of Hebrew bullae from Jerusalem.[134] The three most productive sites of epigraphic Hebrew remains are Arad,[135] Lachish,[136] and Samaria.[137] Names from these sites will be cited as A, L, and S + text/line number.

Ammonite inscriptional material has been gathered together and analyzed by Kent P. Jackson.[138] He has also published a special study on the Ammonite onomasticon.[139] On Moabite, one can consult the Meša inscription[140] and the list of Moabite seals compiled by Felice

---

[132]"I sigilli ebraici," *Bib* 50 (1969) 357-88; "I sigilli ebraici II," *Augustinianum* 11 (1971) 447-54; "Sigilli ebraici III," *AION* 38 (1978) 227-54.

[133]Jerusalem: Israel Exploration Society, 1986.

[134]Yigal Shiloh, "qbwṣt bwlwt ʿbrywt mʿyr dwd," *EI* 18 (1985) 73-87 (in English translation: "A Group of Hebrew Bullae from the City of David," *IEJ* 36 [1986] 16-38).

[135]Yohanan Aharoni, *Arad Inscriptions*, ed. and rev. Anson F. Rainey (Jerusalem: Israel Exploration Society, 1981).

[136]Harry Torczyner (N. H. Tur-Sinai), *Lachish I: The Lachish Letters* (London: Oxford University Press, 1938).

[137]PNN from Samaria will be cited according to the restudy of the ostraca by I. Tracy Kaufman, "The Samaria Ostraca, A Study in Ancient Hebrew Palaeography" (Ph.D. dissertation, Harvard University, 1966).

[138]*The Ammonite Language of the Iron Age*, HSM 27 (Chico: Scholars Press, 1983), pp. 95-98 for his list of Ammonite PNN. Add to his bibliography Felice Israel, "The Language of the Ammonites," *OLP* 10 (1979) 143-59. Jackson's list of Ammonite seals should be expanded (Walter E. Aufrecht, "The Ammonite Language of the Iron Age," *BASOR* 106 [1987] 86; Felice Israel, "Les sceaux ammonites," *Syria* 64 [1987] 141-46).

[139]Kent P. Jackson, "Ammonite Personal Names in the Context of the West Semitic Onomasticon," in *The Word of the Lord Shall Go Forth: Essays in Honor of David Noel Freedman in Celebration of His Sixtieth Birthday*, ed. Carol L. Meyers and M. O'Connor (Winona Lake: Eisenbrauns, 1983), pp. 507-21. See also M. O'Connor, "The Ammonite Onomasticon: Semantic Problems," *AUSS* 25 (1987) 51-64.

[140]H. Donner and W. Röllig, *Kanaanäische und aramäische Inschriften*, 3 vols. (Wiesbaden: Otto Harrassowitz, 1971-76), text #181.

Israel.[141] The Edomite epigraphic remains have been analyzed by Felice Israel.[142] The fundamental work in the study of the Phoenician-Punic onomasticon is that of Frank L. Benz.[143] Additional studies published after Benz partially overlap but also deal with new finds.[144] Jongeling has collected and analyzed the Semitic PNN in Neo-Punic inscriptions.[145]

We turn now to Aramaic PNN written in alphabetic script. For Old Aramaic, most of the texts are to be found in *KAI*. A study of the Old Aramaic onomasticon, which also treats Old Aramaic PNN attested in cuneiform script, was carried out by Mario Liverani.[146] Mohammed Maraqten's study is even broader, including Semitic--mostly Aramaic--PNN in Old and Imperial Aramaic inscriptions (tenth-third centuries B.C.).[147] All the PNN discovered in the Elephantine texts have been collected and analyzed by Michael H. Silverman.[148] Among the West Semitic PNN recorded in the texts are also some Hebrew and Phoenician PNN, and mixed types. A broader work, allegedly treating all the Aramaic PNN from Egypt, is by Walter Kornfeld.[149]

---

[141]"Studi Moabiti I: Rassegna di epigrafia moabiti e i sigilli moabiti," in *Atti della 4ª Giornata di Studi Camito-Semitici e Indoeuropei (Bergamo, Istituto Universitario, 29 novembre 1985)*, ed. G. Bernini and V. Brugnatelli (Milano, 1987), pp. 101-38.

[142]"Miscellanea Idumea," *RivB* 27 (1979) 171-203; idem, "Supplementum idumeum I," *RivB* 35 (1987) 337-56.

[143]*Personal Names in Phoenician and Punic Inscriptions*, Studia Pohl, no. 8 (Rome: Biblical Pontifical Institute, 1972).

[144]Francesco Vattioni, "I sigilli fenici," *AION* 41 (1981) 177-93 (cited as VSP + seal number); idem, "Antroponimi fenicio-punici nell'epigrafia greca e latina del Nordafrica," *Annali del Seminario di studi del mondo classico, Istituto Universitario Orientale, Sezione di archeologia e storia antica* 1 (1979) 153-90. A list of PNN are also included in M-J. Fuentes Estañol, *Vocabulario fenicio*, Biblioteca fenicia, vol. 1 (Barcelona, 1980).

[145]Karel Jongeling, *Names in Neo-Punic Inscriptions* (Groningen, 1984).

[146]"Antecedenti dell'onomastica aramaica antica," *RSO* 37 (1962) 65-76.

[147]*Die semitischen Personennamen in den alt- und reicharamäischen Inschriften aus Vorderasien*, Texte und Studien zur Orientalistik, Band 5 (Hildesheim: Georg Olms, 1988). For the Aramaic seals with an index of PNN, see also Francesco Vattioni, "I sigilli, le monete e gli avori aramaici," *Augustinianum* 11 (1971) 47-87, esp. pp. 47-69.

[148]*Religious Values in the Jewish Proper Names at Elephantine*, AOAT 217 (Kevelaer: Butzon & Bercker; Neukirchen-Vluyn: Neukirchener, 1985). This work is a revision of his dissertation, "Jewish Personal Names in the Elephantine Documents: A Study in Onomastic Development" (Ph.D. dissertation, Brandeis University, 1967).

[149]*Onomastica Aramaica aus Ägypten*, Österreichische Akademie der Wissenschaften, Philosophisch-historische Klasse Sitzungsberichte, Band 333 (Vienna: Österreichische Akademie der Wissenschaften, 1978). In a review article, E.

There remains to mention other treatments of Aramaic PNN. For the study of Palmyrene PNN, the study of Jürgen K. Stark is indispensable.[150] The PNN in the inscriptions from Hatra have been the subject of a study by Sabri Abbadi.[151] Lastly, Nabatean PNN will be cited from the lexicon in the second volume of Jean Cantineau's *Le Nabatéen*.[152]

For the study of pre-Islamic Arabian names the principal work is G. Lankester Harding, *An Index and Concordance of Pre-Islamic Arabian Names and Inscriptions*.[153] It includes all texts up to 1967, and even a few after that date. The various kinds of names are listed according to the Arabic alphabet, and included is all the onomastic material from North Arabian (Liḥyanite, Safaitic, and Thamudic) and South Arabian (Ḥaḍrami, Minaean, Qatabanian, and Sabaean) dialects. Harding's study supplants the enduring work of G. Ryckmans,[154] though the latter work retains value in that it includes a vocalization and interpretation for many of the names. A. R. al-Ansary has studied the relationship of Liḥyanite PNN to other Semitic groups (Amorite, Canaanite in Egyptian sources, Ugaritic, Hebrew, Thamudic, and Safaitic).[155] Lastly West Semitic PNN that occur in Greek inscriptions and papyri were collected and analyzed by Heinz Wuthnow in a study now badly out of date.[156]

Throughout the remainder of this study, the phrases "early West Semitic" (section B. above) and "late West Semitic" (section C. above) have been adopted as a shorthand way to refer to this twofold division.

Lipiński, "Etudes d'onomastique ouest-sémitique," *BO* 37 (1980) 5-10, corrects some of Kornfeld's readings and points out names that were inadvertently omitted.

[150] *Personal Names in Palmyrene Inscriptions* (Oxford: Clarendon Press, 1971).

[151] *Die Personennamen der Inschriften aus Hatra*, Texte und Studien zur Orientalistik, Band 1 (Hildesheim: Georg Olms, 1983).

[152] 2 vols. (Paris: Librairie Ernest Leroux, 1930-32).

[153] Near and Middle Eastern Studies, no. 8 (Toronto: University of Toronto Press, 1971).

[154] *Les noms propres sud-sémitiques*, 3 vols., Bibliothèque Muséon, no. 2 (Louvain, 1934-35).

[155] A. R. al-Ansary, "Lihyanite Personal Names: A Comparative Study," *The Annual of Leeds University Oriental Society* 7 (1969-73) 5-16. This article is based on his "A Critical and Comparative Study of Lihyanite Personal Names" (Ph.D. thesis, Leeds University, 1966).

[156] *Die semitischen Menschennamen in griechischen Inschriften und Papyri des vorderen Orients*, Studien zur Epigraphik und Papyruskunde, Band 1/4 (Leipzig: Dieterich, 1930).

CHAPTER 2

THE NOMINATIVE CASE ENDING *-U*

The Semitic languages originally distinguished three basic case endings in the declension of singular nouns: nominative *-u*, genitive *-i*, and accusative *-a*. These vowels, which are short,[1] are quantitatively distinct from the external case endings in the declension of masculine plural nouns, in which only two cases are distinguished: nominative **-ū* and oblique (= genitive/accusative) **-ī*. The declension of singular nouns is thus triptotic, while that of plural nouns is diptotic. In some Semitic languages, there is a series of singular nouns with diptotic declension.

In Akkadian the basic case endings were retained in their entirety. In the later dialects, such as Neo-Assyrian and Neo-Babylonian, however, the case distinctions became blurred and the endings began to be used indiscriminately or even omitted altogether. Classical Arabic also retained the Proto-Semitic case system in its entirety, whereas in modern vernacular Arabic the case endings have disappeared. In Geʿez, owing to the merger of *i*, *u* > *ĕ*, the nominative and genitive cases have disappeared, since *ĕ* is not retained in word final position; accusative *a* (usually transcribed *ä*), however, remains. In the languages subsumed under early West Semitic, the Proto-Semitic case system was probably retained in its entirety, though most of our evidence (except Ugaritic) is limited to proper names. Among late West Semitic languages, the case endings on singular nouns have generally dropped from use, while those on plural nouns have been modified.

It is the case endings on singular nouns that are pertinent for the study of Canaanite PNN in the Hebrew Bible. In particular, it has long been noted that some Canaanite PNN may have retained the nominative singular case vowel *-u*. The Hebrew reflex of this *-u* vowel has

---

[1]As argued cogently by Sabatino Moscati, "On Semitic Case-Endings," *JNES* 17 (1958) 142-44, and idem, *CGSL* §12.64, who has rebutted the view of Brockelmann, *GVG*, 1:460, that the singular endings were quantitatively ambivalent. For general discussion of case endings, see C. Rabin, "The Structure of the Semitic System of Case Endings," in *Proceedings of the International Conference on Semitic Studies, held in Jerusalem, 19-23 July 1965* (Jerusalem: Israel Academy of Sciences and Humanities, 1969), pp. 190-204.

been referred to as a paragogic vowel[2] or as *waw compaginis* (with reference to the *waw mater lectionis* with which this vowel is marked).[3] Whatever one prefers to call it, the occurrence of this morpheme in Canaanite PNN can best be understood by surveying the use of case endings in early and late West Semitic, with special attention to PNN. This survey focuses on the use of case endings on masculine singular nouns, since only those case endings are relevant for the interpretation of Canaanite PNN. The use of case endings in PNN does not always conform to what we might expect according to the grammar of a language. While one may hesitate to describe their use as arbitrary, nevertheless one must admit that the occurrence or omission of some case endings may be conditioned by a combination of morphological, phonological, and syntactic considerations, not all of which are obvious to the contemporary reader.

I. Early West Semitic

The masculine singular noun in Amorite is characterized by three types of declension: 1) nominative *-u*, genitive *-i*, and accusative *-a*; 2) -Ø ending in all cases; and 3) *-a* in all cases.[4] Gelb has maintained that there is no reason to suppose that the latter two types of declension were used outside of PNN. He supported this assertion by noting that this distribution of declension types in Amorite finds a complete parallel in Old Akkadian; in the latter, of course, there is non-onomastic textual material that establishes the distribution.[5] He attributed the declension type with *-a* in all cases to the predicate state.[6] As examples of the triptotic case system, note nominative *a-ḫu-um*, genitive *a-ḫi-im*, and accusative *a-ḫa-am-ar-ši* (*CAAA*, p. 556), and nominative *me-er-rum*, genitive *me-er-ri-im*, and accusative *me-er-ra-am* (*CAAA*, pp. 622-23). With Amor. PNN one can illustrate how a deviation in the expected

[2] P. Paul Joüon, *Grammaire de l'hébreu biblique* (Rome: Institut Biblique Pontifical, 1923), §93s.

[3] R. Giveon and A. Lemaire, "Sceau phénicien inscrit d'Akko avec scène religieuse," *Sem* 35 (1985) 32; Julius Lewy, "Les textes paléo-assyriens et l'Ancien Testament," *RHR* 110 (1934) 61 n. 77; Bauer, *Ostkanaanäer*, pp. 65-66.

[4] I. J. Gelb, "La lingua degli Amoriti," *RANL* 13 (1958), §3.2.3.1-6.

[5] Ibid.

[6] See especially I. J. Gelb, "The Origin of the East Semitic *Qatala* Morpheme," in *Symbolae linguisticae in honorem Georgii Kurylowicz*, Polska Akademia Nauk, Prace Komisji Jezykoznawstwa, no. 5 (Wroclaw, 1965), pp. 72-80. Contrast C. Rabin, "The Diptote Declension," in *Arabic and Islamic Studies in Honor of Hamilton A. R. Gibb*, ed. George Makdisi (Leiden: E. J. Brill, 1965), pp. 555-56, who compares this *-a* ending with the Arabic diptote declension.

case endings may be due to certain syntactic considerations. PNN from any Semitic language of the type "servant + X," where X = DN or appellative of a deity, are construct phrase PNN. Thus one would expect the *nomen rectum* to end in the genitive case ending *-i*.[7] The Amor. PN *ḫa-ab-du-a-mi-im* (*CAAA*, p. 89), "servant of Amim," illustrates well the expected case ending. Other examples of similar or identical Amor. PNN are *ḫa-ab-du-ᵈa-mi*, *ḫa-ab-du-a-mi*, and *ab-du-a-mi-im* (2x-1x nominative/1x genitive) (*CAAA*, p. 89).[8] Yet the name also appears with the writing *ḫa-ab-du-a-mu-um* (*CAAA*, p. 89), in which the second element ends in a nominative case ending. It is difficult to believe that the last name is semantically and structurally different from the others, and thus means "The servant is Amum." Instead, the case vowel on the second element of *ḫa-ab-du-a-mu-um* may be explained by the phenomenon of nominalization. In this instance, the entire name is treated as a single unit, ending in the nominative case (plus mimation). Examples of nominalization have been observed in Eblaite and Akkadian PNN.[9] A well-known example from Ugaritic PNN will be cited later in this section. Admittedly, some of the deviations in case endings may be due to the syntactic requirements of the sentence in which the PN occurs, but this explanation is not applicable in many cases. Huffmon's study of vocalic endings on the Amor. PNN in the Mari texts has demonstrated that in sentence names the vocalic endings are not merely arbitrary helping vowels.[10] As Huffmon himself emphasizes, the greater regularity in declension of these Amor. PNN is apparent only from an internal study of these names. Amor. PNN from other sites may not exhibit the same degree of homogeneity as those from Mari. Scribal tendencies and onomastic trends may vary in different regions and periods, and these may in part explain differences in the use of case endings.

In the execration texts the nominative case ending *-u* in West Semitic proper names is represented by Egyptian *-w*. These texts contain numerous GNN and PNN from Syria and Palestine dating to the

---

[7]It is difficult to make generalizations about the case ending expected on the *nomen regens* of compound Amor. PNN with **ʿabd-* in first position. The examples cited above all have the nominative case ending *-u*, but other vowels also occur in this position, especially *-i*, rarely *-a*. Note the *-ä* vowel in the construct of Geʿez and Amharic.

[8]Note that Ronald Youngblood, "Amorite Influence in a Canaanite Amarna Letter (*EA* 96)," *BASOR* 168 (1962) 25, analyzes the *-i* vowel on the second element of the WS PN *Rīb-Haddi* as a genitive ending on a *nomen rectum*.

[9]For Eblaite, see Pelio Fronzaroli, "The Concord in Gender in Eblaite Theophoric Personal Names," *UF* 11 (1979) 281; for Akkadian PNN, see Arthur Ungnad, *Grammatik des Akkadischen*, rev. ed. (Munich: C. H. Beck, 1964), §39c.

[10]Huffmon, *APNMT*, pp. 104-17.

first two centuries of the second millennium B.C. Some of these proper names terminate in the case ending itself, whereas others have case ending plus mimation.[11] In the left column the West Semitic proper names in Egyptian transliteration are cited from Sethe's list, and in the right column, the reconstructed Semitic vocable, whenever possible, which ends in the nominative case vowel. No attempt is made here to interpret the names fully. Other examples of the nominative case ending are probably to be found within these lists; for the most part unambiguous examples on easily recognizable Semitic vocables are listed.

e 8	*ʿ-m-mú-ʾa-t(r)*	PN	*ʿ*ammu* "kinsman"
e 10	*ʿ-m-mú-já-k-n*	PN	*ʿ*ammu* "kinsman"
e 11	*ʾa-r-ḥ-b-u*	GN	*rĕḥōb* (biblical GN)
e 11	*ʿpr-u-h-q*	PN	*ʿ*pru* "foster-child"[12]
e 13	*ʿ-m-mú-ta*	PN	*ʿ*ammu* "kinsman"
e 21	*š-m-š-u-ʾil-i-m*	PN	**Šamšu* DN
e 22	*ʾi-l-u-m-q-h-tí*	PN	*ʾ*ilu(m)* "god/El"
e 27	*já-q-r-ʿ-mú*	PN	*ʿ*ammu* "kinsman"
e 30	*já-m-i-l-u*	PN	*ʾ*ilu* "god"

This list is comprised of eight PNN and one GN. With the exception of e 22, the first element of which ends in mimation or enclitic *-m*, the other eight proper names terminate in the simple case vowel *-u*. The eight PNN may be analyzed as follows: one DN (e 21); two occurrences of *ʾ*ilu(m)* (e 22 [DN?], 30); four occurrences of *ʿ*ammu* (e 8, 10, 13, 27); and one occurrence of *ʿ*pru* (e 11). As with kinship terms, the vocable *ʿ*ammu* may be a theophoric element in any of these PNN.

The same procedure is followed in citing West Semitic proper names from Posener's list:

E 3	*n-q-mú-p-ʿa*	PN	**niqmu* "vengeance"
E 4	*ja-tin-h-d-d-u*	PN	**Hadadu* DN
E 6	*ʾab-ś-h-d-d-u*	PN	**Hadadu* DN
E 7	*ʾá-š-h-d-d-u*	PN	**Hadadu* DN
E 8	*p-a-ḥ()l-u-m*	GN	*URUpé-ḫe-lì* (EA GN)
E 8	*ʿ()pr-u-ʿ-nu*	PN	*ʿ*pru* "foster-child"
E 9	*ʾá-p-q-u-m*	GN	*ʾapē/īq* (biblical GN)

[11] On mimation in WS proper names in the execration texts, see pp. 157-59.

[12] According to Helck, *Beziehungen Ägyptens*, p. 47, this is a construct phrase PN.

E 9	*ja-n-k-a-ʾi-lu*	PN	**ʾilu* "god/El"
E 12	*ʿ()pr-u-ʾa-ś-ʾá-p-a*	PN	**ʿpru* "foster-child"
E 14	*ʾa-r-ḥ-b-u-m*	GN	*rĕḥōb* (biblical GN)
E 14	*ja-k-m-š-ʿ-m-mú*	PN	**ʿammu* "kinsman"
E 17	*š-ʿ-p-u-m*	GN	< **s/z/ṣʿp*[13]
E 17	*ḥ-w()r-n-i₂-ʾab-u-m*	PN	**ʾabū(m)* "father"
E 19	*ja-n-ṣ-m-h-d-d-u*	PN	**Hadadu* DN
E 22	*ʿ-m-mú-t-l-a*	PN	**ʿammu* "kinsman"
E 26	*ʿ-ḫ-u-mut*	PN	**ʿḫu*
E 30	*ʿ()pr-u-ja-(...)-mut*	PN	**ʿpru* "foster-child"
E 31-32	*ʿ()pr-u-(...)*	PN	**ʿpru* "foster-child"
E 33-34	*ʾá-p-u-m*	GN	?[14]
E 34	*ʿ-ḫ-u-k-b(!)-k-b(!)*	PN	**ʿḫu*
E 41	*ʿ-m-mú-ʾa-r-u-b-u*	PN	**ʿammu* "kinsman"
E 42	*ʿ-m-mú-(...)*	PN	**ʿammu* "kinsman"
E 43	*š-m-š-u-ʾa-p-a-ʾil-i-m*	PN	**Šamšu* DN
E 46	*(...)-h-d-d-u*	PN	**Hadadu* DN
E 49	*tar-ʿ-m-mú*	PN	**ʿammu* "kinsman"
E 52	*š-mú-ʾab-u*	PN	**šumu* "name"; **ʾabū* "father"
E 54	*ʿ-m-mú-ḥ()r-(...)*	PN	**ʿammu* "kinsman"
E 55	*š-mú-ʿ-nu*	GN	**šumu* "name"
E 55	*ʾab-u-r₂a-h-n-a*	PN	**ʾabū* "father"
E 56	*ʾab-u-(...)-a*	PN	**ʾabū* "father"
E 57	*ja-k-m-š-ʿ-mú*	PN	**ʿammu* "kinsman"
E 58	*ja-r-p-i-l-u*	PN	**ʾilu* "god/El"
E 60	*b-u-tì-š-m-šu*	GN	**Šamšu* DN

This list includes thirty-three proper names, which can be divided into twenty-six PNN and seven GNN. Five GNN (E 8, 9, 14, 17, 33-34) and one PN (E 17) terminate in the nominative case ending plus mimation; the relevant element of the remaining twenty-seven proper names terminates in the simple case vowel (both elements of E 52 terminate in the simple case vowel). The relevant CNN may be summarized as follows, in decreasing order of frequency: **ʿammu* (7x; E 14, 22, 41, 42, 49, 54, 57), **ʿpru* (4x; E 8, 12, 30, 31-32), **ʾabū* (4x; E 17, 52, 55,

[13]So B. Maisler, "Palestine at the Time of the Middle Kingdom in Egypt," *Revue de l'histoire juive en Égypte* 1 (1947) 50.

[14]For various suggestions, see W. F. Albright, "The Land of Damascus between 1850 and 1750 B.C.," *BASOR* 83 (1941) 34-35; René Dussaud, "Nouveaux textes égyptiens d'exécration contre les peuples syriens," *Syria* 21 (1940) 175; Maisler, *Revue de l'histoire juive en Égypte* 1 (1947) 56. The problem of identification is complicated by several similar Amarna GNN.

56), *ʾilu (2x; E 9, 58 [DNN?]), *ʿḫu (2x; E 26, 34), *šumu (2x; E 52, 55), and *niqmu (1x; E 3). For DNN with the nominative case ending, note *Hadadu (5x; E 4, 6, 7, 19, 46) and Šamšu (2x; E 43, 60). In both the Sethe and Posener lists, examples of nominative case endings are found in medial as well as final positions. More PNN with the nominative case ending represented by Egyptian -*w* may be found in the Hayes papyrus (Hayes ##9, 13, 15, 26, 27, 29, 62, 87).

The evidence for the triptotic case system on WS PNN in the Alalakh tablets, the Taanach tablets, and the El Amarna letters has been collected and analyzed by Sivan. His study also includes instances of case endings on WS glosses in the El Amarna letters and on Ugaritic vocables in Akkadian texts from Ras Shamra.[15] Sivan contends that these proper names are characterized by two case systems, triptotic and diptotic.[16] For a detailed treatment of the case endings, one should consult Sivan's work; for our purposes, it is sufficient to cite a few instances of the nominative singular case ending in WS PNN: the EA PNN *ba-lu-mé-er* and *šu-mu-ḫa-d[i]* (Hess, *AmPN*, pp. 83, 239). At Taanach, three WS PNN are constructed with the vocable *ʾilu: *e-lu-ra-p[í?-i?]* (Taan. 12.3); *e-lu-ra-ḫé-ba* (Taan. 4.9); and *e-lu-ra-ma* (Taan. 7.3 [rev.]).[17] On this last name, Thompson notes in passing that the -*u* vowel is the nominative case ending, a common feature of early WS PNN at Mari.[18] For the nominative case ending on a CN functioning as a PN in the Taanach tablets, one may cite *zi-bi-lu* "prince" (l. 4--Glock, *BASOR* 204:19).[19]

Though the Ugaritic script, like other West Semitic scripts, is essentially consonantal, the use of the three *ʾaleph* signs *ʾa*, *ʾi*, and *ʾu* demonstrates that the case system was still in use in this language. The three *ʾaleph* signs indicate case endings on III-ʾ nouns. Regretably, only a few Ug. PNN end in final *ʾaleph*. Two pairs of Ug. PNN display

---

[15]Daniel Sivan, *Grammatical Analysis and Glossary of the Northwest Semitic Vocables in Akkadian Texts of the 15th-13th C.B.C. from Canaan and Syria*, AOAT 214 (Kevelaer: Butzon & Bercker; Neukirchen-Vluyn, Neukirchener, 1984), pp. 114-23.

[16]Ibid, p. 115. See also p. 38 n. 6 above, and Liverani, *RSO* 38 (1963) 131-60, on proper nouns terminating in *-*ānu/a*. For remnants of the diptote declension of GNN in the Hebrew Bible, see Stanislav Segert, "Diptotic Geographical Feminine Names in the Hebrew Bible," *Zeitschrift für Althebraistik* 1 (1988) 99-102. For *a* in EA PNN, see Hess, *AmPN*, pp. 29-30, who writes "The tendency for final vowels to follow their case in WS PNs . . . must be balanced by the frequency of the final *a* vowel, regardless of case, at Amarna."

[17]The first two names are cited according to Sivan's corrected transliterations (*GAGNWS*, p. 200).

[18]Thompson, *Historicity*, p. 30 n. 93.

[19]According to Glock, *BASOR* 204 (1971) 27, perhaps a *qitl* formation with anaptyxis. Compare the Ug. PN ᶠ*pí-zi-ib/bi-li* (Gröndahl, *PTU*, p. 183).

the nominative and genitive case endings: *ʿmlbʾu* and *ʿmlbʾi*; and *bn šmlbʾu* and *šmlbʾi* (*PTU*, p. 154). Other Ug. PNN that attest the case endings are *ʾaḫdbʾu* (*PTU*, p. 308),[20] *ḫlʾi* (*PTU*, p. 138), *bn ḫrʾi* (*PTU*, p. 139), *prʾi* (*PTU*, p. 174), *ʾabrpʾu*, *ʾilrpʾu*, *ʿmrpʾi*, and *ʿbdrpʾu* (*PTU*, p. 180). Gordon notes in his grammar that this last name is a construct phrase type that has been nominalized.[21]

Two points remain to be made on Ug. PNN. First, in at least two compound names the existence of a medial vowel between the name elements may be inferred. That is, when one encounters a writing *x-x*, where *x* represents any consonant, and this writing occurs at the boundary between two nominal elements of a compound name, one may infer the existence of an intervening vowel, because identical consonants that come into contact with one another are not indicated in alphabetic script by double writing.[22] The two Ug. PNN that satisfy these requirements are *ʾdnnʿm* and *šmmlk* (*PTU*, pp. 90, 194). By comparing the first elements of these PNN with the identical vocables in syllabically written PNN one may make suggestions on the quality and nature of the medial vowel. The medial vowel in the PN *ʾdnnʿm* is probably not a case ending at all, but the 1st c.s. pronominal suffix.[23] A comparison of the name *šmmlk* with syllabically written forms of the vocable *šm* indicates two writings with -Ø, one with *-i*, and four with *-u*. Therefore it is possible that the medial vowel in the Ug. PN *šmmlk* is a nominative case ending. Incidentally one may infer the existence of a mood vowel (*-u/-a* ?) in the Ug. PN *yrgbbʿl* (RS 24.246, l. 16 [*Ug* VII, p. 6]).

Second, there is evidence in the Akkadian texts from Ugarit that case endings of PNN were declinable. In text RS 15.89, l. 11 (*PRU* III,

---

[20]This name is cited by Gröndahl in a list of names that are either unclear, or of unknown linguistic origin. The suggestion of Jirku, *ArOr* 37 (1969) 10, is at least plausible; he considers it as a Ug. PN meaning "the brother is strong" (compare Ug. *dbʾat* and the BH root **dbʾ*).

[21]Cyrus Gordon, *Ugaritic Textbook*, Analecta Orientalia, no. 38 (Rome: Biblical Pontifical Institute, 1965), §8.71.

[22]The inference of an intervening vowel is not valid for the writing *n-x*, because there is inconsistency in the assimilation of preconsonantal *n*. For further discussion, see Sivan, *GAGNWS*, pp. 45-47. According to Huehnergard, *Ugaritic Vocabulary*, p. 280, Ugaritic vocables in cuneiform writing evidence complete assimilation of preconsonantal *n*. On the question of the assimilation of *n* in first millennium B.C. Northwest Semitic dialects, see W. Randall Garr, *Dialect Geography of Syria-Palestine, 1000-586 B.C.E.* (Philadelphia: University of Pennsylvania Press, 1985), pp. 40-44.

[23]Likewise with the Amm. *ʾdnnr* (Jackson, *ALIA*, p. 84). This analysis also applies to the EH PN *ʾbbʿl* (S 2.4), and the Ph-P. PN *ʾbbʿl* (Benz, *PNPP*, p. 54), as confirmed by the plene writing *ʾbybʿl* (ibid.) as well as Greek and cuneiform transliterations of the same name (ibid., pp. 257-58). Thus Fuentes Estañol's vocalization of the Ph-P. PN *ʾbbʿl* as "Abbaal" is impossible (p. 57).

p. 53), the Ug. PN *ᶠa-ḫa-tum-milki(LUGAL)* occurs, in which the *nomen regens* ends with the nominative case ending.[24] Twice elsewhere in this text, in syntactic environments requiring the genitive case ending, occurs the form *ᶠa-ḫa-ti-milki(LUGAL)* (ll. 8, 18). One may conclude that while the case endings on many PNN may well have been static, in some instances the case endings were declined according to the syntactic requirements of the context in which the PN

Before concluding this section, it is apposite to discuss briefly the loss of final short vowels in West Semitic. This includes case vowels in the absolute and construct states[25] of singular nouns and the modal vowels on verbs, but we will restrict the discussion to the former as being most relevant to the matter at hand. As will be demonstrated in Chapter 4, the singular noun in Amorite terminated in case ending plus mimation, though there is a considerable inconsistency in the use of mimation in these dialects. Among the late West Semitic languages, the singular noun generally terminates in -Ø ending. Ugaritic and the WS glosses in the Amarna letters represent an intermediate stage, in that the singular noun ended in the case vowel without mimation. As long as mimation characterized the singular noun in West Semitic, the case vowel was protected and thus preserved. This situation prevailed to some extent in Amorite. With the dropping of mimation on the

---

[24]J. Nougayrol's transliteration of the first element of the name as *ᶠa-ḫa-tum-* in l. 11 need not be "corrected" to *ᶠa-ḫa-tu₄-* (so Sivan, *GAGNWS*, pp. 124, 196; see also Huehnergard, *Ugaritic Vocabulary*, p. 294). While it is true that singular nouns did not terminate in mimation (even in the *status rectus*) in these texts, the use of the *tum* sign by the scribe is a sort of historical spelling; in this case it indicates the noun is morphologically feminine and in the nominative case.

[25]Brockelmann's view (*GVG*, 1:475-81) that the construct state of the noun originally had case endings (*pace* BL §65c), finds confirmation in Eblaite, Amorite, Ugaritic, and Amharic (on Amharic, see pp. 9-10). See I. J. Gelb, "Ebla and the Kish Civilization," in *La lingua di Ebla: Atti del Convegno internationale (Napoli, 22-23 aprile 1980)*, ed. Luigi Cagni, Istituto universitario orientale, Seminario di studi asiatici, Series Minor, vol. 14 (Napoli, 1981), pp. 31-32, 50 (he does cite one case in which a noun in the construct state ends in -Ø ending); Huffmon, *APNMT*, pp. 124-25; Gary A. Tuttle, "Case Vowels on Masculine Singular Nouns in Construct in Ugaritic," in *Biblical and Near Eastern Studies: Essays in Honor of William Sanford LaSor*, ed. Gary A. Tuttle (Grand Rapids: William B. Eerdmans, 1978), pp. 253-68; John Huehnergard, "Akkadian Evidence for Case-Vowels on Ugaritic Bound Forms," *JCS* 33 (1981) 199-205; idem, *Ugaritic Vocabulary*, pp. 300-1; idem, "Notes on Akkadian Morphology," in *"Working With No Data": Semitic and Egyptian Studies Presented to Thomas O. Lambdin*, ed. David M. Golomb (Winona Lake: Eisenbrauns, 1987), p. 189 n. 47. Contrast Ziony Zevit, "The Question of Case Endings on Ugaritic Nouns in *Status Constructus*," *JSS* 28 (1983) 225-32, who has voiced a dissenting, though not convincing, opinion on the basis of an occasional undifferentiated use of the *ʾaleph* signs, and see the rebuttal of Huehnergard, *Ugaritic Vocabulary*, p. 300 n. 17.

noun, as attested at Ugarit and in the Amarna letters, the case vowel assumed final position. As West Semitic continued to develop, the final stage was reached, as attested in late West Semitic, in which the singular noun terminated in -Ø ending.

From the development **-vm* > **-v* > **-Ø*,[26] it is evident that the dropping of case vowels could only have occurred after the disappearance of mimation. Ugaritic and the WS glosses in the Amarna letters attest singular nouns without mimation; hence these bodies of textual material have been the starting point for discussions on the question of when case endings were dropped in West Semitic. The complexity of the issues[27] and the fragmentary nature of the evidence prevent a definitive answer to this question; it suffices for our purposes to outline various positions and evaluate them briefly. At one extreme Blau argues that at the time of the Amarna letters (circa 1400 B.C.), the Canaanite case system had already broken down.[28] He points to the gloss *l[i-e]l* (EA 243.13), without case ending, and to the alleged frequent misuse of case endings by the scribes. On the other extreme Friedrich attempted to prove that case vowels were lost between 800-400 B.C.[29] Friedrich's view has not attracted a following. On the other hand, Blau's view strains the evidence a bit. As for the gloss *l[i-e]l*, its cuneiform signs are broken, and Rainey has suggested that it may be restored to read *l[e-l]a*.[30] And as Blau himself admits, the EA glosses ". . . as a rule do have case endings, either in accordance with their syntactic environments (74, 20; 46; 79, 36 in genitive) or standing in the

---

[26]This development is somewhat of an oversimplification. It is necessary to add that one must carefully distinguish the grammatical phenomenon of loss of meaningfulness of the case system and the partial redistribution of the case vowels, and the morphophonetic change from **-v* > *-Ø*.

[27]Case endings probably dropped off in different areas at different times; furthermore, they may have dropped from the construct state before the absolute state (Zellig S. Harris, *Development of the Canaanite Dialects: An Investigation in Linguistic History*, American Oriental Series, vol. 16 [New Haven: American Oriental Society, 1939], pp. 41-42). And perhaps genitive *-i* remained longer than other case endings.

[28]Joshua Blau, "Some Difficulties in the Reconstruction of »Proto-Hebrew« and »Proto-Canaanite«," in *In Memoriam Paul Kahle*, ed. Matthew Black and Georg Fohrer, BZAW 103 (Berlin: Alfred Töpelmann, 1968), pp. 34-35; idem, *On Pseudo-Corrections in Some Semitic Languages* (Jerusalem: Israel Academy of Sciences and Humanities, 1970), pp. 36-37.

[29]Johannes Friedrich, "Der Schwund kurzer Endvokale im Nordwestsemitischen," *ZS* 1 (1922) 3-14.

[30]A. F. Rainey, "Morphology and Prefix-Tenses of West Semitized El ʿAmarna Tablets," *UF* 7 (1975) 404-5. Compare the other attestation of the word in EA 195.13: *li-lá-ma*.

nominative against the context (as 69, 28; 143, 11)."[31] The predominant view is that final short vowels, including case endings, were generally lost after the Amarna period. Nonetheless, Liverani points to a few exceptional forms at Ugarit as evidence that the process of the disuse of case endings had already begun there.[32] Whether the case system began to break down at this early date or somewhat later, it is generally accepted that by the time the Canaanite languages make their historically and epigraphically attested appearances, singular nouns as a rule are no longer characterized by case vowels.

II. Canaanite

For BH direct and indirect evidence indicates the loss of case endings. The direct evidence is the text of the Hebrew Bible as vocalized by the Masoretes. In Masoretic Hebrew final short vowels were either dropped or lengthened.[33] As shown by the Masoretic pointing of singular nominal forms, the final short vowel--a case vowel--was uniformly dropped (e.g., **málku* > **malk* > **málek* > BH *mélek*). In this particular example, the lack of a vowel sign after the third radical, the insertion of the anaptyctic vowel, and the resultant aspiration of the *bgdkpt* letter indicate the loss of the case ending. Indirect evidence consists of the *nota accusativi*, used frequently but not consistently to distinguish between subjective and objective nouns in the absence of case endings, and the absolute feminine singular nominal ending *-â* (< **-at* < **-atu*).

Although case endings were uniformly dropped in SBH, it is generally believed that archaic remnants of case endings survived in isolated instances. In their studies of ancient Hebrew poetry (= ABH), Cross and Freedman claim to have detected remnants of archaic case endings. Not all of the suggestions proposed by Cross and Freedman are of equal merit; each individual passage would have to be evaluated, a desideratum which cannot be attempted in the scope of this study.[34] Generally speaking, case endings were retained only because they were misunderstood and reanalyzed by later readers, such as the

[31]Blau, "Reconstruction," p. 35 n. 30. For additional arguments against Blau, see Sivan, *GAGNWS*, p. 114.

[32]Mario Liverani, "Elementi innovativi nell'ugaritico non lettarario," *RANL* 19 (1964) 179. Huehnergard, however, suggests that these exceptional forms may be nothing more than spelling mistakes (oral communication).

[33]Dennis Pardee, "Letters from Tel Arad," *UF* 10 (1978) 293.

[34]Some of the relevant passages have been discussed by Robertson, *Linguistic Evidence*, pp. 77-110.

Masoretes. For example, Freedman analyzes *ʾēlîm* in the phrase *bĕnê ʾēlîm* (Ps 29:2) as the DN El, plus the genitive case vowel, followed by enclitic *-m*.[35] In this instance the enclitic particle protected the case vowel so that the latter was not dropped. During the transmission of the text, the case vowel was lengthened, and the resultant *-îm* was reanalyzed as the oblique plural morpheme of SBH. Whereas they have posited the retention of genitive and accusative case endings in their studies, I know of no examples cited by them of the preservation of the nominative case ending. According to the grammars, the only examples of the nominative case vowel are to be found in a few proper names,[36] which will be examined in detail in the following section.

Another feature of ABH that merits discussion is the ending *-ô*,[37] which is suffixed to singular nouns in the construct. This construction occurs twelve times in the Hebrew Bible, and it is generally conceded that wherever this construction appears, it is an archaic one.[38] In the earlier editions of GKC (§90 k), the view was entertained that this stressed *-ô* was a remnant of the nominative case ending. W. F. Albright referred to the so-called *littera compaginis -ō* as the survival of a case ending, and that he means the nominative case ending is clear from his reconstruction of BH *bĕnô Bĕʿōr* (< **binu Baʿuri*).[39] From the perspective of historical grammar, this *-ô* may derive from the contraction of an **-aw* diphthong, a (stressed) long **-ā*, or a historical short **-u*. Only if the *-ô* is derived from historical short **-u* can it be considered as the Hebrew reflex of a nominative case vowel. Some scholars have preferred the derivation of *-ô* from the contraction of the **-aw*

---

[35]Freedman, *ZAW* 72 (1960) 104. For other suggestions of genitive case endings retained, see Frank M. Cross, Jr. and David N. Freedman, "A Royal Song of Thanksgiving: II Samuel 22 = Psalm 18," *JBL* 72 (1953) 28 n. 58 (on 2 Sam. 22:24 = Ps. 18:24); and idem, "The Blessing of Moses," *JBL* 67 (1948) 206 n. 53 (on Deut. 33:16).

[36]GKC §90k; Joüon, §93s. Likewise, Ebbe E. Knudsen, "The Mari Akkadian Shift *ia* > *ê* and the Treatment of *l"h* Formations in Biblical Hebrew," *JNES* 41 (1982) 42: ". . . outside proper names there are no unambiguous reflexes of the ancient nominative."

[37]I might add that there is also a suffix *-ô* which is affixed to one-word names, but there is no necessary connection between the two and I have deferred discussion of this onomastic suffix to a later portion of this chapter. See s.v. "yitrô," pp. 98-99.

[38]The most important study of this morpheme is David Robertson, "The Morphemes -y(-ī) and -w(-ō) in Biblical Hebrew," *VT* 19 (1969) 221-23 (= *Linguistic Evidence*, pp. 76-77). The morpheme -y(-ī) will be discussed at pp. 115-17.

[39]W. F. Albright, "The Old Testament and Canaanite Language and Literature," *CBQ* 7 (1945) 18, 22; idem, "The Oracles of Balaam," *JBL* 63 (1944) 232 n. 145.

diphthong[40] or from a long *-ā.[41] The analysis of this ending as a pronominal suffix does not recommend itself.[42] The derivation -ô < *-ā is based on the supposed accusative form of kinship terms, but these forms are not attested, and Canaanite furnishes no evidence to support this reconstruction. By process of elimination, we arrive at -ô < *-u. A positive argument in favor of this derivation may now be added. Barth and Robertson concur that the function of this morpheme is to emphasize construct phrases.[43] That is, they observed that this morpheme is found only on the *nomen regens* of a construct phrase. This distribution of the morpheme does not appear to be fortuitous; elsewhere we noted that in early West Semitic short case vowels were retained in precisely this position.[44] Therefore with good reason the -ô morpheme of ABH may be analyzed as an archaic survival of the nominative case ending.

Outside of the Hebrew Bible, all evidence for the loss (or retention) of case endings must be indirect. In EH the presence of the *nota accusativi* and *-h* marker of the feminine singular absolute imply that case vowels had dropped.[45] The indirect evidence for the loss of case endings among the Transjordanian dialects is slight. The use of the *nota accusitivi* in Moabite intimates that case vowels were not retained in that language.[46] Yet the feminine singular absolute noun ends in *-at.[47] The feminine ending *-at*, however, does not necessarily indicate the retention of case vowels. As Garr rightly stresses, *-at* is an intermediate stage between *-atu* and *-ā.[48] In Ammonite the *nota accusitivi* is not attested and the feminine singular absolute appears to terminate in *-at*. As in Moabite, this feminine suffix may be understood as an intermediate stage. Although no feminine singular absolute nouns appear in Edomite epigraphs, the *nota accusativi* is attested once.[49]

Garr discusses the evidence for the preservation of case endings in Phoenician and concludes that the Byblian dialect, and to a lesser

---

[40]See BL §65m, who analyze this morpheme as the 3rd m.s. pronominal suffix.

[41]Joüon, §93r; Brockelmann, *GVG*, 1:465; and Jakob Barth, "Die Casusreste im Hebräischen," *ZDMG* 53 (1899) 598, derive this -ô from the accusative case vowel of the kinship terms *ʾabā, *ʾaḫā, and *ḥamā.

[42]As observed by Theodor Nöldeke, "Glossen zu H. Bauer's Semitischen Sprachproblemen," *ZA* 30 (1915-16) 165, Semitic languages do not generally place a pronominal suffix immediately before the genitive.

[43]Barth, *ZDMG* 53 (1899) 593-99; Robertson, *VT* 19 (1969) 223.

[44]See p. 44 n. 25.

[45]Gogel, 1:372 and 2:525-27.

[46]Joshua Blau, "Short Philological Notes on the Inscription of Mešaʿ," *Maarav* 2 (1980) 157.

[47]On the feminine suffix *-at* in Moabite, see discussion at p. 203.

[48]Garr, *Dialect Geography*, p. 62.

[49]In l. 3 of the Ḫorvat ʿUza ostracon. See Itzhaq Beit-Arieh and Bruce Cresson, "An Edomite Ostracon from Ḫorvat ʿUza," *TA* 12 (1985) 96-101.

extent, standard Phoenician (Karatepe), may have retained case endings in the singular noun.[50] But the appearance of the *nota accusativi* in standard Phoenician may suggest otherwise. The evidence on the whole is indirect and ambiguous, and consequently it is difficult to evaluate; the interested reader should consult Garr's discussion. Evidence for the retention of the nominative case ending in Punic has been found only on the bound form of the kinship terms **ʾab* and **ʾaḫ*.[51] To summarize: although case endings were occasionally retained in isolated forms (e.g., kinship terms) or archaic dialects (e.g., Old Byblian), the combined weight of the evidence supports the view that case endings were lost throughout the Canaanite languages.[52] Therefore, the retention of the nominative singular case ending *-u* in Canaanite PNN can only be regarded as a genuine archaism.

III. Canaanite PNN in the Hebrew Bible

The principles outlined here govern not only this chapter, but the succeeding chapters as well. Occasionally variations in the format will occur, depending on the particular morphological feature being discussed. The Canaanite PNN are listed according to the order of the Hebrew alphabet. Two main lists are presented in each chapter: 1) probable examples; and 2) dubious examples.[53] Each name will be discussed under the following headings: classification (linguistic and topical), structure, meaning, parallels, and comments. Other headings (e.g., variant spelling[s], sex of the name bearer) will be added where appropriate.

Under the "structure" section names are classified as one-word, construct phrase, nominal-sentence, verbal-sentence, shortened, or hypocoristic PNN. The meaning of most of these terms is transparent; it only needs to be mentioned that shortened names differ from hypoco-

---

[50]Garr, *Dialect Geography*, pp. 61-63. See also the brief remarks of Stanislav Segert, *A Grammar of Phoenician and Punic* (Munich: C. H. Beck, 1976), §52.4; for the retention of the genitive case ending in Phoenician, see Ginsberg, "The Northwest Semitic Languages," pp. 107, 109.

[51]Charles Krahmalkov, "Observations on the Affixing of Possessive Pronouns in Punic," *RSO* 44 (1969) 186; idem, "Studies in Phoenician and Punic Grammar," *JSS* 15 (1970) 184 n. 3; idem, "Comments on the Vocalization of the Suffix Pronoun on the Third Feminine Singular in Phoenician and Punic," *JSS* 17 (1972) 74 n. 2.

[52]In general, this conclusion also holds true for Aramaic. See Garr, *Dialect Geography*, p. 62. For their possible retention at Tell Fakhariyeh, see Stephen A. Kaufman, "Reflections on the Assyrian-Aramaic Bilingual from Tell Fakhariyeh," *Maarav* 3 (1982) 147, 157.

[53]Some chapters include (lists of) ambiguous and non-Canaanite examples.

ristic names in that the latter have a hypocoristic suffix, whereas the former do not.[54] Stated another way, a shortened name plus hypocoristic suffix is a hypocoristic name.

Since citations of biblical references are easily found in the lexica, they are only provided for the classification of the PNN, and when variant spellings are difficult to locate. Hebrew homonyms are denominated I, II, and III according to the convention of KB3. All vocables that are cited in the "parallels" section are PNN unless otherwise indicated, and only those vocables that I consider to be possible parallels (full or partial) are cited.[55] While names have been cited selectively, I have endeavored not to omit any names that might overthrow the interpretation being advocated on any given name. Finally the English spellings of the names discussed have not been normalized in accordance with any major English version of the Bible. Rather I have adopted a simplified transliteration of each name, without diacritic marks, which will enable those conversant with Hebrew to reconstruct the original form of the name. As an example, the name of the well-known Judean king Hezekiah is transliterated in this study as Hizqiyah.

A. *Probable Examples*

The first name to be discussed is the PN Betuʾel. Since it belongs to a series of compound PNN that share a common pattern, it is expedient to review previous scholarship on the study of these names and to make some general introductory remarks on PNN of this type before attempting to interpret and analyze any one of them.

An Excursus on Compound PNN of the Type *C_1ĕC_2ûʾēl

The following nine PNN are included in this series: *bĕtûʾēl, gĕʾûʾēl, ḥammûʾēl* (< **ḥămûʾēl*), *yĕmûʾēl, pĕnûʾēl, pĕtûʾēl, qĕmûʾēl, rĕʿûʾēl,* and *šĕmûʾēl.* Whereas some of these constitute probable examples, upon closer study others turn out to be dubious examples. Already excluded from this list are several names whose readings are textually dubious. The PNN *nĕmûʾēl* and *dĕʿûʾēl* are discussed below and it is concluded that these two names are in all probability textually

[54]Hermann Ranke, *Early Babylonian Personal Names* (Philadelphia, 1905), p. 7, also distinguishes between the two, though preferring to call the former "abbreviated" names.

[55]In the event that parallel names of similar or identical structure are not known, I have cited vocables that contain the same root.

corrupt forms of the PNN *yĕmûʾēl* and *rĕʿûʾēl* respectively. The PN *šĕbûʾēl*, borne by two persons, is also spelled *šĕbūʾēl* and *šûbāʾēl*. Even in those passages that read *šĕbûʾēl* (1 Chr 23:16, 25:4), several manuscripts of the LXX witness a Hebrew *Vorlage* **šwbʾl*. The reading *šĕbûʾēl* may be accounted for by paradigm pressure from the series of PNN of the type **C_1ĕC_2ûʾēl*. Moreover, the element *šĕbû-* does not appear to be a nominal element, as is the case in other PNN of the type **C_1ĕC_2ûʾēl*. The most reasonable approach is to accept the reading *šûbāʾēl*,[56] and to interpret the first element as an imperative (+ paragogic *-ā*?) from the root **šwb* "to return." To cite another example, the PN *lĕmôʾēl* is also attested with the spelling *lĕmûʾēl*. In chapter 4 it will be argued that the vocalization of the name with *-ô-* was the original spelling;[57] again the spelling *lĕmûʾēl* appears to be due to paradigm pressure from the series of PNN of the type **C_1ĕC_2ûʾēl*. Lastly, some PNN in which medial *û* and *î* interchange have been excluded as being textually uncertain.

In addition to treatments in lexica and incidental remarks found in articles and books, three studies of PNN of this type have appeared. The apparent regularity of form of these names furnishes a rationale for the analysis and interpretation of these PNN as a class rather than in isolation from one another. Unfortunately, the interpretations proffered in these studies have been disappointing, in that they are either methodologically unsound or fail to advance our understanding of these PNN. I would like to summarize and to evaluate each of these studies, beginning with the most recent one and moving back in time. I should also add that there is some variation from author to author as to the names included in this class.

The most recent treatment of this class of names is by Fowler in her study of theophoric PNN.[58] She has included thirteen PNN in this class[59] and suggested that their regularity of form points to a common grammatical structure. Though she acknowledged that scholars have identified the medial *û* as a nominative case ending in the PNN *mĕtû-šāʾēl* and *pĕnûʾēl*, she nonetheless remained skeptical:

---

[56]This spelling of the PN is confirmed by the Amor. PNN *šu-ba-ila*(*^{d}DINGIR*), *šu-ba-ḫa-li*, and *šu-ba-ni-ilu*(*DINGIR*) (*CAAA*, p. 642).

[57]See s.v. "lĕmûʾēl," pp. 190-92. Another reason for excluding this PN from the series of names of the type **C_1ĕC_2ûʾēl* is that it is non-Canaanite (i.e., Arabian).

[58]Jeaneane D. Fowler, *Theophoric Personal Names in Ancient Hebrew: A Comparative Study*, Journal for the Study of the Old Testament Supplement Series 49 (Sheffield: JSOT Press, 1988), pp. 122-25. For a general evaluation of this book, see my Review of *Theophoric Personal Names in Ancient Hebrew: A Comparative Study*, by Jeaneane D. Fowler, *JNES* (forthcoming).

[59]*gĕʾûʾēl, dĕʿûʾēl, yĕmûʾēl, yĕʿûʾēl, lĕmûʾēl, mĕtûšāʾēl, nĕmûʾēl, pĕnûʾēl, pĕtûʾēl, qĕmûʾēl, rĕʿûʾēl, šĕbûʾēl*, and *šĕmûʾēl*.

> The evidence for this archaic nominative termination, however, has been deduced from only a few proper names and such evidence, when applied to the above list, continues to violate any formal classification on this basis. Indeed, one would expect theories advanced for any one of these names to be applicable to at least a few others of the same type. When this is not the case, the theory itself may be questionable.[60]

Fowler's own preference is to derive the first element of many, if not all of these PNN, from a III-h root, and to analyze the majority of these names as construct form plus theophoric element.[61]

For a detailed discussion of the names in her list, the reader is referred to the discussion in the rest of this chapter.[62] It suffices to say here, though, that the theory of an archaic nominative case ending is applicable to many of the names within this class.[63] That the initial element of the PNN *gĕʾûʾēl* and *pĕtûʾēl* derive from III-h roots seems probable, but Fowler's predilection to posit III-h roots for other names in this class, even where these roots are not otherwise attested in BH, is methodologically suspect and unnecessary. Finally, her theory that regularity of form implies that all these names are construct types is untenable. The regularity of form of the initial element (*$*C_1\breve{e}C_2\hat{u}$-*) implies that in each case a nominal element is involved, but whether the compound name is a nominal-sentence or a construct phrase is a separate issue. The matter can be resolved only by general structural principles[64] and comparison with other PNN containing the same element.[65]

---

[60]Ibid., pp. 124-25.

[61]Ibid., p. 125. L. Kopf, "Arabische Etymologien und Parallelen zum Bibelwörterbuch," *VT* 8 (1958) 209-10, derived several of these names from III-w roots, interpreting the first element as a perfect verbal form.

[62]Some of the names included in her list are problematic. The PNN Deʿuʾel and Nemuʾel are textually corrupt, and the PN Metushaʾel is of a different pattern altogether!

[63]E.g., *yĕmûʾēl, mĕtûšāʾēl, pĕnûʾēl, qĕmûʾēl,* and *šĕmûʾēl.*

[64]In the most common type of construct phrase PN, the first element is descriptive of the name-bearer. The compound PN of the structure *$*C_1\breve{e}C_2\hat{u}$ʾēl* that belongs to this type is *pĕtûʾēl* "youth of god/El." Also it is likely that the PNN *bĕtûʾēl* "house of god/El" and *pĕnûʾēl* "face of god/El" are of the construct phrase type.

[65]Note, e.g., that the transposition of the nominal elements in the Ug. PNN *ymʾil* and *ʾilym* (*PTU*, p. 144) prove that the biblical PN *yĕmûʾēl* is a nominal-sentence name. Fowler failed to cite these Ug. PNN in her study.

A second treatment of these PNN is to be found in an article by Ben-Ezra.[66] His thesis is that alongside the familiar third masculine singular **qatal* verbal form existed a third masculine singular archaic **qatlu* verbal form. He invokes this putative **qatlu* verbal form to explain certain anomalous *waws* throughout the Hebrew Bible, and he also applies the same approach to the interpretation of this class of PNN. The interpretations he proposes are fanciful, for they are not governed by sound linguistic and philological method and no comparisons of these PNN with similar ones in other ancient Semitic languages are offered.

The third and final study was published by Praetorius just after the turn of the century.[67] In this study Praetorius developed a comprehensive theory for the interpretation of this class of PNN. His article was influential and deemed worthy of bibliographic mention in the standard reference works.[68] While S. R. Driver and Noth expressed reservations on the validity of Praetorius' approach,[69] others, such as Gesenius and Kaila, adopted Praetorius' interpretation of some of the PNN included in this class.[70] Praetorius believed that passive as well as active shortened names of affection were formed from theophoric compound names. From the biblical PN *yišmāʿē(ʾ)l* were formed the shortened PNN *šāmāʿ* and *šammûaʿ*. Now one would expect the passive shortened names to assume the form **qatūl*. He hypothesized that after these **qatūl* base forms had functioned as proper names for a time, they were no longer perceived as participles, and hence they admitted phonological and morphological alterations. In some names, the middle radical was doubled, as in *šammûaʿ*; in others the pretonic short vowel was reduced (e.g., *rĕḥûm*).[71] In still others, the theophoric element was attached at the end and the **qatūl* form was shortened by the loss of the third consonant. Thus, the PN *šĕmûʾēl* derives from **šĕmûaʿ ʾēl*, meaning "heard of God." To be sure, this derivation of the

[66]Akiva Ben-Ezra, "hsywmt û btn"k," *BM* 18 (1972) 113-23, especially pp. 120-22.

[67]Franz Praetorius, "Über einige Arten hebräischer Eigennamen," *ZDMG* 57 (1903) 773-82.

[68]BDB, p. 1028; GKC §90k n. 1; Joüon, §93s n. 3; Noth, *IPN*, pp. 38 nn. 2-3, 39 n. 1.

[69]S. R. Driver, *Notes on the Hebrew Text and the Topography of the Books of Samuel*, 2d ed., rev. and enl. (Oxford: Clarendon Press, 1913), p. 19; Noth, *IPN*, pp. 38 nn. 2-3, 39 n. 1.

[70]GKC §90k n. 1; Lauri G. G. Kaila, *Zur Syntax des in verbaler Abhängigkeit stehenden Nomens im alttestamentlichen Hebräisch* (Helsinki, 1906), pp. 55-57.

[71]Praetorius, *ZDMG* 57 (1903) 774-75.

name Shemu᾿el had been suggested earlier;[72] Praetorius' "genius" was to expand this approach and apply it in a systematic fashion to PNN of the type *C_1*ĕ*C_2*û᾿ēl.* Praetorius then proceeded to make suggestions on the third radical of these PNN (e.g., *pĕtû᾿ēl* < **pĕtûᵃḥ ᾿ēl*). For those names for which no third radical seems likely, he supposed that at a still later stage, names, which were meaningless from the start, were formed mechanically from this scheme.[73]

The weaknesses of Praetorius' view may be described as follows. His whole theory involves a great deal of speculation about name formation for which there is no demonstrable evidence. Also the omission of the third radical of a triradical root in Hebrew PNN is not a common phenomenon, especially in compound PNN. And comparison of PNN from this class with similar or identical names from other Semitic languages suggests interpretations entirely different from those required by Praetorius' view. Driver offers two more criticisms, the one general, the other specific with reference to the name Shemu᾿el.[74] First, Driver rightly emphasizes that PNN of the type passive participle plus DN are practically nonexistent among the proper names of the Hebrew Bible. While the passive participle may be used by itself as a name (e.g., *bārûk*), there are none, or next to none, of the compound variety proposed by Praetorius.[75] Second, if the Praetorius' explanation of the name Shemu᾿el were correct, one would have expected the *᾿aleph* rather than the *ʿayin* to have elided; that is, **šĕmûᵃʿ᾿ēl* > **šĕmûʿē(᾿)l* [on the analogy of *yišmāʿē(᾿)l*] > **šĕmûʿēl.*[76] In short, rather than providing the interpretive key to this class of PNN, Praetorius' approach obscures their structure and meaning. As an initial working hypothesis, it is far better to admit the possibility that the first element of most, if not all, of the PNN belonging to this class derives not from a triradical strong root with loss of the third consonant, but

---

[72]For example, Eberhard Nestle, *Die israelitischen Eigennamen nach ihrer religionsgeschichtlichen Bedeutung* (Haarlem: De Erven F. Bohn, 1876), p. 164.

[73]Praetorius, *ZDMG* 57 (1903) 778.

[74]Driver, *Books of Samuel*, p. 17.

[75]This statement is valid for Canaanite PNN. The only exception is the biblical PN *yĕdîăʿ᾿ēl*, which from the perspective of morphology is not a Canaanite name (**qatīl* is productive in Aramaic). As indicated by WS PNN in cuneiform sources, names of the type passive participle plus DN are common in the Aramaic onomasticon (Zadok, *WSB*, pp. 108-10).

[76]Note especially the GA *hayyišmĕʿēlî* (1 Chr 27:30). Compare also the Amm. PNN *šmʿl* (Jackson, *ALIA*, p. 97) and *hwšʿl* (Pierre Bordreuil, *Catalogue des sceaux ouest-sémitiques inscrits* [Paris: Bibliothèque Nationale, 1986], p. 64). For other examples of the quiescence of *᾿aleph* in PNN, see my "A New Interpretation of an Edomite Seal-Impression," *JNES* (forthcoming).

from a true biradical or a III-weak root. It is with this assumption that we will proceed to study these names.

1. *bĕtû᾿ēl.*

Classification: Can.--son of Nahor (Gen 22:22).

Structure: construct phrase name, *bĕt-* (**qatl* base, BL §61o') + *-û-* nominative case vowel + *-᾿ēl* (**qil* base, BL §61i).

Meaning: "house (= temple) of god/El."

Parallels: Amor. *bīt(dÉ)-il* (*CAAA*, p. 224);[77] Ug. *be-ti-ilim-(DINGIR*^{lim}*)* (*PTU*, p. 330); EA *be-ti-ilu(DINGIR)* (*AmPN*, p. 92); Can. GN *bĕtû᾿ēl* (1 Chr 4:30) = *bĕtûl* (Josh 19:4);[78] Amm. *bt᾿l*;[79] IAram. *bty* (*RVJPNE*, p. 139).

Comments: The meaning of this name is easily understood, despite various attempts to explain it otherwise. The biradical vocable **bt* in PNN must be related to either **bat* "daughter" or **bayt* "house." Since

[77]For discussion of this PN, see Buccellati, *AURIII*, p. 144, who interprets this name as a nominal sentence and translates "the (divine) House is Il." According to Gelb's analysis, the vocable **biyt* occurs in only seven PNN in the Amor. onomasticon (*CAAA*, p. 118), with the syllabic spellings *bi-tu/ti*, *bí-it*, and *bi-é*. Amor. *ī* may possibly derive from *a-yi* (Gelb, *RANL* 13 [1958] §2.3.6).

[78]This GN is not to be confused with the better known Bethel, which in the Hebrew Bible is always spelled *bêt(-)᾿ēl*. Shemaryahu Talmon, "The Ancient Hebrew Alphabet and Biblical Textual Criticism," in *Mélanges Dominique Barthélemy: Études bibliques offertes à l'occasion de son 60e anniversaire*, ed. Pierre Casetti, Othmar Keel et Adrian Schenker, OBO 38 (Fribourg: Éditions Universitaires; Göttingen: Vandenhoeck & Ruprecht, 1981), p. 513, explains the reading in Josh 19:4 as haplography (**bt[w]᾿l* > **bt[w]l*), facilitated by the resemblance between *᾿aleph* and *taw* in ancient Hebrew script. Alternatively, the spelling *bĕtûl* may be a phonetic spelling that arose after the *᾿aleph* quiesced (compare p. 54 and n. 76). At Josh 19:4, the minuscules e, j, g, and p read *βαιθ-* (= **bayt-*). At Josh 15:30, which is a list of the same three GNN mentioned in 19:4, the MT has *kĕsîl* where one would expect the GN Betul. This reading appears to be nothing more than textual corruption and indirectly supports a reconstruction like **btw/yl*, with no *᾿aleph*, as in Josh 19:4. LXX B at Josh 15:30 reads *βαιθηλ* (= **bayt᾿ēl*). Finally, the evidence comes full circle if, as is probable, the GN Betu(e)l of the books of 1 Chronicles and Joshua is to be equated with the GN *bêt-᾿ēl* of 1 Sam 30:27. See Driver, *Books of Samuel*, p. 225; contrast P. Kyle McCarter, Jr., *1 Samuel: A New Translation with Introduction, Notes & Commentary*, AB, vol. 8 (Garden City: Doubleday & Co., 1980), pp. 434, 436, who follows the reading of LXX B (*βαιθσουρ*) and restores Beth-zur.

[79]N. Avigad, "Another Group of West-Semitic Seals from the Hecht Collection," *Michmanim* 4 (1989) 13.

Betu'el is undoubtedly a male,[80] and since PNN with **bat* are predominantly construct phrase PNN borne by females, it is plausible to interpret Betu'el as "house of god/El." The PNN cited above corroborate this interpretation and invalidate the suggestion that Betu'el is a byform of *Metu'el.[81] Baudissin's comparison of the PN Betu'el with the DN Bethel does not recommend itself;[82] there are no certain attestations of this DN before the first millennium B.C.,[83] and the PN Betu'el gives evidence of being an old name with exact parallels among early West Semitic PNN.

Semantic considerations as well as the GN Betu'el may point to this PN as deriving from a GN. However, the use of PNN with the meaning "house of god/El" in Ugaritic and WS PNN in the EA letters makes this assumption questionable.[84] That the first element of Betu'el is not written **byt-* in the MT does not constitute an objection to the proposed interpretation. The PN Betu'el, and other PNN to be discussed below, are vocalized according to the fixed pattern ***C_1*ĕ*C_2*û'ēl.* This fixed pattern is artificial inasmuch as it does not accurately reflect the morphophonology of the initial element of these names. Consequently, the vowel of the initial element is uniformly reduced in propretonic position, regardless of length, and in the PN Yemu'el, the gemination of C_2 is dropped. The artificial pattern ***C_1*ĕ*C_2*û'ēl* even influenced several names that did not belong to this series.[85] In any event, the medial *û* in this PN can only be an archaic survival of the

---

[80]He is described as the "son" (Hebrew *bēn*) of Milkah (Gen 24:15, 24) and Nahor (Gen 24:47) and takes masculine verbal forms (Gen 22:23).

[81]It is surprising that this suggestion is the only one listed in the lexica (BDB, p. 159; KB2, p. 159; KB3, p. 159; Franciscus Zorell, *Lexicon Hebraicum Veteris Testamenti* [Rome: Biblical Institute Press, 1940-84], p. 135). Fowler, pp. 219, 282, inclined toward this view, though elsewhere (pp. 256, 301) she has noted the occurrence of the Akk. cognate *bītu* "temple" in Akk. PNN. That voiced *b* and voiceless *p* alternate according to regular rules of assimilation is clear [W. Randall Garr, "On Voicing and Devoicing in Ugaritic," *JNES* 45 (1986) 45-52], but the evidence for the interchange of *b* and *m* is slight (Moscati, *CGSL*, §8.8). Of the two examples cited by H. Bauer, *ZAW* 48 (1930) 79, the first is textually corrupt (*bĕʿôn* in Num. 32:3, for *bêt baʿal mĕʿôn*) and the second, the PN *minyāmîn*, is far from certain.

[82]Wolf W. G. Baudissin, *Kyrios als Gottesname im Judentum und seine Stelle in der Religionsgeschichte*, 4 parts, ed. Otto Eissfeldt (Giessen: Alfred Töpelmann, 1929), 3:300.

[83]Zadok, *WSB*, p. 60. To be exact, the earliest attestation of the DN Bethel dates to a seventh century B.C. Assyrian treaty between Esarhaddon and Baal of Tyre.

[84]Note also that *ālum* "city" and *bītum* "house" are productive in Akk. PNN (Stamm, *ANG*, pp. 90-91).

[85]Compare *šûbā'ēl*, p. 51, s.v. "lĕmô'ēl," pp. 190-92, and perhaps "rĕʿû," p. 97.

nominative singular case ending.[86] Furthermore, the retention of this vowel on a bound form supports the position that bound forms did originally terminate in a vowel.[87] For other instances of the nominative case vowel on the vocable **bayt-*, compare the WS PN *be-tù-mì-ni* and the GN *[URU]bé-tu-ḫu-li-ia* (Sivan, *GAGNWS*, p. 210). The interpretation proposed here, that Betuʾel means "house of god" and that the medial *û* is the nominative ending, was already suggested before the turn of the century.[88]

2. ***hădôrām.***

Variant spelling: *hădōrām* (2 Chr 10:18).

Classification: Can.--1) son of Toʿu, king of Hamath (1 Chr 18:10); 2) official over corvée labor (2 Chr 10:18).

Structure: nominal-sentence name, *hăd-* (< DN **Hadd-*) + *-ô-* nominative case vowel + *-rām* (< **rwm* "to be high, exalted," 3rd m.s. Qal perfect).

Meaning: "Haddu is exalted."

Parallels: Amor. *a-du-ra-mu* (*CAAA*, p. 556);[89] N/LB *dad-du-ra-am-ma/mu, adad(dIM)-ra-am, adad(dIM)-ra-ma, adad(dIM)-ra-mu* (*WSB*, pp. 45-46).

Comments: The name Hadoram is borne by an Aramean prince and an administrative official of the early Israelite monarchy. In both instances, the name appears to have been altered in antiquity in order to suppress the pagan theophore contained therein. In 2 Sam 8:10 the name of the Aramean prince appears as *yôrām*; yet Josephus and LXX support a reading (H)adoram. The administrative official is called by

---

86In other names to be studied in this section, it will become evident that in PNN Hebrew *û* is the standard reflex for the short nominative case vowel. The explanation for this is that Masoretic Hebrew does not tolerate short vowels in open, pretonic syllables. Short vowels in this position are uniformly lengthened if the propretonic syllable is reducible. One expects, however, for **u* to be lengthened to *ō* in this situation. The representation of **-u* by *-û* may be reckoned as an orthographic idiosyncrasy of PNN. For Hebrew *û* < **ū*, see s.v. "pĕnûʾēl," p. 76 n. 168.

87For further discussion and bibliography, see p. 44 n. 25.

88G. H. Skipwith, "Hebrew Tribal Names and the Primitive Traditions of Israel," *JQR*, o.s., 11 (1898-99) 254.

89For this interpretation, see Buccellati, *AURIII*, p. 131; on the deity **Haddu* in Amor. PNN, see Huffmon, *APNMT*, pp. 156-58.

the name *ʾădōrām* in 2 Sam 20:24 and 1 Kgs 12:18,[90] but by *ʾădōnîrām* in 1 Kgs 4:6 and 5:28. It can hardly be regarded as fortuitous that in two separate instances the pagan DN **Haddu* is either deformed or eliminated altogether from these names. It appears that the Chronicler has preserved the original, unaltered forms of the names.[91]

The name Hadoram, with its variant ʾAdoram, are the only names in the Hebrew Bible with a medial *-ô/ō-* vowel[92] between the two name elements. The *-ô-* vowel may derive from the contraction of an **aw* diphthong, a (stressed) long **ā*, or a historical short **u*. As with the ending *-ô* suffixed to singular nouns in the construct, one may prefer the derivation *ô* < **u*. Or if the reading *-ō-* is preferred, one may still reconstruct *ō* < **u*.[93] In either case the medial vowel may be understood as a Hebrew reflex of the nominative case ending. Some LXX transliterations, however, point to another possibility. In 1 Chr 18:10 LXX B reads Ἰ*δουραὰμ* (= MT *hădôrām*), and other Greek manuscripts support the rendering *ου* after *δ*.[94] 2 Sam 8:10 (MT) reads *yôram*, but LXX B reads Ἰ*εδδουρὰν*,[95] which may reflect a mixed form of the two names.[96] The rendering *ου* indicates that the LXX translators

---

[90]The meaning of the name ʾAdoram is disputed. Tigay, p. 8, suggests as one alternative that **Addu* may be a variant of **Haddu*. Benjamin Mazar, "lmḥqr hšmwt hprṭyym šbmqrʾ," *Leš* 15 (1947) 38-39; idem, "King David's Scribe and the High Officialdom of the United Monarchy of Israel," in *The Early Biblical Period: Historical Essays*, ed. Shmuel Aḥituv and Baruch A. Levine (Jerusalem: Israel Exploration Society, 1986), p. 130) maintains that the initial element of Adoram is the CN **ʾadu* "father." Since the DN **Haddu* is eliminated altogether in the PN Yoram, I am inclined to understand the change *hăd-* > *ʾăd-* as a religiously motivated deformation and thus favor the second view. Maraqten, *SPARI*, p. 51, observes that the writings *d*, *ʾd*, *ʾdd*, and *dd* for *hd(d)* is especially characteristic of *Akkadian* PNN transmitted in Aramaic script.

[91]Note also that the Chronicler preserved certain *baʿal* names that were altered in the MT of Samuel.

[92]Orthographic confusion between *ô* and *ō* is widespread in the biblical text, and therefore one cannot rely upon the difference between plene or defective writing. I will consider both possibilities here.

[93]For *ō* < **u*, compare the DN *milkōm* and the adverbial ending *-ōm* < **-um* (on the latter, see Edward J. Young, "Adverbial *-u* in Semitic," *Westminster Theological Journal* 13 [1951] 151-54).

[94]B *ιδουρααμ*; c_2 *ιλουρααμ*; S *ιδουραμ*; h *αδουρααμ*; g *αδουραν*, AN *δουραμ*.

[95]Again, other Greek witnesses support the rendering *ου*: av *ιεδδουρα*; cegx *ιεδουραν*, a_2 *ιεδουρραν*, o *τον ιεουδδουραν*. Interchange of final *mem* and Grk *ν* is a common phenomenon. See Lea Mazor, "The Origin and Evolution of the Curse upon the Rebuilder of Jericho--A Contribution of Textual Criticism to Biblical Historiography," *Textus* 14 (1988) 9-10 n. 18.

[96]A. Malamat, "Aspects of the Foreign Policies of David and Solomon," *JNES* 22 (1963) 6 n. 23.

understood the vowel as *û*, not *ô*.[97] Since gemination is not consistently expressed in PNN in the Hebrew Bible,[98] one may reconstruct the pre-Massoretic form of the name as **Haddûrām*.[99] Just as in other PNN studied in this chapter, Hebrew *û* in the PN **Haddûrām* is the standard reflex for the short nominative case vowel. The *-ô/ō-* spelling may have arisen as the result of attraction to the *ô* of *yôrām* or the *ō* of *ʾădōnîrām*. In the WS PNN from the execration texts the DNN **Hadadu* and **Šamšu* terminate in the nominative case vowel. Likewise, the DN **Haddu* terminates in the nominative case ending in the PN Hadoram. One may also compare the DN *Yammu in the Can. PN Yemuʾel.[100]

3. *ḥûrām.*

Variant spellings: 1. *ḥîrām* (1 Chr 14:1 K; 2 Chr 4:11 K); 2. *ḥîrôm* (1 Kgs 5:24).

Classification: Ph.--1) king of Tyre (2 Chr 2:2); 2) Tyrian artisan during the time of Solomon (2 Chr 4:11).[101]

Structure: verbal-sentence name, *ḥ-* (< **ʾaḫ*; **qal* base, BL §61h) + *-û-* nominative case vowel + *rām* (< **rwm* "to be high, exalted," 3rd m.s. Qal perfect).

Meaning: "The (divine) brother is exalted."

Parallels: Eblaite *a-ḫu-kam₄* (ARET III:257); Ug. *ʾḫrm* (*PTU*, p. 91), *a-ḫi-ra-mu* (RS 19.42, l. 14 [*PRU* VI, p. 77]); NA *a-ḫi-ra-mu, ḫi-ru-um-mu* (*WSB*, pp. 52, 250); Can. *ʾăḥîrām*, GA *ʾăḥîrāmî*, Ph-P. *ḥrm*, *ʾḥrm* (*PNPP*, p. 263).

---

[97]For further discussion and additional examples, see Batton, p. 33; Könnecke, pp. 23-24.

[98]See s.v. "yĕmûʾēl," p. 65 n. 127, and "ʾăḥûmay," p. 101 and n. 297. Compare also the biblical PNN *mĕpîbōšet* (< **mippîbaʿal*) and *ʾelʿûzay* (< **ʾelʿuzzay*).

[99]For this reconstruction, see André Dupont-Sommer, *Les Araméens* (Paris: A. Maisonneuve, 1949), p. 30; P. Kyle McCarter, Jr., *2 Samuel: A New Translation with Introduction, Notes & Commentary*, AB 9 (Garden City: Doubleday & Co., 1984), p. 250; KB3, p. 229 (one alternative).

[100]See s.v. "yĕmûʾēl," p. 66.

[101]The putative occurrence of this name in 1 Chr 8:5, borne by a Benjaminite, should be emended to Hupham. See s.v. "ḥûpām," p. 175 n. 110, and bibliography cited there.

Comments: The reading of this name with medial *û* is attested in several passages and thus that vowel is sure.[102] The aphaeresis of *ʾaleph* is particularly characteristic of Ph. PNN.[103] For the nominative case vowel on the kinship term **ʾaḫ*, note the Eblaite PN *a-ḫu-kam₄* and the evidence from Punic that the bound form of the kinship terms **ʾab* and **ʾaḫ* retained the nominative case ending.[104] The long case ending may reflect a Proto-Semitic phenomenon--thus *û* < **ū*.[105]

4. *ḥămûṭal.*

Variant spelling: *ḥămîṭal* (2 Kgs 24:18 K; Jer 52:1 K).

Classification: Can.--mother of Jehoahaz and Zedekiah.

Structure: nominal-sentence name, *ḥăm-* (**qal* base, BL §61h) + *-û-* nominative case vowel + *-ṭal* (*qall* base, BL §61w).[106]

Meaning: "The (divine) father-in-law is dew."

Parallels: Ug. *ṭly*, *ṭá-la-ia* (*PTU*, p. 202); WS *ʾbṭl* (Lemaire, *Syria* 63:25); Can. *ʾăbîṭāl* (pausal form). For names with the element **ḥām*, see below, s.v. "ḥammûʾēl," p. 62.

---

[102] 1 Chr 14:1 Q; 2 Chr 2:2, 10, 11, 12; 2 Chr 4:11 (2x--once Q), 16; 2 Chr 8:2, 18; 2 Chr 9:10 Q, 21. Adrien-M. Brunet, "Le chroniste et ses sources (1)," *RB* 61 (1954) 358 n. 4, concluded that the spelling Huram goes back to the Chronicler himself.

[103] Benz, *PNPP*, p. 263, states that original *ʾaleph* is retained in only four Ph. PNN. See also Garr, *Dialect Geography*, p. 50.

[104] See p. 49.

[105] P. Swiggers, Review of *West Semitic Personal Names in the Murašû Documents*, by Michael D. Coogan," *JNES* 42 (1983) 77; Huehnergard, "Notes on Akkadian Morphology," p. 189 n. 46. That kinship terms such as **ʾab*, **ʾaḫ*, and **ḥam* terminated in a long vowel in Proto-Semitic is reconstructed from the forms they take in the construct state and before suffixes in various Semitic languages. The fact, however, that this long vowel is represented in the script by *û* does not support the historical length of the vowel. For further discussion, see p. 57 n. 86.

[106] Franz Praetorius, "Über einige weibliche Caritativnamen im Hebräischen," *ZDMG* 57 (1903) 530-31, analyzed this PN as **ḥāmûṭ* + *-al* cartitative/diminutive ending, relating the first element to the BH CN *ḥōmeṭ* "lizard." This interpretation of the name has been adopted by Noth, *IPN*, p. 39 n. 1; Johann J. Stamm, *Beiträge zur hebräischen und altorientalischen Namenkunde*, OBO 30 (Freiburg: Universitätsverlag; Göttingen: Vandenhoeck & Ruprecht, 1980), p. 126. There is, however, no unambiguous evidence for the existence of an *-al* caritative ending, and the biblical PN *ʾăbîṭāl* (*ʾăbî-* + *ṭāl*) suggests a different segmentation of the PN Hamutal.

Comments: The spelling *ḥămûṭal* occurs in 2 Kgs 23:31, 2 Kgs 24:18 Q, and Jer 52:1 Q. The Kethiv of the last two passages, as well as the LXX and Vulgate, read the PN **ḥmyṭl*. The spelling with medial *û* is the *lectio difficilior* and appears to be the original reading of the name. Since the form of the name with *û* is archaic, it would be difficult to explain how this form arose from an original **ḥmyṭl*. Alternatively, both forms of the names may be genuine variants from different traditions. At any rate, the medial vowel of the form *ḥămûṭal* lines up with *ḥammû-ʾēl*, while the medial *î* of the form *ḥămîṭal* lines up with the EH PNN *ḥmyʿdn* and *ḥmyʾhl*. Along with other kinship terms, the vocable **ḥam* is probably to be interpreted as a divine epithet. The nominative case ending on this kinship term may have been long in Proto-Semitic.[107]

How one analyzes the second element *ṭal* determines whether this name is classified as Canaanite or Aramaic. Two different etymologies have been proposed for the *ṭal* element. Whereas Bauer relates this vocable to Aramaic *ṭal* (< Proto-Semitic **ẓll*) "shadow,"[108] other scholars interpret the vocable as BH *ṭal* (< Proto-Semitic **ṭll*) "dew." The second interpretation appears to be the correct one. From the perspective of lexicon, the vocable **ḥam* occurs in BH, EH, Amm., and Ph-P. PNN--viz., Canaanite PNN. On the other hand, among the scores of Aramaic PNN in NA and N/LB texts, Zadok states that "there are no definite examples of *ḥm* "father-in-law."[109] On the basis of available evidence, the vocable **ḥam* appears to be productive in Canaanite as opposed to Aram. PNN. As for the vocable *ṭal* (< Proto-Semitic **ṭll*), it is found in Ug. and Can. PNN. In fact the Can. PN Abital provides a fitting parallel to Hamutal--both names are nominal-sentence type with a kinship term in first position and *ṭal* in second position. It should be noted that the PN Hamutal was borne by a person who lived during the ninth century B.C. It is not until the exilic and post-exilic periods, especially the latter, that the Aramaic language

---

107One may infer this from the form that *ḥām* takes before suffixes, *ḥamî-* . See p. 60 n. 105; and BL §65f, which contains some unnecessary speculation.

108Bauer, *ZAW* 48 (1930) 76. For *ṭal* "shadow" in Aram. PNN in cuneiform writing, see Fales, *Iraq* 41 (1979) 60-61. According to Silverman, the final element of IAram. *yhwṭl* (*RVJPNE*, p. 149) is Aramaic on account of its phonology. In *JAOS* 89 (1969) 694 n. 20, Silverman has defended his analysis by arguing that the Aramaic root **ṭll* is more commonly used in personal names than the Hebrew *ṭal*. Compare also the phrase *bṭll ʾlh šmyʾ* "in the shadow of the God of heaven" (AP 38:5). On the other hand, Porten, *Archives*, p. 138, has explained IAram. *yhwṭl* as a Hebrew name-type meaning "Yah is (my) dew."

109Zadok, *WSB*, p. 56 n. 4. Silverman, *RVJPNE*, p. 146, claims to have identified this vocable in the IAram. PN *ḥmʾ*, but this name may be a Hebrew name-type at Elephantine.

began to exert an influence on the biblical onomasticon.[110] Therefore it is probable that the PN Hamutal is a Canaanite name, and that the medial *û* vowel is an archaic morphological feature.

5. *ḥammûʾēl.*

Classification: Can.--tribe of Simeon (1 Chr 4:26).

Structure: nominal-sentence name, *ḥamm-* (**qal* ! base, BL §61h) + *-û-* nominative case vowel + *-ʾēl.*

Meaning: "The (divine) father-in-law is god/El."

Parallels: Amor. *^{d}a-mu-da-du*, *^{d}a-mu-ma-lik* (*CAAA*, p. 559);[111] Can. *ḥām*; *ḥămû/îṭal*, BH CN **ḥām*, EH *ḥmyʿdn* and *ḥmyʾhl* (VSE ##324, 412);[112] Amm. *ḥmśgb* (*ALIA*, p. 96), *ḥmywsʿ* (Aufrecht, *BASOR* 266:86); Ph-P. *ḥmbʿl* (*PNPP*, p. 312); Liḥ. and Saf. *ḥmʾl* (*PIAN*, p. 199).

Comments: Other occurrences of the first element of this PN suggest that the gemination of the *m* is secondary.[113] Accordingly, this PN conforms to the pattern *$*C_1\check{e}C_2\hat{u}$ʾēl.* The BH CN **ḥām* occurs four times in the Hebrew Bible (Gen 38:13, 25; 1 Sam 4:19, 21), always with suffixes but never with a geminated *m*. Note also the Can. PN *ḥămû/îṭal*,[114] as well as postbiblical Hebrew *ḥām* and JAram. *ḥāmāʾ*.[115] The

[110]Wagner, p. 151, has observed that Aramaic PNN borne by Israelites are relatively scarce in pre-exilic times.

[111]It is difficult to distinguish between the vocables **ḥamum* and **ʿammum* in Amor. PNN (for the names listed under **ʿammum* and **ḥamum*, see Gelb, *CAAA*, pp. 92-95, 249-50). The situation is complicated further because both vocables may be deified. When the gemination of the *m* is expressed in the script, this spelling points to the vocable **ʿammum*. Those PNN with singular writing of the *m* are problematic. For the Amor. PNN from Mari, Huffmon, *APNMT*, p. 166, has noted several scribal conventions for distinguishing between the two vocables. (The two Amor. PNN cited above are from Mari and derive from the vocable **ḥamum*.) As he himself notes, these conventions do not obtain for Amor. PNN outside of the Mari texts. Gelb (*CAAA*, p. 19) and Huffmon seem to agree that the vocable **ḥamum* is predominantly written *(^{d})a-mu/mi-*, viz. without initial *ḫ*.

[112]All the PNN cited in this section appear to be nominal sentences rather than construct phrases. This analysis is substantiated by these two EH PNN, which are borne by females (the formula on the seals reads "PN *bt* patronym").

[113]On secondary gemination in BH PNN, see s.v. "ḥûpām," p. 143 n. 109, and "šĕpûpām," p. 178 n. 136.

[114]See the preceding entry for discussion.

[115]Marcus Jastrow, *A Dictionary of the Targumim, The Talmud Babli and Yerushalmi, and the Midrashic Literature* (Brooklyn: P. Shalom, 1967), p. 475.

secondary nature of the gemination renders less appealing Lewy's proposal to interpret the element *ḥamm-* as the name of the sun-god.[116] In addition, the suffixed form *ḥmy-* in EH and Amm. PNN indicates a CN, not a DN.[117]

It may be doubted whether the PN *ḥāmûl* is a shortened form of **ḥămûʾēl*, notwithstanding evidence of the versions (LXX B at Gen 46:21 reads *ιεμουηλ*). Actually the evidence from the versions is mixed--e.g., SyrP at Gen 46:21 reads *ḥmwl*. Both the form of the name and the etymology are readily explained. The lack of reduction of the vowel under the *ḥ* may well indicate a **qatūl* base, a common name type in the biblical onomasticon (e.g., *bārûk, zābûd*).[118] Accordingly, the PN Hamul may be analyzed as a **qatūl* base formation from the root **ḥml* "to spare."[119]

6. *yĕmûʾēl.*

Variant spelling: *nĕmûʾēl.*

Classification: Can.--first son of Simeon (Gen 46:10).

Structure: nominal-sentence name, *yĕm-* (< a. DN **Yamm* [cf. CN **yammu*, **qall* base, BL §61w]; or b. DN **Yawm* [cf. CN **yawmu*, **qawl* base[120]]) + *-û-* nominative case vowel + *-ʾēl.*

Meaning: a. "Yammu is god."
b. "Yawmu is god."

Parallels: Amor. *ia-am-mu?-qa-du-um, ia-am-mu-ú* (*CAAA*, p. 597); *mu-tu-ia-ma* (ibid., p. 625); Ug. *ymʾil, ʾilym, ʿbdym, abdu(ÌR)-yammi(A.AB.BA), mlkym, bn ymy, ia-mu-na* (*PTU*, p. 144); *i*[*a*]*-mu-*

One cannot argue from the LXX transliteration *αμουηλ*, as interpreters have been wont to do in the past. In LXX transliterations, there are a great number of inconsistencies in the doubling of consonants (Lisowsky, pp. 143-44).

116Julius Lewy, "The Old West Semitic Sun-God Ḥammu," *HUCA* 18 (1944) 434. He argued that the first element in the PN *ḥammûʾēl* was the masculine counterpart of the the BH CN *ḥammâ* "sun, heat."

117As noted by Tigay, p. 76 n. 10.

118Even in the GA *ḥāmûlî*, this vowel did not reduce. Contrast the reduction of the first vowel of *bĕtûl*, which is shortened from **bĕtûʾēl.*

119This root is productive in the formation of names. Compare the EH PNN *ḥml* (VSE #338; Avigad, *Hebrew Bullae*, #83), *yḥmlyhw* (VSE ##51, 337), and *yḥml* (William G. Dever, "Iron Age Epigraphic Material from the Area of Khirbet el-Kôm," *HUCA* 40-41 [1969-70] 169-72).

120GKC §97; Huehnergard, *Ugaritic Vocabulary*, pp. 265, 303; Joüon, §98f; Sivan, *GAGNWS*, p. 291.

nu (RS 17.430, IV.3 [*PRU* VI, p. 81]); WS *ia-am-mu/ma* (*AT*, p. 136); *aḫi(ŠEŠ)-ia-mi* (Taan. 2.2); EA *ia-ma* (*AmPN*, p. 269); WS *já-m-i-l-u* (e 30); NA *bir-ia-ma-a* (*WSB*, p. 66); N/LB *ia-ma-ʾ*;[121] WS *ḥym* (VSE #8).[122]

Comments: Before the interpretation of this PN can be discussed, the correct reading of the name needs to be established. Two arguments may be mustered to suggest that Yemuʾel is the correct reading and that Nemuʾel is nothing more than a textually corrupt form of Yemuʾel. The first argument requires us to consider the textual evidence in favor of the reading Yemuʾel.

The PN Yemuʾel occurs twice in the Hebrew Bible: Gen 46:10 and Exod 6:15. In Gen 46:10, the SyrH, SyrP, LXX B, and Vulgate all support the reading of the MT. On these two verses the critical apparatus of the Cambridge edition of the LXX contains no evidence that supports a reading Nemuʾel. Though LXX B at Exod 6:15 reads ιεμιηλ (< **ymyʾl*), the MT, SyrH, SyrP, Vulgate, and other Greek manuscripts (AFM, f) support a reading Yemuʾel. The unanimity of textual witnesses in Gen 46:10 and Exod 6:15 strongly suggests that Yemuʾel is the original reading of the name. In Num 26:12, the MT reads Nemuʾel, as does the SyrH, Vulgate, and LXX B.[123] The reading of the SyrP (*ymwʾyl*) is a dissenting witness. In 1 Chr 4:24, the MT, Vulgate, and LXX B read Nemuʾel again, in contrast to the SyrP Yemuʾel. Outside of Num 26:12 and 1 Chr 4:24, where Nemuʾel refers to the first son of Simeon, it is borne by one other person in the Hebrew Bible--a son of Eliab (Num 26:9). Even here, however, the genuineness of the name is in question.[124]

---

[121]Ran Zadok, "Assyro-Babylonian Lexical and Onomastic Notes," *BO* 41 (1984) 39.

[122]Perhaps to be vocalized **(ʾă)ḥîyam*, meaning "My brother is Yamm." See Eduard Y. Kutscher, "lšny ḥwtmwt ʿbryym," in *Kedem: Studies in Jewish Archaeology*, vol. 1, ed. by E. L. Sukenik (Jerusalem, 1942), p. 44. For further discussion of the name, see Tigay, p. 71 and nn. 38-39, and note the possible correspondence between this name and the WS PN *aḫi(ŠEŠ)-ia-mi* from Taanach.

[123]The GA Nemuʾeli also occurs in this verse.

[124]Martin Noth, *Numbers: A Commentary*, The Old Testament Library (Philadelphia: Westminster Press, 1968), pp. 205-6, contended that the PN Nemuʾel in Num 26:9 is the result of transposition of the same name three verses later (v 12). Elsewhere, Eliab's sons appear to be two in number: Dathan and Abiram. Too much weight should not be placed on this argument, for the other passages that mention Eliab's two sons Dathan and Abiram have as their topic the rebellion of Qorah. If a third son of Eliab, named Nemuʾel, did not participate in the said rebellion, then he would receive no mention in these other passages. Nonetheless, doubt still lingers with respect to a third son of Eliab named Nemuʾel on account of the close proximity of the identical name three verses later.

The second argument in favor of the reading Yemu'el is based on extrabiblical occurrences of the same name. The Ug. PN *ym'il* and the WS PN *já-m-i-l-u* are the ancient prototypes of the Can. PN *yĕmû-'ēl.* These extrabiblical attestations of the same name confirm the correctness of the reading Yemu'el. Contrarily, the PN Nemu'el has no onomastic parallels anywhere in the ancient Near East. Neither has an acceptable etymology been suggested for the first element of the name.[125] All things considered, it appears probable that the PN Nemu'el is simply due to textual corruption.[126]

Two different etymologies have been offered for the first element of the name. This element may be derived from **yammu* "sea" and refer to the sea-god, or from **yawmu* "day" and refer to the god of the day. The name as vocalized by the Masoretes permits either derivation.[127] The same interpretive options apply to the Ug. PN *ym'il* and the WS PN *já-m-i-l-u.* Scholars have interpreted the first element in these PNN as the deity "Day" because they claim to have discovered this deity in the Ugaritic texts and in WS PNN.[128] But the evidence presented for a deity "Day" at Ugarit is slight, being confined to one reference in the polyglot god-list.[129] It still has not been proven that this DN is productive in Ug. PNN.[130]

---

[125]For an attempt, see Barr, *Comparative Philology*, p. 182, who then refutes his own suggestion.

[126]For the confusion of the letters *y* (or, as the case may be, *w*) and *n*, see Friedrich Delitzsch, *Die Lese- und Schreibfehler im Alten Testament* (Berlin: Walter de Gruyter, 1920), pp. 111-12, who cited the PN Y/Nemuel as an example of "die Verwechselung von *y* und *n* . . . ."

[127]Since this name is vocalized according to the artificial pattern $*C_1\check{e}C_2\hat{u}$*'ēl*, the lack of gemination is not a decisive argument against deriving the first element from **yammu.*

[128]Hans Bauer, "Die Gottheiten von Ras Schamra," *ZAW* 51 (1933) 92; G. R. Driver, "The original form of the name 'Yahweh': evidence and conclusions," *ZAW* 46 (1928) 7 n. 1; idem, "Theological and Philological Problems in the Old Testament," *JTS* 47 (1946) 156-57 (Driver does not express himself clearly, but he seems to lean toward interpreting the *ym* element as the name of the god of the day); A. Jirku, "Die Keilschrifttexte von Ras Šamra und das Alte Testament," *ZDMG* 89 (1935) 381. In an earlier article, "Zur Götterwelt Palästinas und Syriens," in *Sellin Festschrift: Beiträge zur Religiongeschichte und Archäologie Palästinas, Ernst Sellin zum 60. Geburtstage dargebracht* (Leipzig: D. Werner Scholl, 1927), pp. 85-86, A. Jirku tentatively identifies as a DN the **ym* element of the WS PN Ahiyami (Taanach), the EA PN *Yamiuta* [*sic*] (see Hess, *AmPN*, p. 271), and the Can. PN Yemuel. It is not until his 1935 article, however, that he states that this DN is "Day" rather than the well-known sea-god.

[129]*Ug V*, 137 IV a 17 (pp. 248-49); Huehnergard, *Ugaritic Vocabulary*, pp. 133, 318. Huffmon, *APNMT*, p. 211, cites the phrase *šamši*(^{d}*UTU*^{ši}) *ūmi*(U_4^{mi}) [19.68, l. 46 (*PRU* IV, p. 286)], but the context is broken and the meaning unclear. The deity "Day" is attested in the Aramaic Sefire treaty (A I 12). See the discussion of Ran

Several lines of argument converge to favor a reference to the sea-god in PNN. Although some of the syllabic cuneiform attestations of these two vocables (i.e., **yammu* and **yawmu*) are equivocal, in that the initial cuneiform sign may be read *ya* (**yammu* "sea") or *yu* (**yōmu* < **yawmu* "day"), the cuneiform writings in which the *m* is geminated must be interpreted as referring to the sea-god. Since cuneiform writing does not necessarily reflect geminated consonants, those names with the single writing of the *m* are not necessarily problematic. Moreover, the logographically written Ug. PN *abdv(ÌR)-yammi(A.AB.BA)* proves that the *ym* element in its alphabetically written counterpart *ʿbdym* refers to the sea-god. Therefore, the Can. PN Yemuʾel is best interpreted as a nominal-sentence PN meaning "Yammu is god." This interpretation also obtains for Ug. *ymʾil*[131] and WS *já-m-i-l-u*. This is the first PN of the type **C₁ĕC₂ûʾēl* in which the first element is a DN. As with the Can. PN Hadoram, the DN in Yemuʾel terminates in the nominative case ending *û*. The Amor. PN *ia-am-mu-ú* and the WS PN *ia-am-mu* (Alalakh) may be compared.

7a. *mĕtûšāʾēl.*

Classification: Can.--Qayinite patriarch (Gen 4:18).

Structure: construct phrase name, 1. *mĕt-* (**qul* base, BL §61k) + *-û-* nominative case vowel + *-ša-* relative particle + *-ʾēl.*
2. *mĕt-* + *-û-* nominative case vowel + **šĕʾōl* (revocalization).

Meaning: 1. "man of god/El."
2. "man of (the god of?) Sheol."

Zadok, "On the Historical Background of the Sefîre Treaty," *AION* 44 (1984) 529 n. 1.

[130]Gröndahl, *PTU*, p. 144, lists two PNN, *ʿi-nu-uʾ-mi* and *šlmym*, under the heading *YM*, "day." The meaning suggested for the first name is unlikely, and the second PN could just as well be interpreted as containing the DN Yamm. In the book of Enoch, a fallen angel bears the name *ymʾl* (= Grk ιουμιηλ; Beyer, *ATTM*, p. 734), "day of God," but this late symbolic PN (another angel is named "Night") is hardly decisive for the interpretation of early WS PNN.

[131]As recognized by Gröndahl, *PTU*, p. 144; and Gordon, *UT* §8.62, 19.1106.

Parallels: Amor. *mu-tu-i-la, mu-ut-ḫu-bur* (*CAAA*, pp. 625-26); Ug. *mtbʿl, mu-ut-baʿal*(${}^{d}U^{al}$) (*PTU*, p. 162); WS *mu-*⸢*ut*⸣[*-IŠKUR*] (Taan. 12.4);[132] EA *mu-ut-ba-aḫ-lum* (*AmPN*, p. 190).[133]

Comments: The PNN Metushaʾel and Metushelah are the only two names in the Hebrew Bible that contain the vocable **mut*. It has long been recognized that the similarity between these two names is not isolated but extends to other pairs of names in the genealogies of Gen 4 and 5. Scholars have posited two theories to account for the many similarities: 1) the two genealogical traditions ultimately derive from one original *Vorlage*; or 2) the genealogies were originally separate traditions that partially conflated.[134] Whatever the case may be, the points of correspondence do not extend across the whole Canaanite genealogy of Gen 4:17-24, but only across vv 17-18, where the PN Metushaʾel occurs.[135] The extent of the correspondence can be appreciated best by listing the PNN contained in these two verses with their counterparts from the genealogy of Gen. 5:

Gen 4	Gen 5
qayin	*qênān*
ḥănôk	*ḥănôk*
ʿîrād	*yered*
mĕḥûʾī(y)yāʾēl	*mahălalʾēl*
mĕtûšāʾēl	*mĕtûšelaḥ*
lemek	*lemek*

In the lefthand column, the names have been listed in the sequence in which they are presented in the MT, whereas in the righthand column, the names have been rearranged to facilitate comparison. Two of the PNN are identical (Lemek and Hanok), and the rest approximate one another with variations. The actual sequence of names according to the genealogy of Gen 5 is Qenan, Mahalalʾel, Yered, Hanok, Metushelah,

---

132Cited according to Sivan's transcription (*GAGNWS*, p. 250). On p. 5, he states that he was allowed to see the work that resulted from the reexamination of these tablets by Rainey, Gordon, and Glock.

133This same name is also written *mu-ut-*^{d}*IM* and *mu-ut-*^{d}*IM-me* (*AmPN*, p. 190). I have cited no PNN from the Alalakh tablets on account of the difficulty of distinguishing Akkadian from WS PNN in Wiseman's study. The vocable *mutu* is a lexical item common to Akkadian and early West Semitic.

134The first theory has dominated biblical scholarship. On the second theory, see David T. Bryan, "A Reevaluation of Gen 4 and 5 in Light of Recent Studies in Genealogical Fluidity," *ZAW* 99 (1987) 180-88.

135Claus Westermann, *Genesis 1-11: A Commentary*, transl. J. J. Scullion (Minneapolis: Augsburg Publishing House, 1984), p. 349.

and Lemek. Except for the PNN Qayin/Qenan that head the list, the only point of agreement between the two genealogies is the paternity of Lemek: Metushaʾel in Gen 4, Metushelah in Gen 5. This point of agreement and the correspondence between these two lists of PNN strongly suggest that these two PNN are a doublet, and that the conclusions drawn from the interpretation of one are applicable to the other. Yet the Masoretic versions of the names differ slightly, and it is impossible to determine at what point in the stage of transmission--oral, written, or both--the divergent form(s) arose. Each of these PNN has its own history of interpretation; hence it is expedient to treat each name separately. In this section the interpretation of the PN Metushaʾel will be discussed, always with an eye on the PN Metushelah, and some of the discussion will be relevant for the interpretation of the latter name.

The **mut* element in these PNN may be discussed under three points. First, the overwhelming preponderance of compound PNN with the vocable **mut* "man" in first position are construct phrase theophoric PNN. These names describe the name bearer as a worshiper and protégé of the deity; the *nomen regens* refers to the name bearer, the *nomen rectum* to the deity. Admittedly, a few of these compound PNN may be of the nominal-sentence type, but this type is rare and not pertinent to the names discussed here.[136] Second, the chronological distribution of the word needs to be considered. The vocable **mut* is attested in Akkadian, Eblaite,[137] and early West Semitic PNN. Gelb has isolated approximately 110 PNN in Amorite that contain the vocable **mut*.[138] The occurrence of this vocable in PNN from Ugarit, El Amarna, and Tell Taanach indicates that **mut* continued to be

---

[136]Stamm, *ANG*, pp. 126, 312, analyzes the Akk. feminine (!) PN *ᶠmuti-bāšti* as a nominal-sentence PN ("My husband is my protecting spirit"). Compare also p. 298, for Akk. masculine PNN of type *mut-* + DN that Stamm interprets as nominal sentences. At least one of the PNN he cites [*mu-ti-ilum(DINGIR)*] may be analyzed as a construct phrase type. According to I. J. Gelb, "An Old Babylonian List of Amorites," *JAOS* 88 (1968) 46, the Amor. PN *mu-ti-me-el* is a nominal-sentence name. He analyzes the *i* on *mu-ti-* as a 1st c.s. pronominal suffix. Huffmon, *APNMT*, p. 119, maintains that all the Amor. PNN with *mut-* are of the construct phrase type, and that those Amor. PNN that appear to be exceptions are probably Akk. PNN. It is difficult if not impossible to distinguish Akk. from Amor. PNN in this instance, because the lexical items are common property of both languages. Further, Akkadian name formations may have influenced the Amorite onomasticon, and vice a versa.

[137] In the PN lists in the first four volumes of ARET, only three Eblaite PNN are constructed with the vocable **mut*: *mu-ti-ḫa-lam* (ARET I:234), *mu-ti*, and *mu-ti-iš-ma-a* (ARET IV:258).

[138]Gelb, *CAAA*, pp. 158-60.

productive in the WS onomasticon at a later date. Outside of PNN the vocable is attested in the Ugaritic mythological texts.[139]

While the vocable **mut* continued in use in the Akkadian language until the NA and NB periods,[140] the Canaanite languages are marked by the absence of this word. Outside of the PNN Metushaʾel and Metushelah, the vocable **mut* is not found in Canaanite PNN. In light of the large number of Canaanite PNN that have been preserved, the absence of the vocable is surprising. The only other occurrences of this word among the Canaanite languages are in BH, and even here, the position of this word may be described as marginal, being confined to the plural, mostly in stock expressions.[141] One may conclude that the occurrence of the vocable **mut* in these two Canaanite PNN is a lexical archaism. Both of these names are indeed ancient.

Third, the vocable **mut* assumes various forms in PNN: 1) **mutu-*; 2) **muti-*; and 3) **mut*. In these two Canaanite names this element is written *mĕtû-*, ending with the nominative case vowel *û*. This form may be compared with Amor. *mu-tu-i-la*.[142] For further discussion, one may refer to Huffmon's brief study of the various forms of **mut* in Amor. PNN at Mari.[143] It is frequently not apparent to the contemporary reader why one form is used rather than another.

According to our first proposed structure/meaning, the compound PN Metushaʾel consists of three separate lexemes: 1) *mĕtû-* ; 2) *-šā-* ; and 3) *-ʾēl*. Although names of the type "man of DN" are common in Semitic name formations, the occurrence of the relative particle *ša* in the middle of a construct phrase PN is most unusual. The interpretation of Metushaʾel as a compound PN with three elements is a widely accepted interpretation, and one that is firmly entrenched in Hebrew lexica.[144] This analysis can be traced at least as far back as W. Gese-

---

[139]*UT* §19.569; Joseph Aistleitner, *Wörterbuch der ugaritischen Sprache*, ed. Otto Eissfeldt, Berichte über die Verhandlungen der sächsischen Akademie der Wissenschaften zu Leipzig: Philologisch-historische Klasse, Band 106/3 (Berlin: Akademie, 1963), p. 198 (#1705).

[140]CAD *M*, part 2, p. 316.

[141]KB3, pp. 617-18.

[142]For other Amor. PNN whose initial element is written *mutu-*, see Gelb, *CAAA*, p. 159.

[143]*APNMT*, p. 119.

[144]BDB, p. 607; KB2, p. 582; KB3, p. 618; Zorell, *Lexicon Hebraicum*, p. 487. Other proponents of this interpretation are Cassuto, p. 233; Franz Delitzsch, *A New Commentary on Genesis*, 2 vols., trans. Sophia Taylor (Edinburgh: T. & T. Clark, 1888-94), 1:193-94; Fowler, pp. 115, 123, 271 n. 26; Fritz Hommel, "*ʾăšer*, ursprüngliches Substantiv zu trennen von *še-* (*ša*), ursprünglichem Pronominalstamm," *ZDMG* 32 (1878) 714; Israel, *OLP* 10 (1979) 148 n. 36; Morris Jastrow, Jr., "The Element *bšt* in Hebrew Proper Names," *JBL* 13 (1894) 23-24; Liverani, *RSO* 37 (1962) 72 n. 5; Gary A. Rendsburg, "Evidence for a Spoken Hebrew in Biblical

nius' *Thesaurus philologicus-criticus linguae Hebraeae et Chaldaeae Veteris Testamenti* (1835-40).[145] Although Gesenius cited no Semitic PNN to support his interpretation, Hebrew lexica cite various Akk. PNN of similar or identical structure. It is a pertinent to note the PNN that these lexica cite, and the problems involved with each name.

BDB (p. 607) compares biblical Metushaʾel to *mutu-ša-ili* "man of God," a name which they describe as a "Babylonian form." The only bibliographic source they cite is François Lenormant, *Les origines de l'histoire d'après la Bible et les traditions des peuples orientaux.*[146] In his lexicon, Zorrell (p. 487) also compares the biblical PN to "Assyrian" *mutu-ša-ili.* KB2 (p. 582), on the other hand, lists only the Akk. PN *mutum-ilum* and a bibliographic reference to Stamm's *ANG* (p. 298), where the name is originally cited.[147] KB3 (p. 618) cites the same information included in the KB2 entry on the name, only the third edition adds the Akk. PN **mutu-ša-ili* and a bibliographic reference to Gemser's study of Akkadian PNN.[148]

The entries on the PN Methushaʾel in these lexica may be faulted on several points. If an Akkadian PN **mutu-ša-ili* were attested, it would provide substantial evidence for our first proposed structure/meaning. But this Akk. PN is not attested in any Akkadian source; instead, it was created to provide an apt parallel to the biblical PN Metushaʾel. Although the reader is alerted to this by an asterisk in KB3, one could easily be mislead by the citation of this putative name in the entries in BDB and Zorrell. As early as 1910, Skinner, in his

---

Times" (Ph.D. dissertation, New York University, 1980), p. 78; idem, "Diglossia in Ancient Hebrew as Revealed Through Compound Verbs," in *Bono Homini Donum: Essays in Historical Linguistics in Memory of J. Alexander Kerns*, 2 vols., ed. Yoël Arbeitman & Allan R. Bomhard (Amsterdam: John Benjamins, 1981), 2:667; E. A. Speiser, *Genesis: Introduction, Translation, and Notes*, AB 1 (Garden City: Doubleday & Co., 1964), p. 35; Adrianus van Selms, "A Forgotten God: *Laḥ*," in *Studia biblica et semitica: Theodoro Christiano Vriezen qui munere professoris theologiae per xxv annos functus est, ab amicis, collegis, discipulis dedicata* (Wageningen: H. Veenman & Zonen, 1966), pp. 318-19.

[145]2 vols. (Leipzig, 1835-40), 2:830.

[146]2 vols. (Paris: Maisonneuve, 1880-84), 1:263 n. 1. In this note, Lenormant contended that the biblical PN is ". . . absolument assyrien de forme, *mutu-ša-ili*; bien plus assyrien qu'hébreu." He also referred to F. Hommel, *Zwei Jagdinschriften Asurbanibal's* (Leipzig: J. C. Hinrichs, 1879), p. 22, to the effect that this PN was borrowed from Babylonia. To the best of our knowledge, Hommel was the first (modern?) scholar to compare the biblical PN Metushaʾel to "Assyrian" **mutu-ša-ili.*

[147]KB2 glosses Metushaʾel by "Mann Gottes"; yet the Akk. PN *mutum-ilum* they cite is analyzed by Stamm, *ANG*, p. 298, as a nominal-sentence PN!

[148]Berend Gemser, *De beteekenis der persoonsnamen voor onze kennis van het leven en denken der oude Babyloniërs en Assyriërs* (Wageningen: H. Veenman & Zonen, 1924), pp. 105-6.

commentary on Genesis, correctly stated that "it does not appear that *mutu-ša-ili* occurs as an actual name."[149] Likewise, Tsevat argued that this name is neither Hebrew nor Akkadian, and that he could not find any names of this type among the circa 2600 Akk. PNN listed in Stamm's *ANG* index.[150] Thus there is no reason to continue citing this fictional name-type in the lexica. Apparently the original reason why biblical Metusha᾽el was compared to an *Akkadian* PN was because nineteenth-century scholars had no early West Semitic PNN at their disposal for study and comparison. Therefore, they noticed that the PNN Metusha᾽el and Metushelah were comprised of lexical items found in the Akkadian language, and they concluded that these PNN were actually Akkadian names. The lexica have lost sight of this historical circumstance and continue to cite only Akk. PNN in entries on the name Metusha᾽el. It would be more apposite to cite early West Semitic PNN, such as Amor. *mu-tu-i-la*, which at present provides the closest parallel to Metusha᾽el. Yet it must be underscored that thousands of early West Semitic PNN have come to light in the last century, and not one of them includes a *ša* relative particle intruding between the two elements of a construct phrase name.[151] Therefore, our first proposed structure/meaning should be rejected.

According to our second proposed structure/meaning, the PN Metusha᾽el may be divided into two elements. The difficulty with this approach involves the meaning of the second element, *-šā᾽ēl.* On the analogy of other PNN of the type **mut* + DN, one would expect the second element to be a DN, but a deity named Sha᾽el is unknown. Consequently, some interpreters have suggested that the original vocalization of the second element was lost at some stage in the transmission of the name. Thus Böklen proposed that the final element is to be vocalized **šĕ᾽ōl* "underworld," and the name would mean "Mann der Unterwelt."[152] This interpretation of the PN Metusha᾽el has also been

---

[149]John Skinner, *A Critical and Exegetical Commentary on Genesis*, 2d ed., ICC (Edinburgh: T. & T. Clark, 1930), p. 117.

[150]Matitiahu Tsevat, "The Canaanite God Šälaḥ," *VT* 4 (1954) 45.

[151]A possible exception is the Amor. PN *zu-ú-ša-a-bi*, the analysis of which is problematic. For discussion and bibliography, see Huffmon, *APNMT*, p. 265; Giovanni Garbini, "La parole *zu-ú* nell'onomastica «amorrea»," *AION* 35 (1975) 414-16. The Ph-P. PN *mtršbd᾽* may be another exception, but its interpretation is difficult too (Benz, *PNPP*, pp. 357-58). No certain examples of Akk. construct phrase PNN with *-ša-* separating the two elements of the name are known.

[152]Ernst Böklen, *Adam und Qain im Lichte der vergleichenden Mythenforschung*, Mythologische Bibliothek, Band 1, Heft 2/3 (Leipzig: J. C. Hinrichs, 1907), p. 132 n. 2.

advocated by others, such as Wood,[153] Pope,[154] and Lewy.[155] This ingenious explanation derives support from the PN Metushelah, since, as will be argued below, Shelah is god of the underworld.

The explanation that Methusha'el means "man of Sheol" is plausible, but this interpretation can hardly be regarded as certain. This approach appears inconsistent in its assumption that the original vocalization of the name was lost in transmission, but the original consonantal form of the name remained intact. If we take seriously the view that the PNN Methusha'el and Metushelah form a doublet, one may infer that one of these names, or possibly both, is/are corrupted. And since the interpretation of the PN Methushelah entails less difficulty, it is reasonable to conclude that the PN Methusha'el has been corrupted in transmission. Hommel may well have been correct when he described the PN Metusha'el as a "volkstümliche Umbildung" for the no longer understood Metushelah.[156] The difference between the two names is slight: an interchange of guttural consonants and metathesis of the final two consonants. Some LXX transliterations at Gen 4:18 witness a Hebrew *Vorlage* with **mĕtûšelaḥ*, but these may merely reflect conflation rather than an independent textual tradition.[157] However one understands the problematic final element of this name, the medial *û* in the PN Methusha'el can only be analyzed as the remnant of a nominative case ending. We will now consider the interpretation of the PN Metushelah.

---

[153]W. Carleton Wood, "The Religion of Canaan: The Canaanite Period (1800-1200 B.C.)," *JBL* 35 (1916) 268.

[154]Marvin H. Pope, "Notes on the Ugaritic Rephaim Texts," in *Essays on the Ancient Near East in Memory of Jacob Joel Finkelstein*, ed. Maria de Jong Ellis, Memoirs of the Conneticut Academy of Arts & Sciences, vol. 19 (Hamben, CT: Archon Books for the Academy, 1977), p. 166.

[155]J. Lewy does not appear to have published his view of the PN Metusha'el. In his study of the Canaanite deity Shelah (*VT* 4 [1954] 45), Tsevat refers to Lewy's interpretation of Metusha'el as "man of Sheol" and identifies the source of information as "oral communication." According to the reports on the joint meeting of the Mid-West Branch of the American Oriental Society and Society of Biblical Literature (*Or* 22 [1953] 435; *JBL* 73 [1954] xxii), Lewy presented a paper entitled "Remarks on the Biblical Names Yareb, Methusha'el, Hebron," in which he argued that the PN Methusha'el is synonymous with the "Old West Semitic" PN *mut-ḫubur* "man of (the underworld deity) Ḫubur."

[156]Fritz Hommel, *Aufsätze und Abhandlungen arabistisch-semitologischen Inhalts* (Munich: G. Franz, 1892), p. 222.

[157]Paul de Lagarde, *Orientalia*, 2 vols. (Göttingen: Dieterich, 1880), 2:33-38, endeavored to prove from the LXX and other ancient translations that the PN Metushelah stood originally for Metusha'el.

7b. *mĕtûšelaḥ*.

Classification: Can.--Sethite patriarch (Gen 5:21).

Structure: 1. *mĕt-* + *-u-* nominative case vowel + *-ša-* relative particle + *-laḥ* (DN).
2. *mĕt-* + *-û-* nominative case vowel + *šelaḥ* (DN).

Meaning: 1. "man of Lah."
2. "man of Shelah."

Parallels: Ug. CN *šlḥ*; Can. *šelaḥ*, *šilḥî*, BH CN *šelaḥ*.

Comments: Van Selms has divided the PN Metushelah into three elements and argued for the existence of a deity Lah in the ancient Semitic world.[158] He arrived at this structural analysis of Metushelah by a comparison with the PN Metushaʾel. As argued above, however, the division of the PN Metushaʾel into three elements is untenable because it is without parallel in Semitic name formations; therefore, Van Selm's interpretation of the PN Metushelah cannot be accepted.

In light of the consistency with which compound PNN beginning with **mut-* have a DN in second position, the interpretation of *šelaḥ* as a DN is reasonably assured. While earlier interpreters posited that the name meant "man of the dart/spear,"[159] this meaning did not seem appropriate for a PN. The suggestion that the second element in the name is theophoric goes at least as far back as the late nineteenth century, when Hommel explained Shelah as a corrupt form of *šarraḫu*, the latter said to be the ancient name of the moon-god.[160] Lewy also recognized the PN Metushelah as a theophoric name.[161] The most important study of this PN and the Canaanite deity Shelah is by Tsevat.[162] He has gathered together hints scattered over Semitic languages and religions that combine to point to an underworld deity who was god of the infernal river.

There remains to consider whether there are any references to the deity Shelah outside of PNN.[163] Loretz claims that Ug. *šlḥ* in *KTU*

---

[158] Van Selms, "A Forgotten God," pp. 318-26.

[159] Among others, Emil G. Kraeling, "Metušelach," *ZAW* 40 (1922) 154-55.

[160] Hommel, *Aufsätze und Abhandlungen*, p. 222.

[161] Lewy, *RHR* 110 (1934) 61 n. 77.

[162] Tsevat, *VT* 4 (1954) 41-49; idem, "Additional Remarks to 'The Canaanite God Šälaḥ'," *VT* 4 (1954) 322.

[163] The Can. PNN *šelaḥ* and *šilḥî* appear to be a shortened name, with only the DN retained (on this type, see p. 218 n. 101), and a hypocoristic PN, respectively.

1.14.I.20 is a DN.[164] Lines 15-21a of this passage tell of the misfortune that befell Kirta's family. The passage reaches a climax with the statement *mšbʿthn.bšlḥ ttpl*, which some would translate "the seventh of them fell by ŠLḤ." In support of the claim that Ug. *šlḥ* in line 20 is a DN, it has been noted that in the immediate context (ll. 18-20), the deities Yammu and Rašpu have just been mentioned. Hence a reference to a third deity, the underworld god ŠLḤ, is appropriate at this point in the passage. This interpretation assumes that the Ug. preposition *b* expresses the agent of the verbal action. However, in the similar expression in Job 33:18 and 36:12, the BH preposition *b* has a locative meaning (**ʿbr bšlḥ* "to pass over into the canal"). The parallel syntax between *KTU* 1.14.I.20 and Job 33:18, 36:12 should not pass unnoticed: verb of movement (Ug. **npl*; BH **ʿbr*) + locative use of preposition *b* + object (of preposition) *šlḥ*. It is better, therefore, to interpret Ug. *b* in its locative meaning and translate "a seventh of them fell into the canal/river." This rendering fits the context well, since "to fall into the canal" is an idiomatic expression for death. For the meantime, it appears that the evidence for a DN Shelah is confined to PNN. To summarize, the PN Metushelah is a construct phrase theophoric PN meaning "man of Shelah." The analysis of the medial *û* vowel as a nominative case ending is beyond dispute. The PN Metushaʾel is probably nothing more (or less) than a corrupt form of the PN Metushelah. Whatever the case may be, no meaning can be assigned to the second element of the PN Metushaʾel as pointed by the Massoretes. In the final count of PNN at the end of this chapter, the PNN Metushelah and Metushaʾel are reckoned as only one example.

8. *pĕnûʾēl.*

Variant spelling: *pĕnîʾēl* (1 Chr 8:25 K).

Classification: Can.--1) tribe of Judah (1 Chr 4:4); 2) tribe of Benjamin (1 Chr 8:25 Q).

Tsevat, *VT* 4 (1954) 45, 49, also cites the Ph-P. PNN *ʾšršlḥ* ("Osiris is Shelah") and *ʾbšlḥ* ("the father is Shelah"), but the interpretation of these PNN is uncertain. To fill out the picture, one should also cite the Ph-P. PNN *šlḥ* and *mšlḥ* (Benz, *PNPP*, p. 416), the latter of which may be analyzed as a D-stem participle from a root **šlḥ* "to send." This name raises the possibility that all these names may contain a verbal root **šlḥ* instead of a DN. On a D stem of **šlḥ* "to set free" in Ph. PNN, see the remarks of Fowler, pp. 196-97.

[164]Oswald Loretz, "Der Gott *ŠLḤ*, He. *ŠLḤ* I und *ŠLḤ* II," *UF* 7 (1975) 584-85. In his groundbreaking article (*VT* 4 (1954) 41-49), Tsevat overlooked this important passage, but he later discussed it in a supplementary note (*VT* 4 [1954] 322).

Structure: construct phrase name, *pĕn-* (**qatal* ? base, BL §61n") + *-û-* nominative case vowel + *-ʾēl.*

Meaning: "face of god/El."

Parallels: Amor. *pa-ni-la* (*CAAA*, p. 631); Ug. *pan(IGI)-ili(DINGIR)* (*PTU*, p. 173); WS *pa-ni-la, pa-ni-li* (*AT*, p. 144); WS *pnʾl* (Heltzer, *PEQ* 110:9); Can. GN *pnw-3r* (Shoshenq I list, #54);[165] Can. GNN *pĕnûʾēl, pĕnîʾēl*; EH ⌈p⌉n⌈ʾ⌉l (Beer-sheva ostracon #1.2);[166] Ph-P. *pnsmlt* (*PNPP*, pp. 230, 392); Grk *φανουηλ* (Luke 2:36).

Comments: The proper name Penuʾel is attested as a PN and a GN. The spelling of the name with the medial *û* vowel is not in doubt; it is attested in 1 Chr 4:4 and 1 Chr 8:25 Q as a PN, and in Gen 32:32, Judg 8:8 (2), 9, 17, and 1 Kgs 12:25 as a GN. Contrarily, the spelling Peniʾel is not as well-established; it occurs but twice, in 1 Chr 8:25 K as a PN, and in Gen 32:31 as a GN. In the Gen 32:31, the SamP, SyrP, Vulgate, and the Greek translation of Symmachus witness a reading **pnwʾl*, which agrees with spelling of the GN in the following verse (v 32). The genuineness of the spelling **pnwʾl* for the GN is established by the occurrence of the same GN in the Shoshenq I list (#54 *pnw-3r*), where Egyptian *w* renders Semitic **ū*. In Josephus the GN is uniformly transliterated *φανουηλ* (*NWJ*, p. 122). If the spelling Peniʾel is a genuine variant, and not the product of confusion between *waw* and *yod*, then the first element should be analyzed as the construct form of the plural oblique.[167] This form would be morphological archaism, which was later supplanted by the construct form of the dual in SBH (**panay* > *pĕnê*).

Because the noun **pānē(h)* has developed as a *plurale tantum*, the medial *û* in the PN Penuʾel is to be analyzed as the nominative plural case ending (unless the name represents an archaic singular form), with the first element of the name in the construct state. Since

---

[165]Shmuel Aḥituv, *Canaanite Toponyms in Ancient Egyptian Documents* (Jerusalem: Magnes Press; Leiden: E. J. Brill, 1984), p. 154.

[166]André Lemaire, *Inscriptions hébraïques. Tome 1: Les ostraca.* Littératures anciennes du Proche-Orient, vol. 9 (Paris: Editions du Cerf, 1977), pp. 271-72. Walter Kornfeld, "Zur althebräischen Anthroponomastik ausserhalb der Bibel," *WZKM* 71 (1979) 45, accepts Lemaire's proposed reading.

[167]Rudolph Meyer "Probleme der hebräischen Grammatik," *ZAW* 63 (1951) 226, accepts both forms as genuine variants, and he concludes from the indiscriminate alternation of Penuʾel and Peniʾel that case distinctions were no longer recognized. See also his *Hebräische Grammatik*, 3d ed., 4 vols. (Berlin: Walter de Gruyter, 1966-72), §45 3.a.; BL §65h.

the construct form of the nominative plural case ending was later replaced by the construct form of the dual, the retention of the nominative plural case ending **-ū* in this name may be considered a morphological archaism.[168]

9. *qĕmûʾēl.*

Classification: Can.--1) son of Nahor and father of Aram (Gen 22:21); 2) tribe of Ephraim (Num 34:24); 3) tribe of Levi (1 Chr 27:17).

Structure: 1. verbal-sentence name, **qôm-* (emendation; < **qwm* "to arise," 3rd m.s. Qal perfect) + *-ʾēl.*
2. nominal-sentence name, *qĕm-* (DN?) + *-û-* nominative case vowel + *-ʾēl.*

Meaning: 1. "God/El has arisen."
2. "Qam (theophoric element [DN?]) is god/El."

Parallels: Amor. *qa-mu-ma-a-ḫu-um, qa-mu-ma-a-ḫi, qa-mu-ma-ilu(DINGIR), ba-lum-qa-mu-um* (*CAAA*, pp. 172-73); NA *qa-am-ba-na* (Zadok, *WO* 9:54 n. 138); Nab. *zydqwmw, ʿbdqwmw, ʿbdqwmy* (Cantineau, 2:142); postbiblical Hebrew *qᵉmûʾēl* (name of an angel; Jastrow, *Dictionary*, p. 1384).

Comments: Although the two elements that comprise the compound PN Qemuʾel are well-attested elsewhere in the West Semitic onomasticon, the interpretation of this name is generally considered unclear. Bauer interpreted the PN Qemuʾel in light of his *Mischsprache* theory.[169] He noted that the Qal perfect of the verbal root **rwm* assumes two forms in PNN, *rām* or *rôm* (e.g., the Ph. PN *ḥîrôm*), and he understood these two forms as representing two different strata within BH--Aramaic and Canaanite respectively. Accordingly, Bauer emended *qmwʾl* to **qwmʾl,* thereby eliminating the medial *û* vowel, and he interpreted the first element as a perfect verbal form.[170] The arbitrariness of Bauer's interpretation is apparent; for the *Mischsprache* theory to be applicable to this PN, Bauer has to emend the PN in two

[168]Among names of the type **C₁ĕC₂ûʾēl*, only in the PN Penuʾel does Hebrew *û* represent the long nominative case vowel. The representation of historical long vowels by *matres lectionis* is the norm in biblical orthography. For Hebrew *û* < **u*, see p. 57 n. 86.

[169]Bauer, *ZAW* 48 (1930) 74.

[170]Ibid.

respects: *û* > *ô* and metathesis of *m* and *ô*. Notwithstanding problems with the theory itself,[171] the PN Qemuʾel already belongs to a series of PNN of the type *$*C_1\breve{e}C_2\hat{u}$ʾēl* and therefore it should be interpreted as it stands. Yet one may leave the reading of the name intact and still interpret the first element as a perfect verbal form (**qāmûʾēl* > *qĕmûʾēl*). This approach is superior to Bauer's, but it fails to account for the medial *û*. This vowel cannot be attributed to nominalization; only final vowels are subject to nominalization. Compare, for example, the WS *e-lu-ra-ma* (Taan. 7.3) and the nominalized form Ug. *a-bi-ra-mu* (*PTU*, p. 182). Thus our first proposed structure/meaning fails to explain the medial *û* in the name.

A sounder approach to the PN Qemuʾel is to interpret it in light of other PNN of the type *$*C_1\breve{e}C_2\hat{u}$ʾēl.* Names of this type have a nominal element in the first position and are either construct phrase PNN (e.g., Penuʾel "face of god/El") or nominal-sentence PNN (e.g.,Yemuʾel "Yammu is god"). In other PNN, the element *qam-* appears to be theophoric; thus Qemuʾel may be interpreted as a nominal-sentence PN, meaning "Qam is god/El." Zadok advocated this interpretation and cited the NA PN *Qa-am-ba-na* ("Qam has built, created") as a parallel.[172] The element *qam-* may have attained the status of a DN in this NA PN,[173] but in Amor. PNN it suffices to interpret it as a G participle[174] functioning as a theophoric element. In three of these PNN the enclitic *-ma* is attached to the *qamu-*, suggesting that the participle is the subject.[175] Hence these Amor. PNN must be of the nominal-sentence type. The fourth PN, Amor. *ba-lum-qa-mu-um*, may mean "Qam is

---

171The sound shift **ā* > **ō* in perfect verbal forms is specificially characteristic of Ph.-P. and should not be generalized to Canaanite.

172Ran Zadok, "Historical and Onomastic Notes," *WO* 9 (1977-78) 54 and n. 138. See also his *WSB*, pp. 67-68, where Qam is listed as an epithet or symbol used as a theophoric element in WS PNN.

173Also Nabatean PNN may contain a DN *qwmw/y*. See the list of DNN in Cantineau, 2:170. Whatever the case may be, Fowler, p. 123, errs in her claim that the long vowel *û* makes unlikely the analysis of the first element of Qemuʾel as a DN. Amorite (Huffmon, *APNMT*, pp. 62, 166), Ugaritic, and WS PNN in Egyptian texts (e.g., Hayes list #9: [ʿ]*p-r-ršpw*) furnish evidence for DNN with case endings. See also s.v. "hădôrām," p. 59, and "yĕmûʾēl," p. 66.

174Huffmon, *APNMT*, p. 101; Gelb, *CAAA*, p. 29, lists an entry in his glossary **qāmum*.

175Huffmon, *APNMT*, p. 101. Likewise, Joseph Aistleitner, "Studien zur Frage der Sprachverwandtschaft des Ugaritischen I," *Acta Orientalia Academiae Scientiarum Hungaricae* 7 (1957) 306, observed that *-ma* is attached to the subject in nominal-sentence names. One of his examples is the Amor. PN *qa-mu-ma-ìl*, which he translated "Der Beisteher ist Il_3."

lord."[176] At any rate the Amor. PN *qa-mu-ma-ilu(DINGIR)*, less the enclitic particle, is identical with the biblical PN Qemuʾel. The medial *û* may be analyzed as a nominative case ending.

10. *šĕmûʾēl.*

Classification: Can.--1) Israelite prophet (1 Sam 1:20); 2) tribe of Simeon (Num 34:30); 3) tribe of Issachar (1 Chr 7:2).

Structure: 1. nominal-sentence name, a. *šĕm-* (**qil* base, BL §61i)[177] + *-û-* (< **-uhu*) 3rd m.s. pronominal suffix + *-ʾēl*; or b. *šĕm-* + *-û-* nominative case ending + *-ʾēl.*
2. construct phrase name, *šĕm-* + *-û-* nominative case ending + *-ʾēl.*

Meaning: 1. a. "His name is El"; or b. "Shem (DN) or 'The name' (theophoric element) is god/El."
2. "offspring (< name) of god/El."

Parallels: Eblaite *su-ma-il* (ARET III:298; IV:261); Amor. *sa-mu-i-la* (*CAAA*, p. 635); *sa-mu-ú-i-la* (*CAAA*, p. 636); *su-ma-i-la, su-mi-lu-um* (*CAAA*, p. 637); *su-mu-ilu(DINGIR), su-mu-el, su-mu-i-la* (*CAAA*, p. 638); *ì-lí-su-ú-mu* (*CAAA*, p. 594); WS *šu-um-i-la* (*AT*, p. 147); WS *su-um-ḫa-nu-ta, fsu-mu-la-ilu(DINGIRlu)* (Hazor);[178] EA *šu-um-ad-da, šu-mu-ḫa-d[i]* (*AmPN*, pp. 237, 239); NA *s/šum-ma/mu-il* (*WSB*, p. 108); Ph-P. *šmʾl* (VSP #88); Palm. *šmwʾl* (*PNPI*, p. 115); Saf. *smʾl* (*PIAN*, p. 327); Grk σαμουηλ (Wuthnow, p. 105).

Comments: Of the names constructed according to the pattern $*C_1\breve{e}C_2\hat{u}$ʾ*ēl*, only the PN Shemuʾel is provided with an etiology. However, the meaning that the etiological narrative assigns to this name should not be confused with the original meaning of the name from the perspective of modern philology. Biblical etiologies are wordplays, relying heavily on assonance instead of strict identity of name elements and roots. Moreover, names that are provided with etiologies are

[176]Zadok, *WO* 9 (1977-78) 54 n. 138. On *ba-lu/i* as an appellative or theophoric element ("lord, master"), as opposed to the DN Baal (usually spelled *ba-al*), see Huffmon, *APNMT*, p. 100.

[177]The base of the vocable **švm* varies from language to language: **qil* in BH; **qal* and **qul* in Amorite (Gelb, *RANL* 13 [1958] §2.2.2); and **qal*, **qul*, and **qil* in cuneiform transliterations of WS PNN (Zadok, *WSB*, p. 65).

[178]Hallo and Tadmor, *IEJ* 27 (1977) 2 (obv., ll. 2-3).

generally archaic names[179] that are not readily explained on the basis of the Hebrew lexicon. As aptly stated by Barr, it is "the very strangeness of these names which made them call for an explanation."[180] Hence with the PN Shemu'el there is good reason to believe that the PN is archaic.

According to our structure/meaning 1. a., the PN Shemu'el is interpreted as a nominal-sentence type meaning "His name is El."[181] The inclusion of this view in commentaries--often with little or no discussion and no presentation of other views--might suggest that the meaning "His name is El" is well-founded and beyond reasonable doubt. Unfortunately, the situation is different, as will be shown in the following discussion. Although a complete history of interpretation of the name Shemu'el is not possible within the limits of this study, what can be done is to single out several of the important discussions on this interpretation of the name Shemu'el.

In his commentary on 1-2 Samuel, S. R. Driver[182] traced this interpretation back to Fritz Hommel's *Die altisraelitische Überlieferung in inschriftlicher Beleuchtung*.[183] One of Hommel's purposes was to demonstrate that the biblical names from the time of Abraham onward were in actual use in contemporary inscriptions, and therefore not post-exilic inventions.[184] Hommel argued that the dynasty of Hammurapi was West Semitic, or to be more precise, "Arabian" in origin, and he compared what we nowadays refer to as Amorite PNN with the name formations of the South Arabian inscriptions. He claimed that the most characteristic feature of the South Arabian onomasticon was the use of synonymous terms that served as periphrases for the deity. Prominent among these was the periphrasis **sum-hu* "his name," i.e. God's

---

[179]The archaic nature of these names may be inferred from the incidence of these passages, which are predominantly found at the *beginning* of the biblical story, especially in Genesis. See Johannes Fichtner, "Die etymologische Ätiologie in den Namengebungen der geschichtlichen Bücher des Alten Testaments," *VT* 6 (1956) 373-75.

[180]Barr, *BJRL* 52 (1969-70) 17.

[181]Peter R. Ackroyd, *The First Book of Samuel*, The Cambridge Bible Commentary on the New English Bible (Cambridge: University Press, 1971), p. 26; Aistleitner, *Acta Orientalia Academiae Scientiarum Hungaricae* 7 (1957) 293; Ralph W. Klein, *1 Samuel*, Word Biblical Commentary, vol. 10 (Waco: Word Books, 1983), p. 9; McCarter, *1 Samuel*, p. 62; W. Nowack, *Richter, Ruth u. Bücher Samuelis*, Handkommentar zum Alten Testament (Göttingen: Vandenhoeck & Ruprecht, 1902), p. 7; A. H. Van Zyl, "The meaning of the name Samuel," in *Proceedings of the Twelfth Meeting of Die ou-testamentiese werkgemeenskap in Suid-Afrika* (1969) 126.

[182]Driver, *Books of Samuel*, p. 18.

[183](Munich: G. Franz, 1897), pp. 85-100.

[184]Ibid., p. vi.

name.[185] Thus Hommel understood the Amor. PN *šumu-abi* as a contraction from **šumu-hu-abi*, meaning "His name is my father." Likewise, he assumed that contraction had taken place in the Can. PN Shemuʾel and that it may be interpreted similarly.[186] Any WS PN with the initial element **šumu-* was susceptible to Hommel's line of interpretation. An important modification to Hommel's view was introduced by Giesebrecht, who referred the antecedent of the pronoun to the worshiper who wished to avoid mentioning the name of his god.[187] This is a definite improvement, for elsewhere in the Semitic onomasticon pronominal suffixes consistently find their antecedent in the name-bearer or name-giver instead of the deity (e.g., **ilī* "my god").

The reaction to Hommel's view was mixed. Jastrow criticized Hommel's interpretation of the Can. PN Shemuʾel and the Amor. PNN.[188] Schrader, on the other hand, approved of Hommel's interpretation of the biblical name.[189] Ranke cited Hommel's comparison of Amor. *sa/umu-* with South Arabian *smh*, but he appears to have had some reservations about the comparison, which he expressed by a question mark.[190] T. Bauer rejected Hommel's explanation of Amor. *sumu* as a contraction of **sumu-hu*,[191] but Albright, in a review of Bauer's *Die Ostkanaanäer*, reaffirmed the validity of Hommel's comparison of Sabaean names with their putative Amorite prototypes.[192] Dhorme also accepted Hommel's interpretation of the Amor. PNN.[193] Then in an article responding to the reviews of his book, Bauer presented several arguments against Albright's view of the Amor. PNN.[194] Finally mention should be made of Thureau-Dangin's article published in 1934, which included a discussion of names

---

[185]Ibid., p. 83.

[186]Ibid., p. 99.

[187]F. Giesebrecht, *Die alttestamentliche Schätzung des Gottesnamens und ihre religionsgeschichtliche Grundlage* (Königsberg: Thomas & Oppermann, 1901), pp. 103-13.

[188]Morris Jastrow, Jr., "The Name of Samuel and the Stem *šʾl*," *JBL* 19 (1900) 84, 104 n. 84.

[189]Eberhard Schrader, *Die Keilinschriften und das Alte Testament*, 3d ed. (Berlin: Ruether & Beichard, 1903), p. 225.

[190]Ranke, *Early Babylonian Personal Names*, pp. 217-18.

[191]Bauer, *Ostkanaanäer*, p. 58.

[192]W. F. Albright, Review of *Die Ostkanaanäer*, by Theo Bauer, *AfO* 3 (1926) 125-26.

[193]Édouard Dhorme, "Les amorrhéens," *RB* 37 (1928) 69 n. 2; reprinted in *Recueil Édouard Dhorme: Études bibliques et orientales* (Paris: Imprimerie Nationale, 1951), p. 88 n. 2.

[194]Theo Bauer, "Eine Überprüfung der 'Amoriter'-Frage," *ZA* 38 (1929) 162-63.

compounded with *s/šumu-*.[195] While acknowledging the basic validity of Hommel's comparison of South Arabian PNN with older WS PNN, he was the first to point out the basic flaw in Hommel's line of interpretation. Hommel assumed a complete identity between South Arabian *smh* and early WS *sumu*, and thus concluded that *sumu* must be a contraction of **sumu-hu.* Thureau-Dangin posited that the onomastic formations of the South Arabs differed from those of the (early) West Semites; whereas the former were accustomed to saying "his name," the latter simply said "the name."[196] Accordingly he understood the medial *u* in the Can. PN Shemuʾel and the Amor. *su-mu-el* as the nominative case ending, and he translated these names by "the name (of god) is El" (= structure 1. b. [*šĕm-* = theophoric element]).

Hommel's interpretation of Amor. PNN was to receive support with the publication of Gelb's grammatical sketch of the Amorite language. In his review of Bauer's *Die Ostkanaanäer*, Albright had complained about a "strange gap" created by the absence of any mention of the third person pronouns in the Amorite onomasticon.[197] Gelb claimed to have discovered the missing pronouns in *plene* writings and unwittingly provided support for Hommel's interpretation. Contrary to Akkadian convention, in which *scriptio plena* generally represents long vowels, Gelb boldly asserted that in Amorite such *plene* writings represented an independent syllable. Exceptions were confined to two classes: monosyllabic vocables and GNN.[198] Gelb normalized the spelling *-Cu-ú* as **-uhu* and found graphemic evidence for the existence of the 3rd m.s. pronominal suffix. To be sure, in the select examples which he cited, he did not cite the specific case of *su-mu-ú*,[199] and he even stated that very rarely the 3rd m.s. suffix might be written defectively as *Cu*.[200] Elsewhere in the same study, Gelb concluded that the causative prefix in Amorite was *h*;[201] hence a correlation exists between the Semitic causative prefix and the third person pronouns in Amorite as in other Semitic languages.[202] As indicated by statements

[195]F. Thureau-Dangin, "Un comptoir de laine pourpre à Ugarit d'après une tablette de Ras-Shamra," *Syria* 15 (1934) 137-46, esp. pp. 142-44.

[196]Ibid., p. 142.

[197]Albright, *AfO* 3 (1926) 125-26. Compare Bauer, *Ostkanaanäer*, p. 64.

[198]Gelb, *RANL* 13 (1958) §1.4.

[199]In Aistleitner's treatment of 3rd m.s. pronominal suffixes, he did cite the form *su-mu-ú* (*Acta Orientalia Academiae Scientiarum Hungaricae* 7 [1957] 293-94).

[200]Gelb, *RANL* 13 (1958) §3.1.1.1.6.

[201]Ibid., §3.3.7.6.1-2, 3.3.8.1.5-6. Earlier Bauer, *Ostkanaanäer*, p. 66, came to the same conclusion.

[202]See the important study of E. A. Speiser, "Studies in Semitic Afformatives," *JAOS* 56 (1936) 23-33; reprinted in *Oriental and Biblical Studies: Collected Writings of E. A. Speiser*, ed. J. J. Finkelstein and Moshe Greenberg (Philadelphia:

in his later writings, Gelb apparently never abandoned the view that *plene* spellings, with few exceptions, mark an independent syllable.[203]

I would like to conclude this short history of interpretation with the views of Frank M. Cross, Jr. He is an articulate proponent of this line of interpretation, and he has integrated this view into his reconstruction of patriarchal religion. In his *Canaanite Myth and Hebrew Epic,* Cross interprets the element *sum-* in names to refer to the hypostatized name of the family or clan god, on whom the name bearer calls.[204] As in earlier studies, he cites several Amor. PNN, an Old South Arabian PN, and the biblical PN Shemuʾel as examples of names compounded with *s/šumu-*, and it is evident from the accompanying translations of the names that the medial *u* vowel is understood as a contraction from **uhu* and a marker of the 3rd m.s. pronominal suffix.[205]

Unfortunately, the widespread acceptance of Hommel's view is not matched by a corresponding rigor in argument. If the biblical PN Shemuʾel means "His name is El," then it ought to be spelled **šĕmôʾēl.* The LXX transliterations (e.g., LXX B *σαμουηλ*) confirm the MT vocalization of the medial vowel as *û*; therefore, any suggestion of emending the *û* to *ô* is unwarranted. Hommel recognized this inconsistency,[206] as have others,[207] but they have failed to adjust their interpretation of the PN Shemuʾel. Furthermore, the PN Shemuʾel should be interpreted in light of other PNN of the type **C_1ĕC_2ûʾēl.* In these other names, the medial *û* appears to be either a nominative case ending or the final consonant (*û* < **w*) of a III-weak root. The first analysis is especially applicable to the vocable **šim*, since it is without question a biradical substantive.[208] From the perspective of structure, other names that fit in this series are either construct phrase names or nominal-sentence names, but in neither case does the first element have a pronominal suffix attached to it.[209]

University of Pennsylvania Press, 1967), pp. 404-16. Ugaritic is a notable exception, with *š-* prefix in the causative and *-h* in the third person pronoun.

[203]Gelb, *CAAA*, p. 7; idem, "Ebla and the Kish Civilization," pp. 15-16, where he makes the application to the Eblaite system of writing.

[204]Frank M. Cross, *Canaanite Myth and Hebrew Epic: Essays in the History of the Religion of Israel* (Cambridge: Harvard University Press, 1973), p. 11.

[205]Ibid.

[206]Hommel, *Altisraelitische Überlieferung*, p. 99.

[207]Albright, *AfO* 3 (1926) 126; Van Zyl, pp. 125-26. McCarter, *1 Samuel*, p. 62, frankly admits ". . . the name remains somewhat at variance with the normal morphological development of the language: we expect *šĕmôʾēl.*"

[208]Theodor Nöldeke, "Zweiradikalige Substantive," in *Neue Beiträge zur semitischen Sprachwissenschaft* (Strassburg: Karl J. Trübner, 1910), pp. 140-43.

[209]McCarter, *1 Samuel*, p. 62, does interpret Reuel as "His-friend-is-ʾEl," but this is also at variance with the normal morphological development of the language.

The interpretation of the Amor. PNN is difficult, especially insofar as it involves the spelling *-Cu-ú*. Huffmon provides a thorough discussion of this spelling, and though there may be errors in details, his overall argument justifies the conclusion that this spelling cannot consistently be interpreted as representing the 3rd m.s. pronominal suffix.[210] A comprehensive analysis of this spelling would take us too far afield; it suffices here to highlight some flaws in this interpretation of the Amor. PNN. There are roughly 192 Amor. PNN compounded with the element *sum*, and thirty-eight compounded with *sam*, the latter considered a dialectal variant of the former.[211] Of the names compounded with *sum*, there are only eleven instances of the spelling *su-mu-ú*, and these occur only in final position. The pair of Amor. PNN *su-mu-ia-si-im* and *ia-si-im-su-mu-ú* (*CAAA*, pp. 353, 358) illustrate well the distribution of these spellings. Of the names with *sam*, there are only two instances of the spelling *-Cu-ú*: *sa-mu-ú* and *sa-mu-ú-i-la* (*CAAA*, p. 352). This second name is the only one with the *plene* spelling in first position. In our estimation, it is methodologically suspect to allow a few *plene* writings to dictate the interpretation of the mass of writings *su/amu*, especially since the latter spelling may be understood as representing the nominative case ending. Furthermore, why are there not more occurrences of the uncontracted form of the 3rd m.s. pronominal suffix?

Other objections may be raised against the view that *su/amu* is contracted from **su/am-uhu*. Both Hommel and Cross cite the Amor. PN *su-mu-la-ilu(DINGIR)* (*CAAA*, p. 352), borne by one of Hammurapi's ancestors (first Babylonian dynasty), as an example of the contracted form of 3rd m.s. pronominal suffix.[212] The same name,

---

[210]Huffmon, *APNMT*, pp. 107-16. Huffmon, p. 115, embraces Noth's suggestion that *-Cu-ú* represents an Amorite nominative case ending, statically treated in a foreign name element. In her review of Huffmon's book, Gröndahl concurs with this view (Frauke Gröndahl, Review of *Amorite Personal Names in the Mari Texts: A Structural and Lexical Study*, by Herbert H. Huffmon, *Or* 35 [1966] 450). Contrarily, G. Buccellati, *AURIII*, p. 130, sides with his teacher, Gelb. See also Giorgio Buccellati, Review of *Amorite Personal Names in the Mari Texts: A Structural and Lexical Study*, by Herbert B. Huffmon, *JAOS* 86 (1966) 231-32, for a critique of Huffmon's treatment of the issue. For the spelling *-Cu-ú* in first millennium B.C. WS PNN, see Zadok, *WSB*, pp. 156 and n. 1, 229; idem, *WO* 9 (1977-78) 54 n. 136. And for the cuneiform sign *ú* = *hu* on WS vocables in cuneiform writing, see Sivan, *GAGNWS*, p. 128; Huehnergard, *Ugaritic Vocabulary*, pp. 120, 293; A. F. Rainey, "Notes on the Syllabic Ugaritic Vocabularies," *IEJ* 19 (1969) 108.

[211]Gelb, *CAAA*, pp. 351-55.

[212]Hommel, *Altisraelitische Überlieferung*, p. 98; Cross, *Canaanite Myth and Hebrew Epic*, p. 11. The function of the particle *la* in this PN is contested. If it is the preposition, then this PN may be understood as a construct phrase name (Bauer, *Ostkanaanäer*, pp. 59, 65, 79; Matitiahu Tsevat, in *EM*, s.v. "šĕmûʾēl," 8:71; idem,

however, occurs in a cuneiform tablet found at Hazor, and there it is borne by a female: *ᶠsu-mu-la-ilu(DINGIR^lu)*.[213] Accordingly, this PN cannot be translated "El is indeed *his* (i.e., the name bearer's!) personal god."[214] While Cross translates the Amor. masculine PN *su-mu-a-mi* (*CAAA*, p. 353) by "The (divine) kinsman is his personal god,"[215] the Amor. feminine PN *su-mu-ḫa-mu* (*CAAA*, p. 354) cannot be similarly interpreted. The list of problematic examples may be expanded, and it even includes names with the *uncontracted* writing of the putative 3rd m.s. pronominal suffix.[216] Note, for example, the Amor. feminine PN *a-a-a-bu-ú* (*CAAA*, p. 43), which surely cannot mean "Where is his father?" The element *sum* is also spelled *su-ma*, *su-me*, and *su-mi* (*CAAA*, p. 352), and while some of these may be phonologically conditioned, others remain unexplained on Hommel's view. If *sa-mu-i-la* means "His name is El," then what does *su-ma-i-la* mean (*CAAA*, p. 352)? Finally, Huffmon argues convincingly that this analysis yields a class of names with two pronominal suffixes differing in person, a phenomenon not paralleled elsewhere in Semitic onomastics.[217] It seems reasonable to conclude that Amor. PNN with *su/amu* as the first element need not, and in some cases, cannot be interpreted as containing a 3rd m.s. pronominal suffix. In fact, the system of third singular pronominal suffixes in Amorite needs to be reexamined.[218]

"Die Namengebung Samuels und die Substitutionstheorie," *ZAW* 99 [1987] 254); on the other hand, as an asseverative particle the name should be understood as a nominal-sentence name. The point being made here is not dependent on either analysis; the interpretation of this particle will be discussed below.

[213]Hallo and Tadmor, *IEJ* 27 (1977) 7, justly refer to this name as "Amorite."

[214]So Cross, *Canaanite Myth and Hebrew Epic*, p. 11. Cross' translation of *su/amu* by "personal god" is unusual, but it does not affect the argument here.

[215]Ibid.

[216]See Gelb, *CAAA*, p. 524-26, for a list of names that he analyzes as containing the 3rd m.s. pronominal suffix.

[217]Huffmon, *APNMT*, pp. 112-13.

[218]Part of the problem is that third singular pronominal suffixes are scarce in the WS onomasticon (with the exception of Ph-P. and Neo-Punic; see Benz, *PNPP*, p. 224; Jongeling, pp. 20, 32 and nn. 38, 33). Possible examples of the masculine pronominal suffix in the biblical onomasticon are *ʾĕlîpĕlēhû*, *šĕlōmō(h)*, and perhaps *dôdô* and *yitrô*, though these last two names may be explained otherwise (see s.v. "yitrô," pp. 98-99). For extrabiblical examples, see PNN of the structure **ʾḥʾmh*, s.v. "ʾaḥûmay," pp. 100-101. Albright's statement that third person pronouns are "so common in all Semitic onomastica" (*AfO* 3 [1926] 125-26) is valid for Akkadian but not WS. This makes Gelb's long list of examples highly suspect (*CAAA*, pp. 524-26), especially since it includes seven feminine names. And to make matters worse, there are two possible *š*- stems verbs in Amorite, as well as a personal-demonstrative pronoun formed with *š* (*CAAA*, p. 33)!

Finally a few comments should be made about the South Arabian PNN with the element *smh*.[219] It is appropriate to question the legitimacy of the analogy between Amorite PNN and South Arabian PNN. After all, the difference in time and space between these two onomastica is formidable. Perhaps name formations of the type "his name is . . . ." are particularly characteristic of the South Arabian onomasticon and are not found elsewhere in the WS onomasticon. This assumes that South Arabian *smh* does indeed mean "his name."[220] At any rate, the biblical PN Shemu'el does find ancient antecedents in the Amor. PNN *sa-mu-i-la*, *su-mu-el*, *su-mu-i-la*, and *su-mu-ilu(DINGIR)*, and to cite South Arabian PNN compounded with *smh* in this discussion is unnecessary.

According to structure 1.b., the PN Shemu'el is a nominal-sentence name and the first element is either a DN or a theophoric element. Contrary to the opinion of Theo Bauer, who contended that all names with *sum-* as the initial element were construct phrase names,[221] at least some of the names in this class must be nominal-sentence names. This is especially clear in the pair of Amor. PNN [*su*]-*mu-a-ḫi-ia* and *a-ḫi-su-mu-na* (*CAAA*, pp. 352, 355), in which the position of the elements may be reversed. One may also compare the Amor. PNN of the type *sumu* + *abu/i(m)* (*CAAA*, p. 352) with the WS PN *'ab-š-mú* from Byblos.[222] In addition Huffmon cites Amor. PNN that have a first common plural pronominal suffix attached to the element *sum*.[223] If the first element of the name Shemu'el is a DN, then the name should be translated "Shem is god."[224] Jirku claimed that Shem is a DN in the biblical GN *šĕmîdā'*,[225] and Ginsburger pointed to certain Akk. and Amor. PNN in which he claimed to have detected a Babylonian deity *Sumu*.[226] A bilingual vocabulary list from Ebla indicates that Eblaite

---

[219]A list of these can be found in Harding, *PIAN*, pp. 330-31.

[220]It is not impossible that the vocable *smh* is either a theophoric element, from Arabic *samā* "to be high, elevated" (compare perhaps biblical *rām*), or a DN. Compare the once attested female deity *smht* (see Maria Höfner, "Südarabien," in *Wörterbuch der Mythologie, vol. 1: Götter und Mythen im vorderen Orient*, ed. Hans W. Haussig [Stuttgart: Ernest Klett, 1965], p. 526), and the pair of WS deities Ba'al and Ba'alat, 'An and 'Anat, the one male, the other female. Note also the different spellings in the Sab. PNN *smh'mr* and *smy'mr* (Harding, *PIAN*, pp. 330-31).

[221]Bauer, *Ostkanaanäer*, pp. 59, 65, 79-80.

[222]Helck, *Beziehungen Ägyptens*, p. 64.

[223]Huffmon, *APNMT*, p. 122. Consult Gelb, *CAAA*, p. 354, for a list of Amor. PNN of the type *su-mu-na-*.

[224]As does Zadok, *WO* 9 (1977-78) 54.

[225]Jirku, "Götterwelt Palästinas und Syriens," pp. 84-85.

[226]M. Ginsburger, "Les explications des noms de personnes dans l'Ancien Testament," *RHR* 92 (1925) 6-7.

šum may designate the god Tammuz.[227] The evidence for a DN Shem in the West Semitic pantheon is tenuous, however. In all the names cited, the disputed element is susceptible to interpretation as a theophoric element rather than as a DN.[228] Admittedly, in two Amor. PNN the *sumu* element is preceded by the dingir sign: *^{d}su-mu-a-bu-um* and *^{d}su-mu-ilu(DINGIR)* (*CAAA*, pp. 352-53). But these names were borne by Amorite kings who were deified during their lifetime, and accordingly the determinative goes with the whole name rather than the initial element.[229] Note also that in Amorite the vocable *sa/um* may be combined with unambiguous DNN to form compound theophoric names.[230] To interpret *sa/um* as a DN in these names would create a class of PNN in which two deities are equated; such name formations are rare in Semitic onomastica.

According to our second proposed structure/meaning, the PN Shemu᾿el is analyzed as a construct phrase PN meaning "offspring (< name) of god/El."[231] The vocable **švm* probably originally meant "name," and by a transparent semantic shift, developed the secondary meaning "seed, offspring."[232] Although in Amor. PNN the element

---

[227]See Meir Lubetski, "*ŠM* as a Deity," *Religion* 17 (1987) 2-3; Cyrus H. Gordon, "Notes on Proper Names in the Ebla Tablets," in *Eblaite Personal Names and Semitic Name-Giving*, ed. Alfonso Archi, Archivi reali di Ebla, Studi 1 (Rome: Missione archeologica italiana in Siria, 1988), p. 153.

[228]The following interpreters take **s/švm* to be a theophoric element: H. Bauer, Review of *Die israelitischen Personennamen im Rahmen der gemeinsemitischen Namengebung*, by Martin Noth, *OLZ* 33 (1930) 591; Benz, *PNPP*, p. 419; Maurice Birot, "Trois textes économiques de Mari (II)," *RA* 47 (1953) 167-68; Ruth Hestrin and Michal Dayagi-Mendels, *Inscribed Seals: First Temple Period* (Jerusalem: Israel Museum, 1979), p. 159; Huffmon, *APNMT*, pp. 99-101, 122; Lewy, *HUCA* 18 (1944) 434 n. 39 (this is a change from his earlier view--construct phrase name "son of god"--expressed in *RHR* 110 [1934] 61 n. 77); William L. Moran, "The Hebrew Language in Its Northwest Semitic Background," in *The Bible and the Ancient Near East: Essays in honor of William Foxwell Albright*, ed. G. Ernest Wright (The Biblical Colloquium, 1961; reprint ed.: Winona Lake: Eisenbrauns, 1979), p. 61 n. 75; idem, "Mari Notes on the Execration Texts," *Or* 26 (1957) 343 n. 3; Thureau-Dangin, *Syria* 15 (1934) 142-44.

[229]Walter Sommerfeld, "Untersuchungen zur Geschichte von Kisurra," *ZA* 73 (1983) 217 n. 38. Lubetski, *Religion* 17 (1987) 3, errs in his interpretation of these Amor. PNN.

[230]E.g., Amor. *sa-mu-^{d}da-gan*, *sa-mu-addu(^{d}IM)*, *su-me-^{d}en-líl*, *su-mu-^{d}da-gan*, *su-mu-^{d}a-mi-im*, *su-mu-šamšu(^{d}UTU)* (*CAAA*, pp. 352-54).

[231]Hugo Greßmann, Review of *Die Ostkanaanäer*, by Theo Bauer, *ZAW* 44 (1926) 302; I. Rapaport, *The Hebrew Word* Shem *and Its Original Meaning: The Bearing of Akkadian Philology on Biblical Interpretation* (Melbourne: Hawthorne Press, 1976), pp. 30-47; Bauer, *Ostkanaanäer*, p. 65; Jastrow, *JBL* 19 (1900) 103-4; Tsevat, *EM* 8:71; idem, *ZAW* 99 (1987) 253-54.

[232]Rapaport, *Hebrew Word* Shem, pp. 41-47. Ran Zadok, "Geographical and Onomastic Notes," *JANES* 8 (1976) 119, 125 n. 118, cites Akkadian evidence that

sa/um- predominantly occurs in first position in compound PNN consisting of two nominal elements,[233] and although this order of elements would support a construct phrase analysis, other considerations support the analysis of names of the type *sa/um* + **ʾilu* --and likewise the biblical name Shemuʾel--as nominal-sentence PNN. First, in the once-attested Amor. PNN *ì-lí-su-ú-mu* (*CAAA*, p. 355),[234] the name elements reverse position, a circumstance inconsistent with the construct phrase analysis. Second, alongside names of the type *sa/um* + **ʾilu* are attested parallel names with the particle *la*: *sa-mu-la-ilu(DINGIR)*, *su-mu-la-ilu(DINGIR)*, *su-mu-la-ì-lí*, *su-mu-la-el*, and *su-mu-li-el*[235] (*CAAA*, pp. 352, 354). In these Amor. PNN this particle is best understood as an asseverative particle in a non-verbal sentence.[236]

It appears therefore that slight preference should be accorded the analysis of the biblical PN Shemuʾel as a nominal-sentence PN. But whether one interprets the PN Shemuʾel as a nominal-sentence name or as a construct phrase name, the fact remains that in both cases the medial *û* represents an archaic survival of the nominative case ending.

B. *Dubious Examples*

1. Medial *û*

1. *ʾăbûgayil* (1 Sam 25:18 Q).

Variant spellings: 1. *ʾăbîgayil*; 2. *ʾăbîgal*; 3. *ʾăbīgāyil* (pausal; 1 Sam 25:3).

šum may function as a synonym of *aplu* and *maru*. Gelb, *CAAA*, p. 33, glosses Amor. *šumum* by "name, (male) progeny." Note that even in BH, there is evidence pointing toward this secondary meaning of *šēm* (see BDB, p. 1028 2.c. and especially 1 Sam 24:22, where *šēm* occurs in synonymous parallelism to *zeraʿ* "seed").

[233]Gelb, *CAAA*, pp. 351-55.

[234]The *plene* spelling of the *u* vowel in **sum* does not appear to be significant. Compare the Amor. PNN *ḫa-ìa-su-mu* and *ḫa-ìa-su-ú-mu* (*CAAA*, p. 355).

[235]The form *li* is a phonologically conditioned variant of *la* (Gelb, *RANL* 13 [1958] §2.3.6; John Huehnergard, "Asseverative **law* and Hypothetical **lu/law* in Semitic," *JAOS* 103 [1983] 582).

[236]Huehnergard, *JAOS* 103 (1983) 581, 582 n. 109. Note especially the Amor. PN *su-ma-la-li-a* (*CAAA*, p. 352), translated by Huehnergard, p. 581, as "the Name is indeed for me," in which the asseverative *la* is distinguished from and followed by the preposition *li*. For those who analyze this particle as a preposition, see pp. 83-84 n. 212; and for PNN constructed with the preposition *l*, see discussion s.v. "lĕmûʾēl," p. 192 n. 188.

Classification: Can.--1) wife of Nabal (1 Sam 25:14); 2) sister of David (1 Chr 2:16).

Structure: nominal-sentence name, *ʾăb-* (**qal* base, BL §61h) + *-û-* nominative case vowel + *-gayil* (**qatl* base; < **gyl* "to rejoice").

Meaning: "(My) father is joy."

Parallels: EH *ʾbgyl* (VSE #62).

Comments: This unique spelling of the name occurs only in 1 Sam 25:18 Q and it seems to be the result of textual corruption, stemming from the confusion of *w* and *y* in the square "Aramaic" script. The evidence from the Kethiv and the versions suggests that ʾAbigayil is the original form of the name.[237] Elsewhere the first element of this name is invariably spelled *ʾăbî-*.[238] The interchange of the letters *w* and *y* occurs in other PNN in the Hebrew Bible.[239]

2. *gĕʾûʾēl.*

Classification: Can.--tribe of Gad (Num 13:15).

Structure: 1. *gĕʾû(l)-* (**qatūl* base) + *-ʾēl* (**qil* base, BL §61i; < **gʾl* "to redeem").
2. construct phrase name, *gĕʾû-* (**qatl* base; < **gʾh* "to exalt") + *-ʾēl.*
3. nominal-sentence name, *gĕʾû-* (**qatl* base) + *-ʾēl.*

Meaning: 1. "redeemed by god/El."
2. "majesty of god/El."
3. "God/El is majesty."

Parallels: OAram. *brgʾyh* (*SPARI*, pp. 73, 143).

---

[237]LXX B *αβειγαια*; SyrP *ʾbygl*; and Vulgate *abigail.*

[238]1 Sam 25:14, 18 K, 23, 32, 36, 39, 40, 42; 27:3; 30:5; 2 Sam 2:2; 3:3; 17:25; 1 Chr 2:16, 17; 3:1. In 1 Sam 25:3 alone, we have the spelling *ʾăbīgāyil* (pausal), with *ī* instead of *î.*

[239]Compare the PNN *yzwʾl/yzyʾl; yḥwʾl/yḥyʾl; yʿwʾl/yʿyʾl; mḥwyʾl/mḥyyʾl.* In two pairs of names, Penuel/Peniel and Hamutal/Hamital, there is reason to believe that the forms with *w* are genuine. For further discussion, see s.v. "ḥămû-ṭal," pp. 60-62, and "pĕnûʾēl," pp. 74-76. According to Eshel, pp. 262-63, these variations reflect genuine dialectal distinctions.

Comments: According to our first proposed structure/meaning, the final consonant of the root **gʾl* has been dropped. As mentioned above, Praetorius interpreted all the names of the form **C₁ĕC₂ûʾēl* in this manner. In this instance, however, appeal is made to the LXX B transliteration *γουδιηλ* (with confusion of the Greek capital letters Λ and Δ) to reconstruct the original form of the name **gĕʾūlʾēl*.[240] But Driver's argument that proper names of the structure passive participle plus DN are almost nonexistent in the Hebrew Bible still holds true. Moreover, LXX transliterations provide no evidence for a reading with *l*. The *δ* of *γουδιηλ* may have been borrowed from the immediately preceding PN Gad, by dittography.

According to the second and third structure/meaning, the first element of the name Geʾuʾel derives from the root **gʾh*. Since the vocable *gʾyh* occurs in second position and functions as a theophoric element in the OAram. PN *brgʾyh* "son of Majesty," the Can. PN *gĕʾûʾēl* is in all probability a nominal-sentence name. In this particular name, the medial *û* vowel does not appear to be a remnant of the nominative case vowel. In nouns of the form **qvtl*, in which the third consonant is *w*, the final *w* changes to *û* after the final short vowel drops (**qv́twu* > **qvtw* > **qv́tū* > **qvtū* > **qĕtû*).[241] The development of this class of nouns is analagous to III-y nouns such as *pĕrî* "fruit." Other nouns that may belong to this class are *bōhû*, *tōhû*, *śāḥû*, and *šālû*. The feminine nominal form *gaʾăwâ* (**qatl* base, GKC §84ᵃ c) points to a III-w root.[242] Thus the medial *û* in the name Geʾuʾel is not an archaic nominative ending.[243]

3. *dĕʿûʾēl.*

Comments: Textual corruption. See discussion, s.v. "rĕʿûʾēl," pp. 91-94.

4. *nĕmûʾēl.*

Comments: Textual corruption. See discussion , s.v. "yĕmûʾēl," pp. 63-66.

---

[240]Noth, *IPN*, p. 240.

[241]BL §72g'; George R. Berry, "Original Waw in *l"h* Verbs," *AJSL* 20 (1903-4) 256-57.

[242]For a III-y root, see the OAram. PN *brgʾyh*.

[243]This conclusion was anticipated by Joüon. In a paragraph devoted to the paragogic vowel *û* (§ 93s), he cited the PN Geʾuʾel with hesitation, stating that "p.ê. d'une forme **gaʾw*."

5. *pĕtû'ēl.*

Classification: Can.--father of the prophet Joel (Joel 1:1).

Structure: construct phrase name, *pĕtu-* (**qatl* base, < **pth* I "to be simple") + *-'ēl.*

Meaning: "youth of god/El."

Parallels: BH CNN *petî* I (pausal) "youth," *petî* II (pausal) "simplicity;" Liḥ. and Saf. *fty*; Sab. *fyty*; Sab. *ftym*, *ftyn* (*PIAN*, p. 462).

Comments: Assuming that the reading Petu'el is correct,[244] the interpretation of this PN as a construct phrase name, meaning "youth of god/El," is a plausible suggestion.[245] The development of the noun **pĕtû* is analagous to that of **ga'w*, the noun which comprises the first element of the PN Ge'u'el, only in this case there is no evidence from other nominal forms in BH that the verb **pth* I is an original III-w verb. In fact, from the nominal forms cited above, it would appear that **pth* I is a III-y verb. But in MLArabic the occurrence of various nominal forms of the cognate of this verb, some derived from a III-y root, others from a III-w root,[246] points to the existence of a III-y/III-w doublet.[247] Hence the element **pĕtû* may derive from a III-w root, and this nominal form constitutes indirect evidence for the existence of the III-y/III-w doublet in Can. Therefore the medial *û* in this PN is not a remnant of the nominative case ending.

---

[244]LXX, SyrP, and Old Latin read the first consonant as a *b*, that is, Betu'el, whereas the reading of the MT is supported by the Vulgate and Targum Jonathan.

[245]Fowler, pp. 116, 123, 358; Walter W. Müller, "Altsüdarabische Beiträge zum hebräischen Lexikon," *ZAW* 63 (1975) 313.

[246]Hans Wehr, *A Dictionary of Modern Written Arabic (Arabic-English)*, 4th ed., edited by J. Milton Cowan (Wiesbaden: Otto Harrassowitz, 1979), p. 815. Compare also in Geʿez the III-w verb *fatawa* (Wolf Leslau, *Comparative Dictionary of Geʿez* [Wiesbaden: Otto Harrassowitz, 1987], p. 171).

[247]As noted by Kopf, *VT* 8 (1958) 210 n. 1, the existence of such doublets have frustrated the attempts of Arabic lexicographers to distinguish between III-y and III-w verbs.

6. *rĕʿûʾēl.*

Variant spelling: *dĕʿûʾēl.*

Classification: Can.--1) father-in-law of Moses ? (Exod 2:18); 2) Edomite, son of Esau (Gen 36:4); 3) tribe of Gad (Num 2:14); 4) tribe of Benjamin (1 Chr 9:8).

Structure: 1. construct phrase name, *rĕʿû-* (base unknown; < BH **rʿh* II "to associate with") + *-ʾēl.*
2. nominal-sentence name, *rĕʿû-* (base unknown; < a. BH **rʿh* I "to pasture, graze"; or b. BH **rʿh* II "to associate with") + *-ʾēl.*

Meaning: 1. "friend of god/El."
2. a. "God/El is a shepherd"; b. "God/El is a friend."

Parallels: Ug. *rʿy* (*PTU*, p. 178); Can. *ʾăḥîraʿ*, *rēʿî*; Edom. *rʿʾl* (Israel, *RivB* 27:194).

Comments: Many commentators have assumed that the variant spelling Deʿuʾel represents a genuine name, but several lines of argument may be brought against this assumption. First, the textual evidence in favor of the reading Deʿuʾel is tenuous. The PN Deʿuʾel occurs only four times in the MT (Num 1:14; 7:42, 47; 10:20); in 2:14, however, the MT reads Reʿuʾel. The Vulgate and SamP support a reading **dʿʾl* in each of these verses, but LXX B (*ραγουηλ*) and SyrP (*rʿwʾyl*) read **rʿʾl* throughout the book of Numbers. Since confusion between *r* and *d* is a common scribal error that may occur in either (ancient) Hebrew or (square) Aramaic script,[248] it is easy to account for the variant spelling Deʿuʾel.

Second, it is difficult to provide a satisfactory interpretation of the name. At least two suggestions have been put forward. The element *dĕʿû-* has been derived from the verb **dʿh*, which is attested in only one biblical PN, *ʾeldāʿâ*.[249] In Arabic, *daʿā* means "to call"; thus the PN Deʿuʾel may be translated "invocation of god/El." But this interpretation has several weaknesses. Setting aside the difficult PN Eldaʿah, a verb **dʿh* is not found elsewhere in the West Semitic onomasticon; nor can one find a semantic parallel for a name meaning "invocation of god/El." Though I will argue that the LXX transliteration *ραγουηλ* is not

---

[248]See Delitzsch, *Die Lese- und Schreibfehler*, pp. 105-7 (§104c), who cited Reʿuʾel/Deʿuʾel as an example of the interchange of *r* and *d*.

[249]See Barr, *Comparative Philology*, pp. 23-25, 216, for verses wherein a Hebrew verb **dʿh* has allegedly been identified; Fowler, pp. 118, 122, 125, 341.

a reliable guide for the etymology of the PN Reʿuʾel, nonetheless the LXX transliterations imply that the translators did not derive these names from a common root--Deʿuʾel/*ραγουηλ* versus ʾEldaʿah/*ελδαα*.[250]

Others prefer to derive the first element from the WS root **yd*ʿ "to know." In an important study, Porten identifies eight Israelite PNN that form a group in which the verbal element is in the imperative.[251] He numbers Deʿuʾel among these names and translates it "Acknowledge God." Having noted the textual uncertainty of the reading Deʿuʾel, Stamm raises two additional objections to Porten's view.[252] Since this name occurs in Num 1:5-15, a list that is based on an old tradition,[253] it is scarcely appropriate to explain the name according to prophetic and sapiential sayings (e.g., Prov 3:6) from much later times. Methodologically, it is necessary to compare Deʿuʾel to other names constructed with the root **yd*ʿ, such as *yĕdāʿyāh* and *yādāʿ*; yet the meaning of the root in these names, "to (fore)know," is inappropriate for the name Deʿuʾel. In conclusion, the arguments in favor of regarding the PN Deʿuʾel as a corrupt variant of Reʿuʾel are cogent. Nevertheless, Porten should be credited with recognizing an important category of Israelite names. The exclusion of the PN Deʿuʾel from his list of PNN strengthens his thesis rather than detracts from it.[254]

Opinions are divided over the structural analysis of the name Reʿuʾel. The predominant view is that the PN Reʿuʾel is a construct phrase name (= structure #1).[255] Accordingly, the initial element *rĕʿû-* would describe the name bearer as friend of the deity. Although the

---

[250]Blau, *Polyphony*, pp. 10, 23.

[251]Bezalel Porten, *Archives from Elephantine: The Life of an Ancient Jewish Military Colony* (Berkeley: University of California Press, 1968), p. 144; idem, "'Domla'el' and Related Names," *IEJ* 21 (1971) 47-49. Samuel E. Loewenstamm, in *EM*, s.v. "dĕʿûʾēl," 2:697, proposed that the PN Deʿuʾel may be translated "kinsman of god/El" (note BH *mô/ōdāʿ* "kinsman"), but a noun *dĕʿû* "kinsman" is not known elsewhere.

[252]Stamm, *BHAN*, pp. 149-50.

[253]See Cross, *Canaanite Myth and Hebrew Epic*, pp. 53-54, who noted that the name formations are characteristic of the second millennium B.C.

[254]Note that of the other seven PNN in Porten's list, six of them bear Yahwistic theophores, andtherefore are distinctly Israelite. No. 5 occurs with a Yahwistic theophore (*dmlyh*), as well as an El theophore (*dmlʾl*). In the putative Deʿuʾel, on the other hand, neither of the name elements is distinctly Israelite. And in the list of names in Num 1:5-15 (v 14--Deʿuʾel), not one of the theophoric names is formed with a Yahwistic theophore.

[255]Shmuel Aḥituv, in *EM*, s.v. "rĕʿûʾēl," 7:387; Fowler, pp. 125, 194, 216, 233, 272 n. 49, 360; Edward Lipiński, *Studies in Aramaic Inscriptions and Onomastics 1*, Orientalia Lovaniensia Analecta, no. 1 (Louvain: Leuven University Press, 1975), p. 124; Bernhard Moritz, "Edomitische Genealogien. I.," *ZAW* 44 (1926) 85; Noth, *IPN*, p. 153 n. 2.

element *r῾ occurs in first position in the PN Re῾u᾿el, in the Can. PN ᾿ăḥîra῾ it occurs in second position, with the first slot occupied by a theophoric element. This variation in word order does not support the analysis of Re῾u᾿el as a construct phrase name. If, as appears likely, the element r῾ refers to the deity,[256] then the analysis of the biblical PN Re῾u᾿el as a nominal-sentence name recommends itself.

The meaning "friend" is based on the derivation of the vocable *rē῾û* from BH *r῾h II "to associate with."[257] In PNN, this root, as well as the root BH *r῾h I "to pasture, graze," are difficult to keep apart.[258] In these verbal roots the ῾*ayin* is original. But the LXX B transliteration *ραγουηλ* points to a root with *ǵ*. Consequently, Blau has proposed that the PN Re῾u᾿el is derived from a root **rǵw*;[259] he may well be right, if the development of this PN is from a **qatl* base noun (**ráǵwu* > **raǵw* > **ráǵū* > **raǵū̆* > **rěǵû*). This root may be attested in the Tham. PN *rǵw*, which Harding relates to the Arab. verb *raǵā* "to roar, bellow" (*PIAN*, p. 282). The resultant meaning ("roar of god/El"?) is not paralleled elsewhere in the WS onomasticon. The attempt to derive the PN Re῾u᾿el from the MLArab. *raǵā* (**rǵw*) "to foam, froth" (Wehr, p. 403) fares no better. Therefore, I tentatively suggest that the LXX transliteration *ραγουηλ* represents nothing more than a popular etymology,[260] and that the initial element of the PN Re῾u᾿el is to be derived from either BH *r῾h I or II. Either of these roots provides a suitable

---

[256] In the Punic PN *῾bdr῾* (Benz, *PNPP*, p. 163), the final element refers to the deity. Lambdin's suggestion that *r῾* in this name is the Egyptian deity Re῾a must be greeted with caution because this element is not found in Ph. names from Egypt and Cyprus, where Egyptian deities are common (as noted by Benz, *PNPP*, p. 409).

[257] See Yoël L. Arbeitman, "The Hittite is Thy Mother: An Anatolian Approach to Genesis 23 (ex Indo-Europea Lux)," in *Bono Homini Donum: Essays in Historical Linguistics in Memory of J. Alexander Kerns*, 2 vols., ed. Yoël L. Arbeitman & Allan R. Bomhard (Amsterdam: John Benjamins, 1981), 1:931, who translates biblical Re῾u᾿el as "God is (my) Kinsman." Similarly, Zadok, *WSB*, p. 297 n. 25.

[258] To complicate matters, a third root comes into play with Aram. PNN, the Proto-Semitic root **rḍy* "to desire, to be content," since Proto-Semitic *ḍ* is represented by ῾*ayin* in IAram. (but by *ṣ* in Hebrew). For discussion, see Harald Ingholt, Henri Seyrig, Jean Starcky, and André Caquot, *Recueil des tessères de Palmyre* (Paris: Imprimerie nationale and Librairie orientaliste Paul Geuthner, 1955), p. 157; Stark, *PNPI*, p. 112; Zadok, *WSB*, p. 87 and n. 13; Silverman, *JAOS* 89 (1969) 694; idem, *RVJPNE*, pp. 176-77. In light of the OAram. PN *hdrqy* (Maraqten, *SPARI*, p. 155), where Proto-Semitic *ḍ* is represented by OAram. *q*, the presence of the root **rḍy* in IAram. PNN cannot be contested. Therefore, I have chosen not to interpret the biblical PN Re῾u᾿el in light of numerous Aram. PNN composed with the element *r῾(y)* (e.g., IAram. *r῾dd*, *r῾wy* [*SPARI*, pp. 100, 212-13], *byt᾿lr῾y*, *nbwr῾y*, *r῾wyh*, *r῾ybl(w?)* [*OAA*, pp. 43, 61, 71]; Nab. *r῾y* [Cantineau, 2:147]).

[259] Blau, *Polyphony*, p. 35.

[260] Likewise, Lipiński, *Aramaic Inscriptions*, p. 124, discounts the import of the LXX transliterations.

etymology for the Can. PNN *ʾăḥîraʿ* and *rēʿî*.[261] If, as seems probable, the first element of Reʿuʾel is derived from a III-weak root, then the medial *û* may reflect a change **w > û*, in which case it would not be the remnant of a nominative case ending.

2. Final *û*

Several names ending in *û* in the Hebrew Bible merit consideration. Joüon mentioned three possible examples, the PNN Bokru, Meliku, and Gashmu.[262] As is widely recognized, the last name, Gashmu (Neh 6:6), also spelled Geshem (Neh 2:19), is an Arabian (i.e., non-Canaanite) name, and thus falls outside the scope of this study.[263] I have expanded the following list to include all possible examples, however dubious, of names ending in *û*.

7. *bōkĕrû*.

The genealogy of Gibeon appears in two recensions, 1 Chr 8:29-40 and 9:35-44. According to the MT of 1 Chr 8:38 and 9:44, the second of six sons of Asel bore the putative name Bokeru. The genuineness of this name is in doubt for several reasons. First, the PN Bokeru is unparalleled in the WS onomasticon. Second, this putative name occurs immediately after the name of the first son, and in this position the appellative *bĕkōrô* "his firstborn" would be suitable (cf. v 39). In the Babylonian textual tradition,[264] LXX B (*πρωτότοκος αὐτοῦ*), and SyrP, this vocable is understood as an appellative instead of a PN. Since elsewhere in these two verses (vv 38, 44) the *w* conjunction precedes each PN, its absence before *bōkĕrû* suggests that this vocable is an appellative in apposition to the preceding name, and not another PN.

---

[261]On the PN ʾAhiraʿ, note Blau's remark, *On Polyphony*, p. 29: "Derived, by G at least, from *reʿe* 'friend' with original ʿ? *αχ(ε)ιρε*." Noth, *IPN*, p. 236, is certainly correct in his observation that the derivation of the second element of this name from the verbal root **rʿʿ* is nonsensical. I cannot find the biblical PN *rēʿî* in Blau's study, but the LXX transliterations of zero/vowel mutation point to a root with original *ʿayin*. Compare also the Ug. PN *rʿy* (*PTU*, p. 178).

[262]Joüon, §93s.

[263]For further discussion on this name, see Israel Ephʿal, *The Ancient Arabs: Nomads on the Borders of the Fertile Crescent 9th-5th Centuries B.C.* (Jerusalem: Magnes Press; Leiden: E. J. Brill, 1982), p. 211; Samuel E. Loewenstamm, in *EM*, s.v. "gešem, gašmû," 2:568-69; Isaac Rabinowitz, "Aramaic Inscriptions of the Fifth Century B.C.E. from a North-Arab Shrine in Egypt," *JNES* 15 (1956) 1-9, esp. p. 6.

[264]Paul Kahle, *Der masoretische Text des Alten Testaments nach der Überlieferung der babylonischen Juden* (Leipzig: J. C. Hinrichs, 1902), p. 77.

The only problem remaining is that if Bokeru is taken as an appellative, then there are only five sons named in these verses, and one son is left unaccounted for. This problem may be solved in one of two ways. It is possible that a name dropped out in the transmission of the text (haplography). One may restore the PN ʿAzaryah, either before or after the PN ʿObadyah, on the basis of the Lucianic version of the LXX.[265] Alternatively, one may emend Bokeru to either the PN Beker or Bikri, names which are borne by Israelites elsewhere in the Hebrew Bible, and explain the vocalization Bokeru as contamination from the appellative *bĕkōrô* in v 39.[266] Whichever solution is preferred, it is highly improbable that the final *-û* represents the remnant of a case ending.

8. *bĕnînû.*

Classification: unknown--a Levite (Neh 10:14).

Structure: one-word name (?).

Meaning: unknown.

Parallels: Akk. *bu-na(-a)-nu/ni* (*APN*, p. 65); Ug. *bnn* (*PTU*, p. 119); Amm. *bnny* (*ALIA*, p. 96); Saf. and Min. *bnn* (*PIAN*, p. 511).

Comments: This enigmatic PN occurs in a post-exilic list of Levites. Whereas LXX B renders this name and the preceding name (MT *bānî*) as *υἱοὶ βενιαμειν* (< **bĕnê binyāmîn*), LXX A translates *υἱοὶ βανουαιαι*. On the other hand, the Vulgate (*bani baninu*) agrees with the MT. Although there is evidence for a root **bnn* in West Semitic, this name still strikes one as odd in appearance. Rudolph suggests that this PN be emended to *kĕnānî* on the basis of 9:4, where the pair of PNN Bani and Kenani are reminiscent of Bani and Beninu in 10:14.[267] Loewenstamm compares the South Arabian PN *bnn* and the Akkadian DN *Bunînu*,

---

[265]This solution is preferred by Wilhelm Rudolph, *Chronikbücher*, Handbuch zum Alten Testament, erste Reihe, Band 21 (Tübingen: J. C. B. Mohr [Paul Siebeck], 1955), p. 80.

[266]Dominique Barthélemy, *Critique textuelle de l'Ancien Testament. 1. Josué, Judges, Ruth, Samuel, Rois, Chroniques, Esdras, Néhémie, Esther*, OBO, no. 50/1 (Fribourg: Éditions Universitaires; Göttingen: Vandenhoeck & Ruprecht, 1982), p. 448. The extraneous *w* on Bokru could have arisen by dittography (**bkr wyšmʿʾl* > *bkrw wyšmʿʾl*).

[267]Wilhelm Rudolph, *Ezra und Nehemiah, samt 3. Esra*, Handbuch zum Alten Testament, erste Reihe, Band 20 (Tübingen: J.C.B. Mohr [Paul Siebeck], 1949), p. 152.

also spelled *Bunênu/e*.[268] In the latter case, the PN Beninu may be a shortened name with only the DN retained, for which Stamm cites examples from Akk. PNN.[269] To sum up, the linguistic affiliation, structure, and meaning of this PN are unknown. If the ending of this name in *û* is genuine, it might be traceable to foreign influences, which affected the Israelite onomasticon in the post-exilic period. The name may be excluded from further consideration until it is clarified.

The reading of examples ##9-11 is probably to be attributed to textual corruption, and it suffices to treat them in an abbreviated fashion.

9. *mĕlîkû* (Neh 12:14 Q).

This PN was borne by the head of a priestly family. The Kethiv *mĕlûkî* resulted from dittography of the following *y* (**mlwk ywntn* > *mlwky ywntn*). This *y* was later confused with *w*, giving rise to the Q. The correct form of the name *mallûk* is recorded in v 2 (MT *mallûk*) and supported by LXX B *μαλουχ*. The PN Malluk was a popular name in the post-exilic period, being borne by several other individuals as well (see BDB, p. 576).

10. *sallû* (Neh 12:7).

Elsewhere in the same chapter, this priestly name is spelled *sallay* (v 20), a spelling that looks like it is assimilated to the vocalization of the immediately following vocable *qallāy* (pausal). The same name, borne by a different individual (Benjaminite), is spelled *sallūʾ* (Neh 11:7) or *sallûʾ* (1 Chr 9:7); hence, the spelling *sallû* is a shortening, with omission of the final *ʾaleph*. The same name is spelled *sālûʾ* in Num 25:14, and it appears at Elephantine with the spellings *slwʾ*, *slwʾh*, and *slwh*, of which the last two are feminine names (Silverman, *RVJPNE*, p. 160).

11. *ʿîrû* (1 Chr 4:15).

As noted in the *BHS* textual apparatus, LXX B (*ηρ*) and Vulgate (*Hir*) point to the MT *ʿîrû* as being the result of a misdivision of the text, in which the following *waw* conjunction was misread and attached to

[268]Samuel E. Loewenstamm, in *EM*, s.v. "bĕnînû," 2:281. On the Akk. DN, see Knut L. Tallqvist, *Akkadische Götterepitheta*, Studia Orientalia, no. 7 (Helsinki: Societas Orientalis Fennicae, 1938), p. 277.

[269]Stamm, *ANG*, p. 117. On shortened names with only the DN retained, see pp. 73-74 n. 163, and 218 n. 101.

the preceding PN *ʿîr. Whereas this conjunction is not represented in LXX B, it is in the Vulgate (*Hir et Hela* . . .). The PN ʿIr is also found in 1 Chr 7:12.

12. *rĕʿû* (Gen 11:18-21).

Albright suggested that this PN may be shortened from the PN Reʿuʾel[270] (but compare LXX transliterations). Zadok compares this PN to the NA GN *URUTil Ra-ḫa-a-ú-á*;[271] furthermore, he disputes the comparisons with the NA PN *ra-ʾ-u/ú* (*APN*, p. 186), since the latter is probably an Egyptian name,[272] and with the Aramean tribe *Ru-ʾ-u-a*, since the LXX B *ραγαυ* reflects an original second radical *ǵ*.[273] The LXX rendering of *û* by *αυ* is unusual. Long **ū* is almost always represented in the LXX by *ου*. According to Könnecke, where *αυ* stands for *û*, we are to assume confusion with *ô*.[274] Therefore the name may be vocalized **rĕʿô*. The vocalization *rĕʿû* may be attributed to the similarity between this name and the PN *rĕʿûʾēl*. Baudissin even posits that that the PN Reʿu may be an old DN, but he does not cite any evidence to support his proposal.[275] In this regard one may cite the Punic PN *ʿbdrʿ* (*PNPP*, pp. 409-410), but one must still admit that the evidence in favor of a DN *Rʿ* is slight.[276] Whatever the case may be, it is far from certain that the final *û* represents a nominative case ending.

12. *tōḥû* (1 Sam 1:1).

This name is found in a list of Elqanah's ancestors; in 1 Chr 6:19, the name is spelled *tôaḥ*. The original reading of the name and the etymology remain unknown. The evidence from the versions is not

---

[270]W. F. Albright, "Contributions to Biblical Archaeology and Philology," *JBL* 43 (1924) 388.

[271]Ran Zadok, "West Semitic Toponyms in Assyrian and Babylonian Sources," in *Studies in Bible and the Ancient Near East, Presented to Samuel E. Loewenstamm on His Seventieth Birthday*, 2 vols., ed. Yitschak Avishur and Joshua Blau (Jerusalem: E. Rubinstein, 1978), 1:176; idem, "Notes on the Biblical and Extra-Biblical Onomasticon," *JQR*, n.s., 71 (1980/81) 109-110 and n. 32. For the NA GN, see Simo Parpola, *Neo-Assyrian Toponyms*, AOAT 6 (Kevelaer: Butzon & Bercker; Neukirchen-Vluyn: Neukirchener, 1970), p. 354.

[272]Ran Zadok, "On Some Egyptians in First-Millennium Mesopotamia," *GM* 26 (1977) 65 (#17).

[273]But this LXX transliteration may reflect a popular etymology. See discussion, s.v. "rĕʿûʾēl," pp. 91-94.

[274]Könnecke, p. 24.

[275]Baudissin, *Kyrios als Gottesnamen*, 3:373. See also BDB, p. 946, for further bibliography.

[276]See p. 92 n. 256.

easy to interpret. Following LXX B θοκε and Lucianic θωε, McCarter argues for the Chronicles' version of the name.[277] Even if the form of the name recorded in 1 Samuel is genuine, the name may be from a III-weak root, in which case the final *û* would not be a remnant of a case ending. Until the reading and etymology of this name are clarified, it should remain in the list of dubious examples.

13. *tōʿû* (1 Chr 18:9).

The name of the king of Hamat is spelled *tōʿî* in 2 Sam 8:9, 10. Even in this latter passage, though, LXX A and B (θο[υ]ου) support the spelling of the name found in 1 Chr 18:9. Nevertheless, this name is probably a shortened form of a compound Hurrian name. Thus Toʿu may render Hurrian *teḫ/tiḫ-* "to instruct, inform," though the LXX transliterations imply the *ʿayin* is original.[278] Since the structure, meaning, and linguistic affiliation of the name are unknown, this name must remain in the list of dubious examples.[279]

3. Final *ô*

14. *yitrô*.

Variant spelling: *yeter* (Exod 4:18, but see *BHS* textual apparatus).

Classification: Can.--father of Moses' wife (Exod 3:1).

Structure: one-word or shortened name, *yitr-* (**qatl* base, BL §61j')[280] + *-ô* (< **u*) nominative case ending.

Meaning: "(DN is) preeminent."

Parallels: Amor. *ia-at-ri-im, ia-at-ra-tum, ia-at-ra-il* (*CAAA*, p. 280); Ug. *bn ytr, bn ytrm* (*PTU*, p. 148); NA *it-ru-nu* (*WSB*, p. 116 n. 2);[281] NB *it-ra-a* (Coogan, *Murašû*, p. 28); Can. *yeter, yitrāʾ, yitrān*; GA

---

[277] McCarter, *1 Samuel*, p. 51.

[278] Hurrian *teḫ/tiḫ-* is usually equated with Ug. *tǵ-* (Gröndahl, *PTU*, p. 263).

[279] For further discussion and bibliography, see Y. Ikeda, in *EM*, s.v. "tōʿû, tōʿî," 8:871-72.

[280] In support of the **qatl* base, BL cite Arab. *watru*. According to Wehr, p. 1227, a biform *witru* also is attested. A **qatl* base noun is attested in four Amor. PNN (Gelb, *CAAA*, p. 280). Other PNN cited in the parallels section point to a **qitl* base noun.

[281] Alternatively, this name may be read *id-ru-nu* and derived from the root **ʿdr* (as noted by Zadok).

yitrî; BH CNN *yeter* I and *yitrôn*; Saf., Tham., Qat., and Sab. *wtr*; Had. and Sab. *wtrm*; Sab. *wtrn* (*PIAN*, pp. 633-34).

Comments: Zadok proposes that the *ô* in the PN Yitro represents Proto-Semitic **u*.[282] One may compare the Nab. PN *wtrw* (Cantineau, 2:90), though it is not clear whether the final *w* on this PN represents the nominative case ending. As stated earlier in this chapter, this *ô* can derive from the contraction of an **-aw* diphthong, a (stressed) long **ā*, or a historical short **u*. There is no compelling reason that decides the matter in favor of the derivation of *ô* < **u*. Of these three possible derivations, the second appears plausible with reference to the name Yitro, though the first cannot be ruled out altogether.[283]

According to the second derivation, Yitro is a reduction from an original *Yitron.[284] The final *ô* derives from the long (stressed) *ā* of the derivational nominal suffix **-ānu*. The historical development may be reconstructed as follows (the order of some of the steps remains unknown): **yatrānu* > **yatrōnu* > **yatrōn* > **yitrōn* > *yitrô*. The PN Yitro is comparable to the Can. PN *yitrān*, and differs from it in two respects: Yitro reflects the Canaanite shift (**ā* > **ō*) and the reduction of the final *-n*. Lewy has collected evidence for the loss of final *-n* on names ending in *-ān* and *-ōn*.[285] The loss of the final *-n* has also been seen in the biblical PN *ḥeṣrô* (< **ḥeṣrôn*)[286] and the GN *šîlô* Q/*šîlō(h)* K (Gen 49:10).[287]

---

[282]Zadok, *WSB*, p. 196 n. 12.

[283]Stamm, *BHAN*, p. 294, translates "Sein Rest," understanding the *-ô* as a 3rd m.s. pronominal suffix and thus deriving it from the contraction of the *-aw* diphthong (**ahu* > **au* > **aw* > *ô*). But compare the discussion at p. 84 n. 218.

[284]Theodor Nöldeke, in *EB*, s.v. "Names," 3:3303. Arbeitman, "Hittite is thy Mother," 2:939, states that the suffix *-V̄* is the same suffix (as *-V̄n*) in an alternative shape.

[285]Lewy, *HUCA* 18 (1944) 454 n. 132; idem, "The Late Assyro-Babylonian Cult of the Moon and its Culmination at the Time of Nabonidus," *HUCA* 19 (1945-46) 443 n. 179. Not all of his examples are acceptable. See also Arbeitman, "Hittite is thy Mother," 2:939-40.

[286]Henri Cazelles, in *DBS*, s.v. "Onomastique," 6:740. The name Hesro is attested in 2 Sam. 23:35 K (Q--Hesray) and 1 Chr 11:37. The full name Hesron is also attested in the Hebrew Bible, but it is borne by different individuals.

[287]James A. Montgomery, *A Critical and Exegetical Commentary on the Books of Kings*, ed. Henry S. Gehman, ICC (Edinburgh: T. & T. Clark, 1951), p. 290.

C. *Non-Canaanite Example*

1. *ʾăḥûmay.*

Classification: Aram.--tribe of Judah (1 Chr 4:2).

Structure: 1. nominal-sentence name, *ʾaḥ-* (**qal* base, BL §61h) + *-û-* nominative case vowel + *-m-* + *-ay* hypocoristic suffix.
2. construct phrase name, *ʾaḥ-* + *-û-* nominative case vowel + *-m-* (< **ʾēm*; **qill* base, BL §61b') + *-ay* (< **-î*) 1st c.s. pronominal suffix.

Meaning: 1. "My brother is m_____."
2. "brother of my mother."

Parallels: Akk. *aḫi(ŠEŠ)-um-mi-šu* (*ANG*, p. 302), *a-ḫu-um-mi-ša*;[288] N/LB *aḫi(ŠEŠ)-im-me-e* (*WSB*, p. 356); EH *ʾḥʾmh* (VSE #366; Avigad, *Hebrew Bullae*, #151); Edom. *ʾḥʾmh* (Beit-Arieh and Cresson, *TA* 12 [1985] 97-98); Ph. *ʾḥʾm* (*PNPP*, p. 61); IAram. *ʾḥwm*[*y*] = NB *aḫu(ŠEŠ)-im-mi-e* (*SPARI*, pp. 67, 119); Aram. *ʾḥmh*.[289]

Comments: According to the first interpretation, the *-m* is the first radical of the second element of the name, suffixed with the hypocoristic ending *-ay*.[290] The EH PN *ʾḥmʾ* (S 32.3, 37.2, 38.2, 39.2) has been interpreted in a similar fashion.[291] The second interpretation reconstructs the PN **ʾăḥî-ʾimmî* on the basis of LXX B Αχειμει (contrast LXX A -μαι).[292] The occurrence of the same name in a NB

---

[288] I. J. Gelb, P. M. Purves, and A. A. MacRae, *Nuzi Personal Names*, The University of Chicago Oriental Publications, vol. 57 (Chicago: University of Chicago Press, 1943), pp. 10, 296 (also with different spellings).

[289] Jonathan Rosenbaum and Joe D. Seger, "Three Unpublished Ostraca from Gezer," *BASOR* 264 (1986) 52, Fig. 1.

[290] Noth, *IPN*, p. 40. In a similar fashion, Franz Praetorius, "*Fuʿail* im Hebräischen und Syrischen," *ZDMG* 57 (1903) 524-29, esp. p. 524, interpreted the PN as shortened, but according to the Arabic diminutive form *fuʿail*. He placed it in a series of Hebrew PNN that have *û* in the final root syllable and an *-ay* ending (e.g., *kĕlûbay*).

[291] According to Lemaire, *Inscriptions hébraïques*, p. 50, it is shortened from **ʾḥmlk*, which also occurs in the Samaria ostraca. See also Kornfeld, *WZKM* 71 (1979) 41, who analyzed the EH PN similarly.

[292] As suggested by Theodor Nöldeke, "Kleinigkeiten zur semitischen Onomatologie," *WZKM* 6 (1892) 312; idem, "Names," *EB* 3:3296. Stamm, *BHAN*, p. 76, preferred this interpretation. For Greek ει rendering Hebrew *î*, see αβειβαλου (alongside variant αβιβαλου) "my father is Baal" (Jongeling, p. 225).

text[293] validates the second interpretation; the MT reading *ʾḥwmy*[294] is confirmed and the Akk. version of the name *aḫu(ŠEŠ)-im-mi-e* establishes the meaning "brother of my mother."[295] The emendation of the suffix *-ay* to *-î* on the basis of the LXX B -μει also derives support from structural considerations, since the *-ay* suffix is never attached to construct phrase PNN in the Hebrew Bible. Finally, the intervocalic elision of the *ʾaleph*[296] and the loss of gemination[297] find parallels elsewhere in PNN and therefore occasion no difficulty.

The classification of this name as Aramaic is based on two considerations: 1) the occurrence of an Aram. PN with the same spelling in a NB text; and 2) the nominative case vowel **ū* on the kinship term **ʾaḫ*. The second consideration needs elaboration. In the Hebrew Bible, the nominative case vowel on the kinship term **ʾaḫ* occurs in only two names: ʾAhumay and Huram.[298] In all other PNN the vocable **ʾaḫ* ends in *-î* or *-Ø*. In contrast to Hebrew, Phoenician and Aramaic have retained the nominative case vowel on kinship terms. Therefore, the retention of this vowel in the Ph. PN Huram is expected. Since the PN ʾAhumay does not appear to be archaic name per se,[299] I suggest that the retention of the nominative case vowel points to its Aramaic linguistic affiliation.

IV. Late West Semitic PNN (extrabiblical)

With the exception of *matres lectionis*, vowels are not represented in late West Semitic PNN written in consonantal script. Therefore, for the most part we cannot ascertain how these names were pronounced, nor whether they retained the nominative case vowel. At times it is possible to correlate WS PNN in alphabetic script with their

---

[293]For original publication with handcopies, see Matthew W. Stolper, "Management and Politics in Later Achaemenid Babylonia: New Texts from the Murašû Archive," 2 vols. (Ph.D. dissertation, University of Michigan, 1974), 2:373-76.

[294]The LXX *αχει-* < **ʾḥy-* appears to be a banalization of the text.

[295]Zadok's suggested interpretation of N/LB *aḫi(ŠEŠ)-im-me-e* as "The (divine) brother is with him (?)" may now be corrected.

[296]Compare the biblical PN *ʾiyyôb* < **ʾayya ʾabū* "Where is the father?" and pp. 54 n. 76 and 55 n. 78.

[297]See s.v. "hădôrām," p. 59, and "yĕmûʾēl," p. 65 n. 127.

[298]On the second name, see s.v. "ḥûrām," pp. 59-60. The nominative case ending on the kinship term **ʾaḫ* is found in the Eblaite PNN *a-ḫu-lu* (ARET II:103) and *a-ḫu-kam₄* (ARET III:257); and the Amor. PNN *a-ḫu-um* and *a-ḫu-um-ma-ilu(DINGIR)* (*CAAA*, p. 557).

[299]It does not contain an archaic lexeme (e.g., the PN *mĕtûšelaḥ* contains **mutu* "man") nor does it have exact parallels among early West Semitic PNN (as does, e.g., *yĕmûʾēl*).

counterparts in cuneiform script, and this provides valuable information as to how these names were pronounced. Greek and Latin transliterations of WS PNN may also be utilized to reconstruct the vocalization of WS PNN.

1. *WS PNN in cuneiform writing*

Within the vast corpus of WS PNN in NA and N/LB texts, Zadok has noted that the nominative ending may have been preserved in only four names: 1) N/LB *a-bu-ga-á*; 2) N/LB *a-ḫu-ia-a-li-e*; 3) NA *am-mu-la-di-in*; and 4) N/LB *ḫa-lu-ú-mil-ki* (*WSB*, p. 52-53). To this list Coogan would add NB *aḫu(ŠEŠ)-ú-na-a* and *aḫ(ŠEŠ)-a-bu-ú*, provided that his argument that these names are West Semitic is valid.[300] It should be observed that the nominative case ending in each of these PNN occurs on a kinship term,[301] and that kinship terms in Aramaic (and Phoenician and Punic), in contradistinction to Hebrew, are characterized by the retention of the nominative case vowel in the construct state and before suffixes.

The nominative case ending has also been seen in the name of an Ammonite king and vassal of Assyria in 701/700 B.C., spelled *pa-du-ú-ili(DINGIR)* in the NA document ADD 1110+, and *pu-du-ili(DINGIR)* in the prism inscription of Sennacherib.[302] Zadok has compared this name to other Canaanite PNN of the type $*C_1\breve{e}C_2\hat{u}{}^{\flat}\bar{e}l$ and interpreted it as a nominal-sentence name meaning "Padu is god."[303] Note that in the spelling of the name in the NA document ADD 1110+, the nominative ending would be represented by the *plene* writing *-Cu-ú-*.

2. *Ph-P. PNN*

The Punic name *ḥnwʾl* (*PNPP*, p. 314) appears to retain the nominative case ending, but if we are to judge from Latin transliterations of similar names, such as HANNO, ANNOBAL, then the *w mater lectionis* represents an *o* vowel, and not a *u* vowel. A tantilizing possibility is found on a Phoenician seal discovered at Akko. According to Lemaire's decipherment, the two-line inscription reads (1) *lṣ*[---?] (2) *ʾlwʿzʾ*, with the name *ʾlwʿzʾ* being analyzed as a hypocoristic

---

[300]Coogan, *Murašû*, pp. 12, 68.

[301]Perhaps **ḫalu* "maternal uncle" and **ʿammu* "kinsman" were treated like the kinship terms **ʾaḫū*, **ʾabū*, and **ḫamū*.

[302]Zadok, *WO* 9 (1977-78) 36, 53-55.

[303]Ibid., p. 54.

name from an original *ʾl(y)ʿzr.[304] The reading of this seal is difficult; one line of text is written horizontally, while the second line is written vertically and intersects the horizontal line. To read the name ʾlwʿzʾ, one has to read the four letters of the vertical line (ʾlwʿ) and two letters from the horizontal line (zʾ)! Since this reading yields an archaic morpheme and a name that is unique in the Ph-P. onomasticon, I think it best to consider this PN as a dubious example.

3. *Nabatean PNN*

This group of PNN is especially characterized by a termination in *w*. Though it has been suggested that this final -*w* is possibly the nominative ending,[305] this analysis has met with some objections. After considering the various explanations offered to explain this -*w*, Cantineau concluded that in some instances it may be an abbreviation of a theophoric name, and in others it may indicate the emphatic state.[306] Whatever the case may be, the same suffix has been found on Palm. PNN, on the IAram. PNN *yrḥw* and *plṭw* (*RVJPNE*, pp. 151, 170), and the Amm. PNN *plṭw* (*ALIA*, p. 71). In Nabatean and Palmyrene, it may be a borrowing from Arabic.[307] The fact that this suffix occurs in later Aramaic dialects, and in abundance in Nabatean, suggests that it is a borrowing, and consequently, there is no reason to suppose that the suffix -*w* is the archaic survival of the nominative case ending.

V. Summary

Early West Semitic originally distinguished three basic case endings in the declension of masculine singular nouns: nominative -*u*, genitive -*i*, and accusative -*a*. The nominative case ending -*u* is relevant for this study, since some Canaanite PNN may have retained this case vowel. Examples of these case endings, especially the nominative -*u*, have been drawn from Amorite and Ugaritic PNN, WSS PNN in the

---

304 Giveon and Lemaire, *Sem* 35 (1985) 27-32, and Plate V, b.

305 Zadok, *WSB*, p. 194; idem, "Arabians in Mesopotamia during the Late-Assyrian, Chaldean, Achaemenian and Hellenistic Periods Chiefly According to the Cuneiform Sources," *ZDMG* 131 (1981) 45-46.

306 Cantineau, 2:164-69.

307 For further discussion on this suffix in PNN at Elephantine, see Silverman, *JAOS* 89 (1969) 695 n. 26. Silverman also lists Egyptian and Persian PNN at Elephantine that terminate with -*w* suffix. For NB PNN ending in -*u* from the Murašû archive, see Coogan, *Murašû*, p. 112.

execration texts, the Alalakh tablets, the Taanach tablets, and the El Amarna letters. Several examples are also cited from WS GNN and PNN in the execration texts. In Amorite, some singular nouns were characterized by mimation, and this ending protected the case vowel. With the loss of mimation on singular nouns, as attested in Ugaritic and the WS glosses in the Amarna letters, the case vowel assumed final position. As the WS languages continued to develop, the final stage in the process was reached, in which the singular noun terminated in -Ø ending.

Though there is some disagreement, the predominant view is that final short vowels, including case endings, were lost sometime after the Amarna period. The process of disuse of the case system no doubt varied with respect to time and place. Whatever the case may be, by the beginning of the first millennium B.C., when the Canaanite languages begin to make their appearances, the loss of case endings on singular nouns is the norm. The evidence in favor of this conclusion is both direct and indirect; the direct evidence is the Hebrew Bible as vocalized by the Masoretes, while the indirect evidence consists of certain morphological (feminine nominal ending *-â*) and syntactic developments (the use of the *nota accusativi*) that assume the loss of case endings.

Proper names lie outside the mainstream of language change and are exempt from certain developments that the language undergoes. Those Canaanite PNN in the Hebrew Bible that possess a medial *û*, medial *ô*, or final *û* were studied to see whether these vowels are the archaic survivals of the nominative case ending *u*. The list of probable examples includes the following Canaanite PNN:

1. Betu᾿el
2. Hadoram
3. Huram
4. Hamutal
5. Hammu᾿el
6. Yemu᾿el

7a. Metusha᾿el
7b. Metushelah
8. Penu᾿el
9. Qemu᾿el
10. Shemu᾿el

From this list, one may observe that the nominative case vowel *-u* is only preserved in Can. PNN in medial position. All these PNN are compound PNN; six of these names are constructed according to the pattern *$C_1ĕC_2û$᾿ēl* (##1, 5, 6, 8-10). From the perspective of structure, ##1, 7a-b, and 8 are construct phrase PNN, whereas ##2-6, 9-10 are nominal-sentence PNN. In these PNN Hebrew *û* is the standard reflex for the nominative singular case vowel. Only in the PN/GN Penu᾿el does Hebrew *û* represent the nominative plural case vowel.

The list of dubious examples consists of the following names:

1. ʾAbugayil
2. Geʾuʾel
3. Deʿuʾel (textual corruption)
4. Nemuʾel (textual corruption)
5. Petuʾel
6. Reʿuʾel
7. Bokeru
8. Beninu
9. Meliku
10. Sallu
11. ʿIru
12. Reʿu
13. Tohu
14. Toʿu
15. Yitro

This list may be subdivided into compound PNN with medial *û* (##1-6), one-word names with final -*û* (##7-14), and a one-word or shortened name with final -*ô* (#15). The nominative case vowel occurs in the PN ʾAhumay; this PN is Aram. and therefore constitutes a non-Canaanite example. Finally among late West Semitic PNN (extrabiblical) were cited six WS (Aramaic) PNN in cuneiform writing and one dubious example from Phoenician PNN.

CHAPTER 3

THE *ḤIREQ COMPAGINIS*

While the topics of chapters 2, 4, and 5 are standard morphological features treated in the grammars of several Semitic languages, the topic of this chapter, the *ḥireq compaginis* (hereafter h.c.), is discussed only in Biblical Hebrew. Another difference between the topic of this chapter and those of chapters 2, 4, and 5 is that the h.c. is easily confused with other morphemes (e.g., 1st c.s. pronominal suffix) and thus it is difficult to isolate in PNN. Apart from the perfunctory treatments in the grammars,[1] a study of the h.c. in PNN is scarcely to be found.

In this chapter I intend to remedy this deficiency and to detect historical antecedents of the h.c. in early West Semitic proper names. Since the h.c. is difficult to detect in PNN in the Hebrew Bible, in spite of our generally good knowledge of Hebrew grammar, it follows that any attempt to isolate historical antecedents of this morpheme in early West Semitic will involve proportionately more difficulty, considering that these languages are far less well known than Biblical Hebrew. In the study of a difficult topic, it is important to avoid extreme positions. Extreme scepticism is epitomized by the statement of Albright, who wrote that ". . . the progress in recent research in ancient Oriental onomatology is absolutely opposed to the existence of this formation [the h.c.] in proper names."[2] Other scholars seem to consider any *-i* vowel which is not (part of) a clearly recognizable morpheme as a possible historical antecedent of the h.c. in Hebrew.[3] Many PNN contain a medial *-i*, but the relevance of these vowels for the discussion of the h.c. is questionable for various reasons.

A study of the probable antecedents of the h.c. in early West Semitic PNN needs to be carried out with caution. I intend to limit the

---

[1]BL §65; GKC §90; Joüon, §93.

[2]W. F. Albright, "The Names *Shaddai* and *Abram*," *JBL* 54 (1935) 193.

[3]Hans-Peter Müller, "Das eblaitische Verbalsystem nach den bisher veröffentlichten Personennamen," in *La lingua di Ebla: Atti del Convegno internazionale (Napoli, 22-23 aprile 1980)*, ed. Luigi Cagni, Istituto universitario orientale, Seminario di studi asiatici, Series Minor, vol. 14 (Napoli, 1981), p. 232, cites the phrase *ma-ḫa-ṣí i-da* "to strike with the hand" and refers to the *-i* vowel on the infinitive as 'Ḥireq compaginis'. Moran, "Hebrew Language," p. 60 nn. 49 and 52, cites participles and infinitives from the EA correspondence with the ending *-i*.

study of this morpheme in early West Semitic as follows. First, since the textbook example of this morpheme in the Hebrew Bible is the PN *ʿabdîʾēl* "man of god/El," one may infer that the h.c. is basically a vowel that binds two elements together, and the most likely place it would occur is as a medial vowel in construct phrase names. It is appropriate, therefore, to focus on construct phrase PNN, such as those that commence with **ʿabd-*, and certain GNN of the same structure. Second, these construct phrase PNN will be studied in light of the various forms that the masculine singular noun assumes in the construct state. Before studying early West Semitic PNN, it is necessary to consider briefly the formation of the construct state in Akkadian.

The various forms that the noun assumes in the construct state in Akkadian are dependent upon the syllable structure of the given noun.[4] In construct before nominal genitive, mimation and the preceding short vowel are always dropped. Of particular interest for the study of the h.c. are those nouns to which the vowel *-i* is affixed in the construct state. Although there are some exceptions,[5] most of the nouns that form their construct in this manner fall into two groups: 1) monosyllabic stems with final reduplicated consonant (*ṭuppum* > **ṭupp* > *ṭuppi*); and 2) polysyllabic feminine nouns ending in *-tt* (*nidittum* > **niditt* > *niditti*). Another exception to the first group are nouns like *šarrum* "king," which forms its construct by simplifying the final consonant cluster (*šar*). And some nouns that belong to the second group show another form of the construct. For example, alongside the construct form *napišti* exists also the construct form *napšat*. In the older stages of Akkadian, other nouns exhibit an *-i* vowel in the construct state. Instead of the expected construct form *šum* "name," in Old Assyrian and rarely in Old Babylonian one finds the construct form *šumi*.[6]

It is fortuitous that G. R. Driver and Lewy, independently of one another, and in articles which were published in the same year (1925), compared the construct forms with *-i* vowel in Akkadian with the h.c in Hebrew.[7] Furthermore, Driver argued that this *-i* vowel was not a case vowel but rather a mere helping or binding vowel, which functioned in

---

[4]Von Soden, *GAG* §64.

[5]Such as monosyllabic nouns ending in a single consonant (e.g., *ili*, *qāti*, *bīti*) and a few monosyllabic feminine nouns (*qīšti* "gift").

[6]According to Huehnergard, "Notes on Akkadian Morphology," p. 189, biforms such as *šumi* are due to analogy with *abi* and *aḫi*.

[7]G. R. Driver, "The Origin of 'Ḥireq Compaginis' in Hebrew," *JTS* 26 (1925) 76-77; Julius Lewy, *Forschungen zur alten Geschichte Vorderasiens*, MVAG, vol. 2 (Leipzig: J. C. Hinrichs, 1925), p. 63 n. 2. Driver's citation of Akk. *išdī* "foundation(s!)" is, however, mistaken, for this word is an oblique dual, not a singular.

the construct state to resolve the final consonant cluster.[8] That this *-i* vowel is not a genitive case vowel seems to follow from the fact that it is added to certain nouns only after mimation and the preceding short case vowel are dropped.[9] Nonetheless, this *-i* vowel is easily confused with the genitive case vowel and it may, as Driver himself added, have been reanalyzed as a case ending by the Babylonians and the Hebrews.[10] Nor should this *-i* vowel be reduced to a helping vowel *-ĕ*, as von Soden would have it.[11] Since there is no variation in this vowel, there is no reason why the consistent writing of this vowel should not be taken seriously.[12] To summarize, in Akkadian certain classes of nouns are characterized by affixing an *-i* vowel in the construct state. With other nouns lying outside of these classes, the *-i* vowel functioned as an alternative form of the construct alongside a vowelless form. But the largest number of monosyllabic nouns (**pars/purs/pirs*) that end in a consonant cluster formed their construct through the insertion of a helping vowel of the same quality as the stem vowel.

I. Early West Semitic

In studying the medial vowels in construct phrase proper names, the statement made in the previous chapter bears repeating: the occurrence or omission of some case endings may be conditioned by a combination of morphological, phonological, and syntactic considerations, not all of which are obvious to the contemporary reader. These

[8]As a remote parallel, note that Tigrinya (North Ethiopic Semitic) regularly resolved all noun-final clusters of consonants with an *-i* : Geʿez *kalb* = Tigrinya *kalbi*.

[9]For discussion of the h.c. (and similar phenomena) as a non-case, see Rabin, "Semitic System of Case Endings," pp. 194-95; Huehnergard, "Notes on Akkadian Morphology," p. 190 n. 52.

[10]Driver, *JTS* 26 (1925) 77. It is interesting that in Old Akkadian and to a lesser extent Old Assyrian, the genitive of the construct state ends in *-i* (e.g., *ina bīti* PN "into the house of PN"). See respectively I. J. Gelb, *Old Akkadian Writing and Grammar*, 2d rev. ed., Materials for the Assyrian Dictionary, no. 2 (Chicago: University of Chicago Press, 1961), pp. 145-46, and Karl Hecker, *Grammatik der Kültepe Texte*, Analecta Orientalia, no. 44 (Rome: Pontificium Institutum Biblicum, 1968), pp. 100-101. The retention of the *-i* vowel probably reflects a very archaic state of the language in which case vowels were retained throughout the construct state. Huffmon, *APNMT*, pp. 124-25, has assembled the evidence that suggests that in Proto-Semitic the *nomen regens* originally had case endings. For further bibliography, see p. 44 n. 25, and on the retention of case endings in Ugaritic, see discussion at p. 112 and n. 25.

[11]*GAG* §64e, g-h.

[12]I. J. Gelb, "Notes on von Soden's Grammar of Akkadian," *BO* 12 (1955) 98; Huehnergard, "Notes on Akkadian Morphology," p. 190 n. 52.

considerations aside, one might expect the form of a construct phrase name to be **ʿabdu-ʾili* "servant of god/El," with the *nomen regens* in the nominative case and the *nomen rectum* in the genitive. But a glance at PNN reveals a great deal of variation in vocalic endings. Often these variations from the expected case vowel may be explained by sentence syntax, assimilation, *sandhi* writing, or diptosis, but more often than not the contemporary reader is left without explanation for the choice of vowels. Therefore, one must be careful in drawing conclusions from variation in vowels.

The evidence for an *-i* binding vowel in construct phrase PNN in Amorite is difficult to evaluate. According to Gelb's study of Amorite grammar, the construct state of biradical nouns may end in -Ø, more frequently in *-u*, and rarely in *-i*.[13] He expressed his uncertainty with the termination *-i* by a question mark. The two Amor. PNN that he cited have **bittum* "daughter" or **ʾamtum* "slave girl" as the first element. The first name, *bi-it-ti-ᵈda-gan* (*CAAA*, p. 119), is a feminine construct phrase name, meaning "daughter of Dagan." Yet there is also a feminine name *bi-it-ta-ma-al-ki* (*CAAA*, p. 119), with an *-a* medial vowel rather than an *-i*. The second name cited by Gelb is *am-ti-aš-ta-ra* (*CAAA*, p. 49), apparently a feminine name meaning "slave girl of Aštar." The only other similar Amor. PN is the feminine name *a-ma-at-ᵈba-a-la* (*CAAA*, p. 49), which seems, as is sometimes the case in Akkadian,[14] to exhibit an alternative form of the construct state. The clearest example of the *-i* binding vowel on the *nomen regens* of a biradical noun is **qīštum* "gift."[15] Jean commented that the *nomen regens* frequently received a "voyelle d'appui," which was ordinarily *-u*, but rarely *-i*. The only example he cited of the second is the Amor. PN *qí-iš-ti-ᵈma-ma* (*CAAA*, p. 174).[16] There are, in fact, four other Amor. PNN of identical or similar structure, and unlike the examples cited by Gelb, there is no variation in the binding vowel: *qí-iš-ti-ad-mu*, *qí-iš-ti-li-lim*, *qí-iš-ti-ᵈma-am-ma*, and *qí-iš-ti-ᵈnu-nu* (*CAAA*, p. 174).

In Amor. PNN of the construct phrase type, the variation in medial vowels presents a confusing picture. The vowel on the element **ʿabd-* may be summarized as follows: thirty-three with *-u*; twenty-two with *-i*; two with *-a*; and one with *-e*. In the above-mentioned study of Amorite grammar, Gelb stated that the construct form of triradical roots

---

[13]Gelb, *RANL* 13 (1958) §3.2.4.1.

[14]Compare Akk. *šīmtum* "fate," which predominantly has the construct form *šīmat*, but also *šīmti* in Old Assyrian.

[15]Charles-F. Jean, "Les noms propres de personnes dans les lettres de Mari," in *Studia Mariana*, ed. André Parrot (Leiden: E. J. Brill, 1950), p. 74.

[16]The spelling of the name in his article, *qi-iš-tu-ᵈMa-ma* [*sic*], is a typographical error.

ended in -Ø.[17] All the examples he cited are **qvtl* base. He elaborated upon his position in *CAAA*, p. 7, where he stated that "consonantal clusters are expressed by means of two different signs, the first of which contains the correct vowel plus correct consonant, the second the correct consonant plus any vowel, which becomes silent."[18] One may infer that Gelb would have attached no significance to the final vowel on the element **ʿabd-*. Although Gelb's view adequately explains the variation in vocalic endings, it fails to account for their distribution. If the second vowel in the writing *-vCCv* is arbitrary, why is there not a more even distribution between *-a*, *-i*, and *-u* vowels? In general, Gelb's view that triradical roots of the form **qvtl* end in -Ø in the construct state cannot be accepted. As already illustrated by Akkadian, ancient Semitic languages tend to resolve consonant clusters in the construct state by the insertion of a vowel between the final two consonants, the addition of a vowel after the cluster, or the simplification of the final cluster when the consonants are identical.

To be sure, it is difficult if not impossible to account for each one of the vocalic endings on the element **ʿabd-*. In the Amor. PNN from Mari, Huffmon detects a clear preference for the spelling *(ḫa-)ab-du*.[19] This preference still holds for Amor. PNN from various sites, though not nearly to the same extent as in the sample studied by Huffmon. While forms of **ʿabd-* with the *-u* vowel (thirty-three in number) may be understood as the nominative case ending, it is the forms with *-i*, the statistically next largest group of names (twenty-two in number), which must be explained. In most of these names, the *-i* vowel cannot simply be analyzed as a binding vowel marking the construct state. On the one hand, Huffmon argued that the names at Mari written *(ḫa-)ab-di-* were the product of phonological conditioning in which **-uya-* becomes *-iya-*.[20] On the other hand, Knudsen has stressed that the spellings of Amor. PNN often show *sandhi* features.[21] Therefore, when a spelling such as *ia-an-ti-ni-ilu(DINGIR)* freely varies with *ia-an-ti-in-ilu(DINGIR)*, in which both verbal forms are followed by **ʾilu*, the evidence favors the interpretation of the first spelling as a *sandhi* writing.[22] It is noteworthy that of the twenty-two names that commence with the spelling *(ḫa-)ab-*

---

[17]Gelb, *RANL* 13 (1958) §3.2.4.2.

[18]He went on to add that another way to express the consonantal cluster is by the writing *Cv-vC*, in which boths vowels were silent (*CAAA*, p. 7).

[19]Huffmon, *APNMT*, p. 105.

[20]Ibid.

[21]See Ebbe E. Knudsen, "An Analysis of Amorite: A Review Article," *JCS* 34 (1982)7-8.

[22]Ibid. I might add that of the two names written with *-a* vowel, one, *ab-da-na-ti* (< **ʿabd-* + **ʿanati*; *CAAA*, p. 89) is clearly an instance of *sandhi* writing.

di-, only four names remain that cannot be explained by appeal to phonological conditioning or *sandhi* writing, and in each of these four names, the second element begins with a guttural: *ab-di-ad-du*, *ab-di-a-mi*, *ab-di-a-na-ti*, and *ab-ti-a-na-ti* (*CAAA*, p. 89). Consequently, it is the better part of wisdom to refrain from attaching any importance to these forms.

The search for an *-i* binding vowel in Ugaritic yields meager results. The consonantal nature of the script hinders any attempt to isolate an *-i* binding vowel, since a short *-i* vowel, or even a long *-i* vowel for that matter, would not be indicated in the orthography.[23] A binding vowel might be inferred in a construct phrase PN in which the writing *x-x* (*x* = any consonant) occurs at the boundary between the two nominal elements, but I know of no names that fit these narrow criteria, not to mention that the quality of the inferred medial vowel would remain unknown.

As noted in the previous chapter, the use of the three *ʾaleph* signs *ʾa*, *ʾi*, and *ʾu* on III-ʾaleph nouns indicate that the case system was still in use in Ugaritic. Tuttle argued from III-ʾaleph and III-y nouns that the case vowel was preserved in masculine singular nouns in the construct state.[24] Moreover, Huehnergard has published corroborative evidence from the Akkadian texts written at Ugarit that not only substantiated Tuttle's thesis, but even expanded it to include feminine singular nouns.[25] Therefore, in contrast to the situation in Akkadian, case vowels were retained in the construct state in Ugaritic. In those instances where the noun in construct is preceded by a preposition, or another syntactic environment requiring the genitive, it is probable that the *-i* vowel is a genitive case ending. The retention of case vowels in the construct state in Ugaritic has important implications for the origin of the h.c. To be specific, the Ugaritic situation may lend support to the view that the h.c. is a remnant of the genitive case ending.[26]

---

[23]There are rare instances of the use of *matres lectionis* in Ugaritic to indicate long vowels. The representation of the h.c. by a *y mater lectionis* in BH may imply that the vowel was historically long. Contrarily, it may be that in special environments, such as PNN, short *i* did not (necessarily) shift to *ṣērē* in an open pretonic syllable, but was secondarily lengthened to *ī*. In the absence of corroborative evidence, nothing definitive can be said about the quantity of the vowel.

[24]Tuttle, pp. 253-68.

[25]Huehnergard, *JCS* 33 (1981) 199-205. Earlier but unpublished, Jesse L. Boyd III, "A Collection and Examination of the Ugaritic Vocabulary Contained in the Akkadian Texts from Ras Shamra" (Ph.D. dissertation, University of Chicago, 1975), pp. 289-90, had presented his own list of masculine and feminine nouns that retained the case ending in the construct state. Zevit, *JSS* 28 (1983) 225-32, has questioned this thesis, but the weight of evidence favors it. See also p. 44 n. 25.

[26]Advocates of this view are Barth, *ZDMG* 53 (1899) 593-97; Bauer, *Ostkanaanäer*, pp. 65-66; Robert Gordis, *The Biblical Text in the Making: A Study*

Thus far the discussion has centered upon the construct state of Ugaritic common nouns, whether in alphabetic or syllabic script. According to Gröndahl, there is no standard form which the *nomen regens* assumes in PNN.[27] The *nomen regens* may end in *-u*, *-i*, or *-a*, presumably case vowels; even here, the choice of the vowel is often not clear, though some of the vowels can be explained by the internal structure of the name or the syntactic requirements of the context. The discovery that the *nomen regens* may end in -Ø is unexpected, however.[28] In so conservative a sector of the language as PNN, it is hard to accept Zevit's suggestion that the -Ø ending, as well as the apparent random use of vowels, foreshadows the breakdown of the case system.[29] The consistent use of construct forms from III-ʾaleph nouns in the Ugaritic literary texts points to a situation in which the case system was on the whole intact. Whatever the case may be, the -Ø ending in PNN appears to be the result of Akkadian influence.[30]

In the previous chapter, it was noted that the Ug. feminine PN *ᶠa-ḫa-tum-milki(LUGAL)* (15.89, l. 11 [*PRU* III, p. 53]) is also written *ᶠa-ḫa-ti-milki(LUGAL)* (ll. 8, 18), the second spelling occurring in syntactic environments requiring the genitive case ending. At least in this instance, the case ending on the first element is not static, but is declined according to the demands of the context. This PN is of the construct phrase type, and the *-i* vowel on the *nomen regens* may be analyzed as a genitive case vowel. One can easily imagine a situation where the form ʾAhatimilki, which was the product of the influence of sentence syntax, would assume an existence of its own and begin to be used elsewhere.[31] This process might have been accelerated by the (later) breakdown of the case system, at which point the *-i* vowel may have been reanalyzed as a simple binding vowel.

With these considerations in mind, we may now examine other Ugaritic PNN written in syllabic script. Construct phrase names with **ʿabd-* as the initial element are well documented at Ugarit. With the exception of two names, all these PNN are written logographically without phonetic complement, so that the vowel on the initial element is

---

of the Kethib-Qere, aug. ed. (n.p.: KTAV, 1971), pp. 103-4; GKC §90k (earlier editions); Kaila, pp. 58-59; Joüon, §93l; Nöldeke, *EB* 3:3277; Noth, *IPN*, pp. 33-34.

[27] *PTU*, p. 31.

[28] Ibid.

[29] Zevit, *JSS* 28 (1983) 231.

[30] Huffmon, *APNMT*, p. 105 n. 43, and 119, argues convincingly that the vowelless construct form *mut-* is due to Akkadian influence, all the more likely in this particular case since the vocable *mutu(m)* is common to both Akkadian and Amorite.

[31] Compare the freezing of the genitive vowel in Hebrew in the construct forms *ʾăbî-*, *ʾaḥî-*, and *pî-*.

not indicated. Nevertheless, on the basis of two names, Gröndahl and Sivan normalize the first element of all the other names as *ʿ*abdi-*.[32] The two names in which the vowel on the *ʿ*abd-* element is indicated are *abdi(ÌR*[di]*)-ir-ši* (*PTU*, p. 316) and *ab-di-ḫa-ma-ni* (16.200, l. 3 [*PRU* III, p. 64]). When the contexts in which each of these names appear is consulted, we discover that both names are preceded by the vocable *mār* "son." Thus the vowel on the initial element may be the genitive case ending, declined according to the syntactic requirements of the context. Alternatively, Edzard has explained the *-i* vowel on the first name as *sandhi* writing.[33] This explanation cannot be applied to the name ʿAbdihamani, but it should be noted that sometimes the *nomen rectum* of this name, a name which is attested elsewhere but borne by different persons, shows genuine variation in its declension, sometimes being declined according to the sentence syntax, at other times against the sentence syntax.[34] To sum up, the *-i* vowel on at least one of these two construct phrase names may be a genitive case vowel, but at any rate, it is not clear how the logogram *ÌR* should be normalized in the other names of this kind. There is evidence provided by shortened names for a nominative case vowel on the element *ʿ*abd-*,[35] but this may reflect nothing more than the nominalization of the name.

In the Akkadian texts from Ugarit, Liverani pointed to construct phrase names whose first element terminated with an *-i* vowel, even where the nominative is required, as representing a phenomenon similar to the h.c. in Hebrew.[36] He believed that these names foreshadowed the disintegration of the case system. As examples, he cites two Ug. PNN, *a-ḫi-milki(LUGAL)* (*PTU*, p. 319) and *pí-ṣí-id-qi* (*PTU*, p. 170), and two Ug. GNN, *URUḫal-bi ḫabiri(LÚ.MEŠSA.GAZ)* (11.790, l. 7' [*PRU* III, p. 189]) and *URUḫal-bi ḫuršan(ḪUR.SAG)-ḫa-zi* (11.830, l. 13 [*PRU* III, p. 190]). Although the Ug. PN ʾAhimilki may be a nominal-sentence name,[37] the three other proper names that he cited are

[32]Gröndahl, *PTU*, pp. 104-5; Sivan, *GAGNWS*, pp. 202-3.

[33]D. O. Edzard, Review of *Die Personennamen der Texte aus Ugarit*, by Frauke Gröndahl, *OLZ* 67 (1972) 555. The WS PN *ab-di-ir-šu* (*AT*, p. 125) may be another example.

[34]Note these four spellings, with the sentence syntax indicated in parenthesis after each name: *ÌR-ḫa-m*[*a-n*]*u* (nominative; 16.144, R, l. 13' [*PRU* III, p. 34]); *ÌR-ḫa-ma-nu* (nominative; 16.348 R, l. 6' [*PRU* III, p. 103]); [*ÌR*]- *ḫa-ma-ni* (nominative; 12.34 + 12.43, l. 8 [*PRU* III, p. 193]); *ÌR-ḫa-ma-ni* (nominative; same text, l. 20). For a discussion of the various forms of the *nomen rectum*, see Gröndahl, *PTU*, pp. 33-34.

[35]Ug. *ab-du* (*PTU*, p. 105); *abdu(ÌR*[du]*)* (15.09, B.I.3 [*PRU* III, p. 195]).

[36]Liverani, *RANL* 19 (1964) 179-80.

[37]Pace, Liverani, *RANL* 19 (1964) 180 n. 72. Note, for example, the feminine (!) Amor. PN of similar structure *a-ḫi-ì-lí* (Gelb, *CAAA*, p. 37).

construct phrase names and each occur in a context that calls for the nominative.

WS proper names from other sources, such as the Egyptian execration texts, Alalakh tablets, or Bronze Age texts from Palestine do not contribute any different elements to the discussion. A series of GNN in the EA letters may be relevant in this context, to wit those GNN in which the first element is **gintu* "wine-press." These GNN are of the construct phrase type, and without exception, they exhibit an *-i* vowel on vocalic ending of the initial element. According to Hess, five different GNN are mentioned in the EA letters that commence with the initial element **gintu*: *gi-im-ti^{ki}*; *kín-ti-ki-ir-mi-il*; *gi-ti-ri-mu-ni-ma*; *k*[*ín*]-*ti-aš-na*; and *gi-ti-pa-da-al-la* (*AmPN*, pp. 472, 473, 474, 479, 480.[38] The third one of these GNN, *gi-ti-ri-mu-ni-ma*, occurs in the Hebrew Bible without vocalic ending on the initial element: *gat rimmôn*. The consistency of the *-i* vowel on the initial element of these five GNN, even in different spellings of these GNN and in contexts requiring the accusative case,[39] can hardly be fortuitous. Whether it is a genitive case vowel or merely an *-i* binding vowel cannot be determined; nevertheless, it is as likely a candidate for the historical antecedent of the h.c. in Hebrew as may be discovered in early West Semitic.

II. Canaanite

In this section, the discussion is restricted to Biblical Hebrew, since that language is the only Canaanite language in which the h.c. has been identified. In fact, if the h.c. was historically a short vowel, it would not be indicated in the scripts of the other Canaanite languages, unless these languages shared with Biblical Hebrew the tendency to lengthen secondarily short vowels in certain positions and to mark these secondarily lengthened short vowels by *matres lectionis*. Even if these criteria were met, the h.c. still might not be found in the other Canaanite languages, on account of various other considerations (e.g., genre).

The succinct treatment of the h.c. in the grammars[40] may be supplemented by the study of Robertson.[41] According to his count, the

---

[38]Sivan, *GAGNWS*, p. 220, would add a sixth, reading *^{URU}gin$_x$(KIN)-ti-e-ti* in place of Hess's *URU ^{ki}gam-ti-e-ti* (*AmPN*, p. 470).

[39]EA 250.12, 46. In EA 288.26, 290.9, and 319.5, the context calls for the genitive case.

[40]GKC §90a, k-n; Joüon, §93l-q.

[41]Robertson, *VT* 19 (1969) 212-21. With a few changes, this is an excerpt from his dissertation, which was subsequently published as *Linguistic Evidence* (= pp. 69-76).

h.c. occurs thirty-three times in the Hebrew Bible. In most instances, twenty-seven to be exact, the h.c. is affixed to a participle, while in the remaining six instances, it is affixed to a noun. This list should be considered maximal, since some of the examples listed by him are contestable.[42] In GKC and Joüon, the *-î* suffix on certain Hebrew particles (*biltî, zûlātî, minnî*) is also treated in the section devoted to the h.c. Also the forms that the kinship terms *ʾāb*, *ʾāḫ*, and **ḥām* assume in the construct state are brought into the discussion. While the construct forms of the kinship terms may be helpful in understanding the possible origin of the h.c.,[43] the *-î* suffix on the above-mentioned particles adds little to the discussion.

Unfortunately, a consideration of the h.c. outside of PNN sheds little if any light on the use of this morpheme in PNN. For example, in some PNN, the forms *ʾăbî-*, *ʾăḥî-*, and *ḥămî-* cannot be interpreted as indicative of the construct state. In fact it is questionable whether in PNN these forms should ever be interpreted as construct forms.[44] In addition, twenty-seven of the occurrences noted by Robertson are affixed to participles. Participles are not common among the Canaanite PNN in the Hebrew Bible, and of those PNN that do contain a participle, not one has the h.c. Robertson argued that the *-î* morpheme on these participles marks apposition, and thus it has nothing to do with the construct state.

Nevertheless, two positive contributions result from a study of the h.c. outside of PNN. First, the h.c. is definitely an archaic morpheme. With the exception of two occurrences of this morpheme in Gen 31:39, a prose passage, all the remaining instances are confined to poetry.[45] Second, in the two oldest passages cited by Robertson, Gen 49:11 and Deut 33:16, both of which are examples of ABH, the *-î* morpheme

[42]Francis I. Andersen and David Noel Freedman, *Hosea: A New Translation with Introduction and Commentary*, AB 24 (Garden City: Doubleday & Co., 1980), p. 567, analyze the *ʾōhabtî* of Hos 10:11 not as a participle, as does Robertson, but as a first common singular Qal perfect verbal form.

[43]Barth, *ZDMG* 53 (1899) 597, theorized that the h.c. in such names as the biblical PN *ʿabdîʾēl* was constructed according to the analogy of the construct state of the kinship terms. If this view is accepted, then the origin of the h.c. may be found in the genitive case ending.

[44]For discussion, see section F., "Compound PNN Formed with Kinship Terms," pp. 145-50.

[45]Five of Robertson's thirty-three occurrences are affixed to vocables that are determined by the definite article, and Hurvitz has shown that such mixed forms betray a relatively late stage of BH and hence are archaizing rather than genuine archaisms. See Avi Hurvitz, "Originals and Imitations in Biblical Poetry: A Comparative Examination of 1 Sam 2:1-10 and Ps 113:5-9," in *Biblical and Related Studies Presented to Samuel Iwry*, ed. Ann Kort and Scott Morschauser (Winona Lake: Eisenbrauns, 1985), pp. 117-20.

appears on the *nomen regens* of a construct chain: *bĕnî ʾătōnô* "the colt of his ass" (Gen 49:11) and *šōkĕnî sĕneh* "the dweller of the bush"[46] (Deut 33:16). These two occurrences suggest that the use of *-î* on the *nomen regens* of a construct chain is ancient. Robertson hypothesizes that the original force of the *-î* was to mark bound structures, and later, possibly through association with the *-y* of the *nisbe*, it came to be used to mark apposition. Alternatively, he suggested that we may be dealing with two different morphemes, a *-y* associated with apposition, and a *-y* associated with bound structures.[47] However that may be, it is the *-y* that is associated with bound structures that provides a partial parallel for the use of the h.c. in PNN.

Finally, I would like to conclude this section by citing instances of the h.c. in two GNN and a title in the Hebrew Bible that have been overlooked in previous discussion.[48] In a list of wilderness stations occurs the GN *naḥălîʾēl* "wadi of god/El" (Num 21:19).[49] The second GN, *ʾădāmî hanneqeb*, refers to a site on the border of Naphtali (Josh 19:33).[50] These two GNN are the only GNN in the Hebrew Bible compounded of two nominal elements with a medial *-î* vowel.[51] A medial *-i* binding vowel in EA GNN of the construct phrase type has already been noted above. The last occurrence is in the phrase *ʾădōnî(-)bezeq* in Judg 1:5-7. This phrase has been translated as a PN in some modern translations (e.g., NASV), comparable to the PN ʾAdonisedeq, borne by the king of Jerusalem (Josh 10:1, 3). Some commentators go so far as to emend the phrase in Judges to the PN in Joshua. Against the emendation is the fact that all the textual witnesses confirm the reading of the MT.[52] Nor is it likely to be a PN, because Bezeq is not known to be a DN or divine appellative. From the context of Judges 1, Bezeq is clearly a GN,[53] which also refers to a different locality elsewhere in the Hebrew Bible (1 Sam 11:8). Therefore, the phrase ʾAdoni(-)bezeq must be a title rather than a PN, and it can scarcely be translated other than "lord of Bezeq."[54] Here again we

---

[46]In turn, this phrase functions as the *nomen rectum* of another construct chain, *rĕṣôn šōkĕnî sĕneh* "the favor of the dweller of the bush."

[47]Robertson, *VT* 19 (1969) 221.

[48]Neither GKC nor Joüon mention these examples.

[49]Compare the GN *na-ḫal-li* ^{d}*Ku-si* (Tallqvist, *APN*, p. 257).

[50]The suffix is still preserved in the modern toponym *Dāmiye*.

[51]See the comprehensive lists of compound GNN in Wilhelm Borée, *Die alten Ortsnamen Palästinas* (Leipzig: Eduard Pfeiffer, 1930), pp. 75-98.

[52]LXX B, SyrP, Vulgate, and Targum Jonathan. In Josephus, the metathesized variant of the name is preserved, ἀδωνιζέβεκος (*NWJ*, p. 4).

[53]See KB3, pp. 113-14.

[54]For this analysis, see J. Alberto Soggin, *Judges: A Commentary*, The Old Testament Library (Philadelphia: Westminster Press, 1981), p. 21; Robert G.

have a construct phrase with a medial *-î* vowel between the two nominal elements.

III. Canaanite PNN in the Hebrew Bible

The extent to which the h.c. occurs in Canaanite PNN in the Hebrew Bible is contested. In lexica, grammars, commentaries, and articles, many putative examples have been proffered, some of which can immediately be seen to be untenable, while others are worthy of careful consideration. In general, two large classes of PNN merit consideration: 1) compound PNN with a medial *-î* vowel; and 2) shortened names of these compound PNN, which as the result of the dropping of the second element, terminate in a final *-î* vowel. As an example of these two classes of PNN, we may cite the biblical PNN *ʿabdîʾēl* and *ʿabdî.*

Within the limits of this study, it is impossible to treat in a detailed manner all the names that comprise these two classes. Nor would it be profitable, since upon closer inspection, it becomes apparent that many of these names do not contain the h.c. On the other hand, within these two classes are some PNN that keep coming up in discussions of the h.c. and therefore warrant careful study. Therefore, the names analyzed in this chapter are those names that are usually drawn into service to support the thesis of the h.c. After these names have been discussed, a general treatment of the class of compound PNN with kinship terms will follow; some of the names within this class have been interpreted as containing the h.c. But first it is necessary to make some preliminary remarks about the difficulties involved in isolating the h.c. in Canaanite PNN.

A. *On the Detection of the h.c. in Canaanite PNN*

The main difficulty encountered in studying the h.c. in PNN is that this morpheme is often indistinguishable from various other morphemes that are also represented in the MT by the writing *-î.* The writing *-î* may represent any one of four different morphemes. First, the writing *-î* (< **-iy* < **-iya*) may represent the 1st c.s. pronominal suffix. Examples may be found in the BH PNN *ʾădōnîyāh* and *ʾēlîyāh,* which can only be analyzed as nominal-sentence names meaning "My lord is Yah" and "My god is Yah." Stamm remarks that the pronominal suffix

Boling, *Judges: Introduction, Translation, and Commentary,* AB 6A (Garden City: Doubleday & Co., 1975), p. 55.

has a dual reference, both to the giver of the name and to its bearer: "It expresses a personal utterance at first for the child, until the child is able to make it his own."[55] Alongside forms containing the pronominal suffix are suffixless forms; compare the pairs of BH PNN *ʾēlîyāh* and *yôʾēl* (different persons), and especially the Can. PNN *ʾĕlîʿām* and *ʿammîʾēl*, borne by the same person. The loss of the suffix may be related to position; that is, in a nominal-sentence name, the suffix tends to disappear when at the end of the second element.[56] In the MT there are no exceptions to this rule among the Canaanite PNN.[57] On the whole Canaanite PNN found in extrabiblical sources appear to conform to this structural pattern.[58] In contrast, Aramaic PNN do not fit this pattern, as illustrated by numerous IAram. PNN at Elephantine and the OAram. PN *hdysʿy* "Haddu is my salvation" (*SPARI*, pp. 77, 154).

A second morpheme represented by the writing *-î* (< **-iy* < **-iyy* < **-iyyu*) is the masculine singular form of the gentilic adjective. Among PNN the use of the gentilic suffix is restricted; as examples, note the Can. PN *kûšî* "the one from Kush"[59] and the BH PN *yĕhûdî* "the one from Yehud." The EH PN *bʿlmʿny* "the one from Baalmeon" occurs in S 27.3; compare here the biblical GN *baʿal mĕʿôn* (Num 32:38 and elsewhere). Additional examples in EH PNN are *ngby* "the one from the Negev"[60] and *nby* "the one from Nob."[61] Since this morpheme is not widely used in the formation of PN, and since it is easily identified (GN + *-î*), it may be dismissed from further consideration.

A third morpheme represented by the writing *-î* (< **-iy* < **-iya*) is the hypocoristic suffix. In light of the widespread use of hypocoristic suffixes on West Semitic PNN, it is a pity that the study of hypocoristica has been neglected. The pioneering study of Lidzbarski was a valiant effort and it still retains some of its usefulness, but it is now badly out of date, having been written before every modern study of West Semitic

---

[55] Johann J. Stamm, in *EncJud*, s.v. "Names," 12:804-5.

[56] Cazelles, *DBS* 6:738; Zadok, *TA* 9 (1982) 120.

[57] But note the Can. PN *ʾelʿûzay*, which in LXX A is vocalized ελιωζι (< **ʾelʿuzzî*). Other minor witnesses also support this revocalization (c_2: *αζε*; s: *αζει*; f: *ελιαζι*; dj: *ελιαζι*); contrast LXX B *Ελιαζαι*.

[58] The only exceptions I have encountered are the Ph-P. PN *ʾšmnʾdny* (Benz, *PNPP*, p. 70) and the WS PN *ʾlsmky* (VSE #129). As for the first name, perhaps the 1st c.s. pronominal suffix became fused to the element **ʾdn* so that the resulting form **ʾdny* came to be treated as a unit. On the second name, opinions are sharply divided over its linguistic classification. On the basis of its structure, I suggest it is Aramaic.

[59] The location of the land designated by Kush need not detain us. For various options, see KB3, p. 445.

[60] Avigad, *Hebrew Bullae*, #12.

[61] VSE ##258, 343; N. Avigad, "Titles and Symbols on Hebrew Seals," *EI* 15 (1981) 304-5 (Pl. 57:3).

onomastics.[62] Thompson observes that hypocoristic names appear in our earliest records and thus they should not be considered as being derived from earlier theophoric prototypes (e.g., *yʿqb* < **yʿqbʾl*).[63] The "hypocoristic" name may be a variant in its own right. On the other hand, occasionally the same person bears a theophoric PN and a hypocoristic PN, a circumstance that favors the view that at least some hypocoristic PNN were in fact derived from longer prototypes. The outstanding example of this phenomenon is found in the Brooklyn Museum Aramaic Papyrus #2, where the same individual is called *ʿnnyh* (ll. 2, 11) and *ʿnny* (ll. 7, 9, 10, 11, 12, 13, 14).[64] There is at least one possible example in the Hebrew Bible, *ḥănānî* and *ḥănanyāh* (Neh 1:2 and 7:2), but in this instance there is room for doubt.[65] From such pairs of names, it has been plausibly suggested that the original hypocoristic suffix *-iya*, which was meaningless, was reanalyzed in a Jewish milieu as a theophoric abbreviation of the DN Yah(u).[66] At the same time, the original hypocoristic ending **-iya* may be found on isolated PNN in the Hebrew Bible, such as the PN *baqbuqyāh*.[67]

A fourth morpheme represented by the writing *-î* (< **-ĭ*) is the h.c. The most celebrated example of this morpheme is in the Can. PN *ʿabdîʾēl* "servant of god/El" (see below for further discussion). It should be stated at the outset, that it is not always possible to distinguish between the pronominal suffix, the hypocoristic ending, and the h.c. The best that can be done is to study the structure and semantics of names, and seek to distinguish these morphemes whenever possible. Since the hypocoristic ending is a final termination, it follows that the medial *-î* vowel in compound PNN should be either the pronominal suffix or the h.c. In the compound PN *ʿabdîʾēl*, it would be nonsensical and ill-fitting with the religious piety of the ancient Semites to analyze

---

[62]Mark Lidzbarski, "Semitische Kosenamen," in *Ephemeris für Semitische Epigraphik*, 3 vols. (Giessen: Alfred Töpelmann, 1900-12), 2:1-23.

[63]Thompson, *Historicity*, p. 37. Yaʿaqob would, of course, be a shortened name according to the terminology adopted in this study.

[64]Emil G. Kraeling, *The Brooklyn Museum Aramaic Papyri: New Documents of the Fifth Century B.C. from the Jewish Colony at Elephantine* (New Haven: Yale University Press, 1953; reprint ed., n.p.: Arno Press, 1969), pp. 142-43.

[65]G. C. Tuland, "Hanani-Hananiah," *JBL* 77 (1958) 157-61, defends the view that interprets these two names as variants borne by one person. But see the critique of H. G. M. Williamson, *Ezra, Nehemiah*, Word Biblical Commentary, vol. 16 (Waco: Word Books, 1985), p. 266.

[66]So Jean Margueron and Javier Teixidor, "Un objet à légende araméenne provenant de Meskéné-Emar," *RA* 77 (1983) 80. Contrast Lipiński, *BO* 37 (1980) 4, who sets up an unnecessary opposition in his affirmation that the *-y* on EH PNN is not an abbreviation of the name Yahweh, but rather the final hypocoristic suffix common to the Semitic languages.

[67]Noth, *IPN*, p. 105.

the *-î* writing as a pronominal suffix and to translate this name "My servant is god/El." In this case, semantic considerations call for the analysis of the medial *-î* vowel as the h.c.

For one-word PNN that end with the writing *-î*, this may be the pronominal suffix, the h.c., or the hypocoristic ending. As an example of an ambiguous one-word name, note the Can. PN *zimrî*. Although the h.c. cannot be ruled out entirely in this PN, similar names from the Amorite onomasticon suggest that this PN is susceptible to two different analyses: 1) a shortened name with the DN unexpressed (compare the Amor. PN *zi-im-ri-ilu(DINGIR)* [*CAAA*, p. 129]); or 2) a hypocoristic name, analogous to the Amor. PN *zi-im-ri-ia* (*CAAA*, p. 129).

It should be apparent that structure and semantics are of limited utility when it comes to isolating the h.c. in PNN. Regrettably, that is all we have to go on. As far as semantics is concerned, since many of the compound PNN with medial *-î* are theophoric, it may be helpful to correlate the proposed interpretation of these PNN with kindred religious sentiments expressed in hymns, psalms, and prayers, as well as various epithets and appellatives borne by deities. Porten attempted such a correlation in his study of the Jewish onomasticon at Elephantine.[68] To illustrate, since the Israelite was fond of referring to his god as *ṣûrî* "my rock" (2 Sam 22:3, 47; Ps 18:3, 47; 19:15; 28:1; 62:3, 7; 92:16; 144:1), the Can. PN *ṣûrîʾēl* should be interpreted as a nominal-sentence PN meaning "God/El is my rock."[69] From the perspective of methodology, it is necessary to begin with the two most celebrated examples of the h.c. in PNN, and then proceed to other probable examples that have been proffered. Thus in contrast to the manner of presentation in the other chapters, wherein the Canaanite PNN were listed according to the order of the Hebrew alphabet, in this chapter we will begin with two PNN that contain the most probable examples of the h.c., and building upon what we have learned, then study other examples that have been suggested.

[68]Porten, *Archives*, pp. 135-45.

[69]Likewise, the biblical PN *ṣûrîšadday* is not a construct phrase PN, as Nestle, *Die israelitischen Eigennamen*, p. 46, would have it, but a nominal-sentence PN.

B. *Probable Examples*

1. *ʿabdîʾēl.*

Classification: Can.--tribe of Gad (1 Chr 5:15).
Structure: construct phrase name, *ʿabd-* (**qatl* base) + *-î-* h.c. + *-ʾēl* (**qil* base, BL §61i).

Meaning: "servant of god/El."

Parallels: Amor. *ḫa-ab-di-el, ab-te-il, ḫa-ab-di-ili(DINGIR), ab-di-ili(DINGIR)* (*CAAA*, p. 89); Ug. *ʿbdʾil, ʿbdʾilm, abdv(ÌR)-ili(DINGIR), abdv(ÌR)-ili(DINGIR)-mu* (*PTU*, pp. 104-5); *abdv(ÌR)-i-li* (RS 17.36, ll. 5, 8. 10 [*Ug V*, p. 11]), *abdv(ÌR)-ilim(DINGIR^{lim})* (RS 20.150, l. 9' [*Ug V*, p. 150]), *abdv(ÌR)-ili(DINGIR)-*[*m*]*a* (fragment G, l. 4' [*Ug V*, p. 197]);[70] WS *abdu(ÌR)-ili(DINGIR^{li})* (from Emar);[71] N/LB *ab-di-ili(DINGIR)* (*WSB*, p. 352); Can. *ʿabdĕʾēl*; IAram. *ʿbdʾl* (*SPARI*, pp. 94, 192); Ph-P. *ʿbdʾlm* (*PNPI*, p. 371);[72] Ḥat. *ʿbdʾlhʾ* (*PIH*, p. 136); Saf., Tham., Qat., and Sab. *ʿbdʾl* (*PIAN*, p. 397).

Comments: The PN ʿAbdiʾel is the clearest example of the h.c. in the Hebrew Bible.[73] It stands in contrast with the Can. PN *ʿabdĕʾēl*, which is written with a reduced vowel. From the perspective of semantics, this name must be analyzed as a construct phrase PN. The occurrence of an *-i* binding vowel on the first element of this name has parallels in the early West Semitic proper names (section I.) and biblical GNN (section II.) studied above.

2. *ḥizqîyāh.*

Variant spellings: 1. *ḥizqîyāhû*; 2. *yĕḥizqîyāh*; 3. *yĕḥizqîyāhû.*

---

[70]On the problem of the normalization of *ÌR* at Ugarit, see pp. 113-14.

[71]John Huehnergard, "Five Tablets from the Vicinity of Emar," *RA* 77 (1983) 23 (text 4, l. 27).

[72]On Ph.-P. PNN, Greek and Latin transliterations provide evidence for an *-o-* or *-u-* connecting vowel in some instances. See Benz, PNPP, p. 372; E. Lipiński, Review of *Personal Names in the Phoenician and Punic Inscriptions*, by Frank L. Benz, *BO* 32 (1975) 80; Wuthnow, p. 8.

[73]This textbook example is cited by Joüon, §93m and BL §65g, but it is unaccountably omitted from GKC's list of compound PNN containing the h.c. (GKC §90l).

Classification: Hebrew--1) Judean king, son of Ahaz (2 Kgs 18:11); 2) great-great-grandfather of prophet Zephanyah (Zeph 1:1; =1.[?]); 3) son of Neʿaryah (1 Chr 3:23); 4) head of family of returned exiles (Ezra 2:16); 5) tribe of Ephraim (2 Chr 28:12).

Structure: 1. nominal-sentence name, *ḥizq-* (**qitl* base) + *-î-* 1st c.s. pronominal suffix + *-yāh(û)* (DN).
2. verbal-sentence name, *ḥizq-* (< **ḥzq* "to be strong," 3rd m.s. Qal perfect) + *-î-* h.c. + *-yāh(û)* (DN).

Meaning: 1. "Yah(u) is my strength."
2. "Yah(u) is strong."

Parallels: NA *ḫa-za-qi-a-a-u*, *ḫa-za-qi-a-u*, *ḫa-za-qi-ia*, *ḫa-za-qi-ia-u* (*APN*, p. 88); *ḫa-za-[qi-a/ia-ú]*;[74] BH *ḥizqî*; EH *ḥzq*,[75] *ḥzqyhw* (VSE #321), *ḥ⌈z⌉qyhw* (Ophel ostracon, l. 1);[76] *yḥzq* (VSE #83).

Comments: As this name is pointed in the MT, our first proposed structure/meaning appears to be a fully satisfactory analysis of the PN.[77] Its structure--abstract noun + 1st c.s. pronominal suffix + DN--is one of the most prolific formations among WS PNN. The BH PN *ʿuzzîyāh(û)* "Yah(u) is my strength" would provide an exact semantic and structural analog to this interpretation. Moreover, in Ps 18:2, the psalmist describes Yahweh as "his strength" (MT *ḥizqî*), an appellative which not only echoes the sentiment that finds expression in the PNN Hizqiyah(u) and ʿUzziyah(u), but also attests the existence of a **qitl* base noun from the root **ḥzq*.[78] The only shortcoming of this approach is that it fails to take into account the cuneiform writings of the name Hizqiyah(u).

All of the cuneiform writings agree in vocalizing the first part of the name *ḫa-za-qi-*. This writing appears to be a Qal perfect verbal form plus h.c. If one accepts this analysis, there still remains to explain the MT form *ḥizqîyāh(u)*. On the basis of recognized rules of Hebrew

---

[74] Manfred Görg, "Ein Keilschriftfragment des Berichtes vom dritten Feldzug des Sanherib mit den Namen des Hiskija," *BN* 24 (1984) 16-17, and Plate 1.

[75] P. Bordreuil and A. Lemaire, "Nouveaux sceaux hébreux et araméens," *Sem* 32 (1982) 30-31 #13 (Pl. VI:13).

[76] Lemaire, *Inscriptions hébraïques*, p. 240.

[77] This analysis is preferred by Stamm, *BHAN*, p. 52; KB2, p. 288; David R. Hunsberger, "Theophoric Names in the Old Testament and Their Theological Significance" (Ph.D. dissertation, Temple University, 1969), p. 113.

[78] The masculine singular noun **ḥēzeq* occurs only in Ps 18:2, having been omitted (by scribal error?) in the parallel text 2 Sam 22:2. Note also the feminine singular noun **ḥezqâ* (BDB, p. 305).

phonology, Kutscher has provided an explanation of the MT form of the name.[79] With the h.c., a verbal-sentence name of this type has three short unaccented syllables preceding the tone syllable. Under these circumstances, the second vowel drops and the first vowel would be likely to become *i*.[80] This process may be represented as follows: **ḥazaqîyāh(û)* > **ḥazqîyāh(û)* > *ḥizqîyāh(û)*. The cuneiform writings and the MT form of the name do not contradict one another. Furthermore, the analysis of Hizqiyah(u) as a verbal-sentence name also helps to explain the variant spelling *yĕḥizqîyāh(û)*. Kutscher observed that the forms beginning with *y*- are found almost entirely in the Chronicles, and he has concluded that these forms reflect the post-exilic tendency to form names according to the imperfect verb paradigm.[81] Elsewhere in the Hebrew Bible the name of Jehoiakim's son appears in two different forms, *konyāhû* and *yĕkonyāh*, exhibiting an alternation between perfect and imperfect verbal forms. However one explains the forms beginning with *y*-,[82] it seems probable that this same alternation exists between the variant spellings of the name Hizqiyah(u). That is, the Chronicler correctly understood the first element of the MT form *ḥizqîyāh(û)* to be a perfect verbal form; otherwise he would not have modified[83] the name by replacing the perfect with the imperfect.[84]

---

[79]Kutscher, *Isaiah Scroll*, pp. 104-6.

[80]Ibid., p. 106. On the dropping of the second vowel, see BL §26x'; on the vocalic change *a* > *i*, see J. A. Thompson, "On Some Stamps and a Seal from Lachish," *BASOR* 86 (1942) 26 and n. 15.

[81]Ibid., p. 104. While we may question whether such a tendency existed, Kutscher's observation that these forms are found almost entirely in Chronicles and are therefore late is nevertheless valid. W. F. Albright, "The Names 'Israel' and 'Judah' with an Excursus on the Etymology of Tôdâh and Tôrâh," *JBL* 46 (1927) 165-67, hypothesized that the longer form (i.e., imperfect) was the original form, from which was derived by contraction the shorter form, or imperative. Beegle, *BASOR* 123 (1951) 28-29, accepted Albright's interpretation. Similarly, Fowler, pp. 73, 153, 344, regarded the shorter form as an abbreviation of the longer form (*yĕḥizqîyāh* > *ḥizqîyāh*). This view fails to explain the predominance of the longer form in Chronicles and the cuneiform writings of the name.

[82]Zadok suggests that the forms with *y*- may have arisen from orthographic confusion between *waw* and *yod*: **wḥzqyh(w)* > *yḥzqyh(w)* (oral communication). Whatever the case may be, the form of the name with *y*- is definitely late.

[83]Admittedly, the name as pointed by the Chronicler does not fit the normal pattern of vocalization of an imperfect verbal form. Apparently he sought to preserve the traditional vocalization and, in a mechanical fashion, simply suffixed *yĕ*- to the inherited form [**yĕ*- + *ḥizqîyāh(û)* > *yĕḥizqîyāh(û)*].

[84]Accordingly, the spellings of the name found in the 1QIsa^a with a *w* (*ḥwzqyh*, *yḥwzqyh*), apparently deriving the first element from the **qutl* base noun *ḥōzeq*, reflect the fact that it was no longer realized that the name Hizqiyahu was a verbal-sentence name.

In the Qal stem, the verb **ḥzq* predominantly has a stative meaning, "to be strong." The translation "Yah(u) is strong" yields an acceptable meaning for this name. The most important contribution of this PN to our study stems from the observation that a verbal-sentence PN may contain the h.c. The main difficulty that arises from this observation is that it is sometimes impossible to distinguish verbal-sentence PNN from nominal-sentence PNN. Whenever cuneiform writings of the name are available, these may help to distinguish between verbal and nominal elements. The occurrence of the h.c. in construct phrase PNN and verbal-sentence PNN naturally leads us to consider whether this morpheme is to be found in nominal-sentence PNN. Fowler believed that the h.c. is to be found in nominal-sentence names, particularly where the theophoric element is in the initial position.[85] She admitted that a pronominal suffix may be involved in some cases. Her stance appears hypercritical and ignores the evidence for the pronominal suffix in onomastic formation.[86] In any case, it is impossible to identify the h.c. in nominal-sentence PNN, since in every instance the medial *-î* can be (re?)analyzed as a pronominal suffix. Consequently, the search for the h.c. in nominal-sentence PNN is a meaningless endeavor. My own approach is minimalist; thus I have chosen not to cite any nominal-sentence PNN as examples of the h.c.

3. *ḥizqî.*

Classification: Hebrew--tribe of Benjamin (1 Chr 8:17).

Structure: 1. nominal-sentence name (shortened), *ḥizq-* (**qitl* base) + *-î* 1st c.s. pronominal suffix.
2. verbal-sentence name (shortened), *ḥizq-* (< **ḥzq* "to be strong," 3rd m.s. Qal perfect) + *-î* h.c.

---

[85]Fowler, p. 135.

[86]Compare Hos 2:18, where Yahweh declares that the Israelites will no longer call Him Baʿali "my lord" but rather ʾishi "my man." Although this verse is not discussing onomastic practices, it does testify to the fondness of the Israelites in referring to their god with a pronominal suffix. Yet Fowler, p. 135, claimed that the intermediate *yōd* in names such as *ʾĕlîʾāb* should not be understood as a pronominal suffix! She made the same claim for the biblical PN *ʾûrîʾēl* (ibid.). In Ps. 27:1, though, the psalmist states *yhwh ʾôrî wĕyišʿî* "YHWH is my light and my salvation." In addition, this name belongs to a most pervasive structural type in the WS onomasticon, abstract noun + 1st c.s. pronominal suffix + DN. In the WS PN *id-di-ri-ia-il(DINGIR^{MEŠ})*, which Coogan (*Murašû*, pp. 32, 80) has normalized **ʿidrīʾēl* "God is my help", the scribe has indicated that the intermediate *-i-* vowel is to be understood as a pronominal suffix. It seems likely, therefore, that in other names of this structural type the intermediate *-i-* vowel is to be understood in the same fashion, barring specific evidence to the contrary.

Meaning: 1. "(DN) is my strength."
2. "(DN) is strong."

Parallels: see above, s.v. "ḥizqîyah."

Comments: It is generally recognized that this PN is shortened from the full form *ḥizqîyāh(û).* For the full discussion of that PN, one should consult the preceding entry. Thus the final *-î* vowel is the h.c. If any doubt remains, one should recall that there is no evidence for a **qitl* base noun (from the root **ḥzq*) that is productive in the West Semitic onomasticon. It appears, therefore,that the particular form of this PN may be accounted for by its development along the same lines as the PN Hizqiyah(u), with the additional step of shortening: **ḥazaqîyāh(û) > *ḥazqîyāh(û) > *ḥizqîyāh > ḥizqî.*

4. *yatnîʾēl.*

Classification: Can.--a gatekeeper, son of Meshelemyah (1 Chr 26:2).

Structure: verbal-sentence name, *yatn-* (< **ytn* II "to give," 3rd m.s. Qal perfect) + *-î-* h.c. + *-ʾēl.*

Meaning: "God/El has given."

Parallels: Ug. *ia-ta-nu, ytn* (*PTU,* p. 147); NA *ia-ta-na-e-li* (*WSB,* p. 29),[87] NA *ilu(DINGIR)-iá-ta-a-nu* (*APN,* p. 97); Ph-P. *ytnʾl* (*PNPP,* p. 329); Grk *Ἰαθάν* (Tob 5:13),[88] *Ιατουις* (Jongeling, pp. 38, 236); Latin *Iatunis* (Jongeling, p. 236).

Comments: Rudolph preferred the reading of certain LXX witnesses and reconstructed **nĕtanʾēl* as the original reading.[89] But as a *lectio difficilior* the MT form *yatnîʾēl* should be retained, because it is supported by the Vulg. *Iathanahel* and LXX B *Ἰενουηλ* [< **y(t)nwʾl*]. Noth found this name perplexing; in his name register, he wrote "das 1. Element Imperf. von *tnh* oder Perf. bezw. Nom. von *ytn* ? --In beiden

---

[87]In his "Phoenicians, Philistines, and Moabites in Mesopotamia," *BASOR* 230 (1978) 58-59, Ran Zadok classified this name as Phoenician, despite the lack of the shift **ā > *ō.* Now he classifies the name as Aramaic (private communication).

[88]Already P-E. Dion, "Deux notes épigraphiques sur Tobit," *Bib* 56 (1975) 417, compared this name to biblical *yatnîʾēl,* though he noted that Codex Sinaiticus reads *Ναθαν.*

[89]Rudolph, *Chronikbücher,* p. 170.

Fällen ist keine brauchbare Bedeutung zu finden."[90] The analysis of this name as an imperfect verbal form from the root **tnh* goes back to BDB (p. 1072), and this suggestion may be discarded as being implausible and without parallel in the Canaanite onomasticon.[91] Noth was moving in the right direction when he suggested that the first element of this PN is derived from the root **ytn*. The first element may be parsed as a 3rd m.s. Qal perfect from the root **ytn* II "to give." Note especially the NA PN *ia-ta-na-e-li* (without the h.c.), which supports the analysis of the first element as a Qal perfect[92] rather than a **qatl* base noun **yatn(u)*.[93] This NA PN also rules out the analysis of the first element as a Qal imperfect from the root **ntn*.[94]

Among Northwest Semitic languages the root **ntn* is found in Hebrew (biblical and epigraphic), Amm., Moab., and Aram.,[95] while **ytn* is productive in Ug. and Ph-P. As a generalization, this statement is true; but in light of our increasing knowledge of these languages, it may be qualified. Further, the view that **ytn* is a secondary formation from an older **ntn*[96] stands in need of correction. The more plausible view is that neither of these roots is necessarily derived from the other, but that both of them can be traced back to an original biconsonantal root **tn*,[97] which was expanded to a triconsonantal root by the addition of either *n* or *y*. In some dialects, both of these forms existed side by side, though one form predominated over the other. Here we can only

---

[90]Noth, *IPN*, p. 248.

[91]In the Qal stem, the root **tnh* is only attested once in the entire Hebrew Bible (Hos. 8:10). There is no particular reason to expect it to be found in PNN.

[92]Compare also the element **ytn* in Neo-Punic PNN (Jongeling, pp. 21, 38); the evidence for vocalization points to a 3rd m.s. of the suffix conjugation.

[93]Huffmon, *APNMT*, p. 217, cites a putative Amor. PN *ya-at-nu*, but this PN is not found in Gelb's *CAAA*, nor for that matter in Huffmon's own comprehensive list of Amor. PNN from the Mari texts in chapter two of his study! The Ug. feminine CN *ytnt* "gift" (**yat(a)natu*) and the Ph-P. feminine name *ytnt* (Benz, *PNPP*, p. 329) are attested, but the masculine counterparts appear to be lacking. Compare perhaps the biblical GN *yitnān*.

[94]This was one possibility considered by Samuel E. Loewenstamm, in *EM*, s.v. "yatnîʾēl," 3:953. Zadok, *WSB*, p. 93, has counted only one unambiguous example of an imperfect of the root **ntn* in names from first millennium Mesopotamia.

[95]For the root **ntn* in Aramaic PNN in cuneiform writing, see Zadok, *WSB*, pp. 83-84 and n. 5; F. M. Fales, "L'onomastica aramaica in età neo-assira: Raffronti tra il corpus alfabetico el il materiale cuneiforme," in *Atti del 1o Convegno Italiano sul vicino oriente antico (Roma, 22-24 Aprile 1975)*, Orientis antiqvi collectio, no. 13 (Rome: Centro per le antichità e la storia dell'arte del vicino oriente, 1978), p. 220.

[96]Among others, see Zellig S. Harris, *A Grammar of the Phoenician Language*, American Oriental Series, vol. 8 (New Haven: American Oriental Society, 1936), p. 44.

[97]On the biconsonantal root **tn*, see Andrzej Zaborski, "Biconsonantal Verbal Roots in Semitic," *Prace Jezykoznawcze* 35 (1971) 91.

survey the various pieces of evidence that point to this reconstruction.

In Eblaite occurs the PN *wa-ti-nu* (ARET II:111),[98] which undermines the view that **ytn* was a secondary formation to **ntn* in the second millennium B.C. Amorite has PNN derived from the root(s) **ntn/*ndn*.[99] The Canaanite substratum in the EA letters reflects verbal forms from **ntn* and **ytn*.[100] Despite the predominance of the verbal root **ytn* in Ph-P., on a Ph. seal occurs the PN *bʿlntn* (VSP #95). Avigad has collected other examples of the root **ntn* in Ph-P.[101] In light of this evidence for the root **ntn* in Ph-P., it no longer seems desirable to view the Ph-P. PNN *ntn* and *ntnbʿl* as writing errors for **mtn* and **mtnbʿl*.[102]

Alongside the abundant use of the root **ntn* in BH are found a few isolated vocables derived from the root **ytn*; the evidence is such as to justify the entry **ytn* II "to give" in the Hebrew lexicon.[103] The existence of the pair of roots **ntn* and **ytn* in BH is paralleled by other pairs of roots that show the same alternation in initial consonants-- **yʾw/*nʾw*, **yph/*nph*, **yṣb/*nṣb*, **yqʿ/*nqʿ*, and **yqš/*nqš*.[104] The lAram. PN *ytnʾ* may be derived from the BH root **ytn* II; at least it may be said that Silverman's derivation of this name from the homonym BH **ytn* I "to be strong, constant" does not inspire confidence.[105] Therefore, the use of the root **ytn* "to give" in the formation of Can. PNN should occasion no surprise. The development of the Can. PN *yatnîʾēl*

---

[98]On this name, see Giovanni Pettinato, "Testi cuneiformi del 3. millennio in paleo-cananeo rinvenuti nella campagna 1974 a Tell Mardīkh = Ebla," *Or* 44 (1975) 372; E. Lipiński, "Formes verbales dans les noms propres d'Ebla et système verbal sémitique," in *La lingua di Ebla: Atti del Convegno internazionale (Napoli, 22-23 aprile 1980)*, ed. Luigi Cagni, Istituto universitario orientale, Seminario di studi asiatici, Series Minor, vol. 14 (Napoli, 1981), p. 196.

[99]Gelb, *CAAA*, p. 27.

[100]Sivan, *GAGNWS*, pp. 47, 155, 255, 292.

[101]Nahman Avigad, "Two Phoenician Votive Seals," *IEJ* 16 (1966) 244-45. See also Theodor Nöldeke, "Wechsel von anlautendem *n* und *w* oder Hamza," in *Neue Beiträge zur semitischen Sprachwissenschaft* (Strassburg: Karl J. Trübner, 1910), pp. 192-93.

[102]As suggested by Benz, *PNPP*, p. 364.

[103]KB3, p. 430. For additional evidence for the root **ytn* II in BH, see Nahum M. Sarna, "*ʾytnym*, Job 12:19," *JBL* 74 (1955) 272-73; D. W. Young, "Notes on the Root *ntn* in Biblical Hebrew," *VT* 10 (1960) 457-59. Fowler (pp. 88, 134, 179, 210, 244, 294, 348) has determined the meaning of the biblical PN *yatnîʾēl* by the Arab. cognate *watana* (cognate with BH **ytn* I), but this derivation is unproven and unnecessary.

[104]These pairs are cited by Stanley Gevirtz, "Jericho and Shechem: A Religio-Literary Aspect of City Destruction," *VT* 13 (1963) 62 n. 2.

[105]Silverman, *RVJPNE*, p. 152; idem, *Or* 39 (1970) 481 and n. 1. Contrast Kornfeld, *OAA*, p. 55, and Goldberg, "Northern-Type-Names," p. 125, who relate the lAram. PN *ytnʾ* to BH **ytn* II.

appears to be similar to that of the PN Hizqiyah(u), though the *a* vowel in the first syllable was not reduced to an *i* vowel (**yatanî'ēl* > *yatnî'ēl*).

C. *Ambiguous Examples*

1. *dānîyē(')l.*

Variant spelling: *dānī'ēl* K (Ezek 14:14, 20; 28:3).

Classification: Can.--1) son of David (1 Chr 3:1);[106] 2) priest who returned with Ezra (Ezra 8:2; Neh 10:7); 3) legendary sage [Ezek 14:14; = 4) ?]; 4) hero of the book of Daniel (Dan 1:6).

Structure: 1. verbal-sentence name, *dān-* (< **dyn* "to judge," 3rd m.s. Qal perfect) + *-î(y)-* h.c. + *-ē(')l.*
2. nominal-sentence name, *dān-* (masculine singular Qal participle) + *-î(y)-* 1st c.s. pronominal suffix + *-ē(')l.*
Meaning: 1. "God/El has judged."
2. "God/El is my judge."

Parallels: Eblaite *da-na-il, da-nu-lum* (ARET I:238; III:265); *da-ne-lu* (ARET I:238); *da-nu* (ARET III:265; IV:238);[107] Amor. *da?-ni-ilu(DINGIR), dan-ilu(DINGIR)* (*CAAA*, p. 575);[108] Ug. *dn'il, dn.'il* (*PTU*, p. 96); Can. *dān*; Palm. *dny* (*PNPI*, p. 83); Saf., Tham., and Sab. *dn'l* (*PIAN*, p. 224); Nab. *dny'l* (Cantineau, 2:84).[109]

Comments: Although the form of this name as represented by the spelling *dānîyē(')l* is peculiar, it does not affect the overall inter-

[106]Dubious text; see *BHS* textual apparatus.

[107]On the root **dyn* in Eblaite, see Hans-Peter Müller, "Zum eblaitischen Konjugationssystem," VTSup 36 (1985) 212 and n. 18; idem, "Eblaitischen Verbalsystem," p. 219; Lipiński, "Formes verbales," p. 206; Lucio Milano, "Due rendiconti di metalli da Ebla," *Studi Eblaiti* 3/1-2 (1980) 16 n. g.

[108]Judging from his glossary, Gelb, *CAAA*, p. 17, appears to derive the first element of these PNN from the root **dnn* "to be strong." Those names in which the geminated *n* is expressed in writing (see *CAAA*, p. 294) should be derived from **dnn*, but this is not necessary for the PNN cited above. Huffmon, *APNMT*, p. 90, 182-83, relates Amor. *da?-ni-ilu(DINGIR)* to the root **dyn* "to judge." In his discussion of the Amor. PN *dan-ilu(DINGIR)*, Buccellati, *AURIII*, p. 140, expresses the view that if the *dan-* element is derived from **dnn*, the name is Akkadian, whereas if it is derived from the root **dyn*, the name is Amorite. This approach reflects some uncertainty as to whether the root **dnn* is genuinely Amorite. The root **dnn* has been posited for the biblical GN *dannâ* (KB3, p. 219).

[109]As Cantineau noted, Nab. *dny'l* may be a loan from Hebrew.

pretation of the name.[110] Both spellings of the name exhibit a medial *-î* vowel that can be analyzed in two different ways. Our first proposed structure/meaning analyzes the *-î* vowel as the h.c.,[111] while our second proposed structure/meaning analyzes the same writing as the 1st c.s. pronominal suffix.[112] With this particular name, either interpretation is viable; the element *dān-* is ambiguous because in II-w/y roots the 3rd m.s. Qal perfect and the m.s. Qal participle are formally identical. Further, the PNN in cuneiform writing do not seem to favor one view over the other.[113] Therefore, it is best to classify the PN Daniyʾ(e)l as an ambiguous example.

2. *ʿabdî.*

Classification: Can.--1) tribe of Levi (1 Chr 6:29); 2) individual with a foreign wife (Ezra 10:26).

Structure: 1. construct phrase name (shortened), *ʿabd-* (**qatl* base) + *-î* h.c.
2. construct phrase name (hypocoristic), *ʿabd-* (**qatl* base) + *-î* hypocoristic suffix.

Meaning: 1. and 2. "servant (of DN)."

Parallels: Amor. *ḫa-ab-di-ia, ab-di-ia* (*CAAA*, p. 89); WS *ab?-dì*, [*a*]*b?-dì* (from Emar);[114] Ug. *abdv(ÌR)-ia*, *ʿbdy* (*PTU*, pp. 105-6); WS *ab-di-ia* (*AT*, p. 125); MB *ab-di*, NA *ab-di-i/e*, N/LB *ab-di-ia*, N/LB *ab-di-iá* (*WSB*, pp. 351-52); EH *ʿbdy* (VSE ##172, 291); Ph-P. *ʿbdy* (*PNPP*, p. 371); IAram. *ʿbdy* (Kornfeld, *OAA*, p. 65); Palm. *ʿbdy* (*PNPI*, p. 102); Hat. *ʿbdy* (*PIH*, p. 139); Liḥ, Saf., Min., and Sab. *ʿbdy* (*PIAN*, p. 401); Nab. *ʿbdy* (Cantineau, 2:125); Grk *αβδαιος* (Wuthnow, p. 7). See also the compound PNN listed above, s.v. "ʿabdîʾēl," p. 122.

---

[110]This spelling probably reflects how the name was actually pronounced, perhaps as a result of the quiescence of the *ʾaleph*.

[111]So Kutscher, *Isaiah Scroll*, p. 105; Noth, *IPN*, p. 33; Montgomery, *Books of Kings*, p. 128.

[112]See BDB, p. 193. One may compare the EA PN *ši-ip-ṭì-baʿlu(dIM)* (Hess, *AmPN*, pp. 234-35), which may be translated "Baʿlu is my judgment."

[113]The writing *da-na-* is probably a finite verbal form (G stem), but the same cannot be said for the writing *da-ni-*, which exhibits the same ambiguity in cuneiform writing as does the Can. PN Daniye(ʾ)l.

[114]Huehnergard, *RA* 77 (1983) 22-23 (text 4, seal on reverse and l. 30).

Comments: The PN ʿAbdi may be a shortened name from a fuller form such as ʿAbdiʾel, or it could be a hypocoristicon related to a hypocoristic name such as the ʿAbdiya attested in cuneiform writing. In the first case, the *-î* is the h.c., while in the second, the *-î* is a hypocoristic suffix. Either analysis is equally plausible and has sufficient parallels; therefore the PN ʿAbdi constitutes an ambiguous example.

D. *Dubious Examples*

1. *gabrîʾēl.*

Classification: Can.--an angel in the book of Daniel (Dan 8:16).

Structure: 1. construct phrase name, *gabr-* (**qatl* base) + *-î-* h.c. + *ʾēl.*
2. verbal-sentence name, *gabr-* (< **gbr* "to be strong," 3rd m.s. Qal perfect) + *-î-* h.c. + *-ʾēl.*
3. nominal-sentence name, *gabr-* (**qatl* base) + *-î-* 1st c.s. pronominal suffix + *-ʾēl.*

Meaning: 1. "man of god/El."
2. "God/El has shown himself strong."
3. "God/El is my strong one."

Parallels: WS PNN in NA and N/LB texts:
1. with **qatl* base: NA *gab-ri-ilu(DINGIR)*, N/LB GN *gab-ri-il-lu*, N/LB *gab-ru-ú*, NA *gab-ri-i*, NB *gab-ri-ia*, N/LB *gab-ri-iá* (*WSB*, p. 368); N/LB *abi(AD)-gab-ra* (*WSB*, p. 352); N/LB *adad(dIM)-gab-ri* (*WSB*, p. 353); NA *ilu(DINGIR)-gab-ri*, N/LB *ilu(DINGIR^MEŠ)-gab-ri* (*WSB*, p. 377); NA *na-áš-gab-ri* (*WSB*, p. 383); NA *qa-uš-gab-ri* (*WSB*, p. 388);
2. with **qattāl* base: NA *ga-ab-bar*, *ga-ab-ba-ru*, *gab-ba-ri*, *gab-bar(?)-ru*, *gab-ba-ru* (*APN*, p. 78);[115] N/LB GN *gab-bar-ri* (*WSB*, p. 368); NA *se-ʾ-gab-ba-ri* (*WSB*, p. 392);
3. other writings: N/LB appellative *ga-ba-ri-e* (*WSB*, p. 368); NA *ga-ba-ri* (*APN*, p. 78); N/LB *ga-ba-ri-adad(dIM)*;[116] N/LB *ilu(DINGIR^MEŠ)-ga-bar*, *ilu(DINGIR^MEŠ)-ga-ba-ri* (*WSB*, p. 377);

---

[115]This series of NA PNN is cited from Tallqvist, because he lists each individual spelling separately. See also Zadok, *WSB*, p. 368, who cites them as NA *gab/ga-ab-bar/ba-ru.*

[116]Ran Zadok, *BO* 41 (1984) 38.

NA *ilu(DINGIR)-gab-bi-ri* (*WSB*, p. 377);[117]

Can. *geber*; EH *gbrmgn*;[118] Edom. *qwsg[br]*, *qws⸢g⸣br* (Israel, *RivB* 27:172, 177), *qwsgbr* (*SPARI*, pp. 98, 207-8); OAram. *śʾgbr* (*KAI* 226:1); Aram. *gbrd* (*SPARI*, pp. 74, 147), *gibbār* (Ezra 2:20); Christian Pal. Aram. *gbryl* (*ATTM*, p. 731); Ḥat. *gbrhdd*;[119] Grk *γαβριηλιος* (Wuthnow, p. 38).

Comments: Although the Can. PN Gabriʾel is attested in the Hebrew Bible as the name of an angel, the occurrence of the same name in cuneiform texts and in a Christian Palestinian Aramaic papyrus leaves no doubt that it is a personal name. Noth pointed out that the names of other angels that are found in later Jewish literature, such as Michael, Raphael, and Uriel, are also attested as personal names.[120]

Gesenius and Joüon analyzed the BH PN Gabriʾel as a construct phrase PN containing the h.c.[121] This interpretation of the name is the most popular of the three analyses.[122] Accordingly, the first element *gabr-* would refer to the name bearer, and this PN would find a semantic and structural parallel in PNN in which the first element is **mut-* or *ʾîš* "man." If this PN is actually a construct phrase name, one would not expect to find another compound name in which the same elements appear in reverse order.[123] For example, the Can. PN *ʿabdîʾēl* "servant of god/El" is a construct phrase name, and the transposed form of this name, **ʾēlîʿebed*, is not attested in any Semitic language. Yet the NA PN *ilu(DINGIR)-gab-ri* and the N/LB PN *ilu(DINGIR^{MEŠ})-gab-ri* are composed of the exact same name elements as the BH PN Gabriʾel, but in reverse order; therefore, these names may be nominal- or verbal-sentence PNN, in which the elements can reverse order, but none of them can be construct phrase PNN. A second argument against the first structure/meaning is that the vocables **gabbār* and

---

[117]The unique writing *gab-bi-ri* may reflect a **qattīl* base adjective (Zadok, *WSB*, p. 103).

[118]I. Beit-Arieh, "Tel ʿIra--A Fortified City of the Kingdom of Judah," *Qadmoniot* 18/1-2 (1985) 24.

[119]Vattioni, *Le iscrizioni di Ḥatra*, p. 68 (text #177, l. 1). This name is not found in Abbadi, *PIH*.

[120]Noth, *IPN*, p. 190 n. 1.

[121]GKC §81d, 90l; Joüon, §93m.

[122]BDB, p. 150; KB3, p. 169; Bauer, *Ostkanaanäer*, p. 66; Fowler, pp. 115, 339 ("difficult form, probably construct"); Lewy, *Forschungen*, p. 63 n. 2; Nöldeke, *EB* 3:3277; Barth, *ZDMG* 53 (1899) 597; Zorell, *Lexicon Hebraicum*, p. 141; Edward J. Young, *The Prophecy of Daniel* (Grand Rapids: William B. Eerdmans, 1949), p. 176.

[123]Huffmon, *APNMT*, p. 123 n. 26, recognizes the utility of this argument in distinguishing construct phrase PNN in Amorite.

**gabr*, assuming they are nominal forms, appear to function in PNN as divine epithets.[124]

It is still possible to analyze the medial *-î* as the h.c., if one accepts Noth's interpretation (= second structure/meaning) of the first element as a Qal perfect verbal form.[125] The PN Gabriʾel would have undergone a development similar to that of the PN Hizqiyah(u), except that the *a* vowel in the first syllable did not reduce to *i* (**gabarîʾēl* > *gabrîʾēl*). This interpretation may be considered plausible if cuneiform writings of the type **ga-ba-ri-* in first position are attested, and if a strong case can be made for interpreting the writing **ga-ba-ri* as a Qal perfect verbal form + h.c. In the parallels section, the WS PNN in NA and N/LB texts have been grouped according to orthography. Most of the names reflect either a **qatl* or a **qattāl* base nominal form from the root **gbr* (see above, 1. and 2.). The difference in meaning between these two forms does not concern us and does not affect the analyses of the names proposed here; it suffices to say that the **qattāl* base, with the doubling of the middle radical, is considered to be an intensive form (BL §61jg).[126] Note also that the writing of the **gbr* element with a final *-i* vowel is frequent.[127] Whereas in some of the writings this *-i* vowel was not pronounced and is thus morphologically meaningless,[128] in other cases it may be interpreted as marking the 1st c.s. pronominal suffix. In general, all of these names appear to be nominal-sentence PNN,[129] with both elements preserved, shortened, or shortened with the addition of a hypocoristic suffix.

The cuneiform writings subsumed under 3. have to be considered. The first element of the N/LB PN *ga-ba-ri-adad(dIM)* could

---

[124]Compare here such phrases as OAram. *hdd gbr* in the Tell Fakhariyeh inscription (Aramaic text, l. 12), and BH *ʾēl gibbôr* in the Messianic titulary of Isa 9:5-6.

[125]Noth, *IPN*, pp. 36, 190. Joyce G. Baldwin, *Daniel: An Introduction and Commentary*, Tyndale Old Testament Commentaries (n.p.: Inter-Varsity, 1978), p. 158, also holds this view.

[126]Merely as a convention to distinguish **gabr* from **gabbār*, I have adopted the translations "strong one" and "hero" respectively.

[127]Contrast N/LB *abi(AD)-gab-ra*. In N/LB PN *gab-ru-ú*, the *-u* ending may be related to the fact that the individual who bore this name was Arabian (Zadok, *WSB*, p. 229).

[128]Especially in the N/LB PN *ilu(DINGIR^{MEŠ})-ga-ba-ri*, which varies freely with the N/LB *ilu(DINGIR^{MEŠ})-ga-bar*, both names being borne by the same individual. For discussion and other examples, see Coogan, *Murašû*, p. 96-97; and pp. 151-52 below.

[129]Zadok, *WSB*, pp. 80-81, recognizes those names of the type DN + *gabr* as nominal-sentence PNN. He appears to prefer to interpret some of the other names as of the verbal-sentence type. In the Aram. PN *gbrd*, Maraqten, *SPARI*, p. 147, analyzes *gbr* as a nominal element, but he fails to reflect this analysis in his translation "*Haddu ist stark."

very well be analyzed as a Qal perfect verbal form, analogous to the cuneiform writing *ḫa-za-qi-*. However, geminated consonants are not necessarily expressed in cuneiform writing, and the **qattāl* base nominal form is productive in WS PNN in NA and N/LB texts (see 2. above). We suggest, therefore, that the N/LB PN *ga-ba-ri-adad(dIM)* should be normalized **gabbārī-Adad*, as a nominal-sentence name meaning "Adad is my hero." Two bits of evidence lend support to this interpretation. First, the N/LB *ga-ba-ri-e* is an appellative, and thus it should be normalized as a **qattāl* base nominal form. Second, and more important, the NA PN *ga-ba-ri*, which occurs in the monolith inscription of Shalmaneser III, is elsewhere attested in the same inscription in the writing *gab-ba-ri* (**qattāl* base).[130] This leaves only the N/LB PNN *ilu(DINGIR^{MEŠ})-ga-bar* and *ilu(DINGIR^{MEŠ})-ga-ba-ri* unexplained. The final elements of these names may also be analyzed as a **qattāl* base nouns. Even if they are Qal perfect verbal forms, their significance is overshadowed by the predominance of nominal-sentence type PNN. To sum up, these two names do not provide sufficient reason for interpreting the Can. PN Gabriʾel as a verbal-sentence name.

Therefore, the most plausible interpretation of the BH PN Gabriʾel is as a nominal-sentence name (= third structure/meaning), meaning "God/El is my strong one." This name finds an exact parallel in the NA PN *gab-ri-ilu(DINGIR)* and the N/LB GN *gab-ri-il-lu*; in these names, the cuneiform writing of the first element indicates the same **qatl* base noun as in the Can. PN Gabriʾel. In the works consulted for this study, Albright is the only modern scholar who analyzed the name Gabriʾel as a nominal-sentence PN, having translated it "God is my champion."[131]

2. *ḥannîʾēl.*

Classification: Can.--1) tribe of Manasseh (Num 34:23); 2) tribe of Asher (1 Chr 7:39).

Structure: 1. construct phrase name, *ḥann-* (**qall* base) + *-î-* h.c. + *ʾēl.*
2. verbal-sentence name, *ḥann-* (< **ḥnn* "to show favor," 3rd m.s. Qal perfect) + *-î-* h.c. + *-ʾēl.*
3. nominal-sentence name, *ḥann-* (**qall* base) + *-î-* 1st c.s. pronominal suffix + *-ʾēl.*

130For references, see Tallqvist, *APN*, p. 78.
131Albright, *JBL* 54 (1935) 193 n. 66.

<u>Meaning</u>: 1. "favor of god/El."
2. "God/El has favored."
3. "God/El is my favor."

<u>Parallels</u>: Amor. *an-na-ilu(DINGIR)*, *an-ni-ilu(DINGIR)*, *ḫa-an-ni-ilu(DINGIR)*, *ḫa-an-ni-i-la*, *ḫi-in-ne-ilu(DINGIR)* (*CAAA*, p. 251); Ug. *ḥnʾil* (*PTU*, p. 136); N/LB ^{f}*ḫa-an-na-ʾ*, *ḫa-an-na-a*, ^{f}*ḫa-an-na-a*, *ḫa-an-ni-iá*, *ḫa-an-ni-ia-ʾ* (*WSB*, p. 370); N/LB *ḫi-in-ni-ilu(DINGIR*^{MEŠ}*)*, N/LB *ḫi-in-ni-ʾ-bel(*^{d}*EN)*, N/LB ^{f}*ḫi-in-ni-be-el*, NA *ḫi-(in-)ni*, N/LB *ḫi-in-ni-ia*, N/LB ^{f}*ḫi-in-ni-ia* (*WSB*, p. 373); NA GN *ilu(DINGIR*^{MEŠ}*)-ḫi-ni* (*WSB*, p. 377); Can. *ḥannâ*, *ḥēnādād* (< **ḥēn-hădad*);[132] EH *ḥnʾ* (SO 30.3), *ḥnh* (VSE #351), *ḥnyhw* (VSE #359a), ⸢*ḥ*⸣*nml*⸢*k*⸣ (Shiloh, *IEJ* 36:29); Ph-P. *ḥnbʿl*, *ḥnwʾl*, *bʿlḥn*, *bʿlḥnʾ* (*PNPP*, p. 314); Neo-Punic *ḥnʾ*, *ḥnbʿl* (Jongeling, p. 168); IAram. *ḥnyh* (*OAA*, p. 50), *ḥnʾ* (*SPARI*, pp. 81, 166); Palm. *ḥnbl* (*PNPI*, p. 89); Ḥat. *ḥnšmš* (*PIH*, pp. 111-12); Saf. and Tham. *ḥnʾl* (*PIAN*, p. 205); Nab. *ḥnʾl* (Cantineau, 2:98); Grk *αννηλος*, *ανηλος* (Wuthnow, p. 142).[133]

<u>Comments:</u> Along with the Can. PNN Gabriʾel (see above) and Malki-sedeq (pp. 139-40), Gesenius and Joüon cited the Can. PN Hanniʾel as a clear example of a construct phrase PN containing the h.c.[134] These Hebrew grammarians also propose a similar interpretation for the Ph-P. PN *ḥnbʿl*, of which the transliterations in Greek and Latin sources show an intervening *-i* vowel, or even an *-o* vowel, between the two elements of the name.[135] But since the order of the name elements can reverse, it is unlikely that the Ph-P. PN *ḥnbʿl*, or for that matter the Can. PN *ḥannîʾēl*, are actually construct phrase PNN. From the Ph-P. onomasticon one may cite three pairs of PNN, in which the name elements reverse order: *ḥnbʿl/bʿlḥn*, *ḥnmlqrt/mlqrtḥn*, and *ḥnʿštr/ʿštrḥn* (*PNPP*, p. 314). Another pair of names exhibiting the same alternation are the EH *ḥnyhw* and the IAram. *yhwḥn*. This reversal in the order of the name elements favors the interpretation of

---

[132]Compare this name to the Amor. PNN *an-na-adad(*^{d}*IM)*, *ḫa-an-na-adad(*^{d}*IM)*, and *in-ni-adad(*^{d}*IM)* (Gelb, *CAAA*, p. 251).

[133]The citation of Greek and Latin transliterations of the element **ḥann-* could be greatly multiplied. For a sampling, see Benz, *PNPP*, pp. 314-15; Vattioni, *Annali del Seminario di studi del mondo classico, Istituto Universitario Orientale, Sezione di archeologia e storia antica* 1 (1979) 163-64.

[134]GKC §90l; Joüon, §93m. This interpretation is also found in BDB, p. 337; Hunsberger, p. 267; Nöldeke, *EB* 3:3277. Also Fowler, pp. 120, 345, classified *ḥannîʾēl* as a construct form name.

[135]Ibid.; likewise, Nöldeke, *EB* 3:3277. For the relevant transliterations, see Benz, *PNPP*, pp. 314-15; Jongeling, pp. 33, 226.

this PN as either a nominal- or verbal-sentence name, but not as a construct phrase name.

According to our second proposed structure/meaning, the PN Hanniʾel is a verbal-sentence name meaning "God has favored," and the connecting *-î* vowel is the h.c.[136] If the first element of this name is a verb derived from the root **ḥnn*, one would expect it to be written as a triradical form (cf. Can. PNN *ḥănanʾēl* and *ʾelḥānān*). Noth sought to avoid this difficulty by positing a perfect verbal form **ḥann-* as a biform for *ḥānan*.[137] This is a possible interpretation, but unlikely in this particular case. First, while some geminate verbs take the form $*C_1vC_2(C_3)$ in the 3rd m.s., this development is primarily characteristic of intransitive verbs.[138] The root **ḥnn* is a transitive verb,[139] and throughout the WS onomasticon, there is ample evidence that this verb takes a triradical form.[140] Second, and more importantly, cuneiform writings suggest that **ḥann* is a **qall* base noun. In Amorite, the nominal forms **ḥannu(m)*, **ḥinnu(m)*, and **ḥunnu(m)* are productive in PNN.[141] For WS PNN in NA and N/LB texts, the nominal forms **ḥann* and **ḥinn* are common, and there is even evidence for a nominal form **ḥunn*.[142] Since names are formed indiscriminately with **qall*, **qill*, and **qull* bases from the root **ḥnn*, and since **ḥinn* and **ḥunn* are best analyzed as nominal forms, it follows that **ḥann* should also be a nominal form.

The existence of a **qall* base noun from the root **ḥnn* in Amorite and in WS PNN in cuneiform writing points toward the analysis of the first element of the Can. PN Hanniʾel as a noun (third structure/-meaning). This **qall* base noun is preserved only in the Can. PNN Hanniʾel and Hannah, in contrast to the widely attested BH CN *ḥēn*

136Noth, *IPN*, pp. 35, 187 nn. 3-4.

137Ibid., p. 187 nn. 3-4.

138GKC §67a. Fowler, p. 82 (bottom), 111-12, is unaware of this principle and on p. 112, she even cites some names that are not clearly from geminate roots.

139The active participle *ḥônēn*, attested in BH, points to the transitive nature of the verb. Fowler, p. 80, errs in listing **ḥnn* as a stative verb. For a stative geminate verb in the Hebrew onomasticon, note the BH PN *yôtām* "Yo is perfect" (< **tmm*).

140Compare the following PNN: Amor. *ḫa-na-an-na* (*CAAA*, p. 250); Ug. *ḥnnʾil* (*PTU*, p. 136); N/LB *ḫa-na-na-ʾ* (*WSB*, p. 371); Can. *ḥănanʾēl*; EH *ḥnn* (VSE #49; A 38.6; S 43.2, 45.2, 46.2, 47.1; Avigad, *Hebrew Bullae* ##63, 64), *ḥnnyh* (VSE #23), *ḥnnyhw* (VSE ##24, 25, 50; A 3.3, 16.1); Amm. *ḥnnʾl* (*ALIA*, p. 85); Ph-P. *ḥnn* (*PNPP*, p. 314); IAram. *ḥnnyh* (*RVJPNE*, p. 147); Saf. *ḥnnʾl* (*PIAN*, p. 206).

141Gelb, *CAAA*, pp. 20, 250-51. Huffmon, *APNMT*, pp. 88, 90, and 200, distinguishes **ḫanna*, a verbal form with the *-a* vowel of the perfect, from **ḫanni*, nominal form + pronominal suffix. In some of the names he cites, the *-a* vowel may be attributed to *sandhi* writing rather than indicating a verbal form (e.g., Amor. *an-na-a-ḫi-im* [*APNMT*, p. 200]).

142See names cited above in parallels section and Zadok, *WSB*, pp. 98, 145-46.

(*qill base). The N/LB PN *ḫi-in-ni-ilu(DINGIR^{MEŠ})* differs from the BH PN Hanniʾel only with respect to the base of the first element (*qill versus *qall). With the elements in reverse order, note the NA GN *ilu(DINGIR^{MEŠ})-ḫi-ni*. Zadok interprets these names as nominal-sentence names, meaning "God/El is my favor."[143] Friedrich has argued persuasively that the Ph.-P. PN *ḥnbʿl* is best analyzed as a nominal-sentence name, and should be translated "meine Gnade ist Baal."[144] As with the PN Gabriʾel, Albright correctly interpreted the BH PN Hanniʾel as a nominal-sentence PN meaning "My grace is El."[145] Hence the medial *-î* in the PN Hanniʾel is best understood as a pronominal suffix.[146]

3. *yĕqûtîʾēl.*

Classification: Can. ?--tribe of Judah (1 Chr 4:18).

Structure: 1. verbal-sentence name, *yĕqût-* (< *qwt "nourish" [cf. MLArab. *qāta*, Wehr, p. 930], 3rd m.s. Qal imperfect) + *-î-* h.c. + *-ʾēl.*
2. nominal-sentence name, *yĕqût-* (nominal form, < *yqh "to protect" [cf. MLArab. *waqā*, Wehr, p. 1282] + *-ût* abstract ending) + *-î-* 1st c.s. pronominal suffix + *ʾēl.*

Meaning: 1. "God/El will nourish."
2. God/El is my protection."

143Zadok, *WSB*, pp. 98, 373, 377. See also Coogan, *Murašû*, p. 74, who maintains that names with the element *ḥinn-* are nominal-sentence names.

144Johannes Friedrich, "Zum Phönizisch-Punischen," *ZS* 2 (1924) 10. According to his view, the transliterations with the medial *-i* or *-o* vowel would represent the 1st and 3rd person singular pronominal suffixes respectively. He also cited in this respect the Punic PN *bʿlḥnʾ*, in which the final *ʾaleph* may represent the 3rd m.s. pronominal suffix. Jongeling, pp. 32 and n. 38, 33, arrives at similar conclusions. On 3rd person singular pronominal suffixes in WS PNN, see also p. 84 n. 218.

145Albright, *JBL* 54 (1935) 193 n. 66. See also Porten, *Archives*, p. 137, who analyzes the second element of the IAram. PN *yhwḥn* as a nominal element, translating "Yah is grace/favor."

146If the line of argument in this section is valid, then the pairs of forms *ḥn + DN/*ḥnn + DN attested in Ug. (*PTU*, p. 136), BH, Ph-P. (*PNPP*, p. 314), IAram. (*OAA*, p. 53: *yhwḥn/yhwḥnn*, here with the order of the elements reversed), and Saf. (*PIAN*, pp. 205-6) exhibit an opposition nominal-/verbal-sentence PNN. Also the hypocoristic name *ḥnʾ* attested in EH (SO 30.3), IAram. (*OAA*, p. 50), and Palm. (*PNPI*, p. 89) would be a hypocoristicon of a nominal-sentence name, rather than as generally supposed, a hypocoristicon of a verbal-sentence name. In the Punic and Neo-Punic PN *ḥnʾ* (*PNPP*, p. 314; Jongeling, p. 168), the final *ʾaleph* could be either a hypocoristic suffix or a 3rd m.s. pronominal suffix.

Parallels: NA *ab(AD)-ia-qa* (*WSB*, pp. 88-89).

Comments: According to Noth (= first structure/meaning), the first element of the PN Yequti'el is an imperfect verbal form, derived from a root cognate with Arab. *qāta*, and the medial *-î-* vowel is the h.c.[147] Although this interpretation is possible, another interpretation is slightly to be preferred. The first element of the name has the form of a noun derived from a III-weak root + *-ût* abstract ending,[148] to which the 1st c.s. suffix is attached. The WS root **yqy* "to protect"[149] provides a suitable meaning, "God/El is my protection." The concept of God's protection of the name bearer finds numerous parallels in the WS onomasticon.[150]

4. *yĕśîmī'ēl.*

Classification: Can.--tribe of Simeon (1 Chr 4:36).

Structure: verbal-sentence name, *yĕśîm-* (< **św/ym*, "to set, establish," 3rd m.s. Qal imperfect) + *-ī-* h.c. + *-'ēl.*

Meaning: "God/El will establish."

Parallels: Amor. *ia-si-im-ilu(DINGIR)* (*CAAA*, p. 180); NA *ia-si-me/mì-'-ilu(DINGIR)* (*WSB*, p. 375); N/LB *ilu(DINGIR)-iá-ší-im-m*[*u*] (*WSB*, p. 377).

Comments: This name has been classified as a dubious example because there seems to be some question as to the correct vocalization of the name.[151] In contrast to other instances of the h.c., only in the PN Yasim(i?)'el is the putative h.c. written defectively. When one adds that in manuscripts punctuated according to the Babylonian tradition, the name is written *yĕśîm'ēl*, without any connecting vowel at all, suspicion is cast on the form of the name with the *-ī* connecting vowel.

[147]Noth, *IPN*, pp. 36, 203. This view is also found in KB2, p. 398; KB3, p. 411; Fowler, p. 99, 359; Barr, *Comparative Philology*, p. 182.

[148]For this derivation, see BDB, p. 429 (their preference for a construct phrase PN is to be rejected); Svi Rin and Shifra Rin, "Ugaritic-Old Testament Affinities," *BZ*, n.f., 11 (1967) 175. On nominal formations of this type, see BL §61*α*; and Andreas Eberharter, "Zu den hebräischen Nomina auf *ût*," *BZ* 9 (1911) 113-19, esp. p. 119, where four (other) nomina propria with this ending are listed.

[149]For this root, see KB3, p. 411; *UT* §19.11.43.

[150]Fowler, pp. 75, 286-87.

[151]Noth, *IPN*, p. 36, and Kutscher, *Isaiah Scroll*, p. 105, cite this name as an example of the h.c.

LXX transliterations of this name are so corrupt as to provide no help in determining the reading of this name. The uncertainty over the reading of this name disqualify it from further consideration as an example of the h.c.

5. *malkî-ṣedeq.*

Classification: Can.--Canaanite king of Salem (Gen 14:18).

Structure: 1. construct phrase name, *malk-* (**qatl* base, BL §61r')[152] + *-î-* h.c. + *-ṣedeq* (**qitl* base).
2. nominal-sentence name, *malk-* (**qatl* base) + *-î-* 1st c.s. pronominal suffix + *-ṣedeq* (**qitl* base).

Meaning: 1. "king of righteousness."
2. a. "My king is righteousness"; or b. "My king is Ṣedeq (DN)."

Parallels: Ph-P. *ṣdqmlk* (*PNPP*, p. 345).

Comments: This name occurs twice in the Hebrew Bible (Gen 14:18; Ps 110:4), and in both instances the two main elements are joined by a *maqqeph*. This contrasts with the writing of the name as one word in the Genesis Apocryphon (col. 22, l. 14).[153] Gesenius and Joüon cite the PN Malki-sedeq as a classic example of the h.c.[154] It may be that they, as well as others, were led astray by the popular etymology of the name found in the New Testament book of Hebrews (7:2). The writer

---

[152]The *a* vowel suggests that **malk-* is the CN "king"; compare the PNN *malkîʾēl, malkîyāh(û), malkîrām, malkîšûaʿ*, and *malkām*. On the element **mlk* in biblical PNN, see George C. Heider, *The Cult of Molek: A Reassessment*, Journal for the Study of the Old Testament, Supplement Series 43 (Sheffield: JSOT, 1985), pp. 229-31, who apparently analyzes the *-î* in the PN Malki-sedeq as the pronominal suffix. This analysis precludes the interpretation of the first element of this PN as a DN. Even the vocalization **milk-*, which some have reconstructed on the basis of the LXX, may be interpreted as pointing to a CN (see Tigay, p. 77 n. 18).

[153]Joseph A. Fitzmyer, *The Genesis Apocryphon of Qumran Cave 1: A Commentary*, 2d, rev. ed., Biblica et orientalia, no. 18a (Rome: Biblical Institute Press, 1971), pp. 72-73, 174. In his "'Now this Melchizedek . . .' (Heb. 7,1)," *CBQ* 25 (1963) 312-13, Fitzmyer conjectures that this writing may reflect the period before the popular etymology (= first structure/meaning) had set in.

[154]GKC §90l; Joüon, §93m. See also Lewy, *Forschungen*, p. 63 n. 2; Nöldeke, *EB* 3:3277. William F. Albright, "A Revision of Early Hebrew Chronology," *JPOS* 1 (1920-21) 69 n. 2, also analyzed the medial *-î* vowel as the h.c., translating the name by "legitimate king." In a later article (*JBL* 54 (1935) 193 n. 66), he changed his view and analyzed the medial *-î-* vowel as a pronominal suffix (= structure/-meaning 2.b.).

of Hebrews was influenced by the current popular etymology prevalent in first century Jewish tradition,[155] and it suited his purposes well. The modern philologist, on the other hand, seeks to penetrate behind the popular etymology and determine the original meaning of the name. Our first proposed structure/meaning appears to be a popular etymology, and it is without clear parallel within the Canaanite onomasticon. The Ph.-P. PN *ṣdqmlk* apparently has the same elements in reverse order; if this be the case, then both names must be sentence type names.

On the basis of other Canaanite PNN with the element *malkî-* in first position,[156] our second proposed structure/meaning is the more plausible interpretation of the name. In this name, however, it is difficult to decide whether the second element, *ṣedeq*, is a CN "righteousness" or a DN Ṣedeq. If the BH PN *malkîyāh(û)*, with a DN in second position, is structurally parallel, then one may assume that *ṣedeq* is a DN in the PN Malki-sedeq.[157] The Can. PN *ʾădōnî-ṣedeq* and the Ug. PN *ʾadnṣdq* (*PTU*, p. 90) may be structurally similar and may be translated "My lord is Ṣedeq." Moreover, the fact that Adoni-sedeq was also a king of Jerusalem may suggest that both he and his predecessor, Malki-sedeq, officially worshipped the deity Ṣedeq. However, it is not possible to exclude the meaning of *ṣedeq* as a CN, functioning as a divine epithet, in these names. However that may be, the medial *-î* vowel in the PN Malki-sedeq is best analyzed as a pronominal suffix rather than the h.c.

6. *ṣidqîyāh*.

Variant spelling: *ṣidqîyāhû*.

Classification: Hebrew--1) last king of Judah (2 Kgs 24:17); 2) false prophets, under Ahab (1 Kgs 22:24) and Jeremiah (Jer 21:29); 3) son

---

[155]Fitzmyer, *CBQ* 25 (1963) 312-13.

[156]See p. 139 n. 152.

[157]So BDB, p. 575; BL §65g (but see the reservations expressed in Nachträge und Verbesserungen [Schluß], s.v. p. 524g); Cross, *Canaanite Myth and Hebrew Epic*, p. 209; M. Delcor, "Melchizedek from Genesis to the Qumran Texts and the Epistle to the Hebrews," *JSJ* 2 (1971) 115-16; Roy A. Rosenberg, "The God Ṣedeq," *HUCA* 36 (1965) 161-77; Skinner, pp. 267-68. For the deity *Ṣdq* at Ugarit, see M. C. Astour, "Some New Divine Names from Ugarit," *JAOS* 86 (1966) 282-83; Gröndahl, *PTU*, p. 187. Note also the IAram. PN *ʿbdṣdq* "servant of Ṣdq," published by Javier Teixidor, "Un nouveau papyrus araméen du règne de Darius II," *Syria* 41 (1964) 285-90, and the Ḥad. PNN *ṣdqḏkr* and *ṣdqydʿ*, and the Min. PN *ṣdqyfʿ* (*PIAN*, pp. 369-70).

of Hananiah (Jer 36:12); 4) priest under Nehemiah (Neh 10:2); 5) son of Jehoiakim (1 Chr 3:16).

Structure: 1. verbal-sentence name, *ṣidq-* (< **ṣdq* "to be righteous," 3rd m.s. Qal perfect) + *-î-* h.c. + *-yāh(û).*
2. nominal-sentence name, *ṣidq-* (**qitl* base) + *-î-* 1st c.s. pronominal suffix + *-yāh(û).*

Meaning: 1. "Yah(u) is righteous."
2. "Yah(u) is my righteousness."

Parallels: Amor. *zi-id-qa-addu(dIM), ì-lí-zi-id-qi* (*CAAA*, p. 365); Ug. *ʾilṣdq, ṣdqʾil* (*PTU*, pp. 96, 187); NA *ṣi-id-qí-ilu(DINGIR)*, Saf., Ḥad., Min., Qat., and Sab. *ṣdqʾl* (*PIAN*, p. 369).

Comments: Baudissin conjectured that the first element of the PN Sidqiyah(u) is a verbal form.[158] Kutscher seemed to favor this view too.[159] In the discussion of the PN Hizqiyahu, we already have an exact parallel to the transformation in vocalization that a PN may undergo as a result of the h.c. increasing the number of short vowels before the tone syllable. The process may be reconstructed as follows: **ṣadaqîyāh(û)* > **ṣadqîyāh(û)* > *ṣidqîyāh(û).* Further support for this analysis comes from the BH PNN *yĕhôṣādāq* and *yôṣādāq.* The second element in these two names is a Qal perfect verbal form,[160] and they may be the same name as the PN Sidqiyah(u), except for the transposition of the name elements.

158W. W. G. Baudissin, *Kyrios als Gottesname*, 3:404; idem, *Adonis und Esmun: Eine Untersuchung zur Geschichte des Glaubens an Auferstehungsgötter und an Heilgötter* (Leipzig: J. C. Hinrichs, 1911), p. 247 n. 1; idem, "Der gerechte Gott in altsemitischer Religion," in *Festgabe von Fachgenossen und Freunden: A. von Harnack zum siebzigsten Geburtstag dargebracht* (Tübingen: J. C. B. Mohr [Paul Siebeck], 1921), p. 5.

159Kutscher, *Isaiah Scroll*, p. 105. Noth, *IPN*, p. 36, describes Baudissin's interpretation as "nicht als ganz unmöglich."

160Fitzmyer, *CBQ* 25 (1963) 312 n. 30, analyzes the second element of both of these names as a **qatal* base adjective. But according to the Hebrew lexicon, there is no **qatal* base adjective from the root **ṣdq.* If the second element were adjectival, one would expect *ṣaddîq* or *ṣādō/ôq.* Johann J. Stamm, "Der Name Zedekia," in *De la Tôrah au Messie. Études d'exégèse et d'herméneutique bibliques offertes à Henri Cazelles pour ses 25 années d'enseignement à l'Institut Catholique de Paris*, eds. Maurice Carrez, Joseph Doré, and Pierre Grelot (Paris: Desclée, 1981), p. 231, not only recognizes that these forms are Qal perfects, as does Gröndahl (*PTU*, p. 187), but he suggests that the Qal is being used in the sense of the Hiphil (see also KB3, p. 379).

While at first glance our first proposed structure/meaning appears to be the correct analysis of the name, this view will not hold up under close scrutiny. The basic flaw is that the argument from the analogy of the PN Hizqiyah(u) is not valid for this name. The linchpin in the analysis of the PN Hizqiyah(u) was cuneiform writings of the type *ḫa-za-qi-*. It is also true that the evidence for a **qitl* base noun from the root **ḥzq* is very slight. The situation is just the opposite with the PN Sidqiyahu; the absence of any cuneiform writings of the type **ṣa-da-qi-* may be coupled with the abundant evidence in PNN for a **qitl* base noun from the root **ṣdq*.[161] In light of the widespread evidence for a nominal form **ṣidq(u)*, the analysis of the first element of the PN Sidqiyah(u) as a verbal form becomes gratuitous.

The PN Sidqiyah(u) finds a structural parallel in the NA PN *ṣi-id-qí-ilu(DINGIR)* "God/El is my righteousness," and with the elements reversed, the Amor. PN *ì-lí-zi-id-qi* "My god is my righteousness." Stamm classifies PNN of the type "DN is my _____" as confidence or trust names;[162] accordingly, the PN Sidqiyah(u) is seen to belong to a common structural type. Finally, the thought contained in this name also finds expression in such passages as Ps 4:2, Jer 23:6, and 33:16. Therefore, our second proposed structure/meaning is the more plausible analysis of the name.[163]

E. *Non-Canaanite Examples*

1. Probable Example

1. *zabdîʾēl.*

Classification: Aram.[164]--1) father of one of David's officers (1 Chr 27:2); 2) overseer in Nehemiah's time (Neh 11:17).

---

[161]On **qitl* base nouns from the root **ṣdq*, see Gelb, *CAAA*, pp. 34 (*ṣidqum* "justice"), 365; Huffmon, *APNMT*, pp. 256-57; the Ug. PN *ṣi-id-qa-nu* (*PTU*, p. 187); the WS PN *rabi(GAL)-ṣí-id-qí* (*AmPN*, p. 116); the NA PN *ṣi-id-qa-a* (*WSB*, p. 394); the N/LB PN *zi-id-qí* (*WSB*, p. 116); and the names cited above in the parallels section.

[162]Stamm, "Der Name Zedekia," p. 233.

[163]As argued by Stamm, "Der Name Zedekia," pp. 227-35. For other suggestions, see Lewy, *Forschungen*, p. 63 ("Getreuer Jhwhs"); Roy A. Rosenberg, "Yahweh Becomes King," *JBL* 85 (1966) 301 ("Ṣedeq is Yahweh"). Rosenberg's interpretation is unlikely since names equating deities are rare.

[164]On **zbd* as an Aram. root, see Wagner, pp. 46-47, 151; Coogan, *Murašû*, p. 71.

Structure: 1. nominal-sentence name, *zabd-* (**qatl* base) + *-î-* 1st c.s. pronominal suffix + *-ʾēl* (**qil* base, BL §61i).
2. construct phrase name, *zabd-* (**qatl* base) + *-î-* h.c. + *-ʾēl.*

Meaning: 1. "God/El is my gift."
2. "gift of god/El."

Parallels: N/LB *zab-di-ili(DINGIR)* (*WSB*, p. 399); Palm. *zbdlʾ/h* (< **zbdʾlh*; *PNPI*, p. 85); Saf. *zbdʾl* (*PIAN*, p. 294); Grk *ζαββδηλου*, *ζαβδελα* (Wuthnow, pp. 47-48).

Comments: BDB and Stamm favor our first structure/meaning, which analyzes the medial *-î* vowel as a pronominal suffix.[165] There is little evidence to support this interpretation. In psalms, hymns, and prayers of the Hebrew Bible, nowhere is God referred to as the devotee's gift. Instead, the opposite is true; abundant evidence supports the notion that in PNN, the noun "gift" refers to the name bearer. The basis for this statement is the observation that many names arose out of the circumstances of birth. The etiological narratives of the Hebrew Bible illustrate this name giving context. In Gen 30:20, it is implied that names expressing the idea "to give"[166] may be directly related to childbirth. Leah expresses her joy and thanksgiving at the birth of Jacob by declaring that "God has given me a good gift" (*zĕbādanî ʾĕlōhîm ʾōtî zēbed ṭôb*). One may conclude that the nominal element "gift" in PNN refers to the name bearer, and that PNN of the type "gift + DN" are construct phrase PNN.[167] Therefore, the second structure/meaning is to be preferred, and the PN Zabdiʾel is to be analyzed as a construct phrase name meaning "gift of god/El."[168] In names of this structure, a medial *-î* vowel must be the h.c. Semantically and structurally parallel are PNN of the type **mtn* + DN, which are attested in Ug. (*PTU*, p. 147), Ph-P. (*PNPP*, pp. 229, 356-57), Neo-Punic (Jongeling, pp. 29, 189), EH (VSE ##268, 367, 369; L 1.5), and Palm. (*PNPI*, p. 98) onomastica.

Before concluding the discussion of this PN, it should be added that Loewenstamm suggested as an alternative that the PN Zabdiʾel

[165]BDB, p. 256, who translate "my gift is God"; Stamm, *BHAN*, p. 52.

[166]The verbal roots **ʾwš*, **zbd*, **yhb*, **ytn*, **ntn*, and (Eg.) **pṭ* are used in West Semitic PNN to express this notion. See the remarks of Fowler, pp. 176, 196, 205, 221, 267, 285-86.

[167]In verbal-sentence names, the expressed or unexpressed subject of the verb "to give" is the DN, and in passive participle names, the expressed or unexpressed agent is also the DN.

[168]As recognized by Barth, *ZDMG* 53 (1899) 597; Hunsberger, p. 297; Nöldeke, *EB* 3:3277; Noth, *IPN*, p. 33.

may be a verbal-sentence PN meaning "God/El has given."[169] Zadok proposes the same analysis for the N/LB PN *zab-di-ilu(DINGIR).*[170] This suggestion cannot be lightly dismissed. It is possible that this PN, as well as other PNN that are vocalized *$C_1aC_2C_3$î'ēl*, underwent a development similar to the PN Hizqiyah(u), only without the final step, in which *a* > *i*. This development may be represented as follows: **zabadî'ēl* > *zabdî'ēl*. The pre-Masoretic form of the name Hizqiyah(u) was inferred from the cuneiform writings *ḫa-za-qi-*. With the PN Zabdi'el, however, no cuneiform writings **za-ba-di-* point to the analysis of the first element of this PN as a Qal perfect verbal form. On the contrary, cuneiform writings attest the existence of a **qatl* base noun from the root **zbd*. A popular name in the Murašû archive is the PN Zabdiya. This appears to be a hypocoristic name, construct phrase in structure, meaning "gift (of DN)." According to Coogan, this name occurs a total of twenty-three times, and it is almost always written *zab-di-ia/iá*.[171] It must be conceded that *CvC* signs may be indifferent to vowel quality.[172] Yet the consistency in the orthography suggests that the first element is a **qatl* base nominal element.[173] That the quality of the medial vowel in the *CvC* sign is an *a* vowel can be established from the rare cuneiform writings *za-ab-di-ia/iá*, which is attested three times, two of which are variant writings.[174] When we add the Can. PNN *Zabdî'ēl* and *Zabdî*, and the Greek transliterations cited above, the combined weight of evidence supports the analysis of the first element as a **qatl* base noun.[175] In the Murašû archive, Qal perfect verbal forms from the root **zbd* are easily distinguished, being written *za-bad-du*, *za-ba-du*, or *za-bad-*,[176] but always with a vowel between the

---

[169]Samuel E. Loewenstamm, in *EM*, s.v. "zabdî'ēl," 2:892.

[170]Zadok, *WSB*, p. 399. Zadok has informed me that he now allows for the possibilty that it is a construct phrase PN (oral communication).

[171]Coogan, *Murašû*, pp. 21-22.

[172]Gelb, *BO* 12 (1955) 98; Zadok, *WO* 9 (1977-78) 40 n. 30; idem, *WSB*, p. 117.

[173]Notwithstanding the rare and indeed isolated examples in which the writing **qatl* in cuneiform represents **qatal* (Noth, *IPN*, p. 35; Coogan, *Murašû*, p. 98). Coogan cites only two examples of this practice from the Murašû archive, and it is unwarranted to make sweeping generalizations based on a few unusual writings. In fact, the reason for the spelling of one of the examples cited by Coogan, *^{d}AD.gi-ši-ri-zab-du*, is lack of space (Zadok, *WSB*, p. 80). Excluding this spelling, Zadok, *WSB*, p. 80, has discovered only two instances of this spelling among all the WS PNN in NA and N/LB texts. At any rate each individual case must be evaluated on its own, and with regard to names from the root **zbd*, the interpretation of the writing **zabd-* as indicative of a **qatl* base noun is beyond cavil.

[174]Coogan, *Murašû*, pp. 21-22. Once the variant writing *za-bid-da-a* occurs, but this appears to be a passive participle and not a Qal perfect verbal form.

[175]On the **qatl* base noun from the root **zbd*, see further Zadok, *WSB*, pp. 115, 429 n. 117.

[176]Coogan, *Murašû*, p. 20.

second and third consonants. Even if one still prefers to analyze Zabdiʾel as a verbal-sentence PN, the medial *-î* vowel remains an example of the h.c.

2. Ambiguous Example

1. *zabdî.*

Classification: Aram.--1) tribe of Judah (Josh 7:1); 2) tribe of Benjamin (1 Chr 8:19); 3) an officer of David (1 Chr 27:27); 4) tribe of Levi (Neh 11:17; = *zikrî* [1 Chr 9:15]).

Structure: 1. construct phrase name (shortened), *zabd-* (**qatl* base) + *-î* h.c.
2. construct phrase name (hypocoristic), *zabd-* (**qatl* base) + *-î* hypocoristic suffix.

Meaning: 1. and 2. "gift (of DN)."

Parallels: NA *zab-di-i*, NA *za-ab-di-i*, N/LB *zab-di-e*, N/LB *zab-di-ia*, N/LB *za-ab-di-ia*, N/LB *za-ab-di-ia* (*WSB*, p. 399); IAram. *zbdy* (*RVJPNE*, p. 143), *zbdy* (*SPARI*, pp. 78, 157); Palm. *zbdy* (*PNPI*, p. 85); Hat. *zbdy* (*PIH*, pp. 103-4); Saf. and Min. *zbdy* (*PIAN*, p. 294); Grk *ζαβδαιος* (Wuthnow, p. 47). See also the compound PNN listed s.v. "zabdîʾēl" above.

Comments: Much of what was said above concerning the name Zabdiʾel is also relevant here. In this case, however, the PN Zabdi could be a shortened name from a fuller form such as Zabdiʾel, or it could be a hypocoristicon related to a hypocoristic name such as the Zabdiya attested in cuneiform writing. In the first case, the *-î* is the h.c., while in the second, the *-î* is a hypocoristic suffix.[177] Either analysis is equally plausible and has sufficient parallels; therefore the PN Zabdi constitutes an ambiguous example.

F. *Compound PNN Formed with Kinship Terms*

In general, four kinship terms are productive in the formation of PNN within the Canaanite onomasticon: *ʾāb*, *ʾāḥ*, **ḥām*, and *ʿam*. It is the class of compound names with the kinship terms *ʾāb* and *ʾāḥ* in first

---

[177]On the hypocoristic suffixes *-ī/ē* (spelled *-Ci-i/ia/iá*, *-Ci*[-ʾ]), see Zadok, *WSB*, pp. 153-56.

position that involves peculiar difficulties, owing chiefly to the fact that the termination *-î* on these vocables is susceptible to more than one analysis. Marchel has summarized previous scholarly opinion, and according to his study, three options are available: pronominal suffix, construct state marker, or the h.c.[178] Elsewhere in this chapter, it is assumed that in construct phrase PNN, the h.c. is not readily distinguished from the construct state marker of kinship terms. In fact, Barth maintained that the h.c. in a name such as the Can. PN *ʿabdîʾēl* is formed according to the analogy of the construct state of the kinship terms.[179] The reason some scholars insist on distinguishing the construct state marker from the h.c. is that having rejected the option of the pronominal suffix, they are constrained by semantic considerations to interpret the Can. PN *ʾăbîʾēl* as a nominal-sentence PN meaning "Father is god/El." In this case, the medial *-î* has been analyzed as the h.c., which signifies no more than a vague sort of liaison between the two elements. Another factor that complicates the situation is that the medial *-î* vowel may have been reanalyzed at some time during the use of the name.[180] If this be the case, the lines between the three above-mentioned options become considerably blurred.

I tentatively propose that the preponderance of the compound PNN beginning with a kinship term in first position, and a nominal element in second position, are nominal-sentence PNN, and that the medial *-î* vowel may be understood as the 1st c.s. pronominal suffix.[181] This explanation is in keeping with the minimalist approach that undergirds this study, and it has two advantages. First, the analysis of these PNN as nominal-sentence names, in which the medial *-î* is the pronominal suffix, explains the greatest number of names with the least number of problematic examples. Second, sound methodology dictates that other more common explanations (e.g., pronominal suffix) should first be exhausted before a putative archaic feature is classified as a genuine archaism. To defend this analysis, it is necessary first to refute an argument that supports the interpretation of the medial *-î* as a

---

[178]W. Marchel, *Abba, Père! La prière du Christ et des chrétiens*, Analecta Biblica, no. 19 (Rome: Pontifical Biblical Institute, 1963), pp. 244-46.

[179]Barth, *ZDMG* 53 (1899) 597. Since Phoenician and Aramaic have retained the nominative case vowel on kinship terms (see p. 101), it follows that the *-î*-vowel on Hebrew kinship terms (including **ḥām*, on which see Huehnergard, "Akkadian Morphology," p. 189 n. 45) in the construct singular and before suffixes must be the genitive case vowel.

[180]On this possibility, see Noth, *IPN*, pp. 33-35; Nestle, *Die israelitischen Eigennamen*, pp. 81 n. 1, 129 n. 1.

[181]Many interpreters recognize that most of these names are of the nominal-sentence type, but of those that do, some still maintain that the *-î* is a meaningless binding vowel.

meaningless binding vowel (= the h.c.), and then consider several positive arguments that favor the analysis of this class of names as nominal-sentences with the pronominal suffix attached to the first element.

The main argument in favor of the analysis of the *-î* vowel as the h.c. is pairs of names, in one of which this vowel is omitted, which suggests that it has no significance. Alongside the Can. PN *ʾabrām* we find the name *ʾăbîrām*, and even more telling are those examples where the same individual was called by both forms: *ʾabnēr/ʾăbînēr* (1 Sam 14:50; 51), *ʾabšālôm/ʾăbîšālôm* (2 Chr 11:20; 1 Kgs 15:2), and *ʾabšay/-ʾăbîšay* (2 Sam 10:10; 1 Sam 26:6).[182] Some of the examples that have been cited may be due to textual corruption, but this need not be the explanation in every case. From this alternation of forms, however, it does not necessarily follow that the *-î* vowel is meaningless. The unexpressed assumption in this argument is that the medial *-î* vowel could only be dropped if it were a semantically meaningless binding vowel. It may be countered that the medial *-î* vowel could very well be a semantically meaningful element of the name (i.e., the pronominal suffix), but that it is not an indispensable element of the name. Whether one referred to the deity in a PN as "my father" or simply "father" does not significantly affect the overall meaning of the name. After all, the DN or theophoric element could be omitted altogether in PNN; if such a drastic omission as this is tolerable, then the omission of the pronominal suffix cannot be ruled out in principle.

In another context, Stamm has introduced a useful distinction that may be applied to these names with and without the medial *-î* vowel. He observed that nominal-sentence names may be formulated "neutrally" (without suffix), or "personally" with the first person pronominal suffix.[183] Note the following pairs of BH PNN that exhibit this alternation in formulation: *yôʾāb/ʾăbîyāh(û), yôʾāḥ/ʾăḥîyāh(û)*, and *yôʾēl/ʾēlîyāh(û)*. It is true that the loss of the pronominal suffix may be related to position. Nonetheless, the first member of each pair still attests to the loss of the pronominal suffix, a loss which does not seem to be significantly different than the loss of the same element in medial position. Moreover, the vocable *ʾēl* is the first element of some of the pairs of names that vary between forms with and without the medial *-î* vowel. While forms such as *ʾăbi-* and *ʾăḥî-* are morphologically ambiguous, this is not the case for the form *ʾĕlî*, which can only be

---

[182]For additional examples and discussion, see Noth, *IPN*, pp. 33-34; Thompson, *Historicity*, pp. 22-23; Gottfried Widmer, "Hebräische Wechselnamen," in *Vom Alten Testament: Karl Marti zum siebzigsten Geburtstage*, ed. Karl Budde, BZAW 41 (Giessen: Alfred Töpelmann, 1925), pp. 299-300.

[183]Stamm, *BHAN*, p. 108.

understood as a suffixed form. There are in fact two pairs of compound names in which the first element exhibits the variation *ʾel-/ʾĕlî-*, and where both forms of the pair are borne by the same individual: **ʾelpeleṭ/ʾĕlîpeleṭ* (1 Chr 14:5;[184] 1 Chr 8:39) and *ʾelṣāpān/ʾĕlîṣāpān* (Exod 6:22; Num 3:30). Since the forms can only be analyzed as suffixed and suffixless forms respectively, one may assume that the same variation is present in the compound PNN *ʾabšālôm/ʾăbîšālôm*, in which the first element is the kinship term *ʾāb*. This line of analysis may also be valid for the Can. PN *ʾaḥʾāb*, which appears in the Elephantine texts spelled both with and without the *-y*;[185] yet the possibility that this name is a construct phrase PN cannot be ruled out entirely.

Several positive arguments point to the interpretation of these names beginning with *ʾăḥî-* and *ʾăbî-* as nominal-sentence PNN rather than construct phrase PNN. First, in light of the widespread use of the pronominal suffix in nominal-sentence PNN, and that on the first element (e.g., Can. PN *ṣûrîʾēl* "God/El is my rock"), it is reasonable to conclude that wherever the vocables *ʾāb* and *ʾāḥ* are written with an *-î* termination, this too may be understood as the pronominal suffix. Second, whereas the vocables *ʾāb* and *ʾāḥ* occur predominantly in first position in Canaanite PNN in the Hebrew Bible, their occasional occurrence in second position points to the analysis of compound PNN with kinship terms as being of the nominal-sentence type. Two pairs of these names with their counterparts in reverse position were cited above, *ʾăbîyāh(û)/yôʾāb* and *ʾăḥîyāh(û)/yôʾāḥ*; here we may add two other pairs: *ʾăbîʾēl/ʾĕlîʾāb* and *ʿammîʾēl/ʾĕlîʿām* (same individual). These kinship terms occur in both positions in Amor. PNN and Ugaritic PNN.[186]

The third argument involves the structure of construct phrase PNN. In those construct phrase PNN in which the *nomen regens* is a personal noun, the name is descriptive of the bearer.[187] Hence a concord exists between the gender of the initial element of the name and the sex of the name bearer. Compound names with the vocable

---

[184]But cf. the *BHS* apparatus for evidence for a reading **ʾlyplṭ*).

[185]Silverman, *RVJPNE*, p. 133, analyzes both IAram. PNN as nominal-sentence names. In favor of the nominal-sentence analysis, see Robert Gordis, "ʾmy wʾḥwty' wʿʾḥʾb'," in *The Word and the Book: Studies in Biblical Language and Literature* (New York: KTAV Publishing House, 1976), pp. 45-46 (Hebrew section); and compare the Amor. PNN *a-ḫu-ka-a-bi* and *a-ḫu-um-la-a-bi* (*CAAA*, pp. 556-57).

[186]For Amor. PNN, see Gelb, *CAAA*, pp. 37-45; for Ug. PNN, note especially *ʾabršp/ršpʾab* (Gröndahl, *PTU*, p. 86).

[187]See Noth, *IPN*, p. 12. Huffmon, *APNMT*, p. 123 and n. 12, confirms this for Amor. PNN, but notes that it is not applicable to Akkadian PNN.

ʾāb in first position are used indifferently of men and women in the Hebrew Bible. If these names were construct phrase in structure, then their distribution should be restricted to masculine name bearers. It is necessary to cite only those compound names that are borne by females, and yet their initial element is a masculine kinship term: *ʾăbîgayil*, *ʾăbîyāh*, *ʾăbiḥayil*, *ʾăbîṭāl*, *ʾăbîšag*, *ʾăḥînōʿam*, and *ḥămûṭal*. Examples of this phenomenon could be cited from other WS onomastica;[188] it suffices here to cite instances from the EH onomasticon: *ʾbgyl* (VSE #62), *ʾbyḥy* (VSE #103), *ḥmyʿdn* (VSE #324), and *ḥmyʾhl* (VSE #412). These names pose no problems as nominal-sentence names with the pronominal suffix attached to the first element; since the kinship term is theophoric, the names are to be interpreted as statements about the deity rather than the name bearer.

This section can be concluded by discussing possible exceptions to the generalization that compound PNN with kinship terms in first position are predominantly of the nominal-sentence type. The only possible exceptions are names with *ʾāḥ* as first element. It has been argued from the Ph-P. PN *ʾḥtmlk*[189] that names with *ʾāḥ* as initial element may be construct phrase PNN. Since Milku is a masculine deity, it cannot be contested that this name is construct phrase in structure.[190] This whole question has been discussed at some length by Gray.[191] It suffices to say that no Canaanite PNN in the Hebrew Bible are formed with the element **ʾḥt*, and that the arguments enumerated above imply that names with *ʾāḥ* in first position are predominantly (if not exclusively) nominal-sentence PNN.[192] To judge from the Ph-P. PN *ʾḥtmlk*, the construct phrase analysis is probable only if the second element is a DN (or theophoric element?). But even then, the nominal-sentence analysis cannot be excluded,[193] unless there is gender discord between the kinship term and the DN, as in the Ph-P. PN *ʾḥtmlk*. Canaanite PNN in the Hebrew Bible do not exhibit this gender discord, so the unambiguous evidence in favor of the construct phrase analysis does not exist. To conclude, in compound PNN with kinship terms in first position, the *-î* termination on the vocables *ʾāb* and *ʾāḥ* is not to be

---

[188]Note the Amor. feminine PN *a-bi-šamši(dUTU)* (*CAAA*, p. 555); Ph-P. *ʾbbʿl* (*PNPP*, p. 257); IAram. *ʾbyhw*, *ʾbyhy*, and *ʾbʿšr* (*RVJPNE*, p. 129).

[189]See Benz, *PNPP*, p. 232.

[190]Ibid., p. 231.

[191]G. Buchanan Gray, *Studies of Hebrew Proper Names* (London: Adam & Charles Black, 1896), pp. 75-86.

[192]For pairs that reverse position, note *ʾăḥîyāh(û)/yôʾāḥ*; for a feminine name, note *ʾăḥînōʿam*; and for a verbal-sentence PN with *ʾāḥ* in first position, note *ʾăḥîrām*.

[193]The BH PN *ʾăḥîyāhû* is usually taken as a nominal-sentence PN, meaning "Yahu is my brother" (KB3, p. 32).

analyzed as the h.c.[194] Rather the medial *-î* vowel is best analyzed as the 1st c.s. pronominal suffix.

IV. Late West Semitic PNN (extrabiblical)

One can easily be led astray in attempting to isolate an *-i* binding vowel[195] in late West Semitic PNN. Some of the names are written in syllabic script, while others are written in alphabetic script. Each script has its own advantages and limitations, which must be taken into account as one searches for examples.

1. *WS PNN in cuneiform writing*

In the search for the historical antecedents of the h.c. in early West Semitic, some construct phrase proper names with an *-i* binding vowel on the first element were studied. This would be a good starting point for our discussion of this morpheme in late West Semitic PNN. There are, however, two characteristics of cuneiform orthography that frustrate attempts to detect this binding vowel.

First, the widespread use of logograms to write the first element of construct phrase PNN prevents us from knowing exactly how these names were pronounced and whether an *-i* binding vowel was attached to the *nomen regens.* The use of phonetic complements is not frequent enough to resolve the problem. For example, the first element of construct phrase PNN of the type "servant of DN" is often written *ÌR*. Is this to be normalized **abdu-*, **abdi-*, or **abda-*? Some guidance is provided by construct phrase PNN of the same type in which the first element is written syllabically. In this case, syllabic writings attest all three spellings of the first element.[196] Moreover, the choice of one of these spellings over the other two was often dictated by various orthographic and phonological considerations that are not evident to the contemporary reader.

Another class of construct phrase PNN that may contain an *-i* binding vowel are those in which the vocable **gr* "client" is the first

---

[194]Pace Lewy, *Forschungen*, p. 63 n. 2, who cites the Can. PNN *ʾăbîḥayil* and *ʾăbîšālôm*; and Nöldeke, *EB* 3:3287, who cites the BH PNN *ʾăbîyāhû* and **ʾaḥîyô*. Zadok, *WSB*, pp. 52, cites eight PNN that may contain the h.c. Unfortunately, all these are compound PNN beginning with the kinship terms **ʾab* or **ʾaḫ*. According to the criteria established above, the only one that is a good candidate is the NA *a-ḫi-mil-ki*, a name borne by a Phoenician.

[195]As in the earlier section (I. Early West Semitic) in this chapter, I revert here back to the phrase "*-i* binding vowel," in place of the Hebraeo-centric term "h.c."

[196]See Zadok, *WSB*, pp. 351-52.

element. Lipiński maintains that the sign *GÍR* should be read phonetically *gíri*, and he analyzed the form *gíri* as the construct state supplied with the paragogic *-i* vowel.[197] In support of this normalization, one may compare the syllabically written NA PN *gi-ri-da-di* "client of (A)dad" (*WSB*, p. 369). However, the N/LB PN *gi-ru-adad(dIM)* "client of Adad" (*WSB*, p. 369) frustrates any attempt to make generalizations about the phonetic reading of the sign *GÍR*.

Second, in the cuneiform writing of West Semitic names, vowels (and consonants) are often written that are not etymologically or morphologically significant. That is, these vowels (and consonants) were represented in the script, but they were not pronounced. This scribal convention arose because cuneiform scribes attempted to represent foreign names in their native script. Coogan discusses this problem in his study of WS PNN in the Murašû archive.[198] His comments are of primary relevance for Neo-Babylonian; nevertheless, the orthography of these PNN well illustrates the problems that are encountered elsewhere. The NB PNN *ma-at-tan-ia-a-ma* and *ma-at-ta-ni-ia-a-ma* belong to a list of pairs of names that exhibit different orthographies, yet were borne by the same individual. This variation in orthography indicates that only the consonant was pronounced in the *Cv* sign at the end of the first element.[199] Thus the medial *-i* vowel of the second name was not pronounced and is morphologically meaningless. A plethora of examples support this analysis, so that it cannot seriously be doubted. I have chosen this name in particular for consideration, because names of the type "gift of DN" are construct phrase in structure, and the first element of this name is where one might expect to find an *-i* binding vowel. In this case, the cuneiform writing *ma-at-ta-ni-ia-a-ma* is a false lead.

This second feature of cuneiform writing complicates the search for the *-i* binding vowel in compound PNN. The problem is acute for the bulk of WS PNN which, in contrast to many of those attested in the Murašû archive, are only attested once. The Neo-Babylonian scribes were able to indicate that a final vowel was pronounced by the orthography *Cv-v* or *Cv-ʾ*. But even this orthography can be misleading; note that according to Coogan, the NB PN *ma-at-tan-ni-ʾ-ia-a-ma* reflects the tendency to anticipate the sound of the *-yaw* by adding a junctive *-i*

[197]Lipiński, *BO* 32 (1975) 78. In support of this position, he refers to the study of K. Deller, "Zweisilbige Lautwerte des Typs KVKV im Neuassyrischen," *Or* 31 (1962) 7-26, especially pp. 9-10.

[198]Coogan, *Murašû*, pp. 93-103.

[199]Ibid., p. 96-97. This variation in orthography is characteristic of *cuneiform* writing, and it should be distinguished from the variation that occurs in West Semitic *alphabetic* writing, such as in the Can. PNN *ʾăbšālôm/ʾăbîšālôm*.

to the final consonant of the preceding element.[200] The ambiguities of cuneiform writing may be circumvented when a WS PN in cuneiform writing can be correlated with its counterpart in the Hebrew Bible. The BH PN *ḥizqîyāhû* is represented in cuneiform writing by *ḫa-za-qi-ia/a*. However, this is a unique situation, which is not likely to be duplicated with many other names.

2. *Ammonite PN*

Since vowels are for the most part not represented in late West Semitic PNN written in consonantal script, it is practically impossible to isolate any occurrences of the *-i* binding vowel. The exception to this statement is provided by *matres lectionis*, which would allow us to detect a medial binding vowel in a construct phrase PN. In 1945, G. R. Driver published an Edomite seal which he read *ʿbdybʿl*.[201] He compared it to the Can. PN ʿAbdiʾel and described this name as preserving "the old ending of the construct state."[202] Recent studies on this seal classify it as Ammonite,[203] and Bordreuil corrects the reading of the PN to *ʿbdhbʿl*.[204] With this new reading the putative *-i* binding vowel disappears.[205]

3. *Ph-P. PNN*

At least one name in the Ph-P. onomasticon probably contains an *-i* binding vowel, the Pun. PN *mtnybʿl* (*PNPP*, p. 146). From the perspective of semantics, this name is of the construct phrase type meaning "gift of Baal," and the *-y mater lectionis* should represent an *-i* binding vowel.[206] Benz also cites two other names that he thinks have an *-i* connecting vowel, *mtny* and *ʿzybʿl* (*PNPP*, p. 199), but the *-y* on the first name could just as well be the hypocoristic suffix, and the second name is probably a nominal-sentence PN meaning "Baal is my strength."

---

[200] Coogan, *Murašû*, pp. 99-100.

[201] G. R. Driver, "Seals from ʿAmman and Petra," *QDAP* 11 (1945) 82.

[202] Ibid.

[203] Israel, *Syria* 64 (1987) 142; idem, *Rivista biblica* 35 (1987) 338.

[204] P. Bordreuil, "Les sceaux des grandes personnages," *Le Monde de la Bible* 46/5 (1986) 45.

[205] A. Lemaire has expressed his disagreement with this reading (oral communication). However that may be, Driver's original reading is highly unlikely.

[206] For another explanation of the medial *-y-* in *mtnybʿl*, see Jongeling, p. 43.

V. Summary

Though the h.c. is a morphological feature first identified in Biblical Hebrew, its historical antecedents may be found in early West Semitic PNN. As a binding vowel that connects two elements together, the most likely place to search for it is on the first element of construct phrase proper nouns. Evidence of this kind may be drawn from Amor., Ug., and GNN in the EA letters. Whether the h.c. was originally a genitive case vowel is a moot question. While the Ug. PN *fa-ḫa-ti-milki(LUGAL)*, declined according to the sentence syntax, would support such a notion, the *-i* binding vowel that occurs on the construct form of certain classes of nouns in Akkadian may serve as a counter-argument. And even if it were originally a genitive case ending, it may have later been reanalyzed as a simple binding vowel and thus no longer understood as a case vowel.

The discussion of the h.c. among the Canaanite languages may be restricted to Biblical Hebrew, since only in this language has it been isolated in non-onomastic material. This morpheme has been identified almost exclusively in poetic contexts, which implies that it is an archaic morpheme. The distribution and use of the h.c. in poetry does not shed much light on the distribution and use of this morpheme in PNN. In two old passages (Gen 49:11 and Deut 33:16), however, the h.c. occurs on the *nomen regens* of a construct chain. This usage may constitute a partial parallel with the use of the h.c. in PNN.

The distribution of the h.c. in Canaanite PNN in the Hebrew Bible is contested. The main problem is that the h.c. is easily confused with other morphemes that are productive in PNN: the 1st c.s. pronominal suffix and the hypocoristic suffix. Semantics and structure are of some help in seeking to distinguish these morphemes from one another. Also the vocalization of West Semitic PNN in cuneiform writing enables one better to understand the Masoretic vocalization of many PNN. The list of probable examples includes the following PNN:

1. ʿAbdiʾel
2. Hizqiyah
3. Hizqi
4. Yatniʾel

These names represent two different structural types: construct phrase PN (#1) and verbal sentence PN (##2, 4). Of these verbal-sentence names, #2 is of the structure perfect verbal form + h.c. + DN, wheras #4 has an imperfect verbal form in first position. PN #3 appears to be a shortened name of #2--hence perfect verbal form + h.c.

The list of ambiguous examples consists of the following names:

1. Daniy(ʾ)el
2. ʿAbdi

The following names are considered as dubious examples of the h.c.:

1. Gabriʾel
2. Hanniʾel
3. Yequtiʾel
4. Yesim(i?)ʾel
5. Malki-sedeq
6. Sidqiyah

Among non-Canaanite PNN, the Aram. PN Zabdiʾel represented a probable example of the h.c., and the Aram. PN Zabdi was classified as an ambiguous example.

The h.c. has also been seen in compound PNN beginning with the kinship terms *ʾabî-* and *ʾaḥî-*. An examination of this class of compound PNN reveals that nearly all of these names are of the nominal-sentence type, and that the medial *-î* vowel is best interpreted as a 1st c.s. pronominal suffix rather than as the h.c. The main argument against this position is that the medial *-î* vowel is sometimes omitted for no apparent reason, but it does not follow that the *-î* vowel is necessarily a meaningless binding vowel; it can just as easily be understood as the pronominal suffix. Three arguments are proffered in favor of the analysis of these names as nominal-sentence in structure, with the *-î* vowel understood as the pronominal suffix: 1) the widespread use of the pronominal suffix in PNN, especially on the initial element of compound PNN; 2) the existence of pairs of PNN with the kinship term in first and second position (e.g., *ʾăbîyāh(û)/yôʾāb*); and 3) the lack of concord in feminine names between the initial element (a masculine kinship term) and the sex of the name bearer.

Among late West Semitic PNN, it is difficult to isolate the h.c. As for WS PNN in cuneiform writing, the precise vocalization of the initial element of construct phrase names is often obscured by the use of logograms without phonetic complements. Further, vowels and consonants are often written which are not etymologically or morphologically significant. In the case of the PN Hizqiyah(u), the existence of the h.c. is established by correlating the cuneiform version of the name with its counterpart in BH. An *-i* binding vowel would not normally be expressed in the consonantal writing characteristic of West Semitic alphabetic scripts. Only when *matres lectionis* are used is it possible to isolate the h.c. The Pun. PN *mtnybʿl* is cited as probable example of the h.c.

CHAPTER 4

MIMATION AND ENCLITIC *-M*

Whereas the existence of enclitic *-m*[1] is well-established in West Semitic grammar, the same cannot be said for mimation. After noting the absence of mimation in the Northwest Semitic vocables in Akkadian texts from Canaan and Syria during the fifteenth-thirteenth centuries B.C., Sivan goes so far as to state ". . . it is doubtful if there ever was mimation in Northwest Semitic."[2] This judgment is, in my estimation, an overstatement that disregards some important evidence provided by early West Semitic proper names. It is necessary here to demonstrate the presence of the two *-m* morphemes in West Semitic, starting with the oldest textual material and working forward. Since mimation fell into disuse at an early date in West Semitic, it is necessary first to consider briefly its occurrence in Akkadian and Eblaite to present a complete picture.

In the earlier stages of the Akkadian language (Old Akkadian, Old Babylonian, and Old Assyrian), singular nouns, whether masculine or feminine, as well as feminine plural nouns, terminated in case vowel plus mimation (**-vm*) in the *status rectus.*[3] An exception to this rule occurs in Old Akkadian PNN, in which certain nouns such as *abu* "father" and *aḫu* "brother," when used as appellatives for god, omit mimation.[4] But even here it has been posited that the lack of mimation is only apparent. That is, pre-Sargonic script had not yet fully developed the device of splitting up *CvC* signs to *Cv-vC.* Consequently a *Cv* sign in final position may reflect a closed syllable. Thus mimation was a regular feature of the language, even in PNN, but in certain

---

[1]By enclitic *-m* is meant the morpheme *-m* that is suffixed to a preceding word and thereby loses its own accent, being pronounced as if it were part of the preceding word.

[2]Sivan, *GAGNWS,* p. 124 n. 1.

[3]Von Soden, *GAG* §63c.

[4]Ibid., §63d. See also Gelb, *Old Akkadian,* p. 145, for additional examples of PNN, GNN, and DNN without mimation.

cases the script was not sufficiently developed to reflect it in writing.[5] Mimation fell into disuse during the Old Babylonian period.

In his grammatical sketch of the Eblaite language, Gelb noted that Eblaite does indeed have mimation, though its use, at least in the lexical texts, is inconsistent. He suggested that mimation is used regularly in non-lexical texts.[6] A glance at some of the entries of the PN indices in the first five volumes of ARET reveals isolated instances of mimated forms amidst many non-mimated forms. Especially instructive is the occurrence of both forms of the same name: *a-ʾà-lu* and *a-ʾà-lum* (ARET III:255). For the occurrence of enclitic *-m*, note the PN *a-ba₄-me* (ARET III:256).[7] The basic criterion for distinguishing mimation from enclitic *-m* is morpho-syntactic. Since most West Semitic PNN consist of one, or at most, two elements, syntactic considerations are inadequate to distinguish between the two morphemes. With West Semitic PNN in syllabic cuneiform texts, the most reliable means of distinguishing between the two morphemes lies in the vocalization: whereas mimation is never followed by a vowel,[8] enclitic *-m* is always followed by a vowel.

I. Early West Semitic

The Amorite language is characterized by mimation.[9] In his synopsis of Amorite grammar, Gelb stated that mimation is regular in one-word PNN, with a few exceptions (e.g., less frequent in PNN with the morpheme **-ānu*), but irregular in compound PNN.[10] The existence

---

[5]See Werner Diem, "Gedanken zur Frage der Mimation und Nunation in den semitischen Sprachen," *ZDMG* 125 (1975) 249, who in turn is summarizing Edzard's unpublished remarks.

[6]I. J. Gelb, *Thoughts about Ibla: A Preliminary Evaluation, March 1977*, Syro-Mesopotamian Studies, vol. 1/1 (Malibu: Undena Publications, 1977), p. 19; idem, "Ebla and the Kish Civilization," pp. 30-31, where Gelb noted that the regular declension of the noun is identical with that of Akkadian.

[7]Although enclitic *-m* appears with different vowels, e.g. *-ma/i(e)/u*, the writing *-ma* appears to be the more frequent of the lot. See Sivan, *GAGNWS*, pp. 125-26, and Gröndahl, *PTU*, p. 53. In the following survey of early West Semitic PNN, examples of all three forms of the enclitic will be cited.

[8]Except in the plural morphemes **-ūma* and **-īma*. The possibility that these morphemes are used in PNN is considered below.

[9]Buccellati, *AURIII*, p. 193; Giovanni Garbini, *Il semitico de nord-ovest*, Quaderni della sezione linguistica degli annali, no. 1 (Napoli, 1960), pp. 117-18; Gelb, *RANL* 13 (1958) §3.2.1; Huffmon, *APMNT*, p. 95; Noth, "Mari und Israel," p. 216.

[10]Gelb, *RANL* 13 (1958) §3.2.1.1-2.

of an enclitic particle *-ma*, with a variant *-mi*, has also been observed.[11] Contrasting pairs of PNN, one with and the other without the enclitic particle, are attested: *ila(DINGIR)-ma-a-bi* (*CAAA*, p. 576) versus *i-la-a-bi* (*CAAA*, p. 591); and *mi-il-ki-ilu(DINGIR)* (*CAAA*, p. 623) versus *mi-il-ku-ma-ilu(DINGIR)* (*CAAA*, p. 624). The widespread use of mimation, or perhaps only an archaic scribal tradition, may be inferred from a list of Amorite PNN in an Old Babylonian text from Tell Asmar.[12] Thirteen of the twenty-six Amor. names that are legible terminate in mimation.

The execration texts are an early witness to the existence of mimation in West Semitic. The existence of mimation in proper names in these texts does not prove that mimation was a living feature of early West Semitic at that time. It may have already dropped out of current speech patterns and been retained only in proper names. Only the discovery of West Semitic textual material (i.e., non-onomastic) could settle the issue. Nonetheless its occurrence in West Semitic proper names from Syria and Palestine is hard evidence for the existence of this morpheme in Northwest Semitic. The importance of this material calls for a more detailed treatment. In the following table proper names from Sethe's list are cited in the left column, and similar or identical proper names from other sources (or an apposite Semitic root) in the right column. Ambiguous examples (e.g., e 1 *ʿ3m*) have been excluded from consideration. Further bibliography discussing the identifications is provided in the footnotes. No attempt is made here to settle the debate over which of several possible GNN the execration texts mention. The vocables listed in the right column are pertinent insofar as they help to establish that the form in the execration texts ends in mimation:

e 3	*ʿ-k-r-m*	PN	Amor. *a-ki-rum*; Can. *ʿokrān*[13]
e 4	*ʾay-b-m*	PN	EA *a-ia-ab*; Can. *ʾiyyôb*
e 17	*k-m-r-m*	PN	Taan. *k*[*a-m*]*a-ru*[14]
e 18	*r-q-ḥ-m*	PN	*raqqāḥ* "perfumer"[15]
e 21	*š-m-š-u-ʾil-i-m*	PN	**ʾilum* "god"

[11]Bauer, *Ostkanaanäer*, p. 77; Buccellati, *AUR III*, pp. 124, 200; Gelb, *RANL* 13 (1958) §§2.3.3-4, 3.4.6; Albrecht Goetze, "Amurrite Names in Ur III and Early Isin Texts," *JSS* 4 (1959) 202; Moran, "Hebrew Language," p. 60.

[12]Gelb, *JAOS* 88 (1968) 39-46.

[13]W. F. Albright, "The Egyptian Empire in Asia in the Twenty-First Century B.C.," *JPOS* 8 (1928) 238-39; René Dussaud, "Nouveaux renseignements sur la Palestine et la Syrie vers 2000 avant notre ère," *Syria* 8 (1927) 220.

[14]Dussaud, *Syria* 8 (1927) 225; Albright, *JPOS* 8 (1928) 243-44. For a different suggestion, see Moran, *Or* 26 (1957) 341.

[15]Helck, *Beziehungen Ägyptens*, p. 47.

e 22 *ʿ()r-q-tum*	GN	EA ^{URU}*ir-qa-ta*[16]
e 26 *man-s-m*	PN	Akk. *mi-nu-tum* (?)[17]
e 27-28 *r()w-u-š()l-m-m*	GN	EA ^{URU}*ú-ru-sa-lim*

In total, eight proper names are easily analyzed as exhibiting mimation. One of these, e 22 *ʿ()r-q-tum*, is a feminine noun with mimation, comparable to mimation on Akkadian feminine nouns (e.g., *šarratum*) in the older phases of that language.

From the Posener list, which is to be dated slightly later, note the following mimated forms:

E 8 *p-a-ḫ()l-u-m*	GN	EA ^{URU}*pe-ḫe-li*[18]
E 9 *ʾá-p-q-u-m*	GN	Can. *ʾăpē/îq*[19]
E 14 *ʾa-r-ḥ-b-u-m*	GN	Can. *rĕḥōb*[20]
E 17 *ś-ʿ-p-u-m*	GN	<*s/z/ṣʿp[21]
ḫ-w()r-n-i_2-ʾab-u-m	PN	*ʾabūm "father"[22]
E 19 *s̱-i-r-m*	GN	?[23]
E 20 *b-q-ʿ-tum*	GN	*biqʿatum "valley"[24]
E 25 *ʿ-s-[ta-]r-tum*	GN	Can. *ʿaštārôt*[25]
E 33-34 *ʾá-p-u-m*	GN	?[26]
E 43 *š-m-š-u-ʾa-p-a-ʾil-i-m*	PN	*ʾilum "god"
E 45 *raw-u-š()l-m-m*	GN	EA ^{URU}*ú-ru-sa-lim*
E 54 *ʿ(a)r-q-tum*	GN	EA ^{URU}*ir-qa-ta*[27]

---

[16]Albright, *JPOS* 8 (1928) 245.

[17]Ibid., p. 247; Dussaud, *Syria* 8 (1927) 229.

[18]Albright, *BASOR* 83 (1941) 33; Dussaud, *Syria* 8 (1927) p. 172; Maisler, *Revue de l'histoire juive en Egypte* 1 (1947) 47.

[19]Albright, *BASOR* 83 (1941) 33; Dussaud, *Syria* 21 (1940) 172; Maisler, *Revue de l'histoire juive en Egypte* 1 (1947) 47-48. There is more than one Aphek from which to choose.

[20]Albright, *BASOR* 83 (1941) 33; Dussaud, *Syria* 21 (1940) 172-73; Maisler, *Revue de l'histoire juive en Egypte* 1 (1947) 49. Again, scholars disagree over which Rehob is referred to.

[21]Maisler, *Revue de l'histoire juive en Egypte* 1 (1947) 50.

[22]Albright, *BASOR* 83 (1941) 34 n. 12.

[23]To be identified with either Ser (Josh 19:35) or EA *Ziri-bašani* (Helck, *Beziehungen Ägyptens*, p. 54). Posener, p. 75, states that in one copy a *-u-* is written between the final two consonants.

[24]Maisler, *Revue de l'histoire juive en Egypte* 1 (1947) 51, identifies it with the Lebanon Valley.

[25]Albright, *BASOR* 83 (1941) 33; Dussaud, *Syria* 21 (1940) p. 174; Maisler, *Revue de l'histoire juive en Egypte* 1 (1947) 52.

[26]For discussion, see p. 41 n. 14.

[27]Note the same Semitic root in E 61 *ʿ()r-q-ta*.

E 56 *q-r-q-r-m* GN Can. *qarqōr*[28]

A total of thirteen proper names (eleven GNN and two PNN) exhibit mimation. What is striking is that six of these names end with the writing -*u-m*, which reflects the nominative singular case vowel plus mimation.[29] Posener has noted that three of the five occurrences of E 14 *ʾa-r-ḥ-b-u-m* are written without mimation.[30] The non-mimated form is also found in Sethe's list (e 11-12 *ʾa-r-ḥ-b-u*). It is unclear whether enclitic -*m* occurs on the West Semitic PNN of the execration texts. Dussaud interpreted e 2 *ʾab-i-ja-m-m-u* as a compound name with enclitic -*m* separating the two elements (**ʾabi-ma-ʿammou*), but a different analysis of the name (**ʾabi-yama/imu*) is preferred,[31] and thus the putative enclitic particle disappears. A better candidate for the enclitic -*m* is the GN *q-h-*r_2*-mú* (e 8-10; E 39-40), which appears to represent a triradical root plus enclitic morpheme. The evidence furnished by the West Semitic names in the execration texts indicates that early West Semitic did have mimation.[32]

The West Semitic PNN at Alalakh are found in levels VII (1720-1650 B.C.) and IV (1550-1473 B.C.). Although there are no clear examples of mimation, several names terminate with the enclitic morpheme:

a-bi-ma	(*AT*, p. 126)
ia-ti-ra-ma	(*AT*, p. 137)
bin(DUMU) qa-ṣí-ra-ma	(*AT*, p. 145)[33]
aš-ta-ar-mu	(*AT*, p. 130)
nu-ri-i-el-mu	(*AT*, p. 143)

---

[28]Maisler, *Revue de l'histoire juive en Egypte* 1 (1947) 61, prefers the Qarqor of Judg 8:10 rather than the Syrian Qarqar in the land of Hamath.

[29]Seven if one includes the variant spelling of E 19. See p. 158 n. 23.

[30]Posener, p. 72.

[31]So Albright, *JPOS* 8 (1928) 238; Moran, *Or* 26 (1957) 340.

[32]This conclusion tallies well with the thesis of Diem, *ZDMG* 125 (1975) 239-58, that the singular noun in the Semitic languages was originally characterized by mimation. I. J. Gelb, *Sequential Reconstruction of Proto-Akkadian*, Assyriological Studies, no. 18 (Chicago: University of Chicago Press, 1969), p. 140, reached the same conclusion, though he excepted Arabic which has nunation. Consequently the occurrence of mimation on singular nouns in certain (Old) South Arabian dialects is a matter of archaism rather than innovation. For a discussion of mimation in (Old) South Arabian, see A. F. L. Beeston, *A Descriptive Grammar of Epigraphic South Arabian* (London, 1962), pp. 30-31; idem, "A Sabaean Penal Law," *Le Muséon* 64 (1951) 313-15; idem, *Sabaic Grammar*, Journal of Semitic Studies, Monograph no. 6 (Manchester: University of Manchester, 1984), pp. 30-31.

[33]Reading with Sivan, *GAGNWS*, pp. 125, 261, instead of Wiseman's transliteration *qa-zi-ra-ma*.

u-ri-el-mu (*AT*, p. 151)

Of the twenty-eight West Semitic PNN that occur in the Taanach tablets, none have mimation, and only two end with enclitic *-m*:

bin(DUMU)za-nu-qí-ma (Taan. 4.4)[34]
bin(DUMU)an-⌈t⌉a-m[a] (Glock, *BASOR* 204:20)

Albright claimed that the first two Taanach letters, both written by Canaanites, reflect a high incidence of mimation.[35] If this claim be justified, these letters may reflect an archaic scribal tradition of the area. Nevertheless, scholars agree that mimation ceased to function in Akkadian and West Semitic during the period 1800-1500 B.C.[36] The lack of textual material prevents us from being more specific.[37]

Enclitic *-m* occurs in the Canaanite Amarna letters.[38] Note the following PNN:

a-ad-du-mi (*AmPN*, p. 46)
bin(DUMU) a-zi-mi (*AmPN*, p. 110)
mu-ut-balu(dIM)-me (*AmPN*, p. 190)
ba-lum-me-e (*AmPN*, p. 85)
bá-a-lu-ú-ma (*AmPN*, p. 81)
bi-en-e-lí-ma (*AmPN*, p. 91)

---

[34]As transliterated by Sivan, *GAGNWS*, p. 293, correcting Hrozný's *bin(DUMU) za-nu-ki-ma*. Sivan tentatively suggests the West Semitic root **znq* "to leap." Maisler, "lwḥwt tʿnk," p. 61, also considers the name West Semitic. Contrast A. Gustavs, *ZDPV* 51 (1928) 200, who cites Old Babylonian PNN as possible parallels.

[35]W. F. Albright, "A Prince of Taanach in the Fifteenth Century B.C.," *BASOR* 94 (1944) 26-27.

[36]Albright, *JPOS* 8 (1928) 233-35; idem, *BASOR* 94 (1944) 26; Harris, *Canaanite Dialects*, pp. 32-33; Anton Jirku, "Die Mimation in den nordsemitischen Sprachen und einige Bezeichnungen der altisraelitischen Mantik," *Bib* 34 (1953) 78-80, reprinted in *Von Jerusalem nach Ugarit: Gesammelte Schriften* (Graz: Akademische Druck- u. Verlagsanstalt, 1966), pp. 371-73. It is Moran's opinion that the distribution of *-mi* and *-ma* on the infinitive reflects Canaanite and Akkadian usage respectively (William L. Moran, "The Use of the Canaanite Infinitive Absolute as a Finite Verb in the Amarna Letters from Byblos," *JCS* 4 [1950] 172 n. 34). Be this as it may, the occurrence of the enclitic particle on PNN does not fit this pattern.

[37]Note, however, that in the Akkadian texts at Alalakh, mimation is used consistently in level VII tablets, whereas the breakdown of its use has begun in level IV tablets (George Giacumakis, *The Akkadian of Alalaḫ*, Janua Linguarum, Series Practica, no. 59 [The Hague: Mouton, 1970], p. 44).

[38]Briefly discussed by Robert De Langhe, "L'enclitique cananéenne *-m(a)*," *Le Muséon* 59 (1946) 91-94.

Although the first three PNN present nothing new, new interpretive options have been tendered for the last three names. The PN *ba-lum-me-e* is characterized by mimation and enclitic *-me*. Since cuneiform script does not necessarily reflect geminated consonants, cuneiform writings with single writing of the consonant *-m* may stand for both mimation and the enclitic particle.[39] According to Hess (*AmPN*, p. 81), the name *bá-a-lu-ú-ma* terminates with the nominative masculine plural morpheme **-ūma*, which functions as a plural of majesty or intensity. Furthermore, he analyzes the PN *bi-en-e-lí-ma* as ending with the oblique masculine plural morpheme **-īma*, here as a true plural (*AmPN*, p. 91).[40]

If the West Semitic plural morphemes **-ūma/-īma* do indeed occur in these Amarna PNN, then these plural morphemes may occur in other names as well. It becomes difficult to distinguish between the enclitic *-m* and the plural morphemes **-ūma* and **-īma*, since they are formally identical with one another. In syllabic cuneiform script, the presence of distinctive vowels is usually decisive in distinguishing mimation, one the one hand, from enclitic *-m* and the plural morphemes, on the other. The problem of distinguishing among these morphemes becomes acute in alphabetic script, where, as a rule, vowels are not indicated. In this chapter, it is important, if possible, to distinguish between morphemes terminating in *-m*. First of all, however, it is necessary to determine whether the two Amarna PNN do in fact end in the plural morpheme.

As for the EA PN *bá-a-lu-ú-ma*, Hess appears to base his analysis on the vocable *ba-a-lu-ma*, which occurs in Ugaritic column of the polyglot vocabularies from Ugarit.[41] The other columns of these vocabularies, which give equivalent vocables in other languages, contain singular, not plural nouns, in the slot corresponding to Ug. *ba-a-lu-ma*. As an example, note 130.iii.14' (*Ug V*, pp. 234-35):

Sumerian	Akkadian	Hurrian	Ugaritic
[EN]	[*be*]*-lu*	*e-wi-ri*	*ba-a-lu-ma*

---

[39]The variation in writings may be illustrated from Amor. PNN: *mu-tu-me-el, mu-tum-el, mu-tum-e-el, mu-tum-el(DINGIR), mu-tum-me-el, mu-tum-ma-el* (Gelb, *CAAA*, p. 626).

[40]Sivan, *GAGNWS*, p. 109; and W. F. Albright, "Two Little Understood Amarna Letters from the Middle Jordan Valley," *BASOR* 89 (1943) 11 n. 25, also analyze this PN as terminating in the plural morpheme. For a possible occurrence of the West Semitic oblique dual or plural ending, see the GN *gi-la-di-ma* in the Bronze Age text from Hazor (Hallo and Tadmor, *IEJ* 27 [1977] 8).

[41]130.iii.14'; 137.ii.30', 33' (*Ug V*, pp. 234-35, 244-45). See Huehnergard, *Ugaritic Vocabulary*, p. 114.

Although morphologically plural, Ug. *ba-a-lu-ma* must be semantically singular in light of the vocables in the other columns; therefore, scholars have proposed that the Ugaritic form be understood as a plural of majesty or intensity.[42] This is a possible interpretation, but one may also analyze Ug. *ba-a-lu-ma* as a singular noun plus enclitic *-m*. The advantage of this second analysis is to avoid altogether the grammatical category of the plural of majesty or intensity in Ugaritic.[43] While this category may be generally accepted for certain forms in Biblical Hebrew[44] and other Semitic languages, it is an unusual feature of language, and it is neither necesssary nor essential to appeal to it to explain problematic forms in the West Semitic onomasticon.

Several lines of argument may be advanced to support the analysis of Ug. *ba-a-lu-ma* as singular noun + enclitic *-m*. The deity list published in *Ugaritica VII* (pp. 1-3) has six occurrences of the DN *bʿlm* in the left column, which corresponds to the DN *hdd* in the right column.[45] In the Ugaritic mythological texts, the forms *bʿlm* and *bʿl* alternate, without any discernible pattern of use (e.g., *KTU* 1.2.IV.32). One is hard pressed to explain all these occurrences of *bʿlm* as plurals of majesty; rather it is more plausible to analyze them as singular nouns plus enclitic *-m*. For the enclitic morpheme on the DN Baʿlu, one may compare the EA PNN *mu-ut-balu(dIM)-me* or *ba-lum-me-e* already cited above. On the basis of the Ug. VII deity list and the Ug. mythological texts the analysis of *bʿlm* as a singular noun plus enclitic *-m* seems assured. This same analysis may also be valid for the Ug. *ba-a-lu-ma* in the polyglot vocabularies and for the EA PN *bá-a-lu-ú-ma*.

A similar approach may be applied to the EA PN *bi-en-e-lí-ma*. Instead of the analysis as the oblique plural morpheme **-īma*, the final element may be understood as a genitive singular noun plus enclitic *-m*.

---

[42]Joshua Blau and Jonas C. Greenfield, "Ugaritic Glosses," *BASOR* 200 (1970) 16; Johannes C. de Moor, "The Semitic Pantheon of Ugarit," *UF* 2 (1970) 219, 226; idem, s.v. "*baʿal*," in *TDOT* 2:184; Huehnergard, *Ugaritic Vocabulary*, p. 56 (with a question mark); Stanislav Segert, *A Basic Grammar of the Ugaritic Language, with Selected Texts and Glossary* (Berkeley and Los Angeles: University of California Press, 1984), p. 181; Anson F. Rainey, *IEJ* 19 (1969) 108-9; Sivan, *GAGNWS*, p. 109.

[43]See the critical remarks of Kjell Aartun, *Die Partikeln des Ugaritischen*, AOAT 21/1-2 (Kevelaer: Butzon & Becker; Neukirchener-Vluyn: Neukirchener, 1974-78), 1:51 n. 4.

[44]It has been conjectured that the plural of majesty arose because archaic singular nouns with mimation were later misanalyzed as plural forms. See Norman Walker, "Elohim and Eloah," *VT* 6 (1956) 214-15; and idem, "Do Plural nouns of majesty exist in Hebrew?" *VT* 7 (1957) 208.

[45]For the analysis of the final *-m* of *bʿlm* as the enclitic morpheme, see Astour, *JAOS* 86 (1966) 279 n. 29; Helga and Manfred Weippert, "Die 'Bileam'-Inschrift von *Tell Dēr ʿAllā*," *ZDPV* 98 (1982) 92 n. 70.

Thus the PN may be translated "son of god/El." The arguments in favor of this interpretation are based partly on semantics,[46] and partly on morphology. The West Semitic onomasticon furnishes numerous examples of enclitic -*m* suffixed to the singular noun **ʾilu*. At Alalakh occur the WS PNN *nu-ri-i-el-mu* and *u-ri-el-mu* (*AT*, pp. 143, 151); at Ugarit note the PN [*bin*]-*ili(DINGIR)-ma-ra-kub* (*PTU*, p. 97). Surely the Amor. PNN *zi-im-ri-ilu(DINGIR)* and *zi-im-ri-ilu(DINGIR)-ma* (*CAAA*, p. 651) are identical in meaning, "El/God is my protection," the only difference being that the second PN ends in the enclitic morpheme.[47] The first elements of the Amor. PNN *ila(DINGIR)-ma-ì-la*, *ila(DINGIR)-ma-*^{d}*i-la*, *ila(DINGIR)-ma-a-bi* (*CAAA*, p. 576) are more probably singular nouns plus enclitic -*m* than plurals. Note the following two pairs of Ug. PNN: *ʿbdʾil* and *abdi(ÌR)-ili(DINGIR)* (*PTU*, pp. 104-5); and *ʿbdʾilm* and *abdi(ÌR)-ili(DINGIR)-mu* (*PTU*, pp. 104-5). All four names should probably be translated "servant of god/El." While the second element of the last two names may be interpreted as a plural form, the vocalization of the enclitic -*m* as -*mu*, rather than -*ma*, may be cause for hesitation. The Ph-P. PN *ʿbdʾlm* (*PNPP*, p. 371) may be interpreted in a similar fashion.[48] As parallels to the EA PN *bi-en-e-lí-ma*, note the Amor. PNN *bu-ni-ili(DINGIR)*, *bu-ni-i-la*, *bi-in-i-la*,

---

[46]It seems unlikely that this name should be translated "son of the gods"! See also n. 48.

[47]Note also the Amor. PNN *zi-im-ri-i-lu-ma* (Gelb, *CAAA*, p. 651). Huffmon, *APNMT*, p. 228, has recognized the enclitic particle on the Amor. PNN *zi-im-ri-ilu(DINGIR)-ma* and *zi-im-ri-i-lu-ma*.

[48]Compare the cuneiform version of this Ph-P. name, NA *ab-di-li-mu* (Zadok, *BASOR* 230 [1978] 58). Zadok, p. 60, prefers to interpret the theophoric element as a plural, but why not as a singular noun plus enclitic -*mu* ? For other compound PNN whose second element is -*ʾlm*, see Benz, *PNPP*, p. 267, who interprets this form as a plural of majesty, and Vattioni, *Annali del Seminario di studi del mondo classico, Istituto Universitario Orientale, Sezione di archeologia e storia antica* 1 (1979) 154. Tigay has stated that "Northwest Semitic PNN . . . rarely invoke more than one deity in a single name," but he cited Ph-P. *ʿbdʾlm* as an exception to this rule (p. 6 and n. 5). According to our interpretation, Ph-P. *ʿbdʾlm* would not contradict his observation. Nor would the EA PN *bi-en-e-lí-ma*.

Noteworthy is the phrase *ʾlm nrgl* "the god Nergal" (*CIS* 37.2; 119.2 [= *KAI* 59:2]) in Phoenician inscriptions. For a discussion of Phoenician *ʾlm* meaning "god" rather than "gods," see W. Röllig, "El als Gottesbezeichnung im Phönizischen," in *Festschrift Johannes Friedrich zum 65. Geburtstag am 27. August 1958 gewidmet*, ed. R. von Kienle, A. Moortgat et al. (Heidelberg: Carl Winter, 1959), pp. 403-6. The analysis of the final -*m* of *ʾlm* as enclitic has implications for the interpretation of *ʾlm* in the Hebrew Bible and the Ugaritic texts. For a succinct discussion, see Cross, *Canaanite Myth and Hebrew Epic*, pp. 45-46.

bi-in-i-lí-ia, bu-ni-lum, bu-nu-um-e-lu-um (*CAAA*, pp. 571-73),[49] and the Ug. PNN *bnʾil* and *bin(DUMU)-ili(DINGIR)* (*PTU*, pp. 94, 96). The second element of the two Ug. PNN cannot be interpreted as a plural. In light of this survey of PNN, at least it can be said that the interpretation of EA *be-in-e-lí-ma* as "son of the gods" is questionable. In fact, the balance of evidence slightly favors the interpretation of the second element as a singular noun plus enclitic *-ma*. This is not to say that plural morphemes cannot occur in WS PNN, only that the two EA PNN discussed above are not unambiguous examples of such.

Only in Ugaritic do we have a considerable body of textual material, in addition to a corpus of West Semitic PNN. The statement made above that mimation ceased in West Semitic circa 1800-1500 B.C. is based primarily on the lack of this morpheme on Ugaritic vocables in Ugaritic and Akkadian scripts, and on the West Semitic glosses in the Amarna letters.[50] Nonetheless, it is possible that mimation is retained in Ug. PNN as an archaism. In his grammar, Gordon states that "if the proper names *abm* . . . and *ṣdqm* . . . contain mimation, they are archaistic or borrowed."[51] Though these names could be borrowed from Akkadian, the Ug. PN *špšm* cannot be so explained.[52] Unfortunately, no syllabic writings of Ugaritic PNN end in case vowel plus mimation. Gröndahl mentions one possible example, the PN *ia-qa-rum* (*PTU*, p. 145). But this must be excluded from consideration, since the only occurrence of the PN with this spelling is on a dynastic seal of the nineteenth/eighteenth centuries B.C.[53] In light of its early date, and assuming that the final cuneiform sign is to be read *rum*, the final ending should not be described as "archaizing mimation."[54] The name itself is Amorite, and it may have been coined at a time when mimation was still functional in early West Semitic. When the same PN is written in texts contemporary with the floruit of Ugarit,

---

[49]Knudsen, *JCS* 34 (1982) 11, argues that Amor. had an oblique plural ending in *-īm, which implies a nominative in *-ūm. If this conclusion is accepted, then the only difference between singular and plural in Amor. was the quantity of the case vowel.

[50]For a list of these non-mimated forms in Akkadian script from Ugarit and Amarna, see Sivan, *GAGNWS*, p. 124. For discussion, see Huehnergard, *Ugaritic Vocabulary*, p. 294. For the limited use of mimation in formulas in the Akkadian dialect of Ugarit, see John Huehnergard, *The Akkadian of Ugarit*, HSS 34 (Atlanta: Scholars Press, 1989), pp. 99-100.

[51]*UT* §8.2.

[52]To be sure, the final *-m* on these names could be the enclitic particle.

[53]*PRU* III, p. xxxvi-xliii, pls. xvi-xvii. The same form does occur in Amor. as a PN (Huffmon, *APNMT*, p. 214).

[54]So Gröndahl, *PTU*, p. 145.

the final *-m* is omitted: *yqr* (*KTU* 1.113.26, referring to the same person as Yaqarum on the dynastic seal) and *ia-qa-ri* (12.30 [*Ug V*, p. 18]).

The following is a list of Ugaritic PNN in alphabetic script that terminate in enclitic *-m*, or less likely, mimation:

ʾabm	(*PTU*, p. 86)
ʾibm	(*PTU*, p. 87)
ʾidrm	(*PTU*, p. 90)
ʾaršm	(*PTU*, p. 101)
bn ytrm	(*PTU*, p. 148)
ṣdqm	(*PTU*, p. 188)
špšm	(*PTU*, p. 195)
šrm	(*PTU*, p. 196)

In the Akkadian texts from Ugarit, there are at least three clear writings of the enclitic particle:

[*bin*]-*ili(DINGIR)-ma-ra-kub*	(*PTU*, p. 97)
balu(dIM)-ma-ṣe-ri	(*PTU*, p. 115)
ia-tar-mu	(*PTU*, p. 148)

A fourth name that has been interpreted as terminating in enclitic *-m* is the Ug. PN *abdi(ÌR)milku(LUGAL)-ma* (*PTU*, p. 104). But a comparison with other names suggests that the name may be read *abdi(ÌR)-šarru(LUGAL)-ma*, with the second element referring to the Hurrian deity Šarruma.[55] Two additional putative examples of enclitic *-m* in the middle of alphabetically written compound PNN--*bʿlmṯpṭ* and *bʿlmʿḏr* (*PTU*, p. 116)--are subject to alternative analyses and therefore ambiguous.[56] Finally Singer has collected a number of alleged proper names with the suffix *-m*, which he interprets as a vocative particle.[57] Of the four examples he cites at least two of them are better interpreted as common nouns rather than proper names. The remaining examples are DNN and could be explained as plurals of majesty, or singular nouns followed by enclitic *-m*. At any rate, it is unlikely that the

[55]For this deity in names from Ugarit, see Gröndahl, *PTU*, p. 250, and note especially the Ug. PN *ʿbdṯrm* and the WS PNN *abdi(ÌR)-šar-ru-ma* (Taan. 7.3 [obv.]) and *abdi(ÌR)-ša-ru-ma* (!) (Taan. 4.6 [rev.]). In general, see E. Laroche, "Le dieu anatolien Sarrumma," *Syria* 40 (1963) 277-302.

[56]As noted by Gröndahl, *PTU*, p. 33. Nevertheless, in his review of Gröndahl, André Caquot, "Nouveaux documents ougaritiens," *Syria* 46 (1969) 262, states without hesitation that both of these names contain the "asseverative" particle *-m-*. For the PN *bʿlmṯpṭ*, the one-word Ug. PN *mṯpṭ* (*PTU*, p. 200) points toward a segmentation of the name into *bʿl* + *mṯpṭ*.

[57]Abraham D. Singer, "hʾmʾ hswpytʾ (=mā?) bšpt lwḥwt ʾwgryt," *BJPES* 10 (1943) 59-60.

suffixed *-m* is a vocative particle,[58] and the occurrence of enclitic *-m* on proper names may be established by other, more certain examples. Before concluding the discussion of enclitic *-m* in Ugaritic, it should be stressed that this morpheme is common in Ugaritic texts, appearing with every part of speech.[59] In contrast to mimation, it seems likely that enclitic *-m* was still a regular feature of the language at Ugarit.

II. Canaanite

Since mimation as originally characteristic of the singular died out in West Semitic long before the beginning of the first millennium B.C.,[60] it follows that none of the Canaanite languages possessed mimation as a regular feature of the grammar. In the Hebrew Bible, traces of mimation have been seen in adverbs terminating in *-ām*,[61] common nouns, certain objects associated with prophets,[62] GNN,[63] and in the Amm. DN Milkom. Gelb has collected and analyzed the traces of mimation in BH and other Semitic languages in his fundamental article on mimation and nunation.[64]

Likewise, enclitic *-m* is not a regular feature of Hebrew (biblical and epigraphic), Transjordanian dialects, or Ph-P.[65] It does, however, occur with some frequency in ABH. The standard treatment of the morpheme in BH was published in 1957 by Hummel.[66] Fifteen years

---

[58]Marvin H. Pope, "Ugaritic Enclitic *-m*," *JCS* 5 (1951) 123 n. 8; Robertson, *Linguistic Evidence*, p. 92; de Moor, *UF* 2 (1970) 219.

[59]For a thorough discussion of the morpheme, see Aartun, *Partikeln*, vol. 1 passim.

[60]With the above-mentioned exception of (Old) South Arabian.

[61]BL §65y; Brockelmann, *GVG*, 1:474. In light of EA 137:21, *ri-ka-mi* (compare BH *rêqām*), one may derive these adverbs from the enclitic particle.

[62]According to Jirku, *Bib* 34 (1953) 78-80, accouterments such as urim, tummim, and teraphim were borrowed into Hebrew (which had no mimation) from a language that still possessed it.

[63]The biblical GN Laish, usually written *layîš*, appears once with the variant spelling *lešem* (Josh 19:47). This Syro-Palestinian GN occurs in a Mari text with the Akkadian spelling *la-wi-ši-im*, in the oblique case with mimation. For the publication of the text, see G. Dossin, "La route de l'étain en Mesopotamie au temps de Zimri-Lim," *RA* 64 (1970) 97-106. Note perhaps also the GN *gidʿōm*. For other possible examples among GNN, see Borée, p. 56, though with GNN one must be careful to distinguish other morphemes terminating in *-m*.

[64]Gelb, *RSO* 12 (1930) 229-39 on Hebrew; pp. 239-41 on Ph-P.

[65]This morpheme may occur rarely in Ph-P. For some possible occurrences, see Mitchell Dahood, "G. R. Driver and the Enclitic *mem* in Phoenician," *Bib* 49 (1968) 89-90.

[66]Horace D. Hummel, "Enclitic *mem* in Early Northwest Semitic, especially Hebrew," *JBL* 76 (1957) 85-107.

later, in a carefully executed study, Robertson sifted all of the alleged cases in his published dissertation.[67] He postulates enclitic *-m* as a regular feature of early poetic Hebrew, which leads him to the conclusion that this morpheme had become a rare form in the recent (rather than the remote) past. In addition to the occurrence of this morpheme on nouns, it is also relevant for the study of PNN to note its occurrence on the extended or "poetic" forms of the prepositions *b-*, *k-*, and *l-*.[68]

III. Canaanite PNN in the Hebrew Bible

A final *-m* on a Canaanite PN in the Hebrew Bible may represent several different morphemes, and one must distinguish between these morphemes to determine whether it is an archaic morpheme. Two Canaanite PNN terminate in the oblique plural morpheme; they are *śĕʿōrîm* (1 Chr 24:8) and *ḥû/ūšîm* (1 Chr 8:8, 11). In addition, four Canaanite PNN appear to be formed with the oblique dual morpheme: *ʾappayim* (1 Chr 2:30), *ʾeprayim* (Gen 41:52), *diblayim* (Hosea 1:3), and *šaḥărayim* (1 Chr 8:8).[69] Zadok may well be right in his suggestion that biblical PNN terminating in plural morphemes, masculine *-îm* or feminine *-ôt*, or the dual morpheme *-ayim*, are essentially PNN derived from GNN.[70] However that may be, in the Hebrew Bible the masculine plural and the dual morphemes are normally written with *y mater lectionis* and therefore may be easily identified.

Another possible interpretation is that the final *-m* on biblical PNN is a 3rd m.pl. pronominal suffix.[71] Although the final *-m* on PNN

---

[67]Robertson, *Linguistic Evidence*, pp. 77-110.

[68]See the discussion on the Arabian PN *lĕmôʾēl*, pp. 190-92, and the Amm. PN *mkmʾl*, p. 194.

[69]Charles Fontinoy, "Les noms de lieux en *-ayim* dans la Bible," *UF* 3 (1971) 37, recognizes the dual in at least two of these names, ʾAppayim and Shaharayim.

[70]Ran Zadok in *EM*, s.v. "šm, šmwt ʿşm prṭyym byśrʾl, [g] mwrpwlwgyh," 8:60, cites the PN/GN *ʿănātôt* in support of this assertion. In support of Zadok's suggestion, note that all the proper nouns cited by Sivan, *GAGNWS*, pp. 118-20, under plural and dual case endings in proper nouns, are GNN, with but two putative exceptions: *bi-en-e-lí-ma* and *šu-ma-tu*. As for the first, we have suggested above that it is a singular noun plus enclitic *-ma*, and by Sivan's own admission [*GAGNWS*, p. 276: "fpl. (?): *šu-ma-tu*"], the second is not certainly a plural form. For the *-ayim* ending as a dual morpheme in GNN, see Fontinoy, *UF* 3 (1971) 33-40.

[71]See Stamm, *BHAN*, p. 53, on the Can. PNN *ʾônām* and *malkām*.

is always vocalized *-ām*, as if it were a pronominal suffix,[72] this type of onomastic formation is unknown in early West Semitic or Canaanite PNN.[73] Thus it seems probable that a final *-m* morpheme on Canaanite PNN is either a remnant of mimation or an enclitic *-m*. Since mimation fell into disuse by 1500 B.C., the final *-m* on Ug. PNN, unless an archaism, is more likely the enclitic morpheme than a remnant of mimation. Similarly, the final *-m* morpheme on Canaanite PNN is probably best analyzed as enclitic *-m*.

A. *Probable Examples*

1. *ʾûlām.*

Classification: Can.--1) tribe of Manasseh (1 Chr 7:16-17); 2) tribe of Benjamin (1 Chr 8:39-40).

Structure: one-word name, *ʾûl-* (**qūl* base, BL §61t; < **ʾwl* II "to be in front, strong") + *-ām* enclitic morpheme.

Meaning: "first one, leader."[74]

Parallels: BH CN *ʾûlām* "porch."

Comments: The root **ʾwl* II is not well attested in BH, but it does find good cognates in JAram. *ʾăwal/ʾāwāl/ʾĕwîlâ* "beginning, early season" (Jastrow, *Dictionary*, p. 25), and MLArab. *awwal* "first, chief, principal" (Wehr, pp. 44-45). Mazar also compares Ug. *ʾulm*,[75] but this PN may be Hurrian.[76]

---

[72]Apparently the Masoretes vocalized enclitic *-m* on the analogy of other known morphemes, such as the 3rd m.pl. pronominal suffix or adverbial *-ām* (e.g., *rêqām*).

[73]From the perspective of semantics, it would be nonsensical to translate the Can. PN *pirʾām* "their wild ass."

[74]BDB, p. 17; Noth, *IPN*, p. 231 n. 11; A. Bergman, "Two Hebrew Seals of the *ʿEbed* Class," *JBL* 35 (1936) 223; Joseph J. Devault, "A Study of Early Hebrew Personal Names" (Ph.D. dissertation, The Johns Hopkins University, 1956), p. 56; Friedrich Ulmer, *Die semitischen Eigennamen im Alten Testament* (Leipzig: W. Drugulin, 1901), p. 37.

[75]B. Mazar, "The Military Élite of King David," *VT* 13 (1963) 313 n. 3.

[76]Gröndahl, *PTU*, p. 228.

2. *ʾônām.*

Classification: Can.--1) son of Shobal (Gen 36:23); 2) tribe of Judah (1 Chr 2:26, 28).

Structure: one-word name, *ʾôn-* (**qatl* base, BL §61n'; < **ʾwn* "to be strong") + *-ām* enclitic morpheme.

Meaning: "strength."

Parallels: Can. *ʾôn*, *ʾônān*, BH CN *ʾôn* "strength"; EH *ʾnyhw* (3x);[77] Ph.! *ʾny* (VSE #80); Saf. *ʾwn*, Qat. *ʾwnm* (*PIAN*, p. 87).

Comments: Moritz analyzes this PN as an Afʿal form from a root **wnm* or **ynm*.[78] But the PN *ʾônān*, apparently from the same root and terminating in nunation rather than enclitic *-m*, implies that the final *-m* of *ʾônām* is not the third radical of the root.[79] The form of the name ending in *-m* is, as a rule, viewed as older than the form ending in *-n*.[80] Stamm interprets the final *-m* as a 3rd m.pl. pronominal suffix, translating "their (i.e., the brothers) strength."[81] But as argued above, there appear to be no clear examples of third person plural pronominal suffixes on Canaanite PNN. The EH PN *ʾnyhw* "Yahu is (my) strength" suggests that *ʾôn* may function as a divine epithet.

---

[77]VSE #273; N. Avigad, "A Hebrew Seal Depicting a Sailing Ship," *BASOR* 246 (1982) 59-62, and Fig. 1; Dever, *HUCA* 40-41 (1969-70) 158-62, and Pls. VI:B, VII.

[78]Moritz, *ZAW* 44 (1926) 91.

[79]Noth, *IPN*, p. 225 n. 11.

[80]On the change *m* > *n*, see Moscati, *CGSL* §12.77; Gelb, *RSO* 12 (1930) 237-38; E. Y. Kutscher, *Studies in Galilean Aramaic* (Ramat Gan: Bar-Ilan University, 1976), pp. 58-67; and note the following pseudo-correct PNN: Heb. *šallûn* ! < **šlm* (Neh 3:15 and elsewhere in epigraphic sources); Heb. *ṭbšln* ! < **ṭbšlm* (Tigay, p. 68), WS *mryn* ! < **mrym* (Beyer, *ATTM*, p. 736; Kutscher, *Galilean Aramaic*, p. 62); and Aram. *mnḥn* ! < **mnḥm* (B. Buchanan and P. R. S. Moorey, *Catalogue of Ancient Near Eastern Seals in the Ashmolean Museum, Volume III: The Iron Age Stamp Seals (c. 1200-350 BC)* [Oxford: Clarendon, 1988], p. 44 #291 [Pl. X:291]). The interchange of final *mem* and Grk ν, and of final *nun* and Grk μ, are common phenomena in the LXX. See Mazor, *Textus* 14 (1988) 9-10 n. 18, 12 n. 23. In some of these instances we are dealing with an LXX convention and need not reconstruct a different Hebrew *Vorlage*. Among Ug. PNN we have the pairs *špšm/špšn* and *ʾabm/ʾabn*. At Ugarit, the whole matter of the alternation between *-m* and *-n* is more complex, and may involve Akkadian influence. See the salutary remarks of P.-R. Berger, Review of *Die Personennamen der Texte aus Ugarit*, by Frauke Gröndahl, *WO* 5 (1969-70) 280-81.

[81]Stamm, *BHAN*, p. 53.

3. *ʾăḥuzzām.*

Classification: Can.--tribe of Judah (1 Chr 4:6).

Structure: one-word name, *ʾăḥuzz-* (**qutull* base, BL §61d*α*; < **ʾḫd* "to seize, grasp") + *-ām* enclitic morpheme.

Meaning: "possessor" (BDB, p. 28), or "possession."

Parallels: Can. *ʾăḥuzzat*, BH CN *ʾăḥuzzâ* "possession, inheritance."

Comments: Whereas Noth suggests a vocalization **ʾaḥăzām* on the basis of the PN *ʾaḥăzay* of Neh 11:13,[82] KB3 (p. 32) reconstructs **ʾaḥzām*. The LXX evidence, A *ωχαζαμ* and B *ωχαια*, support neither of these proposals, nor the vocalization of the MT. In any case, Gelb observed that this PN terminates in the suffix *-m*.[83] For the same base form, compare the Can. PN ʾAhuzzat, which terminates in the archaic feminine suffix *-at*.[84]

4. *bilʿām.*

Classification: Can.--son of Beor, a non-Israelite prophet (Num 22:5).

Structure: 1. nominal-sentence name: *bil-* (< DN **Bēl*) + *-ʿām* (**qall* base).
2. verbal-sentence name: *(yi)blĕ-* (< **wbl* "to bring forth, yield," 3rd m.s. G imperfect) + *-ʿām* (**qall* base).
3. one-word name: *bilʿ-* (**qvtl* base,[85] < **blʿ* "to swallow, devour") + *-ām* enclitic morpheme.

Meaning: 1. "Bel is (my) paternal uncle."
2. "The clan brings forth [increase of people]/ the people produces offspring."
3. "swallowing, devouring."

[82]Noth, *IPN*, 179 n. 1. In *BHS*, this PN is vocalized **ʾaḥzay*.
[83]Gelb, *RSO* 12 (1930) 234.
[84]See s.v. "ʾăḥuzzat," p. 205.
[85]**Qatl* (cf. GA *balʿī* in Num. 26:38, and LXX B transliteration *βαλααμ*) or **qitl* (cf. MT vocalization of PN and suffixal form *bilʿô* [Jer 51:44]).

Parallels: Can. *bela*ʿ (three persons), GN *bela*ʿ, GA *bal*ʿ*î*, BH CN *bela*ʿ; OAram. *bl*ʿ*m* (Deir ʿAllā; *SPARI*, pp. 72, 139-40); Liḥ., Saf., and Min. *bl*ʿ; Sab. *bl*ʿ*m* (*PIAN*, p. 116).

Comments: The first interpretation assumes that the initial element of the name is an alternative spelling of the DN Baʿal.[86] It cannot be denied that the spelling Bel does occur in West Semitic PNN.[87] Moreover, the N/LB PNN *Bēl(EN)-am-ma/mu* and *Bēl(dEN)-am-mu* (*WSB*, pp. 362-63) may be cited as exact parallels. Nevertheless, it is more typical of East Semitic than of West Semitic PNN,[88] and its occurrence in West Semitic PNN is often due to Akkadian influence.[89] No other Canaanite PNN in the Hebrew Bible have the DN Baʿal spelled without the ʿ*ayin*,[90] and neither the MT vocalization nor the LXX supports this interpretation.

The second interpretation was advanced by Albright on numerous occasions.[91] Noting that the GN *yiblĕ*ʿ*ām* (Josh 17:11; Judg 1:27; 2 Kgs 9:27) was once written *bil*ʿ*ām* (1 Chr 6:55), Albright theorized that the longer form, an imperfect from the root **wbl*,[92] was the original form, from which was derived by contraction the shorter form, or

[86]BL §61ji; Zadok, *WSB*, p. 70; Stamm, *BHAN*, p. 177 n. 37 (with a question mark); O. Bardenhewer, *Der Name Maria. Geschichte der Deutung Desselben*, Biblische Studien, erster Band, erstes Heft (Freiburg: Herder, 1895), p. 16; Matthias Delcor, "Le texte de Deir ʿAlla et les oracles bibliques de Balaʿam," VTSup 32 (1981) 72-73; René Largement, "Les oracles de Bileʿam et la mantique suméro-akkadienne," in *Mémorial du cinquantenaire 1914-64*, Travaux de l'institut catholique de Paris #10 (Paris: Bloud & Gay, n.d.), p. 38; Bernhard Moritz, "Die Könige von Edôm," *Le Muséon* 50 (1937) 108.

[87]Zadok, *WSB*, pp. 69-71. According to Huffmon, *APNMT*, p. 175, the spelling **bēl* in Amor. PNN is either a loan word or an Akkadianized form of **ba*ʿ*l*. In the EA letters, note the West Semitic PN *be-el-*[*š*]*a-a*[*m-ma*] (Hess, *AmPN*, p. 90), alongside PNN written **ba*ʿ*l-* (Hess, *AmPN*, pp. 81, 83, 85-86). I see no reason why the writing with Bel here may not be considered an Akkadianized form too.

[88]Note that in the WS PN ⌈*ba*⌉*-li-ia-a-ma* "Yaw is lord," the vocable **b*ʿ*l* occurs in its West Semitic form (as opposed to *Bēl*; so Coogan, *Murašû*, pp. 15, 69).

[89]Maraqten, *SPARI*, p. 140, commented that the spelling *bl* is found mainly in Ph-P. PNN and Aramaic inscriptions, especially from Mesopotamia.

[90]The PN *bildad* is often cited as an exception, but the meaning and analysis of this name are most uncertain. The most feasible view is that of E. A. Speiser, "The name Bildad," *AfO* 6 (1930-31) 23, who compares it with Akk. *bil-dAdad*, a form of *apil-dAdad*, both meaning "son of Adad." For another view, see W. F. Albright, "The Name of Bildad the Shuhite," *AJSL* 44 (1927-28) 31-36.

[91]W. F. Albright, "Contributions to the Historical Geography of Palestine," *The Annual of the American School of Oriental Research in Jerusalem* 2-3 (1921-22) 24 n. 10; idem, *JBL* 46 (1927) 165-67; idem, *AJSL* 44 (1927-28) 31-33; idem, *JPOS* 8 (1928) 242-43.

[92]As an aside, the GN *yiblĕ*ʿ*ām* is just as easily derived from the root **bl*ʿ as from the root **wbl*.

imperative (**yabil-ʿammu* > *yiblĕʿām* > *bilʿām*). He contended that other pairs of proper names also show the same alternation between imperfect and imperative and therefore support his theory.

Each pair of proper names cited by Albright would need to be evaluated. Whatever the case may be,[93] the alleged pair of GNN *yiblĕʿām/bilʿām* do not belong here. While the spelling *yiblĕʿām* is sure, occurring three times in the Hebrew Bible and once in the topographical list of Thutmose III,[94] the spelling *bilʿām* is textually suspect. Its sole occurrence is in 1 Chr 6:55, and two Hebrew manuscripts and the versions (LXX, SyrP, Vulgate, and Targum) witness a reading **yiblĕʿām*. The shorter form may have arisen through haplography of the initial *y*.[95] Thus the spelling *bilʿām* is not a genuine variant, and therefore one need not interpret the PN Bilʿam by the GN Yibleʿam.

The third interpretation, that the PN Bilʿam derives from the root **blʿ*, is a plausible interpretation. Thus the final *-m* may be understood as the enclitic morpheme. This analysis avoids the difficulties of the other interpretations and derives its strongest support from the use of the root **blʿ* in other WS PNN.[96]

5. *gaʿtām*.

Classification: Can.--son of Eliphaz (Gen 36:11, 16).

Structure: one-word name, *gaʿ*- (< **gʿh* "to bellow, low") + *-t-* + *-ām* enclitic morpheme.

Meaning: "bellow, low."

Parallel: Ug. *gʿyn* (*PTU*, p. 125), CN *gʿt* "lowing (of an ox)" (*UT* §19.607).

---

[93]One of the pairs cited by Albright (*JBL* 46 [1927] 166), *yĕḥizqîyāh(û)/ḥizqîyāh(û)*, does not exhibit the alleged alternation between imperfect and imperative. See s.v. "ḥizqîyāh," pp. 122-25.

[94]#43: *ja-b-la-ʿá-mú* (Helck, *Beziehungen Ägyptens*, p. 127).

[95]Note MT *yiblĕʿām* and LXX A *βαλααμ* in Judg 1:27. The haplography was facilitated by the preceding word, *yôšĕbê*, which terminated in *-y* (**ywšby yblʿm* > *ywšby blʿm*).

[96]Gray, p. 43 n. 1, recognized that the derivation of the name Balʿam from the root **blʿ* is the most plausible explanation. It may be significant that both Belaʿ (< **blʿ*), an Edom. king (Gen 36:32), and Bilʿam bear the same patronym--son of Beʿor. Maraqten, *SPARI*, p. 140, mentioned as one possibility that the PN *blʿm* derives from the root **blǵ*. But the LXX transliteration *βαλααμ* contradicts this derivation.

Comments: The LXX B transliteration γοθομ implies a pronunciation with *u* or *o*. The Ug. PN *gʿyn* and the Can. PN *gaʿtam* may be derived from a root cognate with BH **gʿh*, "to low, bellow."[97] The Ug. PN would indicate that the *-t-* of the PN Gaʿtam is not part of the root, but a feminine suffix. Compare here the Ug. CN *gʿt*, a feminine nominal form, and perhaps the WS GN *gaʿtôn*.[98]

6. *hōrām*.

Classification: Can.--Can king of Gezer (Josh 10:33).

Structure: one-word name, *hōr-* + *-ām* enclitic morpheme.

Meaning: "mountain."

Parallels: Can. *hārān*, GN *hōr*, GN *bêt hārām* (Josh 13:27) = *bêt hārān* (Num 33:36); BH CN *har*, EH *hryhw* (VSE #273); Ph. *hrbʿl*, Pun. *hr* (*PNPP*, pp. 108, 303).

Comments: According to Loewenstamm and Maisler, the PN Horam and the GN Hor are to be regarded as secondary Canaanite forms of the CN *har*. Furthermore, they consider it feasible that *hōr* "mountain" is to be understood as a theophoric element.[99] The EH PN *hryhw* "Yahu is (my) mountain" and the Ph. PN *hrbʿl* "Baal is (my) mountain" corroborate their interpretation. For semantic parallels, one may compare Hebrew PNN with *ṣûr* and Aramaic PNN with *ṭûr*, both of which derive from Proto-Semitic **ẓr* "mountain, rock."[100]

7. *zētām*.

Classification: Can.--tribe of Levi (1 Chr 23:8).

Structure: one-word name, *zēt-* (**qatl* base, BL §61o') + *-ām* enclitic morpheme.

Meaning: "olive (tree)."

---

[97]For this root in PNN, see Zadok, "Nachbiblische jüdischen Onomastikon," p. 296.

[98]Jastrow, *Dictionary*, p. 262.

[99]Samuel E. Loewenstamm, in *EM*, s.v. "hōrām," 2:855; Maisler, *Revue de l'histoire juive en Egypte* 1 (1947) 46 n. 2. Likewise, Gelb, *RSO* 12 (1930) 230.

[100]For further discussion and additional semantic parallels within Semitic onomastica, see Fowler, pp. 199 n. 34, 221, 224, 251, 286, 324.

Parallels: Can. *zêtān*, BH CN *zayit*; EH *ztn*;[101] NB *za-ta-me-e* (Coogan, *Murašû*, p. 23), NA GN *URUzi-ta-a-nu*.[102]

Comments: This PN belongs to the well-known category of plant names.[103] If the PN cited from the Murašû archive is analagous, the final *-m* should be interpreted as an enclitic particle. As suggested above, the **ztm* form of the name may be viewed as older than the **ztn* form.[104] The PN Zetam is distinct from the biblical PN *zattûʾ* (only attested in postexilic books) and EH PN *ztʾ* (VSE #200 [fifth century B.C.]).[105] These latter two names may be explained in light of Iranian **zāta-* "birth, nature."[106]

8. *ḥûpām.*

Variant spellings: 1. *ḥuppīm*; 2. *ḥuppîm.*

Classification: Can.--tribe of Benjamin (Num 26:39).

Structure: one-word name, *ḥûp-* (**qūl* base) + *-ām* enclitic morpheme.

Meaning: unknown.

Parallels: Can. *ḥuppâ*,[107] GA *ḥûpāmî*, BH CN *ḥuppâ* "canopy, chamber."

Comments: As Nöldeke observed, the GA *ḥûpāmî* of Num 26:39 proves incorrect the plural forms.[108] The variant spellings may be the product of later reanalysis. The gemination of these spellings appears

---

[101] I. Ziffer, "A Hebrew Inscription on a Bronze Bowl in the Haaretz Museum Collection," in *Israel - People and Land*, Eretz Israel Museum Yearbook, Vol. 4, ed. R. Zeevy (Tel Aviv: Eretz Israel Museum, 1986-87), pp. 79-81, Figs. 1-2.

[102] Parpola, *Neo-Assyrian Toponyms*, p. 41 n. 38.

[103] Noth, *IPN*, p. 230.

[104] See p. 169 n. 80.

[105] Walter Kornfeld, "Beiträge zur alttestamentlichen Namensforschung," in *Mélanges bibliques et orientaux en l'honneur de M. Henri Cazelles*, ed. A. Caquot and M. Delcor, AOAT 212 (Kevelaer: Butzon & Bercker; Neukirchen-Vluyn: Neukirchener, 1981), p. 214, and Maraqten, *SPARI*, p. 161, have failed to make this distinction.

[106] Kornfeld, "Beiträge," p. 214; Zadok, *Jews in Babylonia*, p. 113 n. 104.

[107] Fowler, p. 159, has suggested that this name is a short form of an unattested theophoric name, "(DN) has hidden or covered."

[108] Nöldeke, *EB* 3:3301-2.

to be secondary,[109] perhaps due to attraction to the kindred form *ḥuppâ*. It is probable that MT *ḥûrām* (1 Chr 8:5) is textually corrupt and is to be emended to **ḥûpām*.[110]

9. *ḥûšām*.

Variant spelling: *ḥūšām*.

Classification: Can.--Edom. king (Gen 36:34, 35).

Structure: one-word name, *ḥûš-* (**qūl* base) + *-ām* enclitic morpheme.

Meaning: unknown.

Parallels: Can. *ḥûšâ*, *ḥûšay*, *ḥû/ūšîm*; GA *ḥušātî*.

Comments: Two lines of evidence converge to suggest that this PN terminates in enclitic *-m*: 1) the productivity of the root **ḥwš* in Canaanite PNN; and 2) the presence of other Canannite PNN in Gen 36 that terminate in this morpheme.[111] Whether the PN is derived from **ḥwš* I "to make haste" or **ḥwš* II "to feel, enjoy" cannot be determined.[112]

10. *kimhām*.

Variant spelling: *kimhān*.

Classification: Can.--attendant of David (2 Sam 19:38, 39).

---

[109]On secondary gemination, see s.v. "ḥammû'ēl," pp. 62-63; and "šěpûpām," p. 180 n. 136.

[110]KB3, p. 287; Noth, *IPN*, p. 242; J. W. Rothstein and Johannes Hänel, *Das erste Buch der Chronik* (Leipzig: A. Deichertsche, 1927), p. 156; Nehemyah Aloni, *EM*, s.v. "ḥûrām," 3:63.

[111]See s.v., "'ônām," p. 169; "gaʿtām," pp. 172-73; and "ʿîrām," pp. 178-79.

[112]Ernst A. Knauf, "Alter und Herkunft der edomitischen Königsliste Gen 36,31-39," *ZAW* 97 (1985) 245-53, claims that the PN is Arabian, comparing Saf. *ḥsm* and Arabic *al-Ḥusām*. But he ignores the PNN cited above which suggest a hollow root. In another context, Israel Ephʿal, "'Arabs' in Babylonia in the 8th Century B.C.," *JAOS* 94 (1974) 109, has argued that the existence of a root in Arabic does not exclude a name containing that root from being Aramaic (or in this case, Canaanite), provided that the given root is attested in common West Semitic.

Structure: one-word name, *kimh-* (**qitl* base) + *-ām* enclitic morpheme.

Meaning: "of pale complexion."[113]

Parallels: Can. GN *kimhām Q/kĕmôhām* K.

Comments: Alternatively, the PN may mean "blind," on the basis of Syr. *kĕmah* "to be blind" and MLArab. *kamah* "blindness" (Wehr, p. 986).[114] The PNN *kimhām* and *kimhān* are borne by the same person.

11. *malkām.*

Classification: Can.--tribe of Benjamin (1 Chr 8:9).

Structure: one-word name, *malk-* (**qatl* base, BL §61r') + *-ām* enclitic morpheme.

Meaning: "king."

Parallels: Amm. DN *milkōm*; Amm. *mlkmʾwr*, *mlkmgd* (Aufrecht, *BASOR* 266:86); WS *mi-il-ku-*[(?)], *mi-il-ku-ma* (*AT*, p. 142); Ḥaḍ. and Sab. *mlkm*; Saf., Ḥaḍ., Qat., and Sab. *mlkn* (*PIAN*, p. 565).

Comments: Gelb stated that the PN *malkām* is the name of an Ammonite deity.[115] Since the only occurrence of this name in the Hebrew Bible is of a Benjaminite, Gelb apparently confused this PN with the Amm. DN Milkom. The interpretations of the PN *malkām* as a shortened form[116] or of the final *-m* as the 3rd m.pl. pronominal suffix[117] are unparalleled in the Canaanite onomasticon and should therefore be rejected.

12. *mišʿām.*

Classification: Can.--tribe of Benjamin (1 Chr 8:12).

---

[113]Noth, *IPN*, p. 225 n. 5, citing Arab. *kamiha*.

[114]This latter alternative is preferred by Gelb, *RSO* 12 (1930) 234; Eberhard Nestle, "Some Contributions to Hebrew Onomatology," *AJSL* 13 (1896-97) 173; and hesitantly, Nöldeke, *EB* 3:3297.

[115]Gelb, *RSO* 12 (1930) 235.

[116]Noth, *IPN*, p. 118.

[117]Stamm, *BHAN*, p. 53.

Structure: 1. nominal-sentence name, *miš-* (< Ug. *mṯ*) + -*ʿām* (**qall* base).
2. one-word name, *mišʿ-* (< **yṯʿ* "to save, deliver," masculine singular Hiphil participle) + -*ām* enclitic morpheme.

Meaning: 1. "The (divine) lord is kinsman."
2. "Savior, deliverer," or "(DN) saves, delivers."

Parallels: Can. *mêšāʿ*, *mêšāʾ*;[118] Moab. *mêšaʿ* (Hebrew Bible) = *mšʿ* (*KAI* 188:1); Moab. *mšʿ* (2x; Israel, "Epigrafia moabiti," pp. 110-111 ##4,6).

Comments: According to our first proposed structure/meaning, the element *miš-* derives from Ug. *mṯ* "lord," and the meaning of the PN is "The (divine) lord is kinsman."[119] Yadin claimed to have discovered the same element in the EH PNN *ddymš* (VSE #93)[120] and *ʿnmš* (S 24.2), and the IAram. PN *mšlk* (Silverman, *RVJPNE*, p. 181). Actually, Ug. *mṯ* means "lad, son";[121] this change of meaning affects Yadin's proposal to the extent that "lord" is a more plausible divine element than "lad." Still one might modify Yadin's approach and interpret Mishʿam as a profane name meaning "the lad is kinsman."

Even with this modification, Yadin's interpretation has several weaknesses. First, Ug. *mṯ* is probably an Egyptian loan (Eg. *mś* "child"), and it only occurs once in the Ug. onomasticon--*bn mṯ* (*PTU*, p. 161). While a Ug. PN that included this loan word might survive and occur much later, it seems unlikely that the loan word itself would survive and later form an element of the PN Mishʿam. Second, each of the PNN that Yadin cited as containing the element *mš* (< **mṯ*) may better be interpreted otherwise. The IAram. PN *mšlk* may be analyzed as a Pael participle, cognate with vulgar Arab. *sallaka* "to save,

---

118According to Noth, *IPN*, p. 155, this PN, with the hypocoristic suffix -*āʾ*, is a shortened name with the theophoric element omitted. In some LXX manuscripts at 1 Chr 8:9 the PN is transliterated *μω/σα* (Vulgate--*mosa*), which compares favorably with the LXX B transliteration *μωσα* (= MT *mêšaʿ*) in 2 Kgs 3:4.

119First proposed by Yigael Yadin, "ḥwtm ʿbry mtl-g'mh," *EI* 6 (1960) 53-55; accepted by Goldberg, "Northern-Type-Names," p. 75, and N. Avigad, "Ammonite and Moabite Seals," in *Essays in Honor of Nelson Glueck: Near Eastern Archaeology in the Twentieth Century*, ed. James A. Sanders (Garden City: Doubleday & Co., 1970), p. 291. Avigad took the argument a step further by finding Ug. *mṯ* in the Moab. PN *kmšmʾš*. But the final element of the Moab. PN is surely a *m-* preformative noun from the root **ʾwš* "to give." Noth, *IPN*, p. 251, compared the PN Mishʿam to Arab. *misʿāmun* "flowing swiftly (of the river)?", a suggestion which has been passed over in silence by subsequent scholarship.

120Tigay, p. 76 n. 9, inclines toward Yadin's interpretation of this name.

121*UT* §19.1579; *WUS* #1717.

deliver."[122] The EH PN *ʿnmš* may be adequately explained as a verbal-sentence PN, "*ʿn* (DN) has felt/looked over" (<**mw/yš*).[123] Similarly, the EH PN *ddymš* may be interpreted as "My beloved/uncle has felt/looked over."[124] It may be significant that in both EH PNN, the *mš* element is in second position, rather than in first as in the PN *mišʿām*.[125] The combined weight of these objections undermines any confidence in Yadin's interpretation.

Our second proposed structure/meaning analyzes the *mišʿ*-element as a defectively written Hiphil participle from the root **yṯʿ*. It may be the case of a Benjaminite bearing a "Moabite" name, because PNN of this structural type are predominantly (if not exclusively) borne by Moabites (two Moabite seals and PN on Mesha stele) or by Israelites who live near[126] or in the land of Moab.[127] Lastly LXX B transliterates *mišʿām* by *μεσσααμ* (< **mêš(a)ʿām* ?), which may better reflect the original vocalization of the PN than the Masoretic pointing.

13. *ʿîrām*.

Classification: Can.--Edom. ruler (Gen 36:43).

Structure: one-word name, *ʿîr*- (**qīl* base) + *-ām* enclitic morpheme.

---

[122]Silverman, *RVJPNE*, p. 181.

[123]Ran Zadok, Review of *The Extra-biblical Tradition of Hebrew Personal Names from the First Temple Period to the End of the Talmudic Period*, by M. Ohana and M. Heltzer, *WO* 13 (1982) 169; idem, *UF* 17 (1985) 394 n. 123. Note the biblical PN *mû/ūšî*. On the deity *ʿn*, see W. F. Albright, "The Evolution of the West-Semitic Divinity ʿAn-ʿAnat-ʿAttâ," *AJSL* 41 (1925) 73-101; Buccellati, *AURIII*, pp. 134-35; Benz, *PNPP*, p. 380; Gröndahl, *PTU*, p. 110, and see s.v. "(ben-)ʿănāt," p. 217 n. 99. On the other hand, G. A. Reisner, C. S. Fischer, and D. G. Lyon, *Harvard Excavations at Samaria*, 2 vols. (Cambridge: Harvard University Press, 1924), 1:235, followed by Lemaire, *Inscriptions hébraïques*, p. 54, suggested an Eg. derivation of the name.

[124]Assuming that the name is read *ddymš*, rather than *drymš*, and that the *y* goes with the first element of the PN rather than the final element.

[125]Consequently, I consider it improbable that BH Mishʿam is be interpreted as "The kinsman has felt/looked over." Further, the root **mw/yš* is infrequent in PNN, whereas the root **yšʿ* (< **yṯʿ*) is widely attested in PNN.

[126]Shelomo Morag, "mêšaʿ: ʿywnym btkwnwt lšwn šl lhgym ʿbryym qdwmym," *EI* 5 (1958) 138, observes that the PN *mêšāʿ*, borne by Caleb's firstborn (1 Chr. 2:42), occurs in a genealogy of the inhabitants of Ziph--probably Tell Ziph, located in the southeast region of Judah, and hence not far from the border with Moab.

[127]The PNN *mêšāʾ* and *mišʿām* are found in a Benjaminite genealogy of offspring who were born "in the country of Moab" (1 Chr 8:8-12, esp. v 8).

Meaning: "young male donkey."

Parallels: BH CN *ʿayir* (note the suffixal form, *ʿîrōh* [Gen 49:11]), Can. *ʿîrāʾ*, *ʿîrû*,[128] *ʿîrî*; EH *ʿyrʾ*;[129] SArab. *ʿyr*.[130]

Comments: Animal name. On the basis of the parallels adduced, Kornfeld's comparison of this PN with (old) Arab. PNN from the tri-radical root **ʿrm* (MLArab. *ʿarim* "strong;" Wehr, p. 711) would appear to be irrelevant.[131]

14. *pirʾām*.

Classification: Can.--Can. king of Yarmuth (Josh 10:3).

Structure: one-word name, *pirʾ-* (**qatl* base, BL §§61r', 72o)[132] + *-ām* enclitic morpheme.

Meaning: "wild ass."

Parallels: BH CN *pereʾ*; Ug. *priʾ* (*PTU*, p. 174); Saf. *frʾ* (*PIAN*, p. 464).

Comments: Animal name. For other animal names terminating in the enclitic morpheme, compare the Can. PN ʿIram discussed in the preceding entry, the Ph-P. PNN *nmlm* "ant" and *ʿkbrm* "mouse" (*PNPP*, pp. 360-61, 377), and the Liḥ. *ḥmrm* "donkey" (*PIAN*, p. 200).

15. *šûḥām*.

Variant spellings: 1. *ḥūšîm* (Gen 46:23); 2. *ḥūšīm* (1 Chr 7:12).

Classification: Can.--tribe of Dan (Num 26:42).

---

[128]Probably to be read *ʿîr wĕ* with LXX and Vulgate (1 Chr 4:15). See s.v. "ʿîrû," pp. 96-97.

[129]Z. Meshel, "Kuntilat ʿAjrud--An Israelite Site in the Sinai Border," *Qadmoniot* 9/4 (1976) 122.

[130]Müller, *ZAW* 63 (1975) 312. This PN is not to be found in *PIAN*.

[131]Walter Kornfeld, "Die Edomiterlisten (Gn 36; 1C 1) im Lichte des altarabischen Namensmateriales," in *Mélanges bibliques et orientaux en l'honneur de M. Mathias Delcor*, ed. A. Caquot, S. Legasse, and M. Tardieu, AOAT 215 (Kevelaer: Butzon & Bercker; Neukirchen-Vluyn: Neukirchener, 1985), p. 234.

[132]According to KB2, p. 776, the original form was **pĕreʾ*; that is, **qitl* base. The Vulgate reads *Pharam*.

Structure: one-word name, *šûḥ-* (**qūl* base, BL §61r) + *-ām* enclitic morpheme.

Meaning: "pit."

Parallels: Can. *šûaḥ*, *šûḥâ*, GA *šû/ūḥî*, GA *šûḥāmî*, BH CN *šûḥâ* "pit."

Comments: The GA *šûḥāmî*, attested twice (Num 26:42-43), proves that the final *-îm* on the metathetic variant *ḥūšîm* is a reanalysis of the enclitic morpheme as a plural suffix. The variant spelling in Gen 46:23 appears to be textually corrupt in two respects: the enclitic morpheme misread as a plural,[133] and metathesis of the *ḥ* and *š*.[134]

16. *šĕpûpām.*

Variant spellings: 1. *muppîm* (Gen 46:21); 2. *šuppīm* (1 Chr 7:12); 3. *šuppîm* (1 Chr 7:15).

Classification: Can.--tribe of Benjamin (Num. 26:39).

Structure: *šĕpûp-* or *šūp-* (**qatūl* or **qūl* base) + *-ām* enclitic morpheme.

Meaning: unknown.

Parallels: Can. *šĕpûpān*, GA *šûpāmî*, BH CN *šĕpûpōn.*

Comments: The first matter to be settled is the most probable reading(s) of the PN. All other forms of the name argue that the initial letter of the form *muppîm* is undoubtedly corrupt. Furthermore, the GA *šûpāmî* proves that all the forms with a quasi-plural ending *-îm* are incorrect.[135] The variant spellings ##2-3 can be brought closer into line with the GA *šûpāmî* if they are pointed **šūpām*.[136] This reduces the readings of the PN to two: *šĕpûpām* and *šûpām*. Regardless of whether

---

[133]The spelling *ḥūšīm* in 1 Chr 7:12, written without *y mater lectionis*, also implies that we are not dealing with a plural suffix.

[134]For possible examples of metathesis in EH PNN, see my "Edomite Seal-Impression," *JNES* (forthcoming).

[135]As was the case with s.v. "ḥûpām," p. 174; and "šûḥām," p. 180.

[136]As suggested by Rudolph, *Chronikbücher*, p. 66. Again, the gemination appears to be secondary. See s.v. "ḥammûʾēl," pp. 62-63; and "ḥûpām," pp. 174-75, and compare Num 26:39 with 1 Chr 7:12, 15. The Chronicler (or his source) appears to have misunderstood these names.

the PN derives from a geminate (**špp*) or a hollow root (**šwp*), it appears probable that the PN terminates in the enclitic morpheme.

B. *Dubious Examples*

1. *gēršōm.*

Variant spellings: 1. *gēršôm*; 2. *gēršôn*.

Classification: Can.--1) son of Moses (Exod 2:22); 2) son of Levi (1 Chr 6:1);[137] 3) son of Phinehas (Ezra 8:2).

Structure: one-word name, *gērš-* (base unknown; < **grš* I ?, "to drive out") + *-ō/ôm* enclitic morpheme.

Meaning: unknown.

Parallels: Ph-P. *grš* (*PNPP*, p. 107); Saf. and Min.. *jrs* (*PIAN*, p. 158);[138] WS (Arab.) *ga-ra-ši-ú* (*WSB*, p. 219), NA *gír-sa-ʾ* (*WSB*, p. 322 n. 15); Nab. *gršw* (Cantineau, 2:80).

Comments: In the preceding section all the probable examples of the enclitic morpheme are uniformly vocalized *-ām*;[139] here alone among Canaanite PNN do we have the vocalization *-ō/ôm*. One may account for this unique vocalization by positing *gēršôn* (< *gērš-* + *-ôn* [<**-ānu*] derivational nominal suffix) as the original form of the name. The form of the name ending in *-m* was patterned after other Canaanite PNN in which the terminations *-m* and *-n* interchange, only with this name does the form of the name with *-n* appear to be the older of the two.[140] The popular etymology (Exod 2:22; 18:3), which seeks to analyze the word as a compound PN (*gēr* + *šām*, "stranger (was) there"), is based on the later form of the name and, at any rate, ignores the PNN cited above formed from the triradical root **grš*.[141] Thus the PN Gershom is a secondary formation rather than a probable example of a PN terminating in the enclitic morpheme.

---

[137]This individual is referred to by forms of the PN terminating in *-m* and *-n*.

[138]Throughout this study, Arabic j corresponds to Semitic g.

[139]See p. 168 n. 72.

[140]See p. 169 n. 80.

[141]The view of Bauer, *OLZ* 33 (1930), col. 591, who translates "Schätzling of *šwm*," is unduly influenced by the popular etymology and needs no refutation.

2. ***hôhām.***

Classification: Can.--king of Hebron (Josh 10:3).

Structure: one-word name, *hôh-* (**qāl* base ?) + *-ām* enclitic morpheme.

Meaning: unknown.

Comments: Gelb cites this PN as an instance of a name terminating in mimation.[142] LXX B transliterates *αιλαμ* (!). If this PN were derived from a triradical root **hhm*, it would be a **qāqal* base, which is a rare formation (BL §61pβ). The LXX B transliteration and the lack of a recognizable root disqualify this PN from further consideration.

3. *hêmām.*

Variant spelling: *hômām.*

Classification: Can.--son of Seir, the Horite in Edom (Gen 36:22).

Structure: one-word name, *hêm-* (base unknown) + *-ām* enclitic morpheme.

Meaning: unknown.

Parallels: Can. *hêmān*, Saf. *hmm*, *hmmt*, Qat. *hmm*, Sab. *hmmʾl* (*PIAN*, p. 624).

Comments: Again Gelb suggested we see here an Edom. PN terminating in *-m*.[143] But two alternative analyses place this in doubt. First, the North and South Arabian PNN cited above suggest a triradical root **hmm*.[144] Second, Morag proposes to equate Hemam/Homam with the PN Heman; according to him, the roots **ymm/n* are related and mean "lucky, fortunate."[145] Whatever the structure and meaning of this PN, the final *-m* is not certainly the enclitic morpheme.

---

[142]Gelb, *RSO* 12 (1930) 235.

[143]Ibid. BL §61ji recognizes a *-m* suffix here also. Kornfeld, "Edomiterlisten," p. 232, compares the Biblical PN with the MLArab. *hāma* (*haim*, *hayamān*) "to fall in love," apparently understanding the final *-m* as a suffix.

[144]For the BH roots **hmm* I and II, see KB3, p. 241.

[145]Morag, *EI* 5 (1958) 139. In Gen. 36:22, LXX B transliterates *αιμαν* for Hemam. But compare p. 169 n. 80.

4. *ya*ʿ*lām*.

Classification: Can.--son of Esau (Gen 36:5).

Structure: 1. one-word name, *ya*ʿ*l-* (< **yā*ʿ*ēl*) + *-ām* enclitic morpheme.
2. verbal-sentence name, *ya*ʿ*lām* (< **ǵlm* "to be strong, to grow up" [= BH ***ʿ*lm* III], 3rd m.s. Qal imperfect).

Meaning: 1. "mountain-goat."
2. "(DN) is strong."

Parallels: Can. ʿ*ālemet*,[146] BH CNN ʿ*elem*, ʿ*almâ*; Saf. *ǵlm*, *ǵlmt* (*PIAN*, pp. 457-58).

Comments: The two interpretations mentioned above are listed in KB3 (p. 402).[147] In his commentary on Genesis, Westermann lists Yaʿlam as an animal name, thus opting for the first structure/-meaning.[148] The ʿ*ayin* in the BH CN **yā*ʿ*ēl* "mountain-goat" is original (not secondarily from *ǵ*). Contrarily, the LXX B transliteration ιεγλομ indicates that the PN derives from a root which contains *ǵ*.[149] Therefore it is probable that the PN is an imperfect verbal form from a root I-*ǵ* rather than an animal name terminating in the enclitic morpheme.

5. *miryām*.

Classification: Can.--1) sister of Moses and Aaron (Num 26:59); 2) tribe of Judah (1 Chr 4:17).

---

[146]On the derivation of this PN from the root **ǵlm*, see my "The Semitic Root **Ǵlm* and the Hebrew Name ʿAlemet," *ZAW* (forthcoming).

[147]With the qualification that KB3 equivocates between the roots ***ʿ*lm* I (etymological ʿ*ayin* !) and ***ʿ*lm* II.

[148]Claus Westermann, *Genesis 12-36*, transl. John J. Scullion (Minneapolis: Augsburg Publishing House, 1985), p. 567. Likewise W. Robertson Smith, "Animal Worship and Animal Tribes among the Arabs and in the Old Testament," *The Journal of Philology* 9 (1880) 91; and Martin Flashar, "Das Ghain in der Septuaginta," *ZAW* 28 (1908) 212, who, while admitting that the LXX transliteration reflects *ǵ*, explains it as a (false) popular etymology. For the animal name, see the Can. PNN *yā*ʿ*ēl*, *ya*ʿ*lâ/ya*ʿ*ălā*ʾ, BH CN **yā*ʿ*ēl*; Liḥ., Saf., and Sab. *y*ʿ*l* (*PIAN*, p. 676).

[149]As noted by Blau, *Polyphony*, p. 34; Gray, pp. 90-91 n. 5. Theodor Nöldeke, "Bemerkungen über hebräische und arabische Eigennamen," *ZDMG* 15 (1861) 807, understood the PN Yaʿlam as an imperfect verbal form, but he did not specify the root.

Structure: 1. nominal-sentence name, *mir-* (< **marʾ* "lord" + *-yām* (DN).
2. one-word name, *miry-* (< BH **mrʾ* III "to be fat") + *-ām* enclitic morpheme.
3. one-word or shortened name, *miry-* (< Eg. *mry/mryt* "beloved") + *-ām* enclitic morpheme.
4. one-word or shortened name, *miryām* (*m-* preformative noun, < a. WS *râmu* III "to give" [*AHw*, p. 952], or b. WS **rw/ym* "to be high").

Meaning: 1. "Yamm is lord."
2. "plump, corpulent."
3. "Beloved (of DN)."
4. a. "gift (of DN)"; or b. "(DN is ?) the exalted one."

Parallels: Ug. CN *mrym* (*UT* §§19.1550, 2311); Palm. *mrym* (*PNPI*, p. 97); Aram. *mrym, mryn, mrymʾ* (*ATTM*, p. 736); Grk *μαριαμ* (Luke 10:39), *μαρια* (Acts 12:12).[150]

Comments: The interpretation of the PN Miryam involves considerable difficulty, and this has lead to a plethora of suggestions. As regards our first proposed structure/meaning, Zadok has collected a considerable amount of onomastic material for the element *mār* (< **marʾ* "lord") in West Semitic PNN.[151] The main drawback is the total absence of the element *mār* "lord" in both early West Semitic and Canaanite PNN.[152] The appellative *mār* is in fact typically Aramaic,

---

[150]For the passage *mrym* > *mryn* > *mryh* > Grk *μαρια*, see Eduard Y. Kutscher, "The Language of the Genesis Apocryphon," *Scripta Hierosolymitana* 4 (1957) 23 n. 118; reprinted in *Hebrew and Aramaic Studies*, ed. Zeev Ben-Ḥayyim, Aharon Dotan, and Gad Sarfatti (Jerusalem: Magnes Press, 1977), p. 25 n. 118.

[151]Zadok, *WSB*, pp. 64-65. The LXX B transliteration *μαριαμ*, pace MT *miryām*, may imply an original *a* vowel in the first syllable, unless this *a* vowel is due to vowel assimilation (Könnecke, p. 23). For other (unsuccessful) attempts to interpret this name, see Laurence Kutler, "A 'Strong' Case for Hebrew MAR," *UF* 16 (1984) 115-16: "The sea is mighty" (< BH **mar* "strong"); Goldberg, "Northern-Type-Names," p. 73: "strength of Yam or blessed by Yam" (< Ug. **mrr* "to bless, be strong"); D. Volter, "Mirjam," *ZAW* 38 (1919-20) 111-12: "the one whom the sea loves" (< Eg. **mr* "to love").

[152]As evidence that *mār* is contained in Hebrew PNN, Zadok, *WSB*, p. 64, cites Noth, *IPN*, p. 143 n. 2, who in turn cited two PNN: biblical *mrybʿl* and EH *mrnyw* (S 42.3). The etymology of the first name is uncertain, and the second PN should now, in light of Kaufman's restudy of the ostraca, be read *ʾdnyw* (Kaufman, *Samaria Ostraca*, pp. 138, 143). Fowler, p. 215, correctly observes that "Heb. names do not conclusively contain Aram. *mrʾ*." According to Philip C. Hammond, "An Ammonite Stamp Seal from ʿAmman," *BASOR* 160 (1960) 41, the Amm. PN *mrʾl* (*ALIA*, p. 85) should be compared to North Arabian *mrʾl* and be translated "man of El."

and its distribution is restricted to the various dialects of that language.[153] Our second proposed structure/meaning has been championed by Bardenhewer.[154] But it relies on III-y/III-ʾ verb interchange, generally plausible but for which there is no evidence in this case. Further, the root **mrʾ* is not elsewhere attested in Canaanite PNN.[155]

According to our third proposed structure/meaning, Miryam is a *Mischname* composed of the Eg. passive participle *mry* "beloved" plus the enclitic morpheme.[156] In support of this, other Eg. PNN in the family of Moses have been noted.[157] This interpretation seems to account well for the etymology and structure of the PN, but several considerations militate against it. In participle-type names, there is generally a congruence between the gender of the participle and the sex of the name bearer, insofar as the participle is descriptive of the name bearer (e.g., "blessed" or "beloved" by the deity). Since the PN Miryam is borne by a female, one would expect a feminine form of the Eg. passive participle (*mrt/mrʾit/mryt*) to be used.[158] Although the feminine *-t* is often not written when in final position, it is expressed in the script when in non-final position (before the enclitic *-m* in this case); thus its absence in the PN Miryam is difficult to reconcile with the Egyptian derivation of this name.[159] Also a suggested etymology (Eg.

153The restriction of the vocable *mār* to Aramaic has been noted by André Caquot, "Sur l'onomastique religieuse de Palmyre," *Syria* 39 (1962) 251; Hammond, *BASOR* 160 (1960) 40; Maraqten, *SPARI*, p. 53. The interdialectal equivalent in Canaanite is **ʾdn*.

154*Der Name Maria*, pp. 153-54. Also Ludwig Köhler, *Hebrew Man*, transl. Peter R. Ackroyd (London: SCM Press, 1956), p. 33. Bardenhewer's view was criticized by Hubert Grimme, "Der Name Mirjam," *BZ* 7 (1909) 245-51, whose own interpretation ("My [divine] kinsman is the High one") is scarcely probable.

155Gelb, *RSO* 12 (1930) 235, attempts to derive the PN from a root **mrh*, "to be reluctant." This suggestion has little merit.

156Alan H. Gardiner, "The Egyptian Origin of Some English Personal Names," *JAOS* 56 (1936) 195-97; Stamm, *BHAN*, p. 129.

157Perhaps of interest is the remark preserved in 1 Chr 4:17, the only other occurrence of the PN Miryam in the Hebrew Bible (outside of Moses' sister), where Bityah (the mother of Miryam) is described as the daughter of Pharaoh.

158Hermann Ranke, *Die ägyptischen Personennamen*, 3 vols. (Glückstadt: J. J. Augustin, 1935-77), 1:158-61. I might add that the sex of the person named Miryam in 1 Chr 4:17 is not necessarily male, as assumed by BDB, p. 599; KB2, p. 567; KB3, p. 601; and Grimme, "Der Name Mirjam," p. 251. In the New Testament, the Greek forms *μαριαμ* and *μαρια* are only borne by females.

159Manfred Görg, "Mirjam -- ein weiterer Versuch," *BZ*, n.s. 23 (1979) 285-89, did not provide a satisfactory answer to this objection in his attempt to interpret Miryam as an Egyptian name meaning "beloved of Amon" (< **mr-ymn*, with loss of the final *-n*). The complexity of his interpretation robs it of credibility. In another article ("Zum jüdischen Personennamen *MYʾMN*," *BN* 38/39 [1987] 33-35), Görg argued that the EH PN *myʾmn* is to be identified with the Egyptian PN *mry-ymn* "beloved of Amon"! The ad hoc nature of his interpretations is apparent.

mry) that leaves one letter (*-m*) of the name unaccounted for should be viewed with suspicion.[160]

While structure/meaning 4. a. is attractive,[161] the objections raised by Levine are, in my opinion, fatal to it.[162] In short, most if not all the evidence adduced by von Soden to support his interpretation is tenuous. The Amor. PNN that he claims contain this root could just as well be derived from the root **rwm*, "to be high." Structure/meaning 4. b. is Levine's own suggestion, on the basis of the Ugaritic vocable *mrym*. This suggestion yields an acceptable meaning for the PN.[163] From the perspective of morphology, it has an exact analogy in BH. Just as *midyān* occurs as a biform of *mādôn*, both meaning "strife" and derived from the root **dw/yn*, so *miryām* occurs as a biform of *mārôm*, both derived from the root **rw/ym*.[164] Thus the final *-m* on the name is the final consonant of the root **rw/ym*. Therefore, the PN Miryam should not be considered as an Egypto-Can. PN terminating in the enclitic morpheme.

6. *ʿamrām*.

Classification: Can.--1) father of Moses (Exod 6:18); 2) post-exilic individual who married a foreign wife (Ezra 10:34).

Structure: 1. one-word name or shortened name, *ʿamr-* (**qatl* base, <**ʿmr* [cognate with MLArab. *ʿumr* "life, life span," Wehr, p. 753]) + *-ām* enclitic morpheme.
2. verbal-sentence name, *ʿam-* (**qall* base) + *-rām* (<**rwm*, "to be high, exalted," 3rd m.s. Qal perfect).

---

[160] Rita J. Burns, *Has the Lord Indeed Spoken Only Through Moses? A Study of the Biblical Portrait of Miriam*, SBLDS 84 (Atlanta: Scholars Press, 1987), pp. 9-10, derived the first part of the name from Eg. *mry*, but left the final *-m* unexplained.

[161] See Wolfram von Soden, "*Mirjām*--Maria '(Gottes-)Geschenk'," *UF* 2 (1970) 169-72; reprinted in *Bibel und alter Orient: Altorientalische Beiträge zum Alten Testament von Wolfram von Soden*, ed. Hans-Peter Müller, BZAW 162 (Berlin: Walter de Gruyter, 1985), pp. 129-33.

[162] Baruch A. Levine, "Assyriology and Hebrew Philology: A Methodological Re-examination," in *Mesopotamien und seine Nachbarn: Politische und kulturelle Wechselbeziehungen im Alten Vorderasien vom 4. bis 1. Jahrtausend v. Chr*, ed. Hans-Jörg Nissen and Johannes Renger, XXV. Rencontre Assyriologique Internationale Berlin, 3. bis 7. Juli 1978, Teil 1 (Berlin: Dietrich Reimer, 1982), pp. 525-27.

[163] In support of Levine's proposal, note the phrase *mĕrôm ʿam-hāʾāreṣ* (Isa 24:4), where BH *mārôm* is used figuratively and collectively of nobles.

[164] For evidence of a root **rym* "to be high" in Northwest Semitic, see Sivan, *GAGNWS*, p. 266; *UT* §19.2311; and p. 188 n. 172.

Meaning: 1. "life (?)," or "(DN) is life-preserver (?)."
2. "The (divine) kinsman is exalted."

Parallels: Amor. *ḫa-mu-ra-ma* (*CAAA*, p. 585); Can. *rām*, GA *ʿamrāmī*; NA *am-ra-mu* (*APN*, p. 22); N/LB *am-ri-im-me*, NA *a-me-ra-ma* (*WSB*, pp. 55, 103).

Comments: At first glance, our first proposed structure/meaning appears to be the correct analysis of the name.[165] Three arguments may be advanced in support of this interpretation: 1) The root *ʿ*mr* is attested elsewhere in the Israelite onomasticon in the PN *ʿomrî*, borne not only by the famous king but also by three other individuals of the tribes of Israel; 2) When the kinship term *ʿam* "kinsman" occupies first position in compound PNN in the Hebrew Bible, it is elsewhere written *ʿammî-*, and never simply *ʿam-*;[166] and 3) North and South Arabian PNN provide exact parallels.[167]

Each of these arguments has certain weaknesses, and they will be discussed in reverse order. First, it is hardly surprising that North and South Arabian PNN provide exact parallels. These onomastica are rich in both structural variation and vocabulary. Though the root *ʿ*mr* is productive in North and South Arabian, such is not the case with Canaanite PNN in the Hebrew Bible, or even Northwest Semitic. Judging from its distribution, this root is native to Arabic, and not Northwest Semitic.[168] Hence it is unlikely that Moses' father bore a name derived from the root *ʿ*mr*. If possible, one should seek to explain the PN ʿAmram in terms of elements common in Northwest Semitic.

Second, a consideration of compound PNN beginning with *ʾāb* "father" in first position vitiates the second argument. In most compound PNN beginning with *ʾāb*, this kinship term is written *ʾăbî-*. There are, however, some exceptions, most notably the PN *ʾabrām*,

---

[165]Interpreters who derive this PN from the triradical root *ʿ*mr* are Theodor Nöldeke, Review of *Kinship and Marriage in early Arabia*, by W. Robertson Smith, *ZDMG* 40 (1886) 185; Bardenhewer, *Der Name Maria*, p. 16; Brockelmann, *GVG*, 1:396; Gardiner, *JAOS* 56 (1936) 195; Gelb, *RSO* 12 (1930) 234.

[166]See KB3, pp. 798-99, and the PNN *ʿammîʾēl*, *ʿammîhûd*, *ʿammîzābād*, *ʿammînādāb*, and *ʿammîšadday*.

[167]Liḥ., Saf., Thad., Qat., and Sab. *ʿmr*; Saf., Ḥaḍ., Qat., and Sab. *ʿmrm*; Saf., Thad., and Sab. *ʿmm* (*PIAN*, pp. 436, 438).

[168]Of course, archaic vocabulary is often retained precisely in names (Barr, *Comparative Philology*, pp. 181-84). This insight, however, is hardly sufficient to sustain the derivation of the name from the root *ʿ*mr* in light of the total absence--with the possible exception of the PN ʿOmri--of the root in Northwest Semitic and the profuse use of it in South Semitic.

also written *ʾăbîrām.*[169] The compound PNN ʿAmram and ʾAbram are composed of a kinship term in the first position, followed by a Qal perfect verb of the root **rwm*. Finally, it must be admitted that the PN ʿOmri is derived from the root **ʿmr*. Whereas the PN ʿOmri is a **qutl* base noun,[170] the PN ʿAmram would be a **qatl* base. Though both bases may coexist side by side in a language, it may be said that the name ʿOmri does not provide a precise morphological parallel to ʿAmram. Noting the absence of the root **ʿmr* elsewhere in the Israelite onomasticon (or for that matter, in Northwest Semitic), Noth concluded that ʿOmri may have been of Arab descent.[171] The PN he bore appears to point in that direction. Whatever the case may be, the PN ʿOmri does not provide a secure basis upon which to interpret the PN ʿAmram.

A positive argument may be added to these negative arguments. Two of the West Semitic PNN in cuneiform writing cited above cannot be derived from a root **ʿmr*; in fact, they favor the second structure/-meaning: 1) N/LB *am-ri-im-me*, the second element apparently from a root **rym*, a biform of **rwm*;[172] and 2) NA *a-me-ra-ma* (< **ʿammîrām*). Thus as recognized by most scholars,[173] the PN ʿAmram is a Canaanite PN meaning "the (divine) kinsman is exalted," and consequently it does not terminate in the enclitic morpheme.

7. *šimʾām.*

Variant spelling: *šimʾâ.*

Classification: Can.--tribe of Benjamin (1 Chr 9:38).

---

[169]Three other PNN in the Hebrew Bible exhibit the same fluctuation: *ʾabnēr/ʾăbînēr, ʾabšay/ʾăbîšay, and ʾabšālôm/ʾăbîšālôm.* For further discussion, see pp. 145-50.

[170]Despite LXX B *αμβρι*, the NA transcription *ḫum/ḫu-m-ri-i/a* (*WSB*, p. 245) makes this certain.

[171]Martin Noth, "Gemeinsemitische Erscheinungen in der israelitischen Namengebung," *ZDMG* 81 (1927) 20 n. 2; idem, *The History of Israel*, 2d ed. (New York: Harper & Row, 1960), p. 230, n. 1; idem, *IPN*, pp. 63, 222 n. 7. See also James A. Montgomery, "Arabic Names in I. and II. Kings," *The Moslem World* 31 (1941) 266-67, who observed that the lack of a patronym may support Omri's Arab affiliation. The presence of an Arabian name borne by an "Israelite" ruler in the ninth century B.C. poses no historico-chronological problem. See Ephʿal, *The Ancient Arabs*, passim.

[172]Zadok, *WSB*, pp. 84, 103. For **rw/ym* in Ugaritic, see *UT* §19.2311, and see also p. 186 n. 164 above.

[173]Gray, pp. 45, 47, 51; KB3, p. 804; Noth, *ZDMG* 81 (1927) 20 n. 2; 31 n. 1; idem, *IPN*, pp. 16, 33; Thompson, *Historicity*, p. 30; M. Krenkel, "Das Verwandtschaftswort *ʿam*," *ZAW* 8 (1888) 282; Stamm, *BHAN*, pp. 37 n. 3, 68-69, 140.

Structure: one-word name, *šim*ʾ- (**qvtl* base) + -*ām* enclitic morpheme.

Meaning: unknown.

Parallels: Can. *šammā*ʾ; Ph-P. *šm*ʾ (*PNPP*, pp. 419-20); N/LB *šá-ma-*ʾ, *šá-am-ma-*ʾ (*WSB*, p. 119).

Comments: This name has been classified as a dubious example for the following reasons: 1) The meaning and etymology of the PN are unknown; 2) There are no exact parallels that suggest this PN terminates in encltic -*m*; and 3) The exchange of -*m* and -*h* can satisfactorily be explained as nothing more than graphic confusion.[174] In support of this, it should be observed that the PN *šim*ʾ*ām* is transliterated in the LXX A as *σαμα* and in LXX B as *σαμαα*.

Finally two names should be mentioned to complete the list of dubious examples. The PN *hārûm* occurs once, in 1 Chr 4:8. This PN may be related to the PN *hōrām* discussed above (p. 173). It has been excluded from the list of probable examples because of the likelihood of textual corruption.[175] The final name is a Ph-P. PN which appears in two different forms in the MT: *ḥîrôm* and *ḥîrām*. Brockelmann and Gelb have suggested that these PNN terminate with a -*ôm/ām* suffix.[176] But the full name from which these are derived is undoubtedly *ʾ*aḥîrô/ām*, the aphaeresis of the ʾ*aleph* being a common feature of Ph-P. PNN. Thus the -*m* is the final root consonant of the verb **rwm* and not the enclitic morpheme.

C. *Non-Canaanite Examples*

These three PNN have been excluded from the preceding list because of their non-Canaanite linguistic affiliation. On the basis of linguistic criteria alone, one might conclude that these are Canaanite PNN. In each instance, however, topical criteria determine that they are (North or South) Arabian PNN. The first two PNN occur in an

---

174See Samuel Krauss, "Textkritik auf Grund des Wechsels von *h* und *m*," *ZAW* 48 (1930) 321-24, who has collected roughly twenty-five instances of this exchange. For another instance among PNN, note the BH PNN ʾ*ăbîyāh* and ʾ*ăbîyām*.

175Bombergiana reads *hārum*; LXX B *ιαρειμ*. See *BHS* textual apparatus and the comments of Rudolph, *Chronikbücher*, p. 30.

176Brockelmann, *GVG*, 1:396; Gelb, *RSO* 12 (1930) 235.

Arabian genealogy in the book of Genesis, that of the sons of Joktan (Gen 10:26-30).[177]

1. Probable Examples

1. *ʾăbîmāʾēl.*

Classification: Arabian--"son" of Joktan (Gen 10:28).

Structure: nominal-sentence name, *ʾăbî-* + *-ma-* enclitic particle + *-ʾēl* (**qil* base, BL §61i).

Meaning: "My father truly is El/god."

Parallels: Akk. *a-bi$_4$-ilum(DINGIR), a-bi-i-lu-um, a-bu-um-ilum(DINGIR^{lum}), a-bu-um-ì-lum* (*ANG,* p. 297); Eblaite *a-ba$_4$-il* (ARET IV:231); Amor. *a-bi-mi-ki-ilu(DINGIR), a-bu-um-ilu(DINGIR)* (*CAAA,* pp. 554-55); Can. *ʾăbîʾēl;* Sab. *ʾbmʿṯtr* (*PIAN,* p. 15).

Comments: Probably a tribal name. The intervening *-m-*, vocalized as *-mā-* in the MT, is the enclitic morpheme. Hazarmaveth, which appears in the same list (Gen 10:26), has been preserved right up to the present day as the name of a region on the southwest coast of Arabia.

2. *lĕmôʾēl.*

Variant spelling: *lĕmûʾēl.*

Classification: Arabian--king of Massa (Prov 31:1).

Structure: 1. nominal-sentence name, *lĕmû-* (< DN *Lim)+ *-ʾēl* (**qil* base, BL §61i).
2. compound name, *lĕ-* preposition + *-mô-* enclitic particle + *-ʾēl.*

Meaning: 1. "Lim is god."
2. "(Belonging) to god/El."

---

[177]In general, see Fred V. Winnett, "The Arabian Genealogies in the Book of Genesis," in *Translating and Understanding the Old Testament: Essays in Honor of Herbert Gordon May,* ed. Harry T. Frank and William L. Reed (Nashville: Abingdon, 1970), pp. 171-96.

Parallels: Can. *lā'ēl*; IAram. *lnḥy* (Kornfeld, *OAA*, p. 57); Palm. *lmlk'*, *lrmn*, *lšmš*, *lš[mš]'*, *lšmšw*, *lšmšy* (*PNPI*, pp. 29-30, 93); Hat. *lšgl'* (*PIH*, pp. 119-20); Saf. and Sab. *lšms* (*PIAN*, p. 515); Grk λεαστaρτος (< Ph. **l'štrt* [*NWJ*, p. 78]).

Comments: Two lines of evidence support the view that this PN is Arabian. First, in Prov 31:1 he is described as the "king of Massa."[178] Massa is attested elsewhere in the Hebrew Bible (Gen 25:14; 1 Chr 1:30), in the Jabal Ghunaym inscriptions (i.e., North Arabian), and in cuneiform inscriptions as a GN or TN in North Arabia.[179] Second, in Prov 30:1 are mentioned two other PNN--*'āgûr* and *yāqeh*[180]--that are connected to the tribe of Massa. These two PNN have good parallels in the North and South Arabian onomastica.[181]

According to our first proposed structure/meaning, the element *lĕmû* conceals the DN Lim.[182] To support this, Jirku appealed to other PNN of the form **C₁ĕC₂û'ēl* (e.g., Can. *yĕmû'ēl* and Ug. *ym'il*) as well as the *u* vowel, which preserves the old nominal ending *-u(m)*.[183] It is true that the deity Lim is prevalent in West Semitic PNN of the second millennium B.C. found at Mari, Ugarit, and Alalakh.[184]

---

[178]In support of this translation of BH *melek maśśā'*, see Ferdinand Deist, "Prov. 31:1. A Case of Constant Mistranslation," *JNSL* 6 (1978) 1-3; Otto Plöger, *Sprüche Salomos (Proverbia)*, Biblischer Kommentar Altes Testament, Band XVII (Neukirchen-Vluyn: Neukirchener, 1984), pp. 369-70.

[179]F. V. Winnett and W. L. Reed, *Ancient Records from North Arabia*, Near and Middle East Series, vol. 6 (Toronto: University of Toronto Press, 1970), pp. 29, 90-91; Albright, "Tribe of Massa'," pp. 2-7; KB3, p. 604.

[180]I assume the final *h* is consonantal despite the absence of *mappîq* (i.e., the *h* has quiesced in the Masoretic tradition). So also with the theophore *-yh*.

[181]As already noted by Albright, "Tribe of Massa'," p. 7; Eph'al, *JAOS* 94 (1974) 114-15. With reference to *'āgûr*, compare Saf. and Min. *'jr* (*PIAN*, p. 22); on *yāqeh*, compare Qat. and Sab. *yqhmlk* (*PIAN*, p. 681); Min. and Sab. *wqh*, Sab. *wqh'b*, Saf., Ḥaḍ., Min., and Sab. *wqh'l* (*PIAN*, p. 648); Sab. *mlkwqh* (*PIAN*, p. 566); Sab. *'mwqh* (*PIAN*, p. 442).

[182]Anton Jirku, "Das n. pr. Lemu'el (Prov. 31:1) und der Gott Lim," *ZAW* 66 (1954) 151; idem, "Zu einigen Orts- und Eigennamen Palästinas-Syriens," *ZAW* 75 (1963) 87. Others holding this view are Bauer, *OLZ* 33 (1930) 594-95; E. Lipiński, "Le dieu Lim," in *La civilisation de Mari*, XVe Recontre Assyriologique Internationale, ed. J.-R. Kupper (N.p.: Université de Liége, 1967), p. 152 n. 4. The views of Albright, "Tribe of Massa'," pp. 6-7, that Lemu'el is a truncated survival of **Ilīma-El*, or of D. S. Margoliouth, *The Relations between Arabs and Israelites prior to the Rise of Islam*, The Schweich Lectures, 1921 (London: Oxford University Press, 1924), p. 30, that Lemu'el means "belonging to Mauil," are highly implausible.

[183]Jirku, *ZAW* 66 (1954) 151.

[184]In the execration texts, Moran, *Or* 26 (1957) 340-41, finds the DN in the WS PN *m3k3m* (e 16) by normalizing **mlklm*. But Helck, *Beziehungen Ägyptens*, p.

However, no certain attestations of this deity are found in West Semitic PNN from the first millennium B.C.[185] A more decisive argument is that the DN Lim in the Ugaritic PN *yrgblʾim* is written with *ʾaleph.*[186] The MT vocalization with a *u* vowel appears to be the product of paradigm pressure from the series of PNN of the type $*C_1\breve{e}C_2\hat{u}$*ʾēl.* Furthermore, the Arabian origin of the name weakens the hypothesis that the deity Lim is concealed in this name. This leads to our second proposed structure/meaning,[187] which places this PN in the class of prepositional names of the structure *l* + DN,[188] with the intervening *-m-* as an enclitic particle reinforcing the preposition.[189]

2. Dubious Example

1. *ʾalmôdād.*

Classification: Arabian--"son" of Joktan (Gen 10:26).

Structure: 1. *ʾal-* (= **ʾēl*) + *-mô-* enclitic particle + *-dād* (< a. **dwd* "to love," 3rd m.s. Qal perfect, or b. DN Dad [< **Hadad*]).
2. *ʾal-* (= **ʾēl*) + *-môdād* (*m-* preformative noun, < **wdd* "to love").

47, transcribes *m()-l-k-r-m,* which appears preferable in light of the Can. PN *malkîrām* and the Ph-P. PN *mlkrm* (Benz, *PNPP*, p. 408).

185"*Līm* . . . is probably not attested to in names from first-millennium Mesopotamia" (Zadok, *WSB*, p. 279).

186A. Herdner, "Nouveaux textes alphabetiques de Ras Shamra--XXIVe campagne, 1961," in *Ugaritica VII*, Mission de Ras Shamra, vol. 18 (Paris: Geuthner; Leiden: Brill, 1978), p. 6 (RS 24.246, l. 22--*yrgblʾim*). For the DN Lim in Ug. PNN in syllabic script, see Gröndahl, *PTU*, p. 155.

187Proponents of this view are Bauer, *Ostkanaanäer*, p. 57; Fowler, pp. 122-23, 128, 282; James A. Montgomery, *Arabia and the Bible* (Philadelphia: University of Pennsylvania Press, 1934), p. 171 n. 21; Noth, *IPN*, p. 249; Nöldeke, *WZKM* 6 (1892) 314-15; idem, "Einigen Gruppen semitischer Personennamen," in *Beiträge zur Semitischen Sprachwissenschaft* (Strassburg: Karl J. Trübner, 1904), pp. 104-5.

188For other names of this type and further bibliography, see A. Lemaire, "Divinités égyptiennes dans l'onomastique phénicienne," in *Studia Phoenicia IV: Religio Phoenicia*, ed. C. Bonnet, E. Lipiński, and P. Marchetti (Namur: Société des études classiques, 1986), pp. 90-91; Tigay, p. 24 and n. 20; Maraqten, *SPARI*, pp. 107, 176.

189Note the extended forms of the prepositions *l-*, *b-*, and *k-* in BH poetry (*lm-*, *bm-*, and *km-*). Robertson, *Linguistic Evidence*, pp. 109-10, summarizes the distribution of these Hebrew prepositions plus enclitic *-m* in the Hebrew Bible. For enclitic *-m* in South Arabian, see the brief remarks of Beeston, *Descriptive Grammar*, p. 67, and *Sabaic Grammar*, pp. 47-48.

Meaning: 1. a. "Truly El/God loves" or b. "Dad [= Hadad] is truly (my)God."
2. "God/El is a friend."

Parallels: Akk. *mudādum* (*ANG*, p. 248); Amor. *mu-da-du, mu-da-du-um* (*CAAA*, p. 624); Ug. *mddbʿl* (*PTU*, p. 143); Can. *ʾeldād, ʾĕlîdād, mêdād*;[190] NA *mu-da-da* (*WSB*, p. 139), *mu-da-di*;[191] Aram. *mwdd* (*SPARI*, pp. 86, 177); Sab. *mwddm*, Qat. *mwddn* (*PIAN*, p. 574).

Comments: The LXX B transliterates the initial syllable as ελ- in both occurrences of this tribal name in the Hebrew Bible (Gen 10:26; 1 Chr 1:20). Moreover, there is evidence that **ʾil* and **ʾal*, both meaning "god," interchange.[192] Consequently this is a theophoric name.

Our first proposed structure/meaning assumes that the *-mô-* is the enclitic particle.[193] But the widespread occurrence of a vocable **mdd* (< **wdd*) in other PNN argues that the name should be divided according to the second structure, viz. *ʾal-* + *-môdād*. Therefore it is unlikely that this Arabian name contains the enclitic morpheme.

IV. Late West Semitic PNN (extrabiblical)

The appearance of enclitic *-m* on Canaanite PNN in the Hebrew Bible would lead one to search for the same ending on extrabiblical late WS PNN. The following is a list of selected examples:

---

[190]LXX B μωδαδ and the SamP *mwdd* support a reading **môdād*.

[191]Frederick M. Fales, "West Semitic Names from the Governor's Palace," *Annali della facoltà di lingue e letterature straniere di ca' foscari* 13 (1974) 185.

[192]Frederick M. Fales, *Censimenti e catasti di epoca neo-assira*, Centro per le antichità e la storia dell'arte del Vicino Oriente, Studi economici e tecnologici, no. 2 (Rome: Istituto per l'oriente, 1973), p. 16; Zadok, *WO* 9 (1977-78) 42, 54 n. 139; idem, *UF* 17 (1985) 389 n. 23; Stephen A. Kaufman, "The Enigmatic Adad-milki," *JNES* 37 (1978) 107.

[193]For 1. a., see Eshel, pp. 258-59; for 1. b., see W. F. Albright, "The Biblical Tribe of Massaʾ and Some Congeners," in *Studi orientalistici in onore di Giorgio Levi della Vida*, 2 vols., Pubblicazioni dell'istituto per l'oriente, no. 52 (Rome: Istituto per l'oriente, 1956), 1:7. Albright cited no comparative evidence to support his view that Dad is an abbreviation of Hadad. A. Lemaire, "Nouveaux sceaux nord-ouest sémitique," *Sem* 33 (1983) 27-28 #13 (Pl. III:13), has suggested that *ddy* on an Aram. seal might be a hypocoristic of the DN Hadad, and R. Zadok, Review of *Studies in Aramaic Inscriptions and Onomastics I*, by E. Lipiński, *BO* 33 (1976) 227, has cited several additional possible examples. The problem with all these examples, with the possible exception of NA *gi-ri-da-di* (of the structural type client + DN?), is that it is sufficient to interpret *dd(y)* as the CN "paternal uncle" functioning as a theophoric element.

1. *WS PNN in cuneiform writing*

Such names as N/LB *šá-la-am-mu* and NA *sa-lam-me* (*WSB*, pp. 119) cannot be analyzed as terminating in the enclitic morpheme. As noted elsewhere in this study (p. 151), consonants and vowels that are not morphologically significant appear in the cuneiform writing of WS PNN. In the two names cited above, the scribe used a *-Cv* sign at the end of the names to represent a final vowel; the doubling of the final *m* is of no morphological significance. This explanation, however, does not obtain for the NA *sa-la-ma-me* (*WSB*, p. 162), which is a **qatāl* formation from the WS root **šlm*. This name is the cuneiform version of the IAram. PNN *šlwmm* and *šlmm* (see discussion below).

2. *Amm. PN*

The only probable example is the Amm. PN *mkmʾl* (Jackson, *ALIA*, p. 96), meaning "Who is like god/El?" To the best of my knowledge, this is the only PN of its kind in which the preposition is reinforced with enclitic *-m* (contrast Amm. [*m*]*kʾl*; Jackson, *ALIA*, p. 96). It appears that Jackson has failed to pay due attention to this occurrence of enclitic *-m* in this PN. In his synthesis and summation of the Ammonite language (pp. 93-109), he fails to mention it. The occurrence of enclitic *-m* on the Amm. preposition *k-* may be compared to the use of the enclitic particle on the BH prepositions *k-*, *b-*, and *l-*.[194] The use of the enclitic particle with these prepositions occurs predominantly in poetry rather than prose.[195] The archaic nature of poetic language has already been stressed.

3. *Ph-P. and Neo-Punic PNN*

From Ph-P. and Neo-Punic PNN that exhibit enclitic *-m*, the following names may be cited (non-mimated forms are also cited where they exist): *grgš/grgšm* (*PNPP*, p. 299); *mgn/mgnm* (Jongeling, pp. 39, 180), *mtr/mtrm* (*PNPP*, p.357); *nml/nmlm* "ant" (*PNPP*, pp. 360-61); *ʿkbr/ʿkbrm* "mouse" (*PNPP*, p. 377); *qnz/qnzm* (*PNPP*, p. 405). All the above-cited examples, with the exception of *mtr/mtrm*, were noted by Gelb and appear to be probable examples of the enclitic morpheme.[196]

---

[194]See p. 192 n. 189.

[195]Ibid., p. 109. Robertson counts fifty-six total examples of the preposition *k* plus enclitic *-m*, of which fifty-two occur in poetry. Out of these fifty-two, thirty-six examples occur in what he calls archaic poetic Hebrew.

[196]See Gelb, *RSO* 12 (1930) 239-41, who also cites several non-onomastic examples from Ph-P. The interpretation of the final *-m* as the enclitic morpheme is

Benz has discussed the afformative -*m* on Ph-P. PNN and has added a number of additional examples. In some of them the -*m* may represent the initial letter of the apocopated theophoric element *mlk*.[197]

4. *IAram. PNN*

Among the IAram. PNN attested at Elephantine are *šlwmm* and *šlmm* (*RVJPNE*, pp. 72, 80, 125, 182). Silverman is correct in his judgment that the first PN is a Hebrew name-type (*ā > *ō), from the nominal form *šlwm* plus -*m* suffix. He analyzes the second PN--*šlmm* -- as a Qal or Pael perfect with the -*m* suffix. But the -*m* suffix predominantly occurs on nominal rather than verbal forms. Hence the PN *šlmm* could be the same PN as *šlwmm*, with defective writing,[198] or more simply, the Aramaic equivalent of Hebrew *šlwm* "peace." These two PNN should be compared to the NA PN *sa-la-ma-me* (*WSB*, p. 162). Another example among IAram. PNN is the name *šbʿm*. Though this PN is transcribed *šbʿh* in *Aramaic Papyri of the Fifth Century B.C.*, Cowley himself noted that "the *h* is more like *m*."[199] An examination of the photograph confirms that the final consonant should be read as *m*.[200] Lastly Gelb cited additional examples of Aram. CNN and PNN.[201]

5. *North Arabian PNN*

Note the following examples: Liḥ. *ḥmrm* "donkey" (*PIAN*, p. 200); Saf. *jʿlm* (*PIAN*, p. 163); Saf. *ḥrbm* (*PIAN*, p. 182); Saf. *qrḥm* (*PIAN*, p. 479). The occurrence of mimation in North Arabian is discussed further by Gelb.[202]

---

preferred to that of Lidzbarski, who regarded the final -*m* as a plural morpheme in the PN *ʿkbrm* and in several other obscure PNN (Mark Lidzbarski, "Phönizische und aramäische Krugaufschriften aus Elephantine," in *Abhandlungen der königlich preussischen Akademie der Wissenschaften*, Philosophisch-historische Klasse [Berlin: Königlichen Akademie der Wissenschaften, 1912], p. 14).

197Benz, *PNPP*, p. 242-44.

198As suggested by Kornfeld, *OAA*, p. 73.

199A. Cowley, *Aramaic Papyri of the Fifth Century B.C.* (Oxford: Clarendon Press, 1923; reprint ed., Osnabrück: Otto Zeller, 1967), p. 201.

200A. Cowley, "Another Aramaic Papyrus of the Ptolemaic Period," *PSBA* 37 (1915) 217-21, and Pl. XXVI.

201Gelb, *RSO* 12 (1930) 241-43. The IAram. PN *mḥlm* which he cites is probably a PN in the form of a participle (< *ḥlm) rather than a name terminating in enclitic -*m* (so Silverman, *RVJPNE*, p. 146).

202Gelb, *RSO* 12 (1930) 254-57. See also the brief remarks by Harding, *PIAN*, p. 4.

6. *WS PNN in Greek transliteration*

The only clear example to be found in Wuthnow is Grk *σομσουμ* (< **šmšm*).[203]

V. Summary

A study of early West Semitic onomastica suggests that mimation (on singular nouns) and enclitic *-m* were once regular features of the grammar of these languages. Evidence to support this conclusion is drawn from Amorite, and West Semitic proper names in the execration texts, Alalakh tablets, Taanach tablets, and Amarna letters. Mimation appears to have fallen into disuse in early West Semitic and Akkadian during the period 1800-1500 B.C. The absence of the morpheme on Ugaritic vocables in Ugaritic and Akkadian scripts, and a few West Semitic glosses in the Amarna letters, corroborates this statement. Mimation may be retained as an archaism in PNN postdating this period of decline in the use of the morpheme. Although there is at least one clear example of the archaic use of mimation in EA PNN, the lack of any syllabic writings of Ugaritic PNN with the ending case vowel plus mimation leads to ambiguity in the interpretation of the final *-m* on Ugaritic PNN. Unless it is an archaism, this final *-m* is in all likelihood the enclitic morpheme, which was still a regular feature of the poetic language at Ugarit.

Since mimation had fallen into disuse long before the Canaanite languages made their historically and epigraphically attested appearances, it follows that these languages did not possess mimation as a regular feature of their respective grammars. The enclitic morpheme, so amply attested in Ugaritic, had by this time also fallen into disuse, with the exception that it occurs sporadically in ABH.

In light of the propensity for personal names to preserve archaic features of a language, it is hardly surprising that Canaanite PNN in the Hebrew Bible terminate in final *-m*. This *-m* morpheme on Canaanite PNN is either a remnant of mimation or an enclitic *-m*. Since mimation fell into disuse by 1500 B.C., the final *-m* morpheme on Canaanite PNN is probably best analyzed as enclitic *-m*. The following list of sixteen names constitutes the list of probable examples.

---

[203]Wuthnow, p. 111.

1. ʾUlam
2. ʾOnam
3. ʾAhuzzam
4. Bilʿam
5. Gaʿtam
6. Horam
7. Zetam
8. Hupham
9. Husham
10. Kimham
11. Malkam
12. Mishʿam
13. ʿIram
14. Pirʾam
15. Shuham
16. Shephupham

The final -*m* of all these PNN is preceded by a *qāmeṣ* (-*ām*). All the names appear to be simple nominal forms, with the exception of #12 Mishʿam, which is a (nominalized?) participle. Another seven names do not appear to terminate in enclitic -*m* and therefore constitute dubious examples:

1. Gershom
2. Hoham
3. Hemam
4. Yaʿlam
5. Miryam
6. ʿAmram
7. Shimʾam

Three PNN were excluded from the above lists because of their non-Canaanite linguistic affiliation. These are

1. ʾAbimaʾel
2. Lemoʾel
3. ʾAlmodad

Of these Arabian PNN, ##1 and 2 contain the enclitic morpheme; PN #3 constitutes a dubious example. The enclitic morpheme also occurs on extrabiblical late WS PNN. Examples were cited from WS PNN in cuneiform writing and Greek transliteration, and Amm., Ph-P., IAram., and North Arabian PNN.

CHAPTER 5

THE FEMININE MORPHEME *-AT*

The Semitic languages distinguish two genders: masculine and feminine. Whereas the masculine has no special formative, the feminine is mostly indicated by affixing *-(a)t* on the end of a noun. This is not to deny that some nouns, such as **ʾimm-* "mother," are construed as feminine without the formal marker *-(a)t*.

The study of feminine morphemes on PNN affords the opportunity to study the congruence, or lack thereof, between the grammatical gender of the name and the natural gender (i.e., the sex) of the name bearer. In onomastic studies, the phrase feminine name refers to the biological sex of the name bearer. Feminine nouns are well attested in feminine names throughout the WS onomasticon, functioning either as an element in a compound name or as a one-word name. In West Semitic PNN in consonantal script, it is often difficult to determine the biological sex of the name bearer. In some instances, kinship terms, the gender of a gentilic, and general contextual considerations provide some guidance on this matter. Conversely, this problem is minimized with West Semitic PNN in cuneiform script; for the most part the feminine determinative indicates the biological sex of the name bearer.[1]

I. Early West Semitic

Since the feminine morpheme *-(a)t* is recognized by Semitic scholars as the primary feminine sufformative, the following survey is only intended to note its distribution among the various West Semitic languages.

According to Gelb, Amorite possesses three feminine morphemes: *-at*, *-t*, and *-a*.[2] Note the following examples: 1) with *-at*: *a-*

---

[1]An exception to this statement is the omission of the name determinative before PNN that appear in witness lists.

[2]Gelb, *RANL* 13 (1958) §3.2.2. Maurice Birot, "Textes économiques de Mari (IV)," *RA* 50 (1956) 60 n. 1, has suggested that the suffix *-a* is itself a shortened form of *-atum*. Huffmon, *APNMT*, pp. 133-34, cites Birot's view with approval. By

ḫa-tum (*CAAA*, p. 556);[3] *a-lu-pa-tum* (*CAAA*, p., 558); *a-mi-ra-tum* (*CAAA*, p. 559); *a-tam-ra-tum* (*CAAA*, p. 561); *ṭà-ba-tum* (*CAAA*, p. 646); *ta-šu-ba-tum* (*CAAA*, p. 644); 2) with *-t*: *ia-qar-tum* (*CAAA*, p. 604); *a-da-at-ta* (*CAAA*, p. 555); *bi-it-ti-ᵈda-gan* (*CAAA*, p. 571); *bu-tu-um-tum* (*CAAA*, p. 573); *la-ṭà-ab-tum* (*CAAA*, p. 618); *na-kam-tum* (*CAAA*, p. 628); and 3) with *-a*: *a-tam-ra* (*CAAA*, p. 561); *ṭà-ba* (*CAAA*, p. 646); *ta-šu-ba* (*CAAA*, p. 644). The last three PNN, each terminating in *-a*, should be compared with their counterparts in *-at* cited above. In his discussion of feminine morphemes, Huffmon has adopted Gelb's three-fold classification and added several observations.[4] First, he has referred to these three feminine morphemes as hypocoristic suffixes. Second, he has collected five PNN borne by males that have the *-at* suffix. According to him, in these five names the suffix is used in a general, caritative sense, rather than having any feminine connotations. This second observation highlights the fact that there is not always a correlation between the gender of the name and the sex of the name bearer.[5] As regards the first observation, Huffmon is not alone in his use of the term hypocoristic to describe the ending *-at*.[6] It would be more felicitous to say that the feminine suffix *-(a)t* can on occasion be used to form hypocoristica, for it cannot be proven that every PN terminating in *-(a)t* is a hypocoristic name. For example, the Amor. feminine PN *ia-qar-tum* appears to be a one-word name meaning "(the) precious one."

The feminine morphemes *-at* and *-t* are also attested on WS PNN in the execration texts and the Hayes list. The Egyptian method of tran-

---

citing the Ug. PN *ᶠpiddaya*, with the variant *ᶠpidda*, Gröndahl, *Or* 35 (1966) 453, has supported her contention that the suffix *-a* may result from the contraction of the feminine or hypocoristic suffix *-aya*. For a complete list of all Amor. PNN terminating in the suffix *-a*, see Gelb, *CAAA*, pp. 401-4, and note that almost all these names are feminine. Mitchell Dahood, "The Linguistic Classification of Eblaite," in *La Lingua di Ebla: Atti del Convegno internazionale (Napoli, 22-23 aprile 1980)*, ed. Luigi Cagni, Istituto universitario orientale, Seminario di studi asiatici, Series Minor, no. 14 (Napoli, 1981), pp. 180-81, claimed to have detected feminine singular nouns ending in *-a* in Eblaite. Further study of Eblaite grammar is required before one can accede to Dahood's suggestion.

[3]See Gelb, *CAAA*, p. 556, for nine other PNN formed with the element *aḫat-*.

[4]Huffmon, *APNMT*, pp. 133-34.

[5]In Akkadian PNN too, the suffix *-at* is well-attested on names borne by males and females. See Ranke, *Early Babylonian Personal Names*, pp. 14-17; Julius Lewy, "Studies in Akkadian Grammar and Onomatology," *Or* 15 (1946) 376-77; Stamm, *ANG*, p. 113; von Soden, *GAG* §60a.

[6]See also Buccellati, *AURIII*, pp. 129, 176, 183-84, 202; Ranke, *Early Babylonian Personal Names*, pp. 14-17; Lidzbarski, "Semitic Kosenamen," p. 19; Thompson, *Historicity*, p. 47; Cazelles, *DBS* 6:740. Noth, *IPN*, pp. 38-39, has expanded the use of the term hypocoristic suffix to include even the feminine plural ending *-ôt* on PNN in the Hebrew Bible.

scribing foreign words does not permit one to distinguish between these two morphemes; that is, there is no distinct sign to register the presence of an -*a*- vowel before the -*t*.[7] Nevertheless, the occurrence of the same PN or GN in either cuneiform script or another vocalized text (e.g., Hebrew Bible) provides the needed vocalization. Note the following representative examples, cited with corresponding vocalized (or reconstructed) forms: 1) with -*at*: e 22 *ʿ( )r-q-tum*, E 54 *ʿ(a)r-q-tum*, E 61 *ʿ( )r-q-ta*; and EA *URUir-qa-ta*; E 20 *b-q-ʿ-tum* and BH *biqʿâ* (< **biqʿatu*); and 2) with -*t*: Hayes #15 *ʾa-d-u-t-u* (**ʾaduttu* < **ʾaduntu*). Additional examples of feminine PNN with the suffix -*(a)t* are to be found in the Hayes list (##13, 16, 25, 26, 27, 35, 59, 87, 88).

The evidence for the feminine morphemes -*at* and -*t* on WS PNN in the Alalakh tablets, the Taanach tablets, and the El Amarna letters has been collected and analyzed by Sivan. He cites not only PNN from these groups of texts, but also notes the occurrence of these morphemes on WS glosses in the El Amarna letters and on Ugaritic vocables in Akkadian texts from Ras Shamra.[8] Gröndahl has collected the Ug. PNN terminating in -*(a)t*; they consist of no more than nine in number, and most of them are of obscure etymology (*PTU*, pp. 55-56). The existence of both feminine morphemes on Ugaritic nouns written in consonantal script can be inferred on the basis of certain indications. In particular, Gordon mentions the vocalization of *ʾaleph* (*ḫmʾat* = **ḫimʾatu*, "butter" versus *lbʾit* = **labiʾtu*, "lioness"), the assimilation of consonants (mainly *n* [*ʾalmnt* = **ʾalmanatu*, "widow" versus *bt* < **bint*, "daughter"]), and the merging of vowels in nouns from III-weak roots (*ḥmt* = **ḥāmîtu* < **ḥāmiytu*, "(city) wall").[9] In summary, a survey of early West Semitic indicates the existence of two feminine morphemes, -*at* and -*t*, which are productive in feminine, and occasionally, masculine PNN.

II. Canaanite

In the Canaanite languages, the feminine morpheme -*t* is retained in both the construct and absolute states of the noun. The feminine

---

[7]Note, however, a few exceptional examples, cited by Helck, *Beziehungen Ägyptens*, p. 79, in which the *a* vowel is indicated before the feminine -*t*. The validity of these examples is, as noted, dependent on how one views group writing. Burchardt, §170, cites several Canaanite feminine nouns ending in *-*at* that occur as loanwords in Coptic with the ending *-*t* (e.g., BH *ʿăgālâ* = Coptic *aϭoλτe*).

[8]Sivan, *GAGNWS*, pp. 105-7. On Ugaritic vocables in Akkadian texts, ending in -*t* and -*at*, see further Boyd, pp. 286-87; Huehnergard, *Ugaritic Vocabulary*, pp. 295-96.

[9]*UT* §8.3.

morpheme *-at*, however, underwent a change in some of the Canaanite languages. In BH, the feminine morpheme *-at* is preserved only in bound forms--in the construct and before suffixes. In the absolute state, the morpheme *-at* became *-â* [*malkâ* < **malkat(u)*].[10] It is represented in the Masoretic text by *qāmeṣ* and usually by the *mater lectionis -h.* In the area of nouns, exceptions exhibiting final *-at* in the absolute are limited to certain adverbs (e.g., *rabbat*), archaic poetry, and proper nouns.[11] The occurrences of this archaism in ancient poetry have not been studied systematically, and uncertainties of a textual nature are a hindrance. For the meantime, the brief treatment in the grammars must suffice.[12] Several GNN in the Hebrew Bible terminate in *-at* in the absolute. One must be careful to distinguish GNN terminating in *-t* from those terminating in *-at*; only the latter may be termed archaic.[13] Of particular interest is a series of GNN, not necessarily referring to the same locality, which are attested with both *-â* and *-at*: *baʿălat/baʿălâ*; *gibʿat/gibʿâ*; *maʿăkāt/maʿăkâ*; *maʿărāt/mĕʿārâ*; and *ʿayyat/ʿayyâ*.[14] The same alternation between the endings *-â* and *-at* is discovered when one compares certain LXX transliterations with their MT counterparts: MT *ḥăwîlâ*/LXX B *ευειλατ* (Gen. 2:11); MT *ḥărādâ*/LXX B *χαραδαθ* (Num. 33:24); and MT *šorʿâ*/LXX B *σαραθ* (Josh. 19:41).[15] The GNN

---

[10]See discussions in the grammars, viz. BL §62; GKC §80; Joüon, §89.

[11]Joshua Blau, "The Parallel Development of the Feminine Ending *-at* in Semitic Languages," *HUCA* 51 (1980) 18. On the same page, Blau refers to these proper nouns with *-at* in the absolute as "loans." But some of these forms can better be described as archaisms, not loans.

[12]GKC §80g; Joüon, §89n. Where one would expect a treatment of this archaic morpheme is in Robertson, *Linguistic Evidence.* But see ibid., p. 111 n. 1, where he states that "the understanding of the feminine ending *-t* in nouns . . . is so fraught with difficulties that it is the better part of wisdom to omit any consideration of it here."

[13]One must also exclude GNN in which the *-t* is the final consonant of the root and hence not a feminine suffix at all. See Borée, pp. 43-46, whose list is maximal and thus should be used with discretion. Rainey, *BASOR* 231 (1978) 4, is mistaken when he cites the GN *ṣārĕpat* as a feminine noun in which the *-at* is still preserved. He even cites the NA transliteration of the name (*URUṣa-ri-ip-tu*), which clearly indicates that the feminine suffix is *-t*, and not *-at.* Compare here also the Grk transliterations *σαρεπτα* (Luke 4:26) and *σαρεφθα* (*NWJ*, p. 107), both of which confirm the NA transliteration of the name. The combined witness of the NA and Greek transliterations suggest that the Masoretic vocalization is mistaken or reflects the Hebrew and/or Aramaic pronunciation of the GN (*ṣaripta* > **ṣaript* > **ṣaripat* > *ṣārĕpat*, or the like). Lastly, feminine *-at* on GNN in the Hebrew Bible is also discussed by Eshel, pp. 265-66.

[14]On the last pair of GNN, see the comments of Kutscher, *Isaiah Scroll*, p. 115, who notes that the MT *ʿayyat* of Isa. 10:28 has been changed to *ʿyh* in 1QIsa[a].

[15]Batten, pp. 45-46.

terminating in *-at* reflect an earlier linguistic stratum of the language, while those terminating in *-â* reflect a later one.

The situation in EH is identical to that in BH.[16] As evidence for the change **-at* > **-â*, note the following forms: *hnqbh*, *hbrkh*, and *ʾmh* (Siloam tunnel inscription; *KAI* 189); *hrʿh* (A 40:15);[17] and the EH feminine PNN *ḥnh*[18] and *mʿdnh*.[19] The occurrence of these absolute forms of feminine nouns allows us to conclude that in EH, the change **-at* > **-â* took place before roughly 700 B.C.[20] At least two of the Transjordanian dialects retained the **-at* ending on the absolute of the feminine singular noun. For Moabite, the vocables *hmslt* and *hbmt* (*KAI* 181:3, 26) are best analyzed as absolute feminine singular nouns.[21] The evidence for the maintenance of **-at* in Ammonite consists of the following forms: *sdrt* (Amman Citadel, l. 4);[22] and *h.gnt* (Tell Siran, l. 4; cf. BH *gannâ* < **gannat*).[23] According to Israel, the attestations of feminine singular nouns in Ammonite are ambiguous, since most if not all of the forms cited could just as well be plural. Yet the weight of the evidence is in favor of interpreting at least the two above-mentioned nouns as feminine singular absolutes. The Amm. PN *ʿlyh* (*ALIA*, p. 97) does not contradict this conclusion; rather than exhibiting the shift **-at* > **-â*,[24] it is, in all probability, a Yahwistic name

---

16Gogel, 1:375-76.

17Aharoni, *Arad Inscriptions*, p. 71.

18(VSE #351); and Nahman Avigad, "A Note on an Impression from a Woman's Seal," *IEJ* 37 (1987) 18-19, and Pl. 1:A, B.

19N. Avigad, "The King's Daughter and the Lyre," *IEJ* 28 (1978) 146-51.

20The evidence from Old Aramaic proves that the shift took place in some Aramaic dialects at an earlier date. See Garr, *Dialect Geography*, pp. 59-60.

21See the discussion of Blau, *Maarav* 2 (1980) 157 n. 60; idem, *HUCA* 51 (1980) 21-22. Though Blau himself believes the feminine ending *-at* still persisted in Moabite, he attempts to cast doubt on the two above-cited forms by suggesting that *hmslt* could just as well be a plural and that *hbmt* could be vocalized **bāmt/-bamt* (cf. Akk. *bāmtu*). Considering the linguistic affinities of Moabite and BH, the appeal to Akk. *bāmtu* appears unwarranted; rather, one should compare Moab. *hbmt* to BH *bāmâ* (< **bamatu*). Also it is more likely that Mesha (re)built one highway in the Arnon than several (Jer. 48:19-20). Garr, *Dialect Geography*, p. 60, cites Moab. *ryt* "spectacle (?)" (*KAI* 181:12) as an example of a feminine singular absolute noun. But the vocable may be vocalized **rît* (so Blau, *HUCA* 51 [1980] 21).

22See Jackson, *ALIA*, pp. 10, 18-19, whose argument rests upon syntactic considerations.

23Ibid., pp. 36-38. Note that the masculine *singular* noun *hkrm* immediately precedes *h.gnt*. Jackson, ibid., also cites the vocable *nkʾt* in Heshbon 1:4-5. Garr, *Dialect Geography*, p. 59, not only cites *h.gnt*, but also *ʾšḥt* (Tell Siran, l. 5).

24Felice Israel, "Geographic Linguistics and Canaanite Dialects," in *Current Progress in Afro-Asiatic Linguistics: Papers of the Third International Hamito-Semitic Congress*, ed. James Bynon, Amsterdam Studies in the Theory and History

in Ammonite script.[25] As regards Edomite, there is no evidence whether this Transjordanian dialect preserved **-at* in the feminine singular absolute.[26]

In Phoenician **-at* was preserved in the absolute state of feminine singular nouns.[27] Only in later Punic was the *-t* (**-at* > **ōt* > **-ō*) of the feminine absolute state omitted.[28] To sum up, the suffix **-at* on feminine singular absolute nouns was preserved in Moabite, Ammonite, and Phoenician, whereas it shifted to **-â* in BH and EH and to **-ō* in later Punic. The status of the feminine morpheme **-at* in Aramaic will be considered below.[29]

III. Canaanite PNN in the Hebrew Bible

One may be tempted to interpret the one-word names mentioned below as either perfect verbal forms (second person singular, masculine or feminine; or archaic third feminine singular) or as shortened names, with only the *nomen regens* of the construct retained. But the onomastic evidence that would warrant these interpretations is lacking.[30] In this section, we will attempt to determine the sex of the name bearer to see whether it correlates with the grammatical gender of the name.

---

of Linguistic Science; Series IV, Current Issues in Linguistic Theory, vol. 28 (Amsterdam: John Benjamins, 1984), p. 364; idem, *OLP* 10 (1979) 145.

[25]Tigay, p. 87 n. 1; Israel, *OLP* 10 (1979) 145, hinted at this solution, suggesting that the PN *ʿlyh* could be the name of a foreign woman rendered according to non-Ammonite scribal traditions. In fact the Yahwistic theophore is unmistakable here. Compound theophoric PNN formed with the root **ʿlh* are known elsewhere in the Hebrew onomasticon (always with Yahwistic theophore) but not in the Ammonite onomasticon. For other examples of Yahwistic PNN in Ammonite script, note the Amm. seal that reads *ḥnnyh b<n> nwry⌈h⌉* (Aufrecht, *BASOR* 266 [1987] 86).

[26]Israel has suggested that the vocable *lbnt* of the Lachish incense altar inscription be construed as a feminine singular absolute (*RivB* 27 [1979] 179), but this inscription is too obscure to support this conclusion. In the same article (pp. 179-80), Israel cited the weight from Petra, which reads *ḥmšt*, but later argued that this weight should be classified as Aramaic or Ammonite (*RivB* 35 [1987] 339).

[27]Johannes Friedrich and Wolfgang Röllig, *Phönizisch-Punische Grammatik*, 2d rev. ed., Analecta Orientalia, vol. 46 (Rome: Pontificium Institutum Biblicum, 1970), §213; Stanislav Segert, *Phoenician and Punic*, §43.412.

[28]Friedrich and Röllig, §229; Segert, *Phoenician and Punic*, §43.412.2.

[29]See pp. 229-30.

[30]See Michael D. Coogan, "The Use of Second Person Singular Verbal Forms in Northwest Semitic Personal Names," *Or* 44 (1957) 194-97. With the possible exception of Ph. *bʿlʾšrt*, Coogan cites no convincing examples from Canaanite PNN. The six PNN he cites from the Murašû archive appear to be patterned after contemporary Babylonian names.

A. *Probable Examples*

1. *ʾăḥuzzat.*

Classification: Can.--adviser of Abimelek, king of the Philistines (Gen26:26).

Sex of name bearer: male.

Structure: one-word name, *ʾăḥuzz-* (**qutull* base, BL §61da; < **ʾḫḏ* "to seize, grasp") + *-at* feminine suffix.

Meaning: "possession."

Parallels: Can. *ʾăḥuzzām*;[31] BH CN *ʾăḥuzzâ* "possession, inheritance."

Comments: Along with Phicol, ʾAhuzzat[32] belonged to the entourage of Abimelek, the Philistine king of Gerar. His name is classified as Canaanite because the root **ʾḫḏ* is a good Canaanite root,[33] and because Philistine kings generally bore WS PNN.[34] In any case the term "Philistine" does not demand a non-Semitic etymology; its occurrence in the Pentateuch is anachronistic. Not only do general contextual considerations imply that ʾAhuzzat is a male, but he is specifically described as an "adviser," i.e. BH *rēaʿ*, a masculine singular noun. The **qutull* base of the name finds confirmation in LXX B *οχοζαθ* and Vulgate *Ochozath*. Thus it is not necessary to follow Noth's suggestion and revocalize **ʾaḥăzāt*.[35] In the name ʾAhuzzat the feminine suffix is used to form an abstract noun, "possession."

---

[31]See s.v. "ʾăḥuzzām," p. 170.

[32]Although early Jewish exegetes assumed that this vocable was a common noun, Jonathan Safran, "Ahuzzath and the Pact of Beer-Sheba," *ZAW* 101 (1987) 187, defends its understanding as a proper noun.

[33]Görg's attempt to derive the PN ʾAhuzzat from an Egyptian title does not recommend itself (M. Görg, "Die Begleitung des Abimelech von Gerar (Gen 26,26)," *BN* 35 (1986) 24.

[34]Joseph Naveh, "Writing and Scripts in the Seventh-Century B.C.E. Philistia: The New Evidence from Tell Jemmeh," *IEJ* 35 (1985) 9.

[35]Noth, *IPN*, p. 179 n. 1.

2. *běkôrat.*

Classification: Can.--great-grandfather of Kish (1 Sam 9:1).

Sex of name-bearer: male (patrilineal genealogy).

Structure: one-word name, *běkôr-* (**qutul* base, BL §61z‴) + *-at* feminine suffix.

Meaning: "right of first-born."

Parallels: Amor. *ba-ku-ra-tum, bi-ku-ur-tum* (*CAAA*, pp. 569, 571); Akk. CNN *bukru/bukurtu* "son, child/daughter" (*CAD* B, pp. 309-10); MB *fba-ak-ra-tum* (*CAD* B, p. 35); BH CNN *běkō/ôr* and *běkōrâ.*

Comments: The authenticity of this PN is vouchsafed by Amor. *fba-ku-ra-tum*, and thus the emendation of Bekorat to Beker[36] must be met with disapproval. As in the preceding name, the feminine suffix *-at* is used to form an abstract noun. According to Noth, this PN points to the place of the child within the family.[37] McCarter maintains that the versions provide some evidence for the reading **bākîr*, the masculine equivalent of the well-attested feminine PN *běkîrâ.*[38] But this suggestion should be rejected, because the reconstructed noun **bākîr* is unknown to the BH lexicon, and because its feminine counterpart, *běkîrâ*, is in fact never attested as a PN. Moreover, versional evidence may be cited in support of the reading of the MT (LXX A *βεχωραθ* and Vulgate *Bechoreth*).

3. *bāśěmat.*

Classification: Can.--1) daughter of Elon the Hittite[39] and wife of Esau (Gen 26:34); 2) daughter of Ishmael and wife of Esau (Gen 36:2-3);[40] 3) daughter of Solomon and wife of Ahimaaz (1 Kgs 4:15).

Sex of name bearers: female.

---

[36]J. Marquart, *Fundamente israelitischer und jüdischer Geschichte* (Göttingen: Dieterich, 1896), pp. 14-16.

[37]Noth, *IPN*, p. 222.

[38]McCarter, *1 Samuel*, p. 167. Note LXX B *βαχει* and other minor witnesses that suggest an *i* vowel in the second syllable.

[39]Hivite, according to SyrP, LXX B, and SamP.

[40]#1 and #2 are identical according to some commentators.

Structure: one-word name, *bāśĕm-* (**qātil* base ?)[41] + *-at* feminine suffix.

Meaning: "the one fragrant with balsam" or "balsam, spice."

Parallels: Can. *yibśām, mibśām*; BH CN *bōśem*; Sab. *bšm*, Min. and Sab. *bšmt*, Qat. *bšmm*, Tham. *bšmn* (*PIAN*, p. 107).

Comments: If this name is analyzed as a feminine participle, note the lack of the phonological shift **ā > *ō*. It falls into that class of (mostly) feminine names that denote jewelry or cosmetics. Other members of this class are the Can. masculine PNN *yibśām* and *mibśām*; the Can. feminine PN *qeren happûk* "horn of antimony"; and especially the Can. feminine PN *ṣĕrû/ūyâ* (**qatūl* base) "the one fragrant with mastic."

4. *gînat.*

Classification: Can.--parent of Tibni, king of Israel (1 Kgs 16:21-22).

Sex of name bearer: unknown.

Structure: *gîn-* (**qīl* base; < **gyn* "to enclose") + *-at* feminine suffix.

Meaning: "garden, enclosure."

Parallels: Eblaite *gi-na* (ARET I:242); *gi-na-a, gi-na-im* (ARET IV:244); *gi-na-ù* (ARET I:242, III:273, IV:244); Ug. *gn, ʾilgn, gny* (*PTU*, p. 129); *bn gntn, gi-na-ta-na* (*PTU*, pp. 129, 384);[42] Can. *ginnĕtôn*; BH CNN *gan, gannâ, gînâ*; NA *gi-(in-)na-a-a, gi-ni-i/ia* (*WSB*, p. 146), N/LB *gan-na-nu* (*WSB*, p. 133);[43] WS *gnʾ* (*ALIA*, p.

---

[41]Otto Procksch, *Die Genesis, übersetzt und erklärt* (Leipzig: A. Deichert, 1913), p. 207, interprets this name as "eine Femininform *fâʿilatu*," and he translates it "die Balsamduftende." The most frequent LXX B transliteration is *βασεμμαθ*; in Josephus, *βασεμαθη* for the wife of Esau, *βασιμα* for the daughter of Solomon (*NWJ*, p. 25).

[42]For further discussion of the Ug. root(s) **gn(n)*, see M. Dietrich, O. Loretz, and J. Sanmartín, "Zur Ugaritischen Lexikographie (XI)," *UF* 6 (1974) 23-24.

[43]Compare the Aram. CN *gannu* II "garden" attested in cuneiform writing (W. von Soden, "Aramäische Wörter in neuassyrischen und neu- und spätbabylonischen Texten. Ein Vorbericht. I (*agâ* - **mūš*)," *Or* 35 [1966] 8).

96);[44] Ph.-P. *ʾsrgn, gnn* (*PNPP*, p. 297); IAram. *gnt* (*SPARI*, pp. 75, 149); Saf. *jnn, jnnt* (*PIAN*, p. 168).

Comments: Some commentators interpret Ginat as a GN, and they appeal to 2 Kgs 15:10 (*šallum ben-yābēš*) and Judg 3: 31 (*šamgar ben-ʿănāt*) as evidence that in the patronymic formula *x ben y*, the *y* element may be a GN.[45] Admittedly, a similar toponym is attested in the EA letters (*gina* [250.27, 32]), Josephus (*γινη*), and the Talmud (in the Aram. form *gynʾy*).[46] But none of these forms terminate with *-t*, as does the biblical Ginat. Mere similarity of form is not enough to prove identification. Furthermore, in the formulaic *x ben y*, the *y* element almost always refers to the father, or in rare cases, the mother.[47]

The analysis of Ginat as a PN is corroborated by the IAram. PN *gnt*.[48] The PN Ginat corresponds to the CN *gînâ*, which is attested once in the Hebrew Bible (Ezek 42:12). Elliger has discussed the morphology of the two forms, suggesting that they both derive from the geminate root **gnn* (as *mîṣ* < **mṣṣ*).[49] He even proposed that the correct reading is **gnynh*, with the first *n* having dropped out of the text through haplography. In light of pairs of verbs with similar meaning, the one geminate and the other hollow, I prefer to posit the existence of a root **gyn*, biform of the well-known geminate root **gnn*.[50] The sex of

---

[44]Bob Becking, "Kann das Ostrakon ND 6231 von *Nimrūd* für ammonitisch gehalten werden?" *ZDPV* 104 (1988) 66, has argued persuasively that the names on this ostracon are not Ammonite per se.

[45]Thus, a name like Shamgar Ben-ʿAnat would mean Shamgar, who hails from (Beth) Anat. For additional examples and discussion, see W. F. Albright, *JPOS* 1 (1920-21) 55 n. 1; idem, *AJSL* 41 (1925) 84-85; idem, "The Son of Tabeel (Isaiah 7:6)," *BASOR* 140 (1955) 34-35; Albrecht Alt, "Megiddo im Übergang von kanaanäischen zum israelitischen Zeitalter," *ZAW* 60 (1944) 73 n. 4; Noth, *IPN*, p. 123 n. 1.

[46]Samuel Loewenstamm, in *EM*, s.v. "gînat," 2:483-84, for further bibliography.

[47]Neither 2 Kgs 15:10 nor Judg 3:31 is indisputable. On Ben-ʿAnat, see s.v. "(ben)-ʿănāt," pp. 217-18; it suffices to note here that the onomastic parallels are so numerous that it is no longer preferred to interpret ʿAnat as an abbreviation of Beth-ʿAnat. In general, see the critique by A. Van Selms, "Judge Shamgar," *VT* 14 (1964) 301; Daniel I. Block, "'Israel'--'sons of Israel': A study in Hebrew eponymic usage," *Studies in Religion* 13 (1984) 316-17.

[48]The writing **gnt* indicates that the suffix is *-at* [**gin(n)at*]. If the suffix were *-t*, one would expect the writing **gt* (**gitt* < **gint*). Compare also the Ug. PNN *bn gntn* and *gi-na-ta-na* [**qil(l)* base noun + *-at-* feminine suffix + **-ānu* derivational nominal suffix], and the Amm. CN *gnt* (Jackson, *ALIA*, p. 38).

[49]Karl Elliger, "Die grossen Tempelsakristeien im Verfassungsentwurf des Ezechiel (42, 1ff.)," in *Geschichte und Altes Testament*, ed. Gerhard Ebeling, Beiträge zur historischen Theologie, Band 16 (Tübingen: J. C. B. Mohr [Paul Siebeck], 1953), pp. 99-101.

[50]For a list of such pairs, see Zygmunt Frajzyngier, "Notes on the $R_1R_2R_2$ Stems in Semitic," *JSS* 24 (1979) 2. For the geminate root **gnn* in WS PNN in NA and

the name bearer is not unquestionably male. Though not common, the designation of someone as son of a woman is known elsewhere in the Hebrew Bible (Gen 29:12; 2 Kgs 12:22[51]) and in texts from Ugarit.[52] As a semantic parallel to the PN Ginat, compare WS PNN formed with the vocable **karmu* "vineyard."[53]

5. *gĕnūbat.*

Classification: Can.--son of Hadad, the Edomite (1 Kgs 11:20).

Sex of name bearer: male.

Structure: one-word name, *gĕnūb-* (**qatūl* base)[54] + *-at* feminine suffix.

Meaning: 1. "taken by stealth, furtively."[55]
2. "foreigner, stranger."[56]

Parallels: Eblaite *ga-na-ab* (ARET III:272); *ga-na-bù* (ARET III:272, IV:243); Amor. GN *ga-ni-ba-tu-um*;[57] Ug. *gnb*[. (?) (*PTU*, p. 129); Palm. *gnbʾ* (*PNPI*, p. 82); JAram. *gĕnîbāh/ʾ*, CN *gĕnē(y)bâ* "stolen object" (Jastrow, *Dictionary*, p. 259); Heb./Aram. *g*⌈*n*⌉*by*.[58]

Comments: Our first proposed meaning derives the PN from the WS root **gnb* "to steal." If this derivation is accepted, then positive conno-

---

N/LB texts, see Zadok, *WSB*, pp. 133, 146. See also Joseph Naveh, "The Ostracon From Nimrud: An Ammonite Name-List," *Maarav* 2 (1980) 168, who analyzes the WS PN *gnʾ* (cited above) as a hypocoristicon derived from the root **gnn* "to protect." Jackson, "Ammonite Personal Names," p. 512, has already cited the Can. PN *gînat* as a possible cognate of this WS PN.

[51]On this verse, see s.v. "šimʿāt," p. 220.

[52]Anson F. Rainey, "Family Relationships in Ugarit," *Or* 34 (1965) 22 n. 2; idem, "Gleanings from Ugarit," *IOS* 2 (1973) 50 n. 77.

[53]Ug. PNN *kar-mu-nu* and *krmn* (Gröndahl, *PTU*, p. 151), Can. PN *karmî*, and EH PN *krmy* (Avigad, *Hebrew Bullae*, ##68a-b; David Diringer, "On Ancient Hebrew Inscriptions Discovered at Tell Ed-Duweir (Lachish)-I," *PEQ* 74 [1941] 51-52 #15).

[54]The proposal of Montgomery, *Book of Kings*, p. 246, who reconstructed a **gunaibat* diminutive formation on the basis of LXX transliteration, is improbable.

[55]P. le Page Renouf, "The Ḳenbetu and the Semitic South," *PSBA* 10 (1887-88) 376.

[56]Suggested by KB3, p. 191, who cite MLArab. *junub* "guest from a foreign tribe," and Saf. *jnb* (*PIAN*, p. 169; "stranger" according to Ryckmans, 1:62).

[57]Zadok, "Nachbiblische jüdischen Onomastikon," p. 267.

[58]E. Puech, "Inscriptions funéraires palestiniennes: tombeau de Jason et ossuaries (Planches V-VII)," *RB* 90 (1983) 516 #24, and Fig. 5.

tations need to be attached to it, for PNN denoting bad personality traits are not common.[59] The verb can mean "(to) take by stealth (for good purpose)."[60] On the other hand, the second meaning is criticized by Stark as being a secondary derivation from Arab. *janb* "side" and therefore chronologically later than the Palm. PN *gnbʾ*,[61] and the Can. PN Genubat as well. Since the first meaning yields an acceptable sense and is based upon a root common in West Semitic, it appears to be the more plausible solution. Thus the Can. PN *gĕnūbat* finds a etymological cognate in the JAram. PN *gĕnîbāh/ʾ* and a semantic parallel in the NA PN *ga-zi-lu* "robbed."[62] F. Scerbo noted the archaic feminine ending on this name.[63]

6. *ṭāpat.*

Classification: Can.--daughter of Solomon and wife of Ben-Abinadab (1 Kgs 4:11).

Sex of name bearer: female.

Structure: one-word name, *ṭāp-* (< **qall* base, BL §61w) + *-at* feminine suffix.

Meaning: "young/small girl."

Parallels: BH CN *ṭap* I.

Comments: Noth and several other interpreters compare this PN to the JAram. CN *ṭîppāʾ* "drop" (Jastrow, *Dictionary*, p. 533), which in turn is derived from the Aram. verb **ṭwp* (compare also **ṭpp*) "to float,

---

[59]Barr, *BJRL* 52 (1969-70) 22-24; Joseph G. Fucilla, Review of *Onomastica Medio-Assira*, by Claudio Saporetti, *Names* 20 (1972) 138; Joseph Naveh, "The Aramaic Ostracon from Tel Beer-sheba (Seasons 1971-76)," *TA* 6 (1979) 183. Accordingly, Huffmon's gloss "to lie" as the meaning of the Amor. **kzb* (*APNMT*, p. 221) should be corrected to "to be luxuriant" (Gelb, *CAAA*, p. 23).

[60]BDB, p. 170. According to Nöldeke, *EB* 3:3296, this PN is to be placed with other names that allude to the circumstances of the birth. In this instance, the name may hint that the mother died in giving birth to the child.

[61]Stark, *PNPI*, p. 82.

[62]Zadok, *Sources*, p. 28. The JAram. and NA PNN are, of course, **qatīl* base, the morphological equivalent in Aramaic of Hebrew **qatūl*. The most recent discussion of the Can. PN is in J. R. Bartlett, "An Adversary against Solomon, Hadad the Edomite," *ZAW* 88 (1976) 212 n. 22. Barlett does not commit himself on the meaning of the name.

[63]F. Scerbo, *Lessico dei nomi propri ebraici del vecchio testamento* (Firenze: Libreria editrice fiorentina, 1913), p. 37.

drip."[64] As such Tapat would be an Aram. rather than a Can. PN. There are two weaknesses in this explanation of the name. First, the name would have to be revocalized with an *i* vowel in the first syllable. This revocalization ignores the Masoretic pointing and finds no support in the versions.[65] Second, and more important, the meaning "drop" is unsatisfactory. Efforts to justify the appropriateness of this meaning fail miserably.

Rather one should derive this name from the geminate root **ṭpp* I. This verb is attested once in the Hebrew Bible (Isa. 3:16), apparently meaning "to skip about, trip." It is generally assumed that it is a denominative verb from the collective noun *ṭap* (**qall* base). The semantic field of *ṭap* is difficult to define; nonetheless, its use in passages such as Num 14:31 and Deut 1:39 suggest the meaning "children."[66] Accordingly, Tapat is a **qall* base noun, plus *-at* feminine suffix, meaning "young/small girl." This approach avoids both the weaknesses of the above-mentioned view--the MT pointing with an *a* vowel is left intact[67] and the resultant meaning is fitting for a PN borne by a female. This approach assumes that a *daghesh forte* should be inserted in the *p*. The Masoretes were not consistent in the use of *daghesh forte* in PNN, probably because of uncertainties in the reading tradition and ignorance of the morphology and meaning of some of the names.[68]

7. *yĕhôšabʿat.*

Variant spelling: *yĕhôšebaʿ*.

Classification: Hebrew--daughter of Joram, and wife of Jehoiada (2 Kgs 11:2; 2 Chr 22.11 [with *-t*]).

Sex of name bearer: female.

Structure: nominal-sentence name, *yĕhô-* (DN) + *-šabʿ-* (**qatl* base, BL §61l') + *-at* feminine suffix.

---

[64]Noth, *IPN*, p. 226 n. 18; Stamm, *BHAN*, p. 121; Wagner, pp. 61-62; Max Löhr, *Die Stellung des Weibes zu Jahwe-Religion und -Kult* (Leipzig: J. C. Hinrichs, 1908), p. 12.

[65]The LXX transliterations have an *a* vowel in the first syllable; so also Vulgate *Tapheth*.

[66]C. Locher, s.v. "*ṭap*," in *TDOT* 5:347-50. See also 1QpHab. 6:11.

[67]The original short *a* vowel one would expect in a **qall* base noun was lengthened in pretonic position because of the lack of gemination (**ṭappat* > **ṭapat* > MT *ṭāpat*).

[68]On lack of gemination in PNN, see s.v. "hădôrām," p. 59; "yĕmûʾēl," 65 n. 127; and "ʾăḥûmay," pp. 100-101.

Meaning: "Yahweh is seven (i.e, abundance ?)."

Parallels: Can. *šebaʿ*, *ʾĕlîšebaʿ*, *bat-šebaʿ*; GNN *šebaʿ* and *bĕʾēr-šebaʿ*; Ph-P. *šbʿ* (*PNPP*, p. 413); Neo-Punic *šbʿ* (Jongeling, p. 206); NA *apladu(A.U.)-sa-⌈bi⌉-ʾ* (*WSB*, p. 427);[69] EH *šbʿ* (VSE #337, A 38.4, SO 2.6), ⌈*š*⌉*bʿ* (Avigad, *Hebrew Bullae*, #202), *šbʿt*;[70] Can. *šbʿt* (VSE #72);[71] IAram. *šbʿn* (*SPARI*, pp. 102, 216); Saf. *sbʿ*, *sbʿʾl*; Sab. *sbʿm* (*PIAN*, p. 309).

Comments: This is the only Yahwistic PN that terminates in an archaic feminine suffix *-at*. Since the name may be classified as Hebrew, Levin's explanation of the *-at* ending as a Phoenicianism is precluded.[72] The various transliterations of the LXX mostly confirm the MT: ιωσαβεε in 2 Kgs, and ιωσαβεθ in 2 Chr. But readings at variance with the MT occur in both passages: LXX B and Lucianic ιωσαβεε in 2 Chr., and LXX B corrected to ιωσαβεθ (with θ superscripted) in 2 Kgs. Josephus follows the Chronicler's version of the name (ιωσαβεθη; *NWJ*, p. 68). The reading Yehoshabʿat should not be attributed to scribal error. It is the more difficult reading of the two, and the very form *šbʿt* is known elsewhere--on a "Philistine" seal, on a juglet discovered in the Ophel excavations, and perhaps as the second element of the name ʾElishabeth. Two other pairs of PNN in the Hebrew Bible also display the same alternation between simple form and simple form plus *-t*: 1) *mispār* (Ezra 2:2) and *misperet* (Neh 7:7); and 2) *šōmēr* (2 Kgs 12:22) and *šimrît* (2 Chr 24:26--the last form has a *y mater lectionis* as well).

The meaning of the vocable **šbʿ* has been much discussed. The LXX transliteration of zero/vowel mutation for the Hebrew *ʿayin* rules out any relation with Arab. *sabaġa* "to abound, to be abundant."[73]

---

[69]Of uncertain etymology is the NA (probably feminine) PN *se-eb-i-tú* (from **šbʿ* "seven" or **šby* "to deport"?). See Fales, *Iraq* 41 (1979) 69 (col. IV:11).

[70]J. Prignaud, "Scribes et graveurs à Jerusalem vers 700 AV. J.-C.," in *Archaeology in the Levant: Essays for Kathleen Kenyon*, ed. R. Moorey and P. Parr (Warminster: Aris & Phillips, 1978), pp. 136-37 #757 (Pl. XXIb; Fig. 2).

[71]This name is classified as Can., because it is the patronym of a Philistine in Ashkelon.

[72]Saul Levin, "Jocasta and Moses' Mother Jochebed," *Teiresias* 2, Supplement (1979) 50. To complete the argument, it is necessary to add that it is highly unlikely that this PN is a *Mischname*. Similarly, some writers have explained archaic feminine singular absolutes in the Psalms by attributing them to Phoenician influence (Roger T. O'Callaghan, "Echoes of Canaanite Literature in the Psalms," *VT* 4 [1954] 175). In principle, this too is unnecessary, unless Phoenician influence can be advanced on other grounds.

[73]This Arab. etymology was proposed Ludwig Köhler, "Hebräische Vokabeln II," *ZAW* 55 (1937) 165-66; KB2, pp. 370, 944.

Bauer compared the element to Arab. *sab*ʿ "lion," translating the name "Yahweh is lion," but he provides no argumentation to justify this novel interpretation.[74] Other roots that have been suggested are **śb*ʿ "to be sated"[75] and **šb*ʿ "to swear." The Masoretic vocalization of this PN finds ample confirmation in other Can. PNN and GNN. Primae facie, it is difficult to disassociate the vocable **šb*ʿ in proper nouns from the CN *šeba*ʿ/*šib*ʿ*â* "seven." It may be that the number seven in PNN has the connotation of "completeness, abundance";[76] hence the PN Yehoshabʿat would be translated "Yahweh is seven (i.e., abundance)." Whatever the case may be, the spelling Yehoshebaʿ represents the expected masculine form of the numeral (*šeba*ʿ), whereas the spelling Yehoshabʿat evidences the archaic feminine form of the numeral, perhaps in the original unattenuated form (**šab*ʿ*at* > **šib*ʿ*at* > *šib*ʿ*â*).

An Excursus on the PN ʾĕlîšebaʿ

The preceding discussion of the PN Yehoshabʿat leads us to consider the PN ʾElishebaʿ. The name only occurs once in the Hebrew Bible, in Exod 6:23, borne by a daughter of Amminadab. The MT form appears to be a nominal-sentence PN, similar in structure to Yehoshebaʿ, and the meaning of the name would be "My God is seven (i.e., abundance)." Various LXX manuscripts, however, present several variants of the PN. With the exception of LXX A* and the cursive manuscript x, which transliterate *ελισαβε*, all the other textual witnesses favor a form of the name terminating in either *-θ* (*ελ(ε)ισαβεθ*--B and various cursive mss.) or *-τ* (*ελισαβετ*--A_1, F, M, and other cursive manuscripts). To complete the picture, note that in Greek

---

[74]Bauer, *ZAW* 48 (1930) 78.

[75]Note that E. Lipiński, "Apladad," *Or* 46 (1976) 58, normalizes NA *apladu(A.U.)-sa-⌈bi⌉ -*ʾ as **Aplad(ad)-śabi*ʿ "Apladad est opulent."

[76]F. Nötscher, "Bar Kochba, Ben Kosba: der Sternsohn, der Prächtige," *VT* 11 (1961) 450; Stamm, *BHAN*, p. 108-9; KB3, p. 379; and especially Johannes Hehn, "Zur Bedeutung der Siebenzahl," in *Vom Alten Testament, Karl Marti zum siebzigsten Geburtstage*, ed. Karl Budde, BZAW 41 (Giessen: Alfred Töpelmann, 1925), pp. 128-36. Noth, *IPN*, pp. 146-47, develops the notion a bit differently, stressing that God is revealed in the perfection of nature. Hildegard and Julius Lewy, "The Origin of the Week and the Oldest West Asiatic Calendar," *HUCA* 17 (1942-43) 98, n. 395, also derive the **šb*ʿ element from the number seven, but they prefer to interpret it as a theophoric element referring to the Divine Heptad. The last view is criticized by Hehn, p. 131, and considered by Noth, *IPN*, p. 146, n. 3, as "völlig grundlos."

papyri,[77] and invariably in the New Testament (e.g., Luke 1:5), the name is spelled *ελισαβετ*, whereas on a Greek inscription, an ossuary from Jerusalem dating to the first century B.C./A.D., the spelling *ελισαβη* occurs.[78]

One may ask whether the LXX variants of the PN ending in -*τ* or -*θ* are the product of corruption in the LXX or do they reflect a Hebrew *Vorlage* that had a longer form of the name. In their Greek grammar, Blass and Debrunner express the view that the forms of the name ending in a dental are due to corruption in the LXX.[79] This explanation appears likely for those forms of the PN that end in -*θ*. In the LXX of Exod 6:23, the PN is followed by Greek *θυγατερα* "daughter," and by the scribal error of dittography of the initial letter of *θυγατερα*, the reading **ελ(ε)ισαβεθ θυγατερα* would result. But the hypothesis of inner textual corruption fails to explain those forms of the PN that end in -*τ*. The form of the PN ending in -*τ* is the *lectio difficilior*, and more manuscript evidence supports this reading than the form of the name ending in -*θ*. Consequently, it is suggested here that the form of the name ending in -*τ* reflects a genuine variant that was in the Hebrew manuscripts used by the LXX translators. We have already cited other instances in which forms of the name with and without -*t* were transmitted in two different passages of the Hebrew Bible. In the case of Elisheba^ʿ, the variation occurs between two different textual traditions in one verse.

How is the Greek form of the name ending in -*τ* to be explained? According to König, the PN *ʾĕlîšebaʿ* "became combined through a species of popular etymology with *ʾĕlîšabbat* ('God [or 'my God'] is rest')."[80] Köhler hypothesizes that the PN *ʾĕlîšebaʿ* is corrupted from an original PN **ʾĕlîšēbeṭ* "staff of God."[81] Both of these explanations are dubious. The putative PNN cited are scholarly creations rather than genuine PNN--the root **šbṭ* is never used in WS PNN, and the only PN

---

[77]D. Foraboschi, *Onomasticon alterum papyrologicum. Supplemento al Namenbuch di F. Preisigke*. Testi e Documenti per lo studio dell' Antichità, 16. Serie papirologica, 2 (Milano-Varese: Istituto Editoriale Cisalpino, 1971), 104, lists four occurrences.

[78]Wuthnow, p. 44.

[79]F. Blass and A. Debrunner, *A Greek Grammar of the New Testament and Other Early Christian Literature*, trans. Robert W. Funk (Chicago: University of Chicago Press, 1961), §39.2.

[80]Eduard König, "Elisabeth," *ExpTim* 20 (1908-9) 185-86; idem, "Woher stammt der Name 'Maria'?" *ZNW* 17 (1916) 257 n. 1.

[81]Ludwig Köhler, "Septuaginta-Eigennamen und ihre Entartung," in *Festgabe Adolf Kaegi von Schülern und Freunden, dargebracht zum 30. September 1919* (Frauenfeld, 1919), p. 186. In a later article, he retracted this view (Köhler, *ZAW* 55 [1937] 165-66).

with the root **šbt* is the non-theophoric biblical PN *šabbĕtay*, meaning "born on the Sabbath." A more plausible solution is to appeal to the hypothesis of archaism to explain the form of the PN ending in -*τ*.[82] The only drawback to this approach is that Hebrew *-t* is regularly rendered by Greek -*θ* in transliterations. Nevertheless, there are Greek transliterations of Hebrew words in which Hebrew *-t* is rendered by Greek -*τ*.[83]

8. *māḥălat.*

Variant spellings: 1. *maḥălat*; 2. *maḥlat*.[84]

Classification: Can.--1) wife of Esau and daughter of Ishmael (Gen 28:9);[85] 2) wife of Rehoboam (2 Chr 11:18).

Sex of name bearers: female.

Structure: one-word name, *māḥăl/maḥăl/maḥl-* (**maqtal* base; < **ḥlh* II, "to adorn") + *-at* feminine suffix.

Meaning: "jewelry, adornment."

Parallels: Can. *maḥlâ*, *ḥelʾâ*; BH CNN *ḥălî* and *ḥelyâ* "jewelry"; Saf. *ḥly*.[86]

Comments: In his article on Hebrew feminine names, Stamm lists this PN and the PN Mahlah in the subsection entitled "Namen unklarer Deutung," and he suggests possible comparisons with either *maḥălâ/-*maḥălēh* (< **ḥlh* I "to be sick") "sickness" or *mĕḥôlâ* (< **ḥwl* "to

---

[82]While not describing the form as archaic, Coogan, *Murašû*, p. 84 n. 78, does recognize that the PN *ελισαβετ* in the NT may reflect the addition of the feminine ending *-t*.

[83]For further discussion and other examples, see Blass and Debrunner, §39.2; Batton, p. 9; Jongeling, pp. 120-23, 141; Könnecke, p. 13; Eliezer D. Oren and Uriel Rappaport, "The Necropolis of Maresha-Beth Govrin," *IEJ* 34 (1984) 144 (the Aram. PN *bbtʾ* appears in Greek as *βαβάτα* or *βαβαθᾶ*). In commenting on the Greek transcription *βετυλος* (< **bytʾl*), J. T. Milik, "Les papyrus araméens d'Hermoupolis et les cultes syro-phéniciens en Égypte perse," *Bib* 48 (1967) 569 n. 2, remarks that the Semitic -t- is normally rendered by -*τ*- in the Hellenistic period and before, against -*θ*- of the Roman and Byzantine periods.

[84]See *BHS* textual apparatus at 2 Chr 11:18.

[85]In Gen 28:9, SyrP reads Basemat in place of Mahalat. In Gen. 31:3f, the SamP reads Mahalat in place of Basemat.

[86]Harding, *PIAN*, p. 199, relates this PN to Arabic *ḥaliya* "to adorn."

dance") "round dance."[87] The second alternative was suggested, hesitantly, by KB2 (p. 513). The other lexica make no suggestions on the derivation or meaning of the name.[88] Neither of Stamm's suggestions inspire confidence. The differences in root/vowel pattern render the comparison with the vocable *mĕḥôlâ* suspect; one would expect the long vowel to be preserved if the PN Mahalat were from a II-w root. The derivation of this name from the root **ḥlh* I does not appear particular appropriate for PNN, since as a rule names do not emphasize negative qualities.[89] The PN Mahlon "sickness" is a special case--a *nomen omen* in a biblical book (Ruth) replete with such names, and its derivation from the root **ḥlh* I provides a fitting semantic parallel to the rhyming PN Kilyon "withering."[90]

The key to the interpretation of the Can. PN Mahalat is provided by the Can. PN *ḥelʾâ*, borne by one of Ashhur's wives (1 Chr 4:5, 7).[91] This name, as well as the CNN *ḥălî* and *ḥelyâ*, derive from the root **ḥlh* II "to adorn." Therefore I tentatively propose that the PN Mahalat is to be derived from the root **ḥlh* II,[92] and to subsume it under that category of feminine names which Stamm entitles "jewelry and cosmetics."[93] This same root also provides a suitable etymology for the PN *maḥlâ*, borne by a daughter of Zelophehad (Num 26:33 and elsewhere), and by a Manassite (1 Chr 7:18).[94] The PN Mahlah would be the later form of

---

[87]Stamm, *BHAN*, p. 128.

[88]BDB, p. 563; KB3, p. 540; Zorell, *Lexicon Hebraicum*, p. 427.

[89]See p. 210 n. 59.

[90]I prefer the derivation of the PN Mahlon from **ḥlh* I, though it is unusual from the perspective of morphology for a *m*- preformative noun to end in the derivational suffix **-ānu* (as pointed out by Edward F. Campbell, Jr., *Ruth: A New Translation, with Introduction, Notes, and Commentary*, AB 7 [Garden City: Doubleday & Co., 1975], p. 53). While the formation is known elsewhere in BH--e.g., *misdĕrôn* (Judg 3:23) and *maššāʾôn* (Prov 26:26)--it would be more apposite to suggest that the unusual morphology of this PN is a product of the need for this name to rhyme with the following Kilyon. Therefore, it is probably unnecessary to derive the PN Mahlon from an unattested root cognate with MLArab. *maḥala* "to be barren, sterile." The Saf. PNN *mḥl* and *mḥlt* are ambiguous as to their root derivation (< **mḥl* or **ḥl*; Harding, *PIAN*, p. 531).

[91]Noth, *IPN*, p. 223; Stamm, *BHAN*, p. 124. Note that in Cant 7:2, the plural form *ḥălāʾîm* "ornaments" occurs.

[92]M. Margalioth, "The Meaning of the Names Maḥlon and Kilion in the Book of Ruth," in *Studies in Bible and Exegesis: Arie Toeg in Memoriam*, ed. U. Simon and M. Goshen-Gottstein (Ramat-Gan: Bar-Ilan University Press, 1980), pp. 119-21, arrives at the same conclusion, and he even derives the PN Mahlon from this root. But compare n. 90 above.

[93]Stamm, *BHAN*, p. 123.

[94]Again, contra KB2, p. 512, and KB3, p. 539, I assume that the individual named Mahlah in 1 Chr 7:18 is of female sex. Note the readings of two miniscule manuscripts, e2 *μααλαθ* and b *μααδαθ*, which suggest an ending in **-at*.

Mahalat, with the change **-at* > *-â*. Both PNN may be translated "jewelry, adornment." Though Blau considers the PNN Mahalat and Mahlah to be of uncertain etymology,[95] the LXX transliterations with zero/vowel mutation are in accord with the proposed derivation from the root **ḥlh* II (original *ḫ*).[96] Even if one prefers another explanation of the PN, from **ḥlh* I or even **mḥl*, the analysis of the final *-at* as an archaic feminine suffix would still obtain. In light of the evidence adduced for PNN derived from the root **ḥlh* "to adorn," it seems likely that the Palm. PN *ḥly*ʾ (with variant *ḥlyw*) is derived from the same root.[97]

9. *(ben-)*ʿ*ănāt.*

Classification: Can.--father of Shamgar (Judg 3:31; 5:6).

Sex of name bearer: male.

Structure: construct phrase name, *bēn-* (**qil* base, BL §61i) + ʿ*ănāt* (DN, < ***ʿ*an* + *-at* feminine suffix).

Meaning: "(son of) ʿAnat."

Parallels: EA *a-na-ti* (*AmPN*, pp. 59); Ug. *bin(DUMU)-*^{d}*anat(IGI*^{at}*)*, *bn* ʿ*nt* (*PTU*, pp. 111); WS *bin(DUMU)-ḫa-nu-ta* (Hazor; Hallo and Tadmor, *IEJ* 27:2-4); WS *bin(DUMU)-an*⌈*ta*⌉*-m*[*a*] (Taan.; Glock, *BASOR* 204:20, 27); WS *bn* ʿ*nt* (El ʾKhaḍr; Cross, *BASOR* 238:5-7); NA *bur-a-na-te* (*WSB*, p. 38).

Comments: The view that Ben-ʿAnat designates Shamgar as a ruler of Beth ʿAnat has already been discarded.[98] The onomastic data warrants the conclusion that it is a PN rather than a title or gentilic. ʿAnat is a feminine DN, the grammatical counterpart of the masculine DN ʿAn.[99] By analogy with the male deity Baʿal and the female deity

---

[95]Blau, *Polyphony*, p. 58.

[96]Compare MLArab. *ḥalā* "to adorn, grace," and note that the nominal forms *ḥaly* and *ḥilya* (Wehr, pp. 236-37) correspond to the BH CNN *ḥălî* and *ḥelyâ* (**qatl* and **qitl* [+ **-at*] bases).

[97]*Pace* Stark, *PNPI*, p. 88, who opts for a derivation from Arabic *ḫaliyy*, meaning "fresh, juicy herbage."

[98]See s.v. "gînat," p. 208 n. 47.

[99]The following names are constructed with a deity ʿAnu, the masculine counterpart of the deity ʿAnat: EA *bin(DUMU)-a-na* (*AmPN*, p. 109); Ug. *bin(DUMU)-a-nu*, *bn* ʿ*n* (*PTU*, p. 110); Ph. *bn* ʿ*n* (*PNPP*, pp. 89, 380). For a discussion on the DN ʿ*n* in PNN, see p. 178 and n. 123; and Tigay, p. 78 n. 25.

Baʿalat, one may infer that the *-at* endings on ʿAnat and Baʿalat are feminine suffixes. Thus this PN attests to the archaic feminine suffix *-at* on a DN,[100] which in this case either functions as a PN in itself or is an element of a compound PN. Against the possibility that ʿAnat by itself constitutes a PN, it may be argued that DNN as a rule do not function as PNN, and the apparent exceptions to this principle probably belong to that rare class of shortened names in which only the DN is retained.[101] What settles the issue, in my opinion, are the numerous WS PNN of the type Ben-ʿAn(at).[102]

In epigraphic finds, especially first-millennium seals, the term *bēn* is sometimes omitted between the name and its patronym. When the patronym is a compound PN of the type **bn* + DN, the **bn* element may have later been reanalyzed and no longer understood as part of patronym. This reanalysis would have given rise to shortened names, in which only the DN was retained.[103] Hence in the phrase Shamgar Ben-ʿAnat, Ben-ʿAnat may be the patronym of Shamgar, if we assume that the vocable *bēn* has been omitted. At any rate, even if the father's name was simply ʿAnat, this PN, derived from a DN, is an example of the retention of the archaic feminine suffix *-at*.

10. *šimʿāt*.

Classification: Can.--"Amm. mother (?)" of Yozakar (2 Kgs 12:22; 2 Chr 24:26).

Sex of name bearer: female (?).

---

[100]For another archaic morpheme on a DN, compare the Amm. DN Milkom.

[101]So Knauf, *ZAW* 97 (1985) 246; Kutscher, "lšny ḥwtmwt ʿbryym," p. 45; Noth, *IPN*, p. 123 n. 1; Ranke, *Early Babylonian Personal Names*, p. 8 n. 2; Stamm, *ANG*, p. 117; Tigay, pp. 24 and n. 18, 67 n. 15, 75, 76 n. 9, 77 nn. 15-16; 79 n. 26, 88 n. 6; Manfred Weippert, "Jau(a) mār ḫumrî--Joram oder Jehu von Israel?" *VT* 28 (1978) 116. Both Hess, *AmPN*, p. 59, and M. Dietrich and O. Loretz, "Der Amarna-Brief VAB* 2, 170," in *Beiträge zur alten Geschichte und deren Nachleben: Festschrift für Franz Altheim zum 6.10.1968*, ed. Ruth Stiehl and Hans E. Stier, 2 vols. (Berlin: Walter de Gruyter, 1969-70), 1:23, interpret EA *a-na-ti* in this fashion. In the WS onomasticon there are a good number of examples of this phenomenon. See the examples cited by Frank M. Cross, "An Interpretation of the Nora Stone," *BASOR* 208 (1972) 17-18; Baruch Halpern, "Yaua, Son of Omri, Yet Again," *BASOR* 265 (1987) 83; add the Can. PNN *rešep* (1 Chr 7:25) and *šelaḥ* (Gn 10:24; for discussion, see s.v. "mětûšelaḥ," pp. 73-74 n. 163), and the Moab. PN *kmš* (Israel, "Epigrafia moabiti," p. 115 #14).

[102]See especially J. T. Milik, "An Unpublished Arrow-Head with Phoenician Inscription of the 11th-10th Century B.C.," *BASOR* 143 (1956) 3-6. PNN of the type *bn(t)-ʿAnat* also occur in Egyptian documents (ibid., p. 5).

[103]Ibid., p. 5 n. 15.

Structure: 1. one-word name, *šim*ʿ- (**qitl* base) + *-at* feminine suffix.
2. shortened name, *šim*ʿ- (< **šm*ʿ "to hear," 3rd m.s. Qal perfect) + *-at* feminine suffix.

Meaning: 1. "hearing, report."
2. "(DN) has heard."

Parallels: Can. *šemaʿ*, *šimʿâ* = *šimʿā*ʾ, *šimʿî*, *šimʿôn*; GAA *šimʿātîm*, *šimʿônî*; BH CNN *šēmaʿ*, **šemaʿ*; IAram. *šmʿy* (*SPARI*, pp. 103, 220); Saf., Min., and Sab. *smʿ*, Saf. and Tham. *smʿt*, Sab. *smʿm*, *smʿn* (*PIAN*, pp. 328-29).

Comments: The archaic feminine suffix *-at* is easily recognized on this PN, but the function of this suffix depends on the overall analysis of the name. According to our first proposed structure/meaning, the PN *šimʿāt* is a nominal form, **qitl* base plus *-at* feminine suffix. Thus Shimʿat would be a feminine noun, and the feminine suffix in this case would be used to form an abstract noun, meaning "hearing, report."[104] This form of the name may be compared to the Can. PN *šimʿâ*, which reflects the change **-at* > *-â*. In the parallels section, I have cited PNN that would favor the analysis of *šimʿāt* as a nominal form. Some of these PNN may be analyzed differently, and the bases of the Can. PNN are not always as straightforward as they might appear at first glance. LXX transliterations sometimes point to a **qat(a)l* base rather than a **qitl* base.[105] It may be that the MT pointing should be explained as attenuation in some instances.

According to our second proposed structure/meaning, Shimʿat is a shortened name[106] from a verbal-sentence PN of the type **šāmaʿ* + DN, meaning "(DN) has heard." The feminine suffix would not indicate a feminine nominal form, but functions as a hypocoristic suffix on a shortened name. In his study of hypocoristic PNN, Lidzbarski noted that verbal-sentence names are often shortened according to the analogy of nominal forms.[107] For example, just as the hypocoristic suffix *-î* reminds one of the first person pronominal suffix, so the shortened form of the name bears a likeness to the suffixed form of the noun. This may

---

[104]The plural GA *šimʿātîm* also attests the same basic form (1 Chr 2:55).

[105]Note, for example, the LXX B transliteration *σαμαθ* for the Can. PN *šimʿāt* at 2 Chr 24:26.

[106]Noth, *IPN*, pp. 38, 185; Stamm, *BHAN*, p. 115; and apparently Tigay, p. 80 n. 34.

[107]Lidzbarski, "Semitische Kosenamen," 2:12.

imply, in a circuitous way, that a **qitl* base noun did exist, for it provided the model after which the shortened form was patterned. This second interpretation of the PN cannot be lightly dismissed, because verbal forms from the root **šmʿ* are productive in Canaanite PNN.[108] However, it has not yet been proven that the feminine suffix *-at* functioned as a hypocoristic suffix on Canaanite PNN.[109] All things considered, it is more likely that Shimʿat is to be analyzed as a **qitl* base noun plus archaic feminine suffix *-at*. Even if the hypocoristic interpretation of this name is preferred, the PN Shimʿat still ends in archaic feminine *-at*.

2 Kgs 12:22 makes no mention of the nationality of Shimʿat; in 2 Chr 24:26, however, the Chronicler adds the gentilic *hāʾammônît* "the Ammonitess" after the name. Thus the Chronicler understood Shimʿat as a matronym. Graham has argued against the historical reliability of the Chronicler's version.[110] Of importance here is Graham's argument that the Chronicler borrowed the GA *hāʿammōnî* from Ezra 9:1 and added it to his text. Though there are errors in detail,[111] the overall thrust of his argument may be valid. Since there is some question as to the historical reliability of this information, I have indicated this uncertainty by a question mark in the classification section. Likewise, since the gentilic adjective in 2 Chr 24:26 is the only indicator of the sex of the name bearer, some doubt remains as to whether the name bearer is female. It is possible, though it cannot be proven, that the sex of the name bearer is female, though she is not of Ammonite extraction.[112]

---

[108]Can. PN *šāmāʿ*; BH PN *šĕmaʿyāh(û)*; EH PNN *šmʿyhw* (VSE #40; A 27.2, 31.5, 39.2, 8; L 4.6, 19.4); Amm. PN *šmʿl* (*ALIA*, p. 97); Edom. PN *šmʿʾl* (Israel, *RivB* 27:194); Ph-P. PNN *šmʿbʿl*, *šmʿmlk*, *bʿlšmʿ* (Benz, *PNPP*, p. 421).

[109]For its use on Amor. PNN, see Huffmon, *APNMT*, p. 133. The use of the feminine suffix as a hypocoristic ending may have fallen into disuse long before the first millennium B.C. It is not attested as a hypocoristic suffix on Ug. PNN, unless in the compound hypocoristic suffix *-yt* (Gröndahl, *PTU*, p. 54).

[110]M. Patrick Graham, "A Connection Proposed Between II Chr 24,26 and Ezra 9-10," *ZAW* 97 (1985) 256-58.

[111]The link proposed by him between 2 Chr 24:26 and Ezra 9-10 is weakened if the name of the first assassin is read as Yozakar. This is certainly the preferred reading of the name (see Barthélemy, *Critique textuelle de l'Ancient Testament*, p. 400). Also Graham argues that the Chronicler altered the name of the parent of the second assassin from a masculine to a feminine form (*šōmēr* in 2 Kgs 12:22; *šimrît* in 2 Chr 24:26), so that it corresponded to the name of the first parent, the PN *šimʿāt*. But this fails to explain why the Chronicler wrote *šimrît*, instead of the expected **šimrāt*. Also note the difference in spelling between *hāʿammōnî* (Ezra 9:1--no *w mater lectionis*) and *hāʾammônît* (2 Chr 24:26--with *w mater lectionis*).

[112]For the designation of someone as the son of a woman, see p. 209 n. 52.

11. *šimrāt.*

Classification: Can.--one of the "sons" of Shimei (1 Chr 8:21--tribe of Benjamin).

Sex of name bearer: unknown.

Structure: 1. one-word name, *šimr-* (**qitl* base) + *-at* feminine suffix. 2. shortened name, *šimr-* (< **šmr* "to guard, protect," 3rd m.s. Qal perfect) + *-at* feminine suffix.

Meaning: 1. "guard, protection."
2. "(DN) has protected."

Parallels: Amor. *ši-im-ra-al-la* (*CAAA*, p. 641); *sa-ma-ri-a-du*, *sa-ma-ri-ilu(DINGIR)* (*CAAA*, p. 635); Can. *šemer*, *šimrî*, *šimrît*, *šimrôn*, GA *šimrōnî*, GN *šimrôn*; BH CN *šomrâ*; Liḥ., Saf., and Tham. *smr*; Qat. and Sab. *smrt*; Sab. *smrm*; Tham. *smrn* (*PIAN*, p. 328).

Comments: Much of the discussion on the name Shimʿat is, *mutatis mutandis*, applicable to the PN *šimrāt*. Again the archaic feminine suffix *-at* is easily recognized on this PN, but the function of this suffix is disputed. Our first proposed structure/meaning analyzes the PN *šimrāt* as a nominal form, **qitl* base plus *-at* feminine suffix. Thus Shimrat would be a feminine noun, and the feminine suffix in this case may be used to form an abstract noun, meaning "guard, protection." An analogous nominal form is the BH CN *šomrâ* (**qutl* base + *-â* [< **-at*] feminine suffix). In the parallels section, I have cited several PNN that would favor the analysis of *šimrāt* as a nominal form.[113] The Amor. PN *ši-im-ra-al-la* does attest a **qitl* base noun (**śimrum*).[114] The Can. PN *šemer* is either **qitl* or **qatl* base.[115] But the Can. PN *šimrî*, apparently a **qitl* base noun, is sometimes vocalized in the LXX as if it were a Qal perfect verbal form (e.g., LXX B *σαμαρ* in 1 Chr 4:37).

---

[113]According to Gelb, *CAAA*, p. 32, the Amor. PNN *sa-ma-ri-a-du* and *sa-ma-ri-ilu(DINGIR)* are verbal-sentence PNN, with the G stem of the verb **śmr*. But this analysis does not account for the *ri* sign. A common structure for nominal-sentence PNN is noun + 1st c.s. pronominal suffix + DN. Accordingly, these two PNN may consist of **qatal* base nouns as the first element and be translated "DN is my guard/protection."

[114]Gelb, *CAAA*, p. 32.

[115]LXX B transliterates *σεμμηρ* in 1 Chr 6:31 and 7:34; *σημηρ* in 1 Chr 8:12.

As with the preceding name, our second proposed structure/-meaning analyzes Shimrat as a shortened name[116] from a verbal-sentence PN of the type **šamar* + DN, meaning "(DN) has guarded." Verbal forms from the root **šmr* are productive in Canaanite PNN.[117] In view of the lack of evidence for the feminine suffix *-at* functioning as a hypocoristic suffix on Canaanite PNN, it is more likely that Shimrat should be analyzed as a **qitl* base noun plus archaic feminine suffix *-at.* Nothing can be said about the sex of the name bearer.

12. *tôqhat* K.

Variant spellings: 1. *toqhat* Q; 2. *tiqwâ.*[118]

Classification: Can.--father-in-law of Huldah the prophetess (2 Chr 34:22).

Sex of name bearer: male.

Structure: one-word name, *t-* preformative (**taqt(a)l* base ?, < **yqh* "to obey") + *-at* feminine suffix.

Meaning: "obedience."

Parallels: Ug. *ʾaqht* (*PTU*, p. 100); Can. *qĕhāt*, BH CN **yĕqāhâ*; NA *ia-a-qí-e* (*WSB*, p. 93 and n. 6); IAram. *yqh*, *yqyh* (*OAA*, p. 54); North and South Arab. PNN.[119]

Comments: According to Zadok, this PN ends in the feminine suffix *-at.*[120] Since the root **yqh* is productive in the formation of names in West Semitic,[121] and since the spelling *tôqhat* (< **tawqhat)* appears to

---

[116]Noth, *IPN*, pp. 38, 177; Stamm, *BHAN*, p. 134; and apparently Tigay, p. 80 n. 34.

[117]BH PN *šĕmaryāh(û)* (borne by four persons); EH PNN *šmryhw* (VSE ##362, 363; A 18.4), *šmryw* (VSE #214; S 1.1-2, 13.2, 14.2, 21.1-2); Ph-P. *šmrbʿl*, *ʾršmr*, *ʾšmnšmr*, *bʿlšmr* (Benz, *PNPP*, p. 421).

[118]I agree with Noth, *IPN*, p. 260, that the reading *tiqwâ* in 2 Kgs 22:14 is nothing more than a "Erleichterung" for the more difficult reading. Tiqwah may be attested as a post-exilic name in Ezra 10:15.

[119]See s.v. "lĕmûʾēl," p. 191 n. 181 for a list of North and South Arab. names with the root **wqh.*

[120]Zadok, *EM* 8:60.

[121]All the PNN cited may be derived from this root. For the derivation of the Ug. PN *ʾaqht* from this root, see Baruch Margalit, "Ugaritic Lexicography IV: The Name AQHT," *RB* 95 (1988) 211-14; J. C. de Moor, Review of *Die Personennamen der Texte aus Ugarit*, by Frauke Gröndahl, *BO* 26 (1969) 106 (with some

point to this root, then it is probable that the name ends in the archaic feminine suffix *-at*.

B. *Dubious Examples*

1. *ʾeprāt.*

Variant spelling: *ʾeprātāh.*

Classification: Can.--the second wife of Caleb (1 Chr 2:19).

Sex of name bearer: female.

Structure: *ʾepr-* (base unknown) + *-at* feminine suffix.

Meaning: "territory ?"

Parallels: Can. *ʾeprayim*, GN *ʾeprātāh*, GA *ʾeprātî.*

Comments: Three lines of evidence converge to suggest that the PN ʾEphrat is derived from a toponym: 1) In 1 Chr 2:50 and 4:4, it is written with the *-āh* locative ending; 2) its predominant use in the Hebrew Bible is as a GN for several different localities (KB3, p. 78); and 3) the etymology of the word is suited for a GN.[122] In his study of the suffix *-at* on PNN and GNN, Eshel issues a caveat that the *-at* ending on

---

reservation). For a different proposal, see K. Aartun, "Herkunft und Sinn des Namens *Aqht* im ugaritischen Material," in *Scripta Signa Vocis: Studies about Scripts, Scriptures, Scribes and Languages in the Near East, presented to J. H. Hospers*, ed. H. L. J. Vanstiphout et al. (Groningen: Egbert Forsten, 1986), pp. 9-14 (*ʾaqht* < **ʾqh* + *-t* "objection, protest").

[122]The etymology of ʾEphrat(ah) can hardly be divorced from that of ʾEphraim. J. Heller, "Noch zu Ophra, Ephron and Ephraim," *VT* 12 (1962) 339-41, compares the latter PN with Akk. *eperu*, which means not only "dust," but also "territory." For an older etymology, see Friedrich Schulthess, "Zwei etymologische Versuche," *ZAW* 30 (1910) 61-63, who compares these PNN to the JAram. and Mishnaic Hebrew root **ʾpr*, "pasture-ground," which is related to Akk. *appārum* "marshy meadow," itself a loanword from Sumerian. Compare also the NA GN *URUap-paru* (< Aram.) "reed marsh/bed, lagoon" (Zadok, *WSB*, p. 205). Manuscript Kaufmann gives the vocalization *ʾappār* for the Hebrew. According to Eduard Y. Kutscher, "Mittelhebräische und Jüdisch-Aramäisch im neuen Köhler-Baumgartner," VTSup 16 (1967) 163 (reprinted in *Hebrew and Aramaic Studies*, ed. Zeev Ben-Ḥayyim, Aharon Dotan, and Gad Sarfatti [Jerusalem: Magnes Press, 1977], p. 161), this vocalization rules out any connection with Hebrew *ʾeprayim*. Whichever etymology is preferred, both of them are well-suited for a GN.

GNN may be the product of a late development, i.e. a shortening from the locative form.[123] In light of the evidence suggesting that we are dealing with a PN < GN, then it is probable that the PN ʾEphrat is nothing other than a secondary formation from the GN that ended with *-āh* locative ending.

2. *golyāt.*

Classification: unknown--Philistine (1 Sam 17:4).

Sex of name bearer: male.

Structure: one-word name.

Meaning: unknown.

Comments: The PN Golyat has been cited as a name terminating in the feminine suffix *-at.*[124] Scholars agree that the original home of the Philistines was located somewhere in the Aegean. That the Philistines who settled in Palestine generally bore WS PNN attests to the influence of Canaanite culture. The case of the PN Golyat, however, appears to be exceptional; no satisfactory explanation of this name has ever been advanced on the basis of WS grammar and vocabulary. Assuming for the sake of argument that the final *-at* is the feminine suffix, one possible root is **glh* "to uncover," but this analysis is hardly persuasive. Nor does comparison with the PN *γωλωτ*, attested in a Greek inscription from El-Arish, shed any light.[125] With good reason one may suspect

---

[123]Eshel, p. 266.

[124]Driver, *Books of Samuel*, p. 139; idem, *A Treatise on the Use of the Tenses in Hebrew*, 2d ed., rev. and enl. (Oxford: Clarendon Press, 1881), p. 261 n. 1; Henry P. Smith, *A Critical and Exegetical Commentary on the Books of Samuel*, ICC (Edinburgh: T. & T. Clark, 1899), p. 155; Stanley A. Cook, "Notes on Semitic Inscriptions III.," *PSBA* 26 (1904) 126; Nöldeke, *EB* 3:3303; GKC §80g; Joüon, §89n. BL §62v cite the PN Golyat in a list of PNN terminating in the feminine ending, but add the qualification (n. 3) that with a Philistine name it is not certain whether the final *-at* is the feminine ending.

[125]Raphael Tonneau, "Épigraphie grecque du Négeb," *RB* 36 (1927) 93. In his review of KB2, Paul Humbert stresses the uncertainty of the reading of this PN and that it may well represent nothing but a late derivation of the Arabic name of Goliath, *ǵālūt* (Paul Humbert, Review of *Lexicon in Veteris Testamenti libros*, by Ludwig Köhler and Walter Baumgartner, *TZ* 6 [1950] 61). The MT *golyāt*, LXX B *γολιαθ*, and the transliteration in Josephus (*γολιαθος*, *-αθης*; *NWJ*, p. 35) all line up together, over against Grk *γωλωτ*.

that the name is non-Semitic, as was the PN Akish, the Philistine king of Ekron.[126]

3. *mānaḥat.*

Classification: Can.--son of Shobal (Gen 36:23; 1 Chr 1:40).

Sex of name bearer: male.

Structure: one-word name, *m*- performative noun (< **nwḥ*)[127] + -*at* feminine suffix.

Meaning: "rest, quietness?"

Parallels: Can. GN *mānaḥat*, GA *mānaḥtî.*

Comments: See discussion below, s.v. "naḥat."

4. *naḥat.*

Classification: Can.--1) son of Reʿuʾel (Gen 36:13); 2) tribe of Levi (1 Chr 6:11 = English 6:26);[128] 3) overseer in time of Hizqiyah (2 Chr 31:13).

Sex of name bearers: male.

Structure: one-word name, *na(w)ḥ*- (**qatl* base ?) + -*at* feminine suffix.

Meaning: "rest, quietness ?"

Parallels: Can. *mānaḥat*, GN *mānaḥat*, GA *mānaḥtî*, BH CNN *naḥat* I "strength"[129] and II "quietness, rest."

---

[126]McCarter, *1 Samuel*, p. 291, speculates that the name may be Anatolian, comparing the final -*yat* of Golyat to similar Hittite and Lydian endings. For an attempt to derive the PN Golyat from Egyptian, see M. Görg, "Goliat aus Gat," *BN* 34 (1986) 17-21.

[127]BDB, p. 630; KB2, p. 539; KB3, p. 565; BL §77i.

[128]In place of Nahat, 1 Chr 6:19 (= English 6:34) reads Toah, and 1 Sam 1:1 reads Tohu.

[129]Previously the BH CN *naḥat* I, which occurs once in the Hebrew Bible (Isa. 30:30), has been understood as deriving from the verb *nāḥat*, "to go down, descend." Robert M. Good, "Hebrew and Ugaritic *NḤT*," *UF* 17 (1985) 153-56, argues persuasively that *naḥat* I is instead derived from a root **nḥt*, common to Ug.

Comments: According to S. R. Driver and Zadok, the final *-at* of the PN *naḥat* is the feminine termination.[130] Driver also cites in this regard the Can. PN *mānaḥat*.[131] Since these two PNN appear to be related, whatever is said about the PN Nahat may be applied to Manahat.

To analyze the final *-at* as the feminine suffix, one must derive the PN Nahat from the II-weak root **nwḥ*. This is the derivation proposed for the CN *naḥat* in grammars and lexica.[132] Although nowhere explicitly stated, the raison d'être for this derivation appears to be semantic considerations; that is, both the root **nwḥ* and the CN *naḥat* are associated with the concept of "rest, quietness." Nevertheless, from the perspective of morphology it is difficult to derive *naḥat* from a II-weak root **nwḥ*.[133] In forms derived from the II-weak root **nwḥ*, one expects a *u* class vowel, in most cases *ô*, between the *n* and the *ḥ*. Note the following derived forms: PN *nôḥâ*, GNN *yānôaḥ* and *yānôḥâ*, CN *mĕnû/ūḥâ*, and the CN and PN *mānôaḥ*.[134] Although there is some diversity in nominal formations, no nominal forms provide an analogy for the derivation *naḥat* < **nwḥ*. The closest analogy is BH *bōšet* < **bwš*, but even here, the expected *u* class vowel occurs, and the feminine ending is *-t* (> *-et*) and not *-at*.

A segholate noun such as *naḥat* may be derived from a triradical root **nḥt*, a I-weak root (see BL §61g), or a III-weak root (e.g., *delet*). In light of Ug. *nḥt* and *nḫt*, and BH **nḥt* "to descend" and **nḥt* "to be strong," the first alternative should not be lightly dismissed. Moreover,

(G and D stems) and BH (D stem), meaning "to be strong" (G), "to strengthen" (D). Manfred Görg, "Marginalien zur Basis *NḪT*," *BN* 32 (1986) 20-21, cites Eg. evidence for a root **nḫt*, meaning "(to be) strong, to strengthen." Finally, Svi Rin, "Ugaritic-Old Testament Affinities," *BZ*, n.f., 7 (1963) 24-25, had already suggested the meaning "strength" for *naḥat* in Isa 30:30, though he appealed to Ug. *nḫt* in *KTU* 1.3.IV.3.

[130]Driver, *Books of Samuel*, p. 139; Zadok, *EM* 8:60.

[131]Ibid. Likewise, Nöldeke, *EB* 3:3303, sees in Manahat the retention of the archaic feminine ending.

[132]BDB, p. 629; KB2, p. 611; KB3, p. 654; Bernhard Stade, *Lehrbuch der hebräischen Grammatik* (Leipzig: F. C. W. Vogel, 1879), §201d; Justus Olshausen, *Lehrbuch der hebräischen Sprache* (Braunschweig: Friedrich Vieweg & Sohn, 1861), §164c; Eduard König, *Historisch-kritisches Lehrgebäude der hebräischen Sprache*, 2 vols. (Leipzig: J. C. Hinrichs, 1881-97), vol. 2, part 1, §91. Contrast Friedrich Delitzsch, *Prolegomena eines neuen hebräischen-aramäischen Wörterbuchs zum Alten Testament* (Leipzig: J. C. Hinrichs, 1886), pp. 118-20, who dissents, deriving the noun from the triradical root **nḥt*, "to descend." On the derivation of the PN Manahat from the root **nwḥ*, see p. 225 n. 127.

[133]That *naḥat* in the MT of Qoh. 6:5 is rendered by *nwḥt* in 4Q4:6 proves nothing, since the latter form reflects Aramaic influence (Kutscher, *Isaiah Scroll*, pp. 201-3).

[134]To cite additional examples, note BH *šûḥâ* "pit," from the II-w root **šwḥ*, and BH *bûšâ* "shame," from the II-w root **bwš*.

in Job 36:16, the CN *naḥat* functions as a masculine noun.[135] Unfortunately, the LXX transliterations of the PNN Nahat and Manahat are of no help in ascertaining the root; they exhibit genuine inconsistency in their rendering of the *ḥ*.[136] To conclude, the PN Nahat may share the meaning of the CN *naḥat*. If this be so, then morphological considerations suggest that both nouns are to be derived from BH **nḥt* "to descend." A semantic development from an action "to descend" to a resultant state "rest" occasions no difficulty. A theory of biconsonantalism would account for the semantic overlap between the roots **nwḥ* "to rest" and **nḥt* "to descend." On the other hand, the PN and the CN may be mere homonyms. Whatever the case may be, it is more probable that the final *-t* is part of the root in the PNN Nahat and Manahat, rather than the archaic feminine suffix *-at*.

5. *ʿašwāt.*

Classification: unknown--tribe of Asher (1 Chr 7:33).

Sex of name bearer: unknown.

Structure: one-word name, *ʿašw-* (**qatl* base ?) + *-at* ? feminine suffix.

Meaning: unknown.

Comments: I have classified this PN as a dubious example for the following reasons. First, the reading of the name is uncertain. The MT *ʿašwāt* is not supported by the versions: LXX A and B read *ασειθ* (< **ʿšyt* ?),[137] whereas the Vulgate reads *Asoth* (< **ʿăśôt* ?). Some Hebrew manuscripts have *ś* in place of *š*.[138] Second, there is no root **ʿšw* in Northwest Semitic to provide an acceptable etymology for the name. Noth accepts the reading with *ś* and compares the PN with MLArab. *ʿašā* ("to be dim-sighted, to be night blind" [Wehr, p. 719]).[139] The Palm. PN *ʿšy* (*PNPI*, p. 107) and the Hat. PN *ʿšy* (*PIH*, p. 156)

---

[135]Contrast the feminine BH CN *šaḥat*, which may be derived from the triradical root **šḥt* (**šaḥattu* > **šaḥatt* > *šaḥat*) or from a III-weak root *šāḥâ* "to bow down." In either case, the feminine ending is *-t*.

[136]Blau, *Polyphony*, p. 46.

[137]Lucianic *ασσουαθ* may reflect the consonantal *w*, but then double *σ* becomes difficult.

[138]See *BHS* textual apparatus. LXX transliterations do not distinguish between sibilants.

[139]Noth, *IPN*, p. 228 n. 3, who also cites Arab. *ʿašwatun*.

have also been related to this Arabic root. But each of these names, as well as the EH PN *ʿšy* (VSE #243), may not be related at all, if they are from the common BH root **ʿśh* "to do, make." But if *š* is the correct reading in the biblical PN, and if it is a genuinely Hebrew name, then it cannot be related to the Arabic root. It is tenuous to base an etymology on a disputed consonant. Because of uncertainty concerning the structure and root of the name, it is necessary to consider it as a dubious example.[140]

6. *rîpat.*

Variant spelling: *dîpat.*[141]

Classification: Anatolian ?--"son" of Gomer (Gen 10:3).

Structure: one-word name.

Meaning: unknown.

Comments: BL §62v mentions Ripat as an example of the archaic feminine suffix *-at* preserved in the absolute state. Though there is a suitable Can. etymology available for this TN,[142] the place it occupies in the Table of Nations, between Ashkenaz and Togarmah, all three as "sons" of Gomer, suggests strongly that it is a non-Semitic and probably Anatolian name.[143]

IV. Late West Semitic PNN (extrabiblical)

The following PNN are cited as evidence for the preservation of the archaic feminine suffix *-at* on extrabiblical late West Semitic PNN.

---

[140]Without providing an etymology, Zadok, *EM* 8:60, states that this name ends in *-t*, rather than *-at*. His analysis would presuppose a revocalization of the MT. If he is correct, then this PN should definitely be excluded from further consideration. In "Notes on the Prosopography of the Old Testament," *BN* 42 (1988) 45, Zadok ponders whether *ʿšwt* might be a metathesis of **šwʿt* (> **šwʿh/šwʿʾ*).

[141]Whereas the variant spelling occurs in the MT of 1 Chr. 1:6, other Hebrew manuscripts, LXX A and B, the Vulgate, and Josephus read Ripat. On the confusion of *r* and *d*, see s.v. "rĕʿûʾēl," p. 91 n. 248.

[142]BH **rîpâ*, "groat(s)."

[143]For further discussion of the "sons" of Gomer, see Westermann, *Genesis 1-11*, p. 506.

1. *WS PNN in alphabetic writing*

The only known examples have already been cited in the discussions of the PNN Yehoshabʿat and Ginat. The PN *šbʿt* occurs twice, once on a seal (which reads *lʿbdʾlʾb bn šbʿt ʿbd mtt bn ṣdqʾ* "(belonging) to Abdʾelʾab, son of Shabʿat, servant of Mititt(i), son of Sidqa"),[144] and a second time incised on a juglet discovered in the Ophel excavations.[145] The IAram. PN *gnt* was discovered on an ostracon from the fifth century B.C.[146]

2. *WS PNN in cuneiform writing*

Aramaic as well as Hebrew underwent the change **at* > *â* in the feminine singular absolute of the noun. In a discussion of names borne by females, Zadok has isolated nine Aramaic PNN occurring in N/LB texts which end in *-at*:

> *ᶠa-qu-ba-tu₄*
> *ᶠdi-di-(in-)na-tu₄*
> *ᶠdu-da-ti*
> *ᶠḫa-ba/ma-ra-na-tú*
> *ᶠia-ba-ba-ti*
> *ᶠia-a-qar-ra-tu₄*
> *ᶠna-si-ka-tu₄*
> *ᶠna-tin-na-tu₄* (*WSB*, p. 170)
> *ᶠṭu-na-tu₄* (*Sources*, p. 24)

He remarks that "the number of feminine names ending in **-â* greatly exceeds that of the names ending in *-at*," and then provides a list of twenty-one PNN ending in **-â* from NA and N/LB documents (*WSB*, pp. 170-71).[147] These two groups of PNN represent two different strata of the Aramaic language, an earlier one with the feminine ending *-at*, and a later one with the feminine ending *-ā*. He even cites one instance from N/LB documents in which the name of the same woman is written

---

[144]VSE #73. For a photograph of the seal, see Naveh, *IEJ* 35 (1985) 9, and Pl. 2A. Cook, *PSBA* 26 (1904) 166, noted the retention of the "old feminine ending" on this PN and compared it to PNN in the Hebrew Bible with the same ending.

[145]See p. 212 n. 70.

[146]See p. 208.

[147]In Review of *West Semitic Personal Names in the Murašû Documents*, by Michael D. Coogan, *IEJ* 28 (1978) 291, Ran Zadok adds NA *ᶠṭa-li-ia-a*, and in *Sources*, p. 24, he adds N/LB *ᶠgu-zu-um-ma-a* and N/LB *ᶠšá-(an-)na-a*, raising the total to twenty-four.

in both forms: *ᶠa-qu-ba-tu₄* and *ᶠa-qu-ba-ʾ* (*WSB*, p. 170). Other evidence indicates that Aramaic scribes were uncomfortable with the feminine morpheme *-at* in the absolute state and occasionally even hypercorrected Akkadian proper nouns to conform to the norms of the current Aramaic grammar. Fales notes the correspondence between the NA PN *ᶠar-ba-ìl-šar-rat* = *ʾrblsr*, the GN *ᵁᴿᵁḫa-an-du-a-te* = *ḥdwh*, and the GN *Ekallāte* = *ʾglh*, in which the Aramaic scribes either dropped the feminine *-at* or adjusted it to **-â*.[148]

3. *WS PNN in Greek transliteration*

I tentatively cite two examples that appear to end in the feminine suffix *-at*: Grk *γαδιμαθος* (< **gdymt*) and *οασιχαθος* (< **wšykt*).[149]

V. Summary

The feminine marker on early West Semitic PNN is *-at* or *-t*. Examples are to be found on Amorite PNN, and on WS PNN in the execration texts, Alalakh tablets, Taanach tablets, and the El Amarna letters. Gelb, who is followed by Huffmon, has recognized a feminine morpheme *-a* on Amor. PNN, which may be a shortened form of *-atum*. In Ugaritic, the feminine morphemes *-at* and *-t* continue to be productive in the formation of feminine nouns. In early West Semitic, these morphemes occur primarily on feminine PNN, and occasionally on masculine PNN as well.

In the Canaanite languages, the feminine morpheme *-t* is retained in both the construct and absolute states of the noun. While the feminine morpheme **-at* is preserved in both the absolute and construct states of the noun in Moabite, Ammonite, and Phoenician, it shifted to **-â* in the absolute state of the noun in BH and EH. ABH most likely preserves some remnants of *-at* in the absolute state. In light of certain feminine singular absolute nouns in EH, which provide a *terminus ad quem* for the shift **-at* > **-â*, the change must have taken place sometime before 700 B.C. In the Hebrew Bible, the following Canaanite PNN end in the feminine suffix *-at* and thus constitute probable examples:

---

[148] Frederick M. Fales, "On Aramaic Onomastics in the Neo-Assyrian Period," *OrAnt* 16 (1977) 66. For other possible examples, see idem, "Assyro-Aramaica: Three Notes," *Or* 53 (1981) 66; idem, "Note di semitico nordoccidentale," *Vicino Oriente* 5 (1982) 82-83.

[149] Wuthnow, pp. 133, 137.

1. ʾAhuzzat
2. Bekorat
3. Basemat
4. Ginat
5. Genubat
6. Tapat
7. Yehoshabʿat
8. Mahalat
9. (Ben-)ʿAnat
10. Shimʿat
11. Shimrat
12. Toqhat

In PNN ##1-8 and 12, the Masoretes represented the *a* vowel with *pataḥ*, whereas PNN ##9-11 are vocalized with *qāmeṣ*. I can find no rationale behind this difference in vowel notation. With the exceptions of PN #7, a nominal-sentence name, and PN #9, a construct phrase name, the remaining PNN appear to be one-word names.

These twelve PNN may be contrasted with Canaanite PNN in the Hebrew Bible that exhibit the shift **-at* > *-â* in the absolute state of the feminine noun. It is often difficult to distinguish the feminine suffix *-â* (< **-at*) from the hypocoristic suffix *-ā*, which can be written with either *h* or *ʾaleph mater lectionis*. I have attempted to exclude ambiguous examples; the following PNN should probably be included in the group: Bilhah, Deborah, Dinah, Delilah, Zebudah, Zilpah, Hoglah, Helah, Huldah, Hannah, Huppah, Yedidah, Yemimah, Yerushah, Leah, Mahalah, Milkah, Noah, Naamah, Naarah, Eglah, Azubah, Atarah, Aksah, Ophrah, Puah, Peninah, Sibyah, Sillah, Sipporah, Seruah, Qesiah, Reumah, Rinnah, Rispah, and Shiprah. This list, which totals thirty-six PNN, shows that most PNN in the Hebrew Bible that end in the feminine morpheme reflect the shift **-at* > *-â*. Furthermore, in this second list the congruence between the grammatical gender of the name and the sex of the name bearer is greater than in the list of PNN terminating in *-at*. There is congruence in thirty-four out of thirty-six PNN--roughly ninety-five percent. More accurate figures could be attained, but only after careful study of all PNN in the Hebrew Bible ending in *-â*, a task which exceeds the limits of this study.

As dubious examples I cite the following PNN, some of which may not even be Canaanite:

1. ʾEphrat
2. Golyat
3. Manahat
4. Nahat
5. ʿAshwat
6. Ripat

Among extrabiblical late WS PNN, the Can. PN *šbʿt* (2x) and the IAram. *gnt* terminate in the feminine suffix *-at*. From N/LB texts may be cited nine Aram. PNN that terminate in the feminine suffix *-at*. Two possible examples are to be found in WS PNN in Greek transliteration.

CHAPTER 6

CONCLUSIONS

The purpose of this study was to test the hypothesis that enjoys a certain popularity among Semitists, that Semitic proper names, and in particular the group studied here, viz., Canaanite PNN, contain archaic morphological features. From a preliminary study of Canaanite PNN, it became apparent that morphology would be the most profitable area for investigation. Accordingly the inquiry was limited to a particular set of archaic morphological features, and a close examination of all putative examples has shown that a significant number of probable cases of each archaic feature exist.

The study was purposely conducted in such a way as to organize the putative examples of each feature into categories of probable and dubious cases; only with the morphological archaism of the *ḥireq compaginis* was a third category deemed necessary, ambiguous cases. A total of eighty-four putative examples were considered, and those names that could be classified as Canaanite were sorted into one of the three above-mentioned categories.[1] The approach may be characterized as "minimalist," and it is possible, therefore, that the resultant lists of probable examples of each feature will be expanded in the course of future research.

Thus the primary accomplishment of this inquiry has been to place the study of archaism of Canaanite PNN in the Hebrew Bible on a firm foundation of detailed examination of all the evidence. It has been demonstrated that Canaanite PNN do retain the following archaic morphological features: 1) the nominative case vowel *-u*; 2) the *ḥireq compaginis*; 3) enclitic *-m*; and 4) the feminine morpheme *-at* in the absolute state. While the net yield of the morphological features contained in this 'mini-grammar' is meager, a proper perspective ensures the importance of this inquiry. In the reconstruction of the older stages of Northwest Semitic, piecemeal evidence from a variety of

[1]The net yield of non-Canaanite PN is as follows: a) Aram.: 1. ʾAhumay (probable example of the nominative case vowel); 2. Zabdiʾel (probable example of the h.c.); 3. Zabdi (ambiguous example of the h.c.); b) Arabian: 1. ʾAbimaʾel and 2. Lemoʾel (probable examples of enclitic *-m*); 3. ʾAlmodad (dubious example of enclitic *-m*).

different sources must be synthesized to obtain as full a picture as possible. The retention of these archaic morphological features in Canaanite PNN is another important piece of evidence.

A secondary accomplishment of this study is the analysis and interpretation of an important sector within the Canaanite onomasticon of the Hebrew Bible. Many of these names, borne by individuals marginal to the flow of the narrative of the Hebrew Bible, were poorly understood until now; as a result of this study, new interpretations have been proffered for some of the names.

The results obtained in this study may be compared with archaic morphological features preserved in ABH. Whereas ABH and Canaanite PNN both attest the nominative (singular) case ending *-u*, the *ḥireq compaginis*, enclitic *-m*, and the feminine morpheme *-at* in the absolute state, only PNN preserve a morphological feature not found in ABH: the nominative plural case vowel *-ū*.[2] Our final task is to study each group of these names containing morphological archaisms to see whether any patterns emerge, and then to synthesize the results for each group of names as a whole.

The best way to get an overview of each group of names is to list them and to note their distribution in the books of the Hebrew Bible. Many of these PNN are found in Chronicles, and for chronological purposes, it is pertinent to note in which portion of Chronicles they are to be found: 1 Chr 1-9--from Adam to David; 1 Chr 10-29--time of David; 2 Chr 1-9--time of Solomon; and 2 Chr 10-36--kings of Judah, ending with Cyrus, king of Persia.

I. The Nominative Case Vowel *-u*

Name	Biblical books			
	Torah	F Prophets	L Prophets	Writings
1. Betu᾽el	Gen			
2. Hadoram				1 Chr 10-29; 2 Chr 10-36
3. Huram				1 Chr 1-9, 10-29; 2 Chr 1-9
4. Hamutal		2 Kgs	Jer	

[2] See s.v. "pĕnû᾽ēl," pp. 74-76.

5. Hammu'el					1 Chr 1-9
6. Yemu'el	Gen, Ex				
7a. Metusha'el	Gen				1 Chr 1-9
7b. Metushelah	Gen				1 Chr 1-9
8. Penu'el					1 Chr 1-9
9. Qemu'el	Gen, Num				1 Chr 10-29
10. Shemu'el	Num	1 Sam		Jer[3]	Ps,[4] 1 Chr 1-9, 10-29; 2 Chr 10-36[5]

Any attempt to detect patterns must take into consideration the uncertainty of the enterprise. It has already been noted that the linguistic classification of many of the names studied cannot be carried out with precision beyond a certain level and at best is provisional in nature. The same problem afflicts any attempt to date names, since names may be older or younger than the texts in which they are found. Nevertheless, certain generalizations can be made. Names that retain the nominative case vowel *-u* are found predominantly in the time before David. The only names which continue in use after the time of David are the Ph. PN Huram, and the Can. PNN Hadoram and Shemu'el. The reuse of the name Shemu'el, which is found even in the postbiblical period, is understandable.

With the exception of the PNN Hadoram, Huram, Hamutal, and Metushelah, the remaining names of this group, six in number, are of the structural type $*C_1\breve{e}C_2\hat{u}{}^{\prime}\bar{e}l$. This onomastic formation appears to be ancient; it is likely that this is a non-Hebrew name type native to the Canaanite[6] onomasticon.[7]

---

[3]Jer 15:1, a reference to the famous Israelite prophet.

[4]Ps 99:6; see the preceding note.

[5]2 Chr 35:18; see the preceding note.

[6]Viz., Canaanite as opposed to Israelite. Here I use the term "Canaanite" not in its linguistic sense, but ethnically to refer to the non-Israelite population who resided in Canaan.

[7]This is immediately evident for the Can. PNN Betu'el, Yemu'el, and Qemu-'el. As for the PNN Hammu'el and Shemu'el, each of these names include lexemes (**ḥām* and *šēm*) that are not productive in the Israelite onomasticon. This leaves only the name Penu'el, borne by individuals from the tribes of Judah and

II. The *Ḥireq Compaginis*

Name	Biblical books			
	Torah	F Prophets	L Prophets	Writings
1. ʿAbdiʾel				1 Chr 1-9
2. Hizqiyah		2 Kgs	Zeph	Prov, Neh, 1 Chr 1-9
3. Hizqi				1 Chr 1-9
4. Yatniʾel				1 Chr 10-29

In contrast to the names in the previous group, not one of these names is attested in the Torah.

III. Enclitic *-m*

Name	Biblical books			
	Torah	F Prophets	L Prophets	Writings
1. ʾUlam				1 Chr 1-9
2. ʾOnam	Gen			1 Chr 1-9
3. ʾAhuzzam				1 Chr 1-9
4. Bilʿam	Num, Deut.	Josh	Mic	Neh[8]
5. Gaʿtam	Gen			1 Chr 1-9
6. Horam	Josh			
7. Zetam				1 Chr 10-29

Benjamin; but this proper name is first attested in the Hebrew Bible as a Canaanite GN.

[8]All references to the same person, the non-Israelite prophet.

8. Hupham	Num		
9. Husham	Gen		1 Chr 1-9
10. Kimham		2 Sam	
11. Malkam			1 Chr 1-9
12. Mish‘am			1 Chr 1-9
13. ‘Iram	Gen		1 Chr 1-9
14. Pir’am		Josh	
15. Shuham	Num		
16. Shephupham	Num		

The list of PNN retaining enclitic *-m* is longer than any of the other lists, consisting of sixteen names. Excluding the PNN Zetam and Kimham, these PNN are first attested in the pre-Davidic period, and they are not attested in the Hebrew Bible for later periods.

Two patterns should be noted. First, four of the names that terminate in the enclitic morpheme are, according to biblical tradition, borne by Edomites and all stem from the same chapter in the Hebrew Bible--Gen 36.[9] The other pattern that emerges from a study of this list of PNN is that five of the names are borne by individuals from the tribe of Benjamin (’Ulam, Hupham, Malkam, Mish‘am, and Shephupham).[10] This is the highest concentration of PNN retaining archaic morphology that is traceable to a single tribe.[11]

[9]They are ’Onam, Ga‘tam, Husham, and ‘Iram. Of these PNN, the PN ’Onam is also borne by an Israelite (1 Chr 2:26).

[10]Of these PNN, only the PN ’Ulam is borne by a individual from another tribe--Manasseh (1 Chr 7:16-17).

[11]Already cited in this study (p. 17 n. 64) is the conclusion of Goldberg, "Northern-Type-Names," p. 101, that Canaanite divine elements are most prevalent in PNN traceable to the tribe of Benjamin.

IV. The Feminine Morpheme *-at*

Name	Torah	F Prophets	L Prophets	Writings
		Biblical books		
1. ʾAhuzzat	Gen			
2. Bekorat		1 Sam		
3. Basemat	Gen	1 Kgs		
4. Ginat		1 Kgs		
5. Genubat		1 Kgs		
6. Tapat		1 Kgs		
7. Yehoshabʿat				2 Chr 10-36
8. Mahalat	Gen			2 Chr 10-36
9. (Ben-)ʿAnat		Judg		
10. Shimʿat		2 Kgs		2 Chr 10-36
11. Shimrat				1 Chr 1-9
12. Toqhat				2 Chr 10-36

It should be remembered that feminine PNN are much less frequently attested in the Hebrew Bible than masculine PNN, and to some extent, this affects any conclusions drawn from this list. Some of these PNN (##1, 3, and 8) are first attested early in the biblical narrative, while the others are randomly dispersed throughout the rest of the Hebrew Bible.

V. Synthesis

The sum total of names contained in these four lists is forty-two.[12] This number represents a small percentage of the total number of Canaanite PNN in the Hebrew Bible. This sum total may be broken down as follows, in decreasing order of frequency: sixteen PNN (enclitic *-m*), twelve PNN (feminine morpheme *-at*), ten PNN (nominative case vowel *-u*), and four PNN (*ḥireq compaginis*). Many of the names that comprise this list are first attested in the earlier periods which are recorded in the Hebrew Bible. In broad terms, these PNN may be described as preexilic; with few exceptions, these PNN were not reused in the postexilic period.[13] Lastly, on the basis of the Hebrew Bible, names with the Yahwistic theophore are relatively late;[14] therefore, it is not surprising that there are only two Yahwistic PNN in the entire list: Hizqiyah and Yehoshabʿat.

With few exceptions, it has not been possible to determine the specific Canaanite dialect to which each of these names belong. Nonetheless, it seems reasonable to suggest that the retention of archaic morphological features is not proper to any particular Canaanite dialect to the exclusion of the others. If this suggestion is accepted, then one may infer that these Canaanite dialects ultimately derive from a parent language in which these morphological features were productive.

---

[12]Of the other forty-two PNN that were considered, six were non-Canaanite (see p. 233 n. 1), and the remaining thirty-six constituted dubious examples.

[13]Tigay, p. 17 and n. 57, speaks of an "inertia in onomastic habits," which would well explain the use of names with archaic features in later periods.

[14]Thompson, *Historicity*, p. 36 n. 141.

Appendix

The Feminine Morpheme *-(a)y*

The most celebrated example of archaism among Canaanite PNN of the Hebrew Bible is the feminine PN Saray. Before discussing this PN, we shall consider the West Semitic evidence for the existence of a Proto-Semitic feminine ending **-ay*, which would have coexisted with the feminine ending *-(a)t*. Whatever the original situation, the feminine ending *-ay* fell into desuetude in West Semitic, occasionally being retained as an archaism in proper nouns and a few uninflected forms.[1] The only exception to this generalization is Arabic, in which the *-ay* feminine ending is still productive in forming adjectives.[2] The evidence for the existence of this feminine morpheme in early West Semitic is to be found in Amorite and Ugaritic.[3]

I. Early West Semitic

The detection of the feminine ending *-ay* in PNN may be described as hazardous, since the feminine ending is easily confused with the hypocoristic suffixes *-uya*, *-iya*, and *-aya*.[4] The possibility that the gentilic suffix *-iy(y)u* might also appear on PNN only makes matters worse. In Amorite, the first common singular pronominal suffix is exceptionally written *-ya*, but this writing most probably reflects Babylonian influence and need not be considered further in the analysis of

---

[1]Moscati, *CGSL* §12.33; Brockelmann, *GVG*, 1:412. Theodor Nöldeke, *Compendious Syriac Grammar*, 2d ed., rev., transl. James A. Crichton (London: Williams & Norgate, 1904), §83, lists seven Syriac nouns that retain this old feminine ending.

[2]W. Wright, *A Grammar of the Arabic Language*, 3d ed., 2 vols. (Cambridge: Cambridge University, 1971), 1:184.

[3]In his discussion of the feminine suffix *-ayu*, Albrecht Goetze, "The Akkadian Masculine Plural in *-ānū/ī* and its Semitic Background," *Language* 22 (1946) 130 n. 44, appeals to Amorite names ending in *-y* in the execration texts. These names have been excluded from further consideration, because there is no evidence that this final *-y* is a feminine morpheme.

[4]On these hypocoristic suffixes, see the brief remarks by Hess, *AmPN*, p. 326; Sivan, *GAGNWS*, pp. 99-100. The hypocoristic suffix *-(a)ya* also occurs on Akkadian PNN (Stamm, *ANG*, pp. 113, 242-43).

Amor. PNN.[5] In principle, the vowel which precedes the *-y* may provide some help; hence the hypocoristic suffixes *-uya* and *-iya*, as well as the gentilic *-iy(y)u*, are distinguishable from the feminine ending *-ay*. But the hypocoristic suffix *-aya* is homographous with the feminine ending *-ay*. Moreover, in Ugaritic PNN written in consonantal script, the precise vocalization is often unknown, except in those cases in which the same PN occurs in Akkadian script. A partial solution to the problem of distinguishing hypocoristic *-aya* from feminine *-ay* will become evident in the treatment of Amor. PNN.

Gelb does not mention a feminine ending *-ay* in his brief treatment of Amorite grammar. In his chapter on hypocoristica, Huffmon notes a hypocoristic ending *-a(y)a*, "found mostly with feminine names."[6] He lists only three names, two of which are feminine. From such a short list, it seems unreasonable to conclude that this suffix is found mostly with feminine names. The publication of Gelb's comprehensive list affords the opportunity to study all Amor. PNN that end in a suffix *-aya*. According to Gelb's morphemic analysis, sixty-five names end in *-aya* (*CAAA*, pp. 436-37). Twenty-eight of these PNN are feminine names; furthermore, this number may be minimal, since Gelb ordinarily lists as feminine only those PNN that are preceded by the feminine determinative *SAL*, and this determinative is omitted before names occurring in witness lists. Considering that feminine PNN are not nearly so extensively attested as masculine PNN in any Semitic language, the proportion of feminine PNN (28 out of 65 = 43 percent) is high. This percentage can be contrasted with that of the feminine PNN ending in *-iya*: 17 feminine PNN out of 126 = 13 percent.[7] Not enough names end in *-uya* to draw any conclusions.[8] In a study of Akkadian PNN from Mari, Rasmussen lists seven PNN that end in *-aya*, of which at least five are feminine.[9]

The "high" percentage of feminine PNN ending in final *-aya* is unusual. For at least some of these PNN, I propose that the *-aya* ending is a feminine morpheme. When some of these PNN ending in *-aya* are compared with other PNN from the same root, it becomes probable that the *-aya* ending is an alternative feminine ending to the common *-at*.

---

[5]Gelb, *RANL* 13 (1958) §3.1.1.1.2-3.

[6]Huffmon, *APNMT*, p. 135.

[7]Gelb, *CAAA*, pp. 464-66, registered his uncertainty about three PNN in this list, one feminine and two masculine, by a question mark. I have included these in the above calculation. Huffmon's statement that at Mari the hypocoristic ending *-iya* is found only with masculine PNN stands in need of correction (*APNMT*, p. 135). Two of the seventeen feminine PNN are from Mari.

[8]Gelb, *CAAA*, p. 493, lists only two, *a-ḫa-tu-ia* and *bu-zu-a-ia*, and the second appears to terminate in *-aya*.

[9]Rasmussen, p. 191.

Both feminine endings are attested in the pair of feminine PNN *ḫu-ra-za-a-ia* and *ḫu-ra-za-tum* (*CAAA*, p. 588). These can be contrasted with the masculine PNN *ḫu-ru-zum*, *ḫu-ru-za-an*, and *ḫu-ru-za-nu-um* (*CAAA*, p. 588).[10] Note also the following pairs or sets of PNN:

Feminine PNN	Masculine PNN
ia-pu-ḫa-ia *ia-pu-ḫa-tum*	*ia-pu-ḫu* *ia-pu-ḫu-um* (*CAAA*, p. 604)
iz-za-a-ia	*iz-za-an* (*CAAA*, p. 611)
sa-bi-ra-a-ia *sa-bi-ra-tum*	*sa-bi-ru* *sa-bi-ru-um* (*CAAA*, p. 634)

For most of the twenty-eight feminine PNN ending in -*aya*, comparable masculine and feminine PNN from the same root are not attested. To complicate matters, neither the roots nor the meanings of many of the PNN are known with a reasonable degree of probability. To sum up, it seems likely that in at least four feminine PNN, the final ending -*aya* can be understood as a feminine morpheme. How high this number should be raised is impossible to determine in light of our deficient knowledge of the Amorite language.

In Ugaritic texts, the feminine morpheme *-*ay* has been identified on certain common nouns and adjectives, such as *ṣrry* (*KTU* 1.16.I.19)[11] and *brky* (*KTU* 1.5.I.16). The last instance is noteworthy, since in the parallel text RS 24.293, l. 6 (*Ug V*, p. 559), the ordinary feminine form *brkt* occurs. Another occurrence is the noun *nʿmy*, which occurs in two passages. In *KTU* 1.5.VI.5-7, the noun *nʿmy* stands in parallelism to the feminine form *ysmt*:

*m*ǵny l nʿmy . ʾarṣ . d*br* *l ysmt . šd . š*ḥl mmt*	We reached "Loveliness," the steppe-land, "Delightfulness," the coastal plain of the realm of the dead.

[10]The last two names end in the suffix *-*ān(um)*, which occurs almostly exclusively on masculine PNN (I. J. Gelb, "On the Morpheme *ān* in the Amorite Language," in *Languages and Areas: Studies Presented to George V. Bobrinskoy* [Chicago, 1967], p. 47). The -*ān* suffix is used in Arabic to form masculine adjectives. See Goetze, *Language* 22 (1946) 129-30.

[11]Johannes C. de Moor, "Studies in the New Alphabetic Texts from Ras Shamra I," *UF* 1 (1969) 172 n. 33.

The other passage, *KTU* 1.17.II.41-42 is difficult to interpret; nevertheless, it is clear that the noun *nʿmy* occurs in parallelism with *ysmsmt*, again a feminine form.[12]

The feminine ending *-ay* has also been seen on certain proper nouns. Richardson correlates Ug. GNN ending in *-y* with their counterparts in Akkadian script.[13] Since the Akkadian spellings [*Ca(-a)*] often do not reflect the consonant *y*, he proposed that the Ugaritic spellings with *-y*, interpreted as feminine endings, are historical spellings. Hence those Ugaritic spellings that omit the *-y* demonstrate that the original *-aya* has contracted and was no longer pronounced in current speech.[14] It is difficult to decide whether these GNN actually attest the feminine morpheme *-ay*. If Richardson's argument stands up under scrutiny, then GNN also attest this feminine ending.

Most of the evidence for the feminine ending **-ay* in Ugaritic comes from a series of feminine names.[15] Foremost among the feminine names cited are those of the three "daughters" of Baal, *pdry*, *ṭly*, and *ʾarṣy* (*KTU* 1.3.III.6-7). The DN *pdry* is vocalized in an Akkadian text as *dpi-id-ra-i* (17.116, l. 3 [*PRU* IV, p. 132]); in this instance, there is no *a* vowel following the feminine morpheme *-ay*. The DN *ṭly* may be compared to the feminine PN *fṭá-la-ia* (*PTU*, p. 202),[16] which, as in Amor. PNN, exhibits an *a* vowel after the ending *-ay*. Other feminine names often cited as apparently ending with the feminine suffix **-ay* are *ḥry* (Kirta's wife), *dnty* (Dnil's consort), *dmgy* (Athirat's handmaiden), and *rḥmy*, another name of Ashera.[17] Richardson expresses the view that all these names could be interpreted as hypocoristic forms, rather than instances of the feminine morpheme *-(a)y*.[18] Some of these names, however, are DNN, and hypocoristic suffixes are not generally suffixed to DNN.[19] Nonetheless, Richardson's suggestion

---

[12]The text is discussed by Baruch Margalit, "Restorations and Reconstructions in the Epic of Aqht," *JNSL* 9 (1981) 84-85; idem, "Lexicographical Notes on the *Aqht* Epic (Part 1: KTU 1.17-18)," *UF* 15 (1983) 75.

[13]M. E. J. Richardson, "Ugaritic Place Names with Final *-y*," *JSS* 23 (1978) 298-315.

[14]Ibid., pp. 314-15. See also Huehnergard, *Ugaritic Vocabulary*, p. 290 n. 109.

[15]*UT* §8.54; Joseph Aistleitner, *Untersuchungen zur Grammatik des Ugaritischen*, Berichte über die Verhandlungen der sächsischen Akademie der Wissenschaft zu Leipzig, Philologisch-historische Klasse, Band 100/6 (Berlin: Akademie, 1954), p. 22.

[16]According to J. T. Milik, "Giobbe 38,28 in siro-palestinese e la dea ugaritica *Pdry bt ar*," *RivB* 3 (1958) 253, the spelling Talaya reflects the oblique case.

[17]On female deities whose names end in *-y*, see de Moor, *UF* 2 (1970) 225-26; and especially S. Ribichini and P. Xella, "Il dio PDR," *UF* 16 (1984) 267-68.

[18]Richardson, *JSS* 23 (1978) 314 n. 4.

[19]Unless the DNN are functioning as (shortened) PNN!

that the *-(a)y* suffix on feminine PNN is not necessarily a feminine morpheme is well-taken. Gröndahl assembles other examples of feminine PNN that end in *-aya/-a-a*, and in some of these, the final ending must be hypocoristic.[20] She also cites four feminine PNN ending in the hypocoristic suffix *-iya*, and two ending in *-uya* (*PTU*, p. 56). To this total may be added masculine PNN that end in hypocoristic *-aya*; one of the clearest examples is the PN *nu-ú-ma-ia*, which is also attested with a compound hypocoristic suffix as *nu-ú-ma-ia-nu* (*PTU*, p. 163).

To summarize, in Ugaritic one may posit the existence of a feminine ending *-(a)y*.[21] A stronger case can be built from occurrences of this morpheme on common nouns, adjectives, and DNN than from the human onomasticon; in the latter case, it becomes difficult to distinguish the feminine ending from hypocoristic suffixes.[22] The feminine ending *-(a)y* may very well have been an archaism in Ugaritic. The common nouns and adjectives, and even the occurrences on proper nouns--mostly borne by deities or semi-divine individuals--all stem from poetic texts. As is well-known, poetry tends to retain the archaic features of a language. The combined evidence from Amorite and Ugaritic points to a feminine morpheme **-ay*. Even in these languages it appears to be an archaic morpheme, its use being restricted to feminine proper nouns in both languages, and a few anomalous nouns and adjectives in Ugaritic poetic texts.

---

[20]Gröndahl, *PTU*, p. 56. The *-(a)y(a)* ending on names such as ^{f}*a-ba-ia*, ^{f}*bi-tá-ia*, and *ʾaḫty* cannot be the feminine morpheme, for obvious reasons. Consult also her discussion of hypocoristic suffixes, pp. 50-51. Mario Liverani, Review of *Die Personennamen der Texte aus Ugarit*, by Frauke Gröndahl, *OrAnt* 7 (1968) 291, distinguishes between a feminine suffix *-Ca-a* and a masculine suffix *-Ca-ia*, which he tentatively suggests differed also in vocalization (**-ay* and **-āya* respectively). I find it unlikely that this difference in orthography is indicative of different suffixes.

[21]Aartun, *Partikeln*, 1:45 n. 6, also reached this conclusion. He describes the vocables ending in this morpheme as "reine Nominalbildungen." In Ugaritic, this suffix appears to function as a nominal and adjectival suffix.

[22]Cross, *Canaanite Myth and Hebrew Epic*, p. 56 n. 45, has posited the existence of two series of closely related adjectival suffixes (**-i/a/u-yya* and **-ī/ā/ū-ya*), from which are derived the feminine *-ay*, gentilic, hypocoristic, and other unnamed suffixes. The gentilic *-iy(y)* can be distinguished from the feminine *-ay*, because the former is a masculine suffix, subject to expansion with regard to gender and number.

II. Canaanite

Since the feminine ending *-ay* is rare and archaic in early West Semitic, its absence in the Canaanite languages is expected. Traces of this morpheme have been seen in such forms as BH *gōbay* "locusts."[23]

III. Canaanite PNN in the Hebrew Bible

A. *Probable Example*

1. *śāray.*

Variant spelling: *śārâ.*

Classification: Can.--first wife of Abr(ah)am (Gen 11:29).

Sex of name bearer: female.

Structure: one-word name, *śār-* (**qall* base, BL §61w) + *-ay* feminine suffix.

Meaning: "princess."

Parallels: Amor. *šar-ra-a-ia, šar-ra-ia, šar-ri-ia* (*CAAA*, p. 186);[24] Ug. *šry* (RS 24.323, l. 2);[25] BH CN **śarâ*; NA *ᶠsa-ra-a-a*, N/LB *ᶠšar-ra-a* (*WSB*, p. 171);[26] Palm. *sr*ʾ (*PNPI*, p. 102).

---

[23]See further Adrianus Van Selms, "Some Reflections on the Formation of the Feminine in Semitic Languages," in *Near Eastern Studies in Honor of William Foxwell Albright*, ed. Hans Goedicke (Baltimore: John Hopkins Press, 1971), p. 427, who cites several BH nouns ending in *-ê*.

[24]According to Gelb, *CAAA*, p. 186, these three Amor. names may be analyzed as **šarr* + **a/ija*. In his glossary (*CAAA*, p. 33), he lists **šarrum* "king"; **šarratum* and **šarra* "queen."

[25]M. Dietrich and O. Loretz, "Beschriftete Lungen- und Lebermodelle aus Ugarit," in *Ugaritica VI*, ed. Claude F. A. Schaeffer et al., Mission de Ras Shamra, vol. 17 (Paris: Missione archéologique de Ras Shamra and librairie orientaliste Paul Geuthner, 1969), pp. 172-73. Rainey, *IOS* 3 (1973) 50, was the first to compare this PN to biblical Saray. For Ug. PNN with the masculine form *šr*, see Gröndahl, *PTU*, p. 196, and for the Ug. CN *šr* "prince," see *UT* §19.2477.

[26]As acknowledged by Zadok, *WSB*, p. 310 (§11261) n. 6, the N/LB name may be Akkadian as well. The NA name is also uncertain, for in transliterations of WS PNN Assyrian *s* transliterates both WS *ś* and *š* (see Ran Zadok, in *EM*, s.v. "śārâ, śāray," 8:391).

Comments: The feminine PN Saray/Sarah occurs fifty-five times in the Hebrew Bible. In Genesis, the distribution of the two forms overlaps at Gen 17:15, a pivotal verse in which both forms of the name occur. From Gen 11:29 to 17:15, the name is uniformly spelled *śāray* (seventeen times); from Gen 17:15 and throughout the rest of the book, the name is spelled *śārâ* (thirty-seven times). The only other occurrence of the name is in Isa 51:2, where, as one might expect, the name is spelled *śārâ*. In postbiblical Aramaic texts, both forms recur, the archaizing *śāray* in columns 19-20 of the Genesis Apocryphon (which elaborates on events before Gen 17:15), and *śārâ* in the Testament of Levi and in an inscription on an amulette from Arbela.[27]

In the past there have been attempts to derive these two names from different roots. Although Geers recognized that Sarah is the feminine form of *śar* "prince," he derived Saray from a root **śrh*, "to contend, persevere."[28] While not defining the meaning of the *-y* form of the name, Richardson contends that the change of name is not merely a change in spelling, but reflects Sarah's ennobled position as the result of the birth of Isaac.[29] Könnecke even appealed to the distinction in the LXX transliterations--MT *śāray*/LXX *σαρα* and MT *śārâ*/LXX *σαρρα*--as evidence that the first name derives from the root **śrh*, the second from the root **śrr*.[30] Any distinction which is based on the LXX transliterations is ill-founded. Considering that the LXX is inconsistent in the doubling of consonants,[31] it appears reasonable to see in the LXX transliterations *σαρα* and *σαρρα* nothing other than an ad hoc orthography for distinguishing between two similar names. In fact there is little justification for deriving Saray and Sarah from two different roots, or for that matter, for seeing a change of meaning involved in the change of name.

Zadok presents two explanations to account for the suffixes *-ay* and *-â*: 1. morphological--the two forms of the name exhibit two different feminine suffixes, *-ay* and *-â* (< **-at*); and 2. phonological--the Sarah form arose from the contraction of the ending of the Saray form

---

[27]For references, see Beyer, *ATTM*, p. 740.

[28]Geers, *AJSL* 27 (1910-11) 303. In an article published earlier, Nestle, *AJSL* 13 (1896-97) 175, sought to relate both forms of the name to the root **śrh* "to contend." The root **śrh* has also been seen in the BH PN *śĕrāyāh(û)* and the EH PNN *śryhw* (VSE #334; Avigad, *Hebrew Bullae*, ##37, 167; idem, "The Seal of Seraiah (son of) Neriah," *EI* 14 [1978] 86-87) and *śrmlk* (VSE #333; P. Bordreuil and A. Lemaire, "Nouveaux sceaux hébreux et araméens," *Sem* 32 [1982] 30 #12).

[29]Richardson, *JSS* 23 (1978) 314.

[30]Könnecke, p. 18.

[31]Lisowsky, pp. 143-44.

(*-ay* > *-â* > *-ā*).[32] In other words, the *-â* on the form Sarah may be either the SBH feminine suffix or the contracted form of the archaic feminine suffix *-ay*. The simpler explanation of the two is the phonological one, because the Sarah form of the name can be directly related to the Saray form by contraction. On the other hand, the morphological one assumes there is no direct relation between the suffixes of the two forms of the name. Commentators have noted that the absence of an etiology to explain the change of name is remarkable. But an etiology would be out of place in this instance, since the change from Saray > Sarah entailed no change in meaning. In any event, the change of the name Saray to Sarah reflects a stage in which the suffix *-ay* was no longer understood as a feminine morpheme. Assuming that the Sarah form arose by contraction, the *-â* ending would have been reanalyzed as the SBH feminine suffix. The Sarah form, however it arose, is definitely a later form of the name.

IV. Late West Semitic PNN (extrabiblical)

The rarity of the feminine morpheme *-ay* in early West Semitic makes it unlikely that it will be found in extrabiblical late WS PNN. I cite the following PNN for the sake of thoroughness; I consider these names as uncertain examples.

1. *WS PNN in cuneiform writing*

Zadok lists three feminine names that terminate in *-ay(ya)*: NA *ᶠnin-qa-a-a*, *ᶠsa-ra-a-a*,[33] and *ᶠsa-ar-ḫa-a-a* (*WSB*, p. 171). These names may terminate in the hypocoristic suffix *-aya*.

2. *Ph-P. PNN*

With hesitation Benz (*PNPP*, pp. 241-42) has cited three feminine Ph-P. PNN that end in *-y*, though the names themselves are very obscure: excluding the final *-y*, *brqny* and *grgšy* are both quadra-consonantal, whereas *ʾšṣpty* is a (compound?) name composed of five consonants.

[32] Zadok, *EM* 8:391; as a parallel to the proposed contraction, compare the Ug. feminine PN *ᶠpí-id-da-ia* with the variant spelling *ᶠpí-id-da* (*PTU*, p. 170).

[33] On this name, see also p. 246 n. 26.

V. Summary

Evidence for the existence of a feminine morpheme -*(a)y* is to be found in Amorite and Ugaritic PNN, as well some common nouns and adjectives in Ugaritic. Some of the forms cited for the existence of this morpheme are ambiguous; this is especially true with regard to PNN, since the hypocoristic suffix is virtually indistinguishable from this feminine morpheme. The rarity of feminine -*(a)y* in early West Semitic implies that it may already have been archaic among those languages. The only Canaanite PNN in the Hebrew Bible retaining this suffix is the feminine name Saray. Lastly possible examples of this suffix have been suggested for Ph-P. PNN and WS PNN in cuneiform writing. None of these, however, are certain.

Bibliography

Aartun, Kjell. *Die Partikeln des Ugaritischen.* Alter Orient und Altes Testament, Band 21/1-2. Kevelaer: Butzon & Bercker; Neukirchen-Vluyn: Neukirchener, 1974-78.

_______. "Herkunft und Sinn des Namens *Aqht* im ugaritischen Material." In *Scripta Signa Vocis: Studies about Scripts, Scriptures, Scribes and Languages in the Near East, presented to J. H. Hospers,* pp. 9-14. Edited by H. L. J. Vanstiphout et al. Groningen: Egbert Forsten, 1986.

Ackroyd, Peter R. *The First Book of Samuel.* The Cambridge Bible Commentary on the New English Bible. Cambridge: University Press, 1971.

Abbadi, Sabri. *Die Personennamen der Inschriften aus Hatra.* Texte und Studien zur Orientalistik, Band 1. Hildesheim: Georg Olms, 1983.

______. *Arad Inscriptions.* Edited and revised by Anson F. Rainey. Jerusalem: Israel Exploration Society, 1981.

Aḥituv, Shmuel. *Canaanite Toponyms in Ancient Egyptian Documents.* Jerusalem: Magnes Press; Leiden: E. J. Brill, 1984.

______. S.v. "rĕʿûʾēl." In *Enṣîqlôpedyâ Miqrāʾît,* 7:387.

Aistleitner, Joseph. *Untersuchungen zur Grammatik des Ugaritischen.* Berichte über die Verhandlungen der sächsischen Akademie der Wissenschaft zu Leipzig: Philologisch-historische Klasse, Band 100, Heft 6. Berlin: Akademie, 1954.

_______. "Studien zur Frage der Sprachverwandtschaft des Ugaritischen I." *Acta Orientalia Academiae Scientiarum Hungaricae* 7 (1957)251-307.

_______. "Studien zur Frage der Sprachverwandtschaft des Ugaritischen II." *Acta Orientalia Academiae Scientiarum Hungaricae* 8 (1958) 51-98.

_______. *Wörterbuch der ugaritischen Sprache.* Edited by Otto Eissfeldt. Berichte über die Verhandlungen der sächsischen Akademie der Wissenschaften zu Leipzig: Philologisch-historische Klasse, Band 106, Heft 3. Berlin: Akademie, 1963.

al-Ansary, A. R. "Lihyanite Personal Names: A Comparative Study." *The Annual of Leeds University Oriental Society* 7 (1969-73) 5-16.

Albright, William F. "A Revision of Early Hebrew Chronology." *Journal of the Palestine Oriental Society* 1 (1920-21) 49-79.

______. "Contributions to the Historical Geography of Palestine." *The Annual of the American School of Oriental Research in Jerusalem* 2-3 (1921-22) 1-46.

______. "Contributions to Biblical Archaeology and Philology." *Journal of Biblical Literature* 43 (1924) 363-93.

______. "The Evolution of the West-Semitic Divinity ʿAn-ʿAnat-ʿAttâ." *American Journal of Semitic Languages and Literatures* 41 (1925) 73-101.

______. Review of *Die Ostkanaanäer*, by Theo Bauer. *Archiv für Orientforschung* 3 (1926) 124-26.

______. "The Names 'Israel' and 'Judah' with an Excursus on the Etymology of Tôdâh and Tôrâh." *Journal of Biblical Literature* 46 (1927) 151-85.

______. "The Name of Bildad the Shuhite." *American Journal of Semitic Languages and Literatures* 44 (1927-28) 31-36.

______. "The Egyptian Empire in Asia in the Twenty-First Century B.C." *Journal of the Palestine Oriental Society* 8 (1928) 223-56.

______. *The Vocalization of the Egyptian Syllabic Orthography.* American Oriental Series, vol. 5. New Haven: American Oriental Society, 1934.

______. "The Names *Shaddai* and *Abram.*" *Journal of Biblical Literature* 54 (1935) 172-204.

______. "The Land of Damascus between 1850 and 1750 B.C." *Bulletin of the American Schools of Oriental Research* 83 (1941) 30-36.

______. "A Case of Lèse-Majesté in Pre-Israelite Lachish, with Some Remarks on the Israelite Conquest." *Bulletin of the American Schools of Oriental Research* 87 (1942) 32-38.

______. "A Teacher to a Man of Shechem about 1400 B.C." *Bulletin of the American Schools of Oriental Research* 86 (1942) 28-31.

______. "Two Little Understood Amarna Letters from the Middle Jordan Valley." *Bulletin of the American Schools of Oriental Research* 89 (1943) 7-17.

______. "A Prince of Taanach in the Fifteenth Century B.C." *Bulletin of the American Schools of Oriental Research* 94 (1944) 12-27.

______. "The Oracles of Balaam." *Journal of Biblical Literature* 63 (1944) 207-33.

______. "The Old Testament and Canaanite Language and Literature." *Catholic Biblical Quarterly* 7 (1945) 1-31.

______. "Northwest-Semitic Names in a List of Egyptian Slaves from the Eighteenth Century B.C." *Journal of the American Oriental Society* 74 (1954) 222-33.

______. "The Son of Tabeel (Isaiah 7:6)." *Bulletin of the American Schools of Oriental Research* 140 (1955) 34-35.

______. "The Biblical Tribe of Massa' and Some Congeners." In *Studi orientalistici in onore di Giorgio Levi della Vida*, 1:1-14. 2 vols. Pubblicazioni dell'istituto per l'oriente, no. 52. Rome: Istituto per l'oriente, 1956.

______. "An Ostracon from Calah and the North-Israelite Diaspora." *Bulletin of the American Schools of Oriental Research* 149 (1958) 33-36.

Albright, William F., and Lambdin, Thomas O. "New Material for the Egyptian Syllabic Orthography." *Journal of Semitic Studies* 2 (1957) 113-27.

Algeo, John. *On Defining the Proper Name.* University of Florida Humanities Monograph, no. 41. Gainesville: University of Florida Press, 1973.

Aloni, Nehemyah. S.v. "ḥûrām." In *Enṣîqlôpedyâ Miqrā'ît*, 3:63.

Alt, Albrecht. "Megiddo im Übergang vom kanaanäischen zum israelitischen Zeitalter." *Zeitschrift für die alttestamentliche Wissenschaft* 60 (1944) 67-85.

Andersen, Francis I., and Freedman, David N. *Hosea: A New Translation with Introduction and Commentary.* Anchor Bible, vol. 24. Garden City: Doubleday & Co., 1980.

Arbeitman, Yoël L. "The Hittite is Thy Mother: An Anatolian Approach to Genesis 23 (ex Indo-Europea Lux)." In *Bono Homini Donum: Essays in Historical Linguistics in Memory of J. Alexander Kerns*, 1:889-1026. 2 vols. Edited by Yoël L. Arbeitman & Allan R. Bomhard. Amsterdam: John Benjamins, 1981.

______. "Luwio-Semitic and Hurro-Mitannio-Semitic Mischname-Theophores in the Bible, on Crete, and at Troy." *Scripta Mediterranea* 3 (1982) 5-53.

Archi, Alfonso. *Testi amministrativi: assegnazioni di tessuti.* Archivi reali di Ebla testi, vol. I. Rome: Missione archeologica italiana in Siria, 1985.

Archi, Alfonso, ed. *Eblaite Personal Names and Semitic Name-giving. Papers of a Symposium held in Rome, July 15-17, 1985.* Archivi reali di Ebla, Studi 1. Rome: Missione archeologica italiana in Siria, 1988.

Archi, Alfonso, and Biga, M. G. *Testi amministrativi di vario contenuto.* Archivi reali di Ebla testi, vol. III. Rome: Missione archeologica italiana in Siria, 1982.

Astour, Michael C. "Some New Divine Names from Ugarit." *Journal of the American Oriental Society* 86 (1966) 277-84.

Aufrecht, Walter E. "The Ammonite Language of the Iron Age." *Bulletin of the American Schools of Oriental Research* 266 (1987) 85-95.

Avigad, Nahman. "Two Phoenician Votive Seals." *Israel Exploration Journal* 16 (1966) 243-51.

_______. "Ammonite and Moabite Seals." In *Essays in Honor of Nelson Glueck: Near Eastern Archaeology in the Twentieth Century*, pp. 284-95. Edited by James A. Sanders. Garden City: Doubleday & Co., 1970.

_______. "A Bulla of Jonathan the High Priest." *Israel Exploration Journal* 25 (1975) 8-12.

_______. "The King's Daughter and the Lyre." *Israel Exploration Journal* 28 (1978) 146-51.

_______. "The Seal of Seraiah (son of) Neriah." *Eretz-Israel* 14 (1978) 86-87.

_______. "Titles and Symbols on Hebrew Seals." *Eretz-Israel* 15 (1981) 303-5.

_______. "A Hebrew Seal Depicting a Sailing Ship." *Bulletin of the American Schools of Oriental Research* 246 (1982) 59-62.

_______. *Hebrew Bullae from the Time of Jeremiah: Remnants of a Burnt Archive.* Jerusalem: Israel Exploration Society, 1986.

_______. "A Note on an Impression from a Woman's Seal." *Israel Exploration Journal* 37 (1987) 18-19.

_______. "Another Group of West-Semitic Seals from the Hecht Collection." *Michmanim* 4 (1989) 7-21.

Baldwin, Joyce G. *Daniel: An Introduction and Commentary.* Tyndale Old Testament Commentaries. N.p.: Inter-Varsity, 1978.

Bardenhewer, O. *Der Name Maria. Geschichte der Deutung Desselben.* Biblische Studien, erster Band, erstes Heft. Freiburg: Herder, 1895.

Barr, James. *Comparative Philology and the Text of the Old Testament.* Oxford: Clarendon Press, 1968.

_______. "The Symbolism of Names in the Old Testament." *Bulletin of the John Rylands University Library of Manchester* 52 (1969-70) 11-29.

_______. "The Nature of Linguistic Evidence in the Text of the Bible." In *Languages & Texts: The Nature of Linguistic Evidence*, pp. 35-57. Edited by Herbert H. Paper. Ann Arbor: University of Michigan, 1975.

Barth, Jakob. "Die Casusreste im Hebräischen." *Zeitschrift der deutschen morgenländischen Gesellschaft* 53 (1899) 593-99.

Barthélemy, Dominique. *Critique textuelle de l'Ancien Testament. 1. Josué, Juges, Ruth, Samuel, Rois, Chroniques, Esdras, Néhémie, Esther.* Orbis biblicus et orientalis, vol. 50/1. Fribourg: Éditions Universitaires; Göttingen: Vandenhoeck & Ruprecht, 1982.

Bartlett, J. R. "An Adversary against Solomon, Hadad the Edomite." *Zeitschrift für die alttestamentliche Wissenschaft* 88 (1976) 205-26.

Batten, Loring W. "The Septuagint Transliteration of Hebrew Proper Names." Ph.D. dissertation, University of Pennsylvania, 1893.

Baudissin, Wolf W. G. *Adonis und Esmun: Eine Untersuchung zur Geschichte des Glaubens an Auferstehungsgötter und an Heilgötter.* Leipzig: J. C. Hinrichs, 1911.

______. "Der gerechte Gott in altsemitischer Religion." In *Festgabe von Fachgenossen und Freunden: A. von Harnack zum siebzigsten Geburtstag dargebracht*, pp. 1-23. Tübingen: J. C. B. Mohr (Paul Siebeck), 1921.

______. *Kyrios als Gottesname im Judentum und seine Stelle in der Religionsgeschichte.* 4 parts. Edited by Otto Eissfeldt. Giessen: Alfred Töpelmann, 1929.

Bauer, Hans. "Die hebräischen Eigennamen als sprachliche Erkenntnisquelle." *Zeitschrift für die alttestamentliche Wissenschaft* 48 (1930) 73-80.

______. Review of *Die israelitischen Personennamen im Rahmen der gemeinsemitischen Namengebung*, by Martin Noth. *Orientalistische Literaturzeitung* 33 (1930) 588-96.

______. "Die Gottheiten von Ras Schamra." *Zeitschrift für die alttestamentliche Wissenschaft* 55 (1933) 81-101.

Bauer, Hans, and Leander, Pontus. *Historische Grammatik der hebräischen Sprache des Alten Testament.* Halle: Max Niemeyer, 1922.

Bauer, Theo. *Die Ostkanaanäer: Eine philologisch-historische Untersuchung über die Wanderschicht der sogenannten "Amoriter" in Babylonien.* Leipzig: Asia Major, 1926.

______. "Eine Überprüfung der 'Amoriter'-Frage." *Zeitschrift für Assyriologie* 38 (1929) 145-70.

Becking, Bob. "Kann das Ostrakon ND 6231 von *Nimrūd* für ammonitisch gehalten werden?" *Zeitschrift des deutschen Palästina-Vereins* 104 (1988) 59-67.

Beegle, Dewey M. "Proper Names in the Dead Sea Isaiah Scroll (DSIa), With a Detailed Examination of the Use of the Vowel Letters Waw and Yod." Ph.D. dissertation, The Johns Hopkins University, 1952.

______. "Proper Names in the New Isaiah Scroll." *Bulletin of the American Schools of Oriental Research* 123 (1951) 26-30.

Beeston, A. F. L. *A Descriptive Grammar of Epigraphic South Arabian*. London, 1962.

______. "A Sabaean Penal Law." *Le Muséon* 64 (1951) 305-15.

______. *Sabaic Grammar*. Journal of Semitic Studies, Monograph no. 6. Manchester: University of Manchester, 1984.

Beit-Arieh, Itzhaq. "Tel ʿIra--A Fortified City of the Kingdom of Judah." *Qadmoniot* 18/1-2 (1985) 17-25.

Beit-Arieh, Itzhaq, and Cresson, Bruce. "An Edomite Ostracon from Ḥorvat ʿUza." *Tel Aviv* 12 (1985) 96-101.

Ben-Ezra, Aqiva. "hsywmt û btn"k." *Beth Mikra* 18 (1972-73) 113-23.

Benz, Frank L. *Personal Names in the Phoenician and Punic Inscriptions*. Studia Pohl, no. 8. Rome: Biblical Institute Press, 1972.

Berger, P.-R. Review of *Die Personennamen der Texte aus Ugarit*, by Frauke Gröndahl. *Die Welt des Orients* 5 (1969-70) 271-82.

Bergman, A. "Two Hebrew Seals of the *ʿEbed* Class." *Journal of Biblical Literature* 35 (1936) 221-26.

Bergsträsser, Gotthelf. *Hebräische Grammatik*. 2 vols. Leipzig: F. C. W. Vogel, 1918-29.

Berry, George R. "Original Waw in *l"h* Verbs." *American Journal of Semitic Languages and Literatures* 20 (1903-4) 256-57.

Beyer, Klaus. *Die aramäischen Texte vom Toten Meer*. Göttingen: Vandenhoeck & Ruprecht, 1984.

Biga, M. G., and Milano, L. *Testi amministrativi: assegnazioni di tessuti*. Archivi reali di Ebla testi, vol. IV. Rome: Missione archeologica italiana in Siria, 1984.

Birot, Maurice. "Trois textes économiques de Mari (II)." *Revue d'assyriologie et d'archéologie orientale* 47 (1953) 161-74.

______. "Textes économiques de Mari (IV)." *Revue d'assyriologie et d'archéologie orientale* 50 (1956) 57-72.

Blass, F., and Debrunner, A. *A Greek Grammar of the New Testament and Other Early Christian Literature*. Translated by Robert W. Funk. Chicago: University of Chicago Press, 1961.

Blau, Joshua. "Some Difficulties in the Reconstruction of »Proto-Hebrew« and »Proto- Canaanite«." In *In Memoriam Paul Kahle*, pp. 29-43. Beiheft zur Zeitschrift für die alttestamentliche Wissenschaft, Band 103. Edited by Matthew Black and Georg Fohrer. Berlin: Alfred Töpelmann, 1968.

______. *On Pseudo-Corrections in Some Semitic Languages*. Jerusalem: Israel Academy of Sciences and Humanities, 1970.

______. "The Historical Periods of the Hebrew Language." In *Jewish Languages: Themes and Variations*, pp. 1-13. Edited by Herbert H. Paper. Cambridge, MA: Association for Jewish Studies, 1978.

_______. "The Parallel Development of the Feminine Ending *-at* in Semitic Languages." *Hebrew Union College Annual* 51 (1980) 17-28.

_______. "Short Philological Notes on the Inscription of Mešaʿ." *Maarav* 2 (1980) 143-57.

_______. *On Polyphony in Biblical Hebrew.* Proceedings of the Israel Academy of Sciences and Humanities, vol. 6, no. 2. Jerusalem: Israel Academy of Sciences and Humanities, 1982.

_______. S.v. "Hebrew Language. Biblical." In *Encyclopaedia Judaica,* 16:1568-83.

Blau, Joshua, and Greenfield, Jonas C. "Ugaritic Glosses." *Bulletin of the American Schools of Oriental Research* 200 (1970) 11-17.

Block, Daniel I. "'Israel'--'sons of Israel': A study in Hebrew eponymic usage." *Studies in Religion* 13 (1984) 301-26.

Böklen, Ernst. *Adam und Qain im Lichte der vergleichenden Mythenforschung.* Mythologische Bibliothek, Band 1, Heft 2/3. Leipzig: J. C. Hinrichs, 1907.

Boling, Robert G. *Judges: Introduction, Translation, and Commentary.* Anchor Bible, vol. 6A. Garden City: Doubleday & Co., 1975.

Bordreuil, Pierre. *Catalogue des sceaux ouest-sémitiques inscrits.* Paris: Bibliothèque Nationale, 1986.

_______. "Les sceaux des grandes personnages." *Le Monde de la Bible* 46/5 (1986) 45.

Bordreuil, Pierre, and Lemaire, André. "Nouveaux sceaux hébreux, araméens et ammonites." *Semitica* 26 (1976) 45-63.

_______. "Nouveau groupe de sceaux hébreux araméens et ammonites." *Semitica* 29 (1979) 71-84, Plates III-IV.

_______. "Nouveaux sceaux hébreux et araméens." *Semitica* 32 (1982) 21-34.

Borée, Wilhelm. *Die alten Ortsnamen Palästinas.* Leipzig: Eduard Pfeiffer, 1930.

Botterweck, G. Johannes, and Ringgren, Helmer, eds. *Theological Dictionary of the Old Testament.* Translated by John T. Willis. 6 vols. Grand Rapids: William B. Eerdmans, 1974-.

Boyd, Jesse L., III. "A Collection and Examination of the Ugaritic Vocabulary Contained in the Akkadian Texts from Ras Shamra." Ph.D. dissertation, University of Chicago, 1975.

Brockelmann, Carl. *Grundriss der vergleichenden Grammatik der semitischen Sprachen.* 2 vols. Berlin: Reuther & Reichard, 1908-13.

Brønno, Einar. "Some Nominal Types in the Septuagint. Contributions to Pre-Masoretic Hebrew Grammar." *Classica et Mediaevalia* 3 (1940) 180-213.

______. "Einige Namentypen der Septuaginta. Zur historischen Grammatik des Hebräischen." *Acta orientalia* (Copenhagen) 19 (1943) 33-64.

Brooke, Alan E.; McLean, Norman; and Thackeray, Henry St. J., eds. *The Old Testament in Greek According to the Text of Codex Vaticanus.* 3 vols. Cambridge: Cambridge University Press, 1906-.

Brovender, Chaim. S.v. "Hebrew Language. Pre-Biblical." In *Encyclopaedia Judaica*, 16:1560-68.

Brown, Francis; Driver, S. R.; and Briggs, Charles A. *A Hebrew and English Lexicon of the Old Testament.* Oxford: Clarendon Press, 1976.

Brunet, Adrien-M. "Le chroniste et ses sources (1)." *Revue biblique* 61 (1954)349-86.

Bryan, David T. "A Reevaluation of Gen 4 and 5 in Light of Recent Studies in Genealogical Fluidity." *Zeitschrift für die alttestamentliche Wissenschaft* 99 (1987) 180-88.

Buccellati, Giorgio. Review of *Amorite Personal Names in the Mari Texts: A Structural and Lexical Study*, by Herbert B. Huffmon. *Journal of the American Oriental Society* 86 (1966) 230-33.

______. *The Amorites of the Ur III Period.* Pubblicazioni del seminario di semitistica, Ricerche 1. Napoli: Istituto orientale di Napoli, 1966.

Buchanan, B., and Moorey, P. R. S. *Catalogue of Ancient Near Eastern Seals in the Ashmolean Museum, Volume III: The Iron Age Stamp Seals (c. 1200-350 BC).* Oxford: Clarendon Press, 1988.

Burchardt, M. *Die altkanaanäischen Fremdwörter und Eigennamen im Ägyptischen.* 2 vols. Leipzig: J. C. Hinrichs, 1909-10.

Burns, Rita J. *Has the Lord Indeed Spoken Only Through Moses? A Study of the Biblical Portrait of Miriam.* Society of Biblical Literature Dissertation Series, no. 84. Atlanta: Scholars Press, 1987.

Bynon, Theodora. *Historical Linguistics.* Cambridge: Cambridge University Press, 1977.

Campbell, Edward F., Jr. *Ruth: A New Translation with Introduction, Notes, and Commentary.* Anchor Bible, vol. 7. Garden City: Doubleday & Co., 1975.

Cantineau, Jean. *Le Nabatéen.* 2 vols. Paris: Librairie Ernest Leroux, 1930-32.

Caquot, André. "Sur l'onomastique religieuse de Palmyre." *Syria* 39 (1962) 231-56.

______. "Nouveaux documents ougaritiens." *Syria* 46 (1969) 241-65.

Cassuto, Umberto. *A Commentary on the Book of Genesis, Part II: From Noah to Abraham.* Translated by Israel Abrahams. Jerusalem: Magnes Press, 1964.

Cazelles, Henri. S.v. "Onomastique." In *Dictionnaire de la Bible, Supplément*, 6:732-44.

Clay, Albert T. *Personal Names from Cuneiform Inscriptions of the Cassite Period.* Yale Oriental Series, vol. 1. New Haven: Yale University Press, 1912.

Coogan, Michael D. "Patterns in Jewish Personal Names in the Babylonian Diaspora." *Journal for the Study of Judaism* 4 (1973) 183-91.

______. "The Use of Second Person Singular Verbal Forms in Northwest Semitic Personal Names." *Orientalia* 44 (1975) 194-97.

______. *West Semitic Personal Names in the Murašû Documents.* Harvard Semitic Monographs, no. 7. Missoula: Scholars Press, 1976.

Cook, Stanley A. "Notes on Semitic Inscriptions III." *Proceedings of the Society of Biblical Archaeology* 26 (1904) 164-67.

Cowley, A. "Another Aramaic Papyrus of the Ptolemaic Period." *Proceedings of the Society of Biblical Archaeology* 37 (1915) 217-21, Plate XXVI.

Cowley, A. *Aramaic Papyri of the Fifth Century B.C.* Oxford: Clarendon Press, 1923; reprint ed., Osnabrück: Otto Zeller, 1967.

Cross, Frank M., Jr. "The Canaanite Cuneiform Tablet from Taanach." *Bulletin of the American Schools of Oriental Research* 190 (1968) 41-46.

______. "An Interpretation of the Nora Stone." *Bulletin of the American Schools of Oriental Research* 208 (1972) 13-19.

______. *Canaanite Myth and Hebrew Epic: Essays in the History of the Religion of Israel.* Cambridge: Harvard University Press, 1973.

______. "Newly Found Inscriptions in Old Canaanite and Early Phoenician Scripts." *Bulletin of the American Schools of Oriental Research* 238 (1980) 1-20.

Cross, Frank M., Jr., and Freedman, David N. "The Blessing of Moses." *Journal of Biblical Literature* 67 (1948) 191-210.

______. "A Royal Song of Thanksgiving: II Samuel 22 = Psalm 18." *Journal of Biblical Literature* 72 (1953) 15-34.

Dahood, Mitchell. "G. R. Driver and the Enclitic *mem* in Phoenician." *Biblica* 49 (1968) 89-90.

______. "The Linguistic Classification of Eblaite." In *La lingua di Ebla: Atti del Convegno internazionale (Napoli, 22-23 aprile 1980)*, pp. 177-89. Istituto universitario orientale. Seminario di studi asiatici, Series Minor, vol. 14. Edited by Luigi Cagni. Napoli, 1981.

Deist, Ferdinand. "Prov. 31:1. A Case of Constant Mistranslation." *Journal of Northwest Semitic Languages* 6 (1978) 1-3.

De Langhe, Robert. "L'enclitique cananéenne *-m(a)*." *Le Muséon* 59 (1946)89-111.

Delcor, Matthias. "Melchizedek from Genesis to the Qumran Texts and the Epistle to the Hebrews." *Journal for the Study of Judaism* 2 (1971) 115-35.

______. "Le texte de Deir ʿAlla et les oracles bibliques de Balaʿam." Vetus Testamentum, Supplement 32 (1981) 52-73.

Delitzsch, Franz. *A New Commentary on Genesis.* 2 vols. Translated by Sophia Taylor. Edinburgh: T. & T. Clark, 1888-94.

Delitzsch, Friedrich. *Prolegomena eines neuen hebräisch-aramäischen Wörterbuchs zum Alten Testament.* Leipzig: J. C. Hinrichs, 1886.

______. *Die Lese- und Schreibfehler im Alten Testament.* Berlin: Walter de Gruyter, 1920.

Deller, K. "Zweisilbige Lautwerte des Typs KVKV im Neuassyrischen." *Orientalia* 31 (1962) 7-26.

de Moor, Johannes C. "Studies in the New Alphabetic Texts from Ras Shamra I." *Ugarit-Forschungen* 1 (1969) 167-88.

______. Review of *Die Personennamen der Texte aus Ugarit,* by Frauke Gröndahl. *Bibliotheca orientalis* 26 (1969) 105-8.

______. "The Semitic Pantheon of Ugarit." *Ugarit-Forschungen* 2 (1970) 187-228.

______. *The Seasonal Pattern in the Ugaritic Myth of Baʿlu, According to the Version of Ilimilku.* Alter Orient und Altes Testament, Band 16. Kevelaer: Butzon & Bercker; Neukirchener-Vluyn: Neukirchener, 1971.

______. S.v. "Baal." In *Theological Dictionary of the Old Testament,* 6 vols., 2:181-92. Edited by G. Johannes Botterweck and Helmer Ringgren. Grand Rapids: William B. Eerdmans, 1974-.

Devault, Joseph J. "A Study of Early Hebrew Personal Names." Ph.D. dissertation, The Johns Hopkins University, 1956.

Dever, William G. "Iron Age Epigraphic Materials from the Area of Khirbet El-Qôm." *Hebrew Union College Annual* 40-41 (1969-70) 139-204.

Dhorme, Édouard. "Les amorrhéens." *Revue biblique* 37 (1928) 63-79. Reprinted in *Recueil Édouard Dhorme: Études bibliques et orientales,* pp. 81-99. Paris: Imprimerie Nationale, 1951.

Diem, Werner. "Gedanken zur Frage der Mimation und Nunation in den semitischen Sprachen." *Zeitschrift der deutschen morgenländischen Gesellschaft* 125 (1975) 239-58.

Dietrich, M., and Loretz, O. "Beschriftete Lungen- und Lebermodelle aus Ugarit." In *Ugaritica VI,* pp. 165-79. Mission de Ras Shamra, vol. 17. Edited by Claude F. A. Schaeffer. Paris: Mission archéologique de Ras Shamra and librairie orientaliste Paul Geuthner, 1969.

______. "Der Amarna-Brief VAB* 2, 170." In *Beiträge zur Alten Geschichte und deren Nachleben. Festschrift für Franz Altheim zum 6. 10. 1968*, 1:14-23. 2 vols. Edited by Ruth Stiehl and Hans E. Stier. Berlin: Walter de Gruyter, 1969-70.

Dietrich, M.; Loretz, O.; and Sanmartín, J. "Zur Ugaritischen Lexikographie (XI)." *Ugarit-Forschungen* 6 (1974) 19-38.

______. *Die keilalphabetischen Texte aus Ugarit. Einschließlich der keilalphabetischen Texte außerhalb Ugarits. Teil 1: Transkription.* Alter Orient und Altes Testament, Band 24/1. Kevelaer: Butzon & Bercker; Neukirchen-Vluyn: Neukirchener, 1976.

Dion, P-E. "Deux notes épigraphiques sur Tobit." *Biblica* 56 (1975) 416-19.

Diringer, David. *Le iscrizioni antico-ebraiche palestinesi.* Florence: Felice Le Monnier, 1934.

______. "On Ancient Hebrew Inscriptions Discovered at Tell Ed-Duweir (Lachish)-I." *Palestine Exploration Quarterly* 74 (1941) 38-56.

Donner, H., and Röllig, W. *Kanaanäische und aramäische Inschriften.* 3 vols. Wiesbaden: Otto Harrassowitz, 1971-76.

Dossin. G. "La route de l'étain en Mésopotamie au temps de Zimri-Lim." *Revue d'assyriologie et d'archéologie* 64 (1970) 97-106.

Driver, G. R. "The origin of 'Ḥireq Compaginis' in Hebrew." *Journal of Theological Studies* 26 (1925) 76-77.

______. "The original form of the name 'Yahweh': evidence and conclusions." *Zeitschrift für die alttestamentliche Wissenschaft* 46 (1928)7-25.

______. "Seals from ʿAmman and Petra." *Quarterly of the Department for Antiquities in Palestine* 11 (1945) 81-82.

______. "Theological and Philological Problems in the Old Testament." *Journal of Theological Studies* 47 (1946) 156-66.

______. "Hebrew Poetic Diction." Vetus Testamentum, Supplement 1 (1953)26-39.

Driver, S. R. *A Treatise on the Use of the Tenses in Hebrew.* 2nd ed., rev. and enl. Oxford: Clarendon Press, 1881.

______. *Notes on the Hebrew Text and the Topography of the Books of Samuel.* 2d ed., rev. and enl. Oxford: Clarendon Press, 1913.

Dupont-Sommer, André. *Les Araméens.* Paris: A. Maisonneuve, 1949.

Dussaud, René. "Nouveaux renseignements sur la Palestine et la Syrie vers 2000 avant notre ère." *Syria* 8 (1927) 216-33.

______. "Nouveaux textes égyptiens d'exécration contre les peuples syriens." *Syria* 21 (1940) 170-82.

Eberharter, Andreas. "Zu den hebräischen Nomina auf *ût*." *Biblische Zeitschrift* 9 (1911) 113-19.

Edgerton, W. F. "Egyptian Phonetic Writing, from its Invention to the Close of the Nineteenth Dynasty." *Journal of the American Oriental Society* 60 (1940) 473-506.

Edzard, D. O. "*mNingal-gāmil, fIštar-damqat*. Die Genuskongruenz im akkadischen theophoren Personennamen." *Zeitschrift für Assyriologie* 55 (1962) 113-30.

_______. Review of *Die Personennamen der Texte aus Ugarit*, by Frauke Gröndahl. *Orientalistische Literaturzeitung* 67 (1971) 551-55.

_______. *Verwaltungstexte verschiedenen Inhalts*. Archivi reali di Ebla testi, vol. II. Rome: Missione archeologica italiana in Siria, 1981.

_______. *Hymnen, Beschwörungen und Verwandtes aus dem Archiv L. 2769*. Archivi reali di Ebla testi, vol. V. Rome: Missione archeologica italiana in Siria, 1984.

Elliger, Karl. "Die grossen Tempelsakristeien im Verfassungsentwurf des Ezechiel (42,1ff.)." In *Geschichte und Altes Testament*, pp. 97-103. Beiträge zur historischen Theologie, Band 16. Edited by Gerhard Ebeling. Tübingen: J. C. B. Mohr (Paul Siebeck), 1953.

Eph'al, Israel. "'Arabs' in Babylonia in the 8th Century B.C." *Journal of the American Oriental Society* 94 (1974) 108-15.

_______. *The Ancient Arabs: Nomads on the Borders of the Fertile Crescent 9th-5th Centuries B.C.* Jerusalem: Magnes Press; Leiden: E. J. Brill, 1982.

Eshel, Ben-Zion. "lhgym whgywt lpy šmwt šbmqrʾ." In *mwgš lkbwd hprwpʾ n. h. ṭwr-syny lmlʾt lw šbʿym šnh*, pp. 243-78. Publications of the Society for the Study of the Bible in Israel, vol. 8. Edited by Menahem Haran and B. Z. Luria. Jerusalem: Society for the Study of the Bible in Israel, 1960.

Fales, Frederick M. *Censimenti e catasti di epoca neo-assyria*. Centro per le antichità e la storia dell'arte del Vicino Oriente. Studi economici e tecnologici, no. 2. Rome: Istituto per l'oriente, 1973.

_______. "West Semitic Names from the Governor's Palace." *Annali della facoltà di lingue e letterature straniere di ca' foscari* 13 (1974) 179-88.

_______. "On Aramaic Onomastics in the Neo-Assyrian Period." *Oriens antiquus* 16 (1977) 41-68.

_______. "L'onomastica aramaica in età neo-assira: Raffronti tra il corpus alfabetico el il materiale cuneiforme." In *Atti del 1º Convegno Italiano sul vicino oriente antico (Roma, 22-24 Aprile 1975)*, pp. 199-229. Orientis antiqvi collectio, no. 13. Rome: Centro per le antichità e la storia dell'arte del vicino oriente, 1978.

______. "A List of Assyrian and West Semitic Women's Names." *Iraq* 41 (1979) 55-73.

______. "Note di semitico nordoccidentale." *Vicino Oriente* 5 (1982) 75-83.

______. "Assyro-Aramaica: Three Notes." *Orientalia* 53 (1984) 66-71.

Fichtner, Johannes. "Die etymologische Ätiologie in den Namengebungen der geschichtlichen Bücher des Alten Testaments." *Vetus Testamentum* 6 (1956) 372-96.

Fitzmyer, Joseph A. "'Now This Melchizedek . . .' (Heb. 7:1)." *Catholic Biblical Quarterly* 25 (1963) 305-21.

______. *The Genesis Apocryphon of Qumran Cave 1: A Commentary.* 2d, rev. ed. Biblica et orientalia, no. 18a. Rome: Biblical Institute Press, 1971.

Flashar, Martin. "Das Ghain in der Septuaginta." *Zeitschrift für die alttestamentliche Wissenschaft* 28 (1908) 194-220.

Fleischer, Wolfgang. "Zum Verhältnis von Name und Apellativum im Deutschen." *Wissenschaftliche Zeitschrift der Karl-Marx-Universitat Leipzig, Gesellschafts- und Sprachwissenschaftliche Reihe* 13 (1964) 369-78.

Fontinoy, Charles. "Les noms de lieux en *-ayim* dans la Bible." *Ugarit-Forschungen* 3 (1971) 33-40.

Foraboschi, D. *Onomasticon alterum papyrologicum. Supplemento al Namenbuch di F. Preisigke.* Testi e Documenti per lo studio dell' Antichità, 16. Serie papirologica, 2. Milano-Varese: Istituto Editoriale Cisalpino, 1971.

Fowler, Jeaneane D. *Theophoric Personal Names in Ancient Hebrew: A Comparative Study.* Journal for the Study of the Old Testament Supplement Series, no. 49. Sheffield: JSOT Press, 1988.

Frajzyngier, Zygmunt. "Notes on the $R_1R_2R_2$ Stems in Semitic." *Journal of Semitic Studies* 24 (1979) 1-12.

Freedman, David N. "Archaic Forms in Early Hebrew Poetry." *Zeitschrift für die alttestamentliche Wissenschaft* 72 (1960) 101-7.

______. *Pottery, Poetry, and Prophecy: Studies in Early Hebrew Poetry.* Winona Lake: Eisenbrauns, 1980.

Friedrich, Johannes. "Der Schwund kurzer Endvokale im Nordwestsemitischen." *Zeitschrift für Semitistik und verwandte Gebiete* 1 (1922) 3-14.

______. "Zum Phönizisch-Punischen." *Zeitschrift für Semitistik und verwandte Gebiete* 2 (1924) 1-10.

Friedrich, Johannes, and Röllig, Wolfgang. *Phönizisch-Punische Grammatik.* 2d rev. ed. Analecta Orientalia, vol. 46. Rome: Pontificium Institutum Biblicum, 1970.

Fronzaroli, Pelio. "West Semitic Toponymy in Northern Syria in the Third Millennium B.C." *Journal of Semitic Studies* 22 (1977) 145-66.

———. "The Concord of Gender in Eblaite Theophoric Personal Names." *Ugarit-Forschungen* 11 (1979) 275-81.

Fucilla, Joseph G. Review of *Onomastica Medio-Assira*, by Claudio Saporetti. *Names* 20 (1972) 138-39.

Fuentes Estañol, Marie-José. *Vocabulario Fenicio.* Biblioteca Fenicio, vol. 1. Barcelona, 1980.

Garbini, Giovanni. *Il semitico de nord-ovest.* Quaderni della sezione linguistica degli annali, no. 1. Napoli, 1960.

———. "La parole *zu-ú* nell'onomastica «amorrea»." *Annali dell'istituto orientali di Napoli* 35 (1975) 414-16

Gardiner, A. H. "The Egyptian Origin of Some English Personal Names." *Journal of the American Oriental Society* 56 (1936) 189-97.

Garr, W. Randall. *Dialect Geography of Syria-Palestine, 1000-586 B.C.E.* Philadelphia: University of Pennsylvania Press, 1985.

———. "On Voicing and Devoicing in Ugaritic." *Journal of Near Eastern Studies* 45 (1986) 45-52.

Geers, F. W. "Das endschwache Zeitwort in hebräischen Eigennamen." *American Journal of Semitic Languages and Literatures* 27 (1910-11)301-11.

Gelb, I. J. "La mimazione e la nunazione nelle lingue semitiche." *Rivista degli studi orientali* 12 (1930) 217-65.

———. *Inscriptions from Alishar and Vicinity.* Oriental Institute Publications, vol. 27. Researches in Anatolia, vol. 6. Chicago: University of Chicago Press, 1935.

———. "Notes on von Soden's Grammar of Akkadian." *Bibliotheca orientalis* 12 (1955) 93-111.

———. "La lingua degli Amoriti." *Rendiconti della classe di scienze morali, storiche e filologiche della Accademia Nazionale dei Lincei* 13 (1958) 143-64.

———. "Sumerians and Akkadians in Their Ethno-Linguistic Relationship." *Genava* n.s., 8 (1960) 258-71.

———. "The Early History of the West Semitic Peoples." *Journal of Cuneiform Studies* 15 (1961) 27-47.

———. *Old Akkadian Writing and Grammar.* 2d rev. ed. Materials for the Assyrian Dictionary, no. 2. Chicago: University of Chicago Press, 1961.

———. "Ethnic Reconstruction and Onomastic Evidence." *Names* 10 (1962)45-52.

———. *A Study of Writing.* rev. ed. Chicago: University of Chicago Press, 1963.

______. "The Origin of the West Semitic *Qatala* Morpheme." In *Symbolae linguisticae in honorem Georgii Kurylowicz*, pp. 72-80. Polska Akademia Nauk. Prace Komisji Jezykoznawstwa, no. 5. Wroclaw, 1965.

______. "On the Morpheme *ān* in the Amorite Language." In *Languages and Areas: Studies Presented to George V. Bobrinskoy*, pp. 45-48. Chicago, 1967.

______. "An Old Babylonian List of Amorites." *Journal of the American Oriental Society* 88 (1968) 39-46.

______. *Sequential Reconstruction of Proto-Akkadian.* Assyriological Studies, no. 18. Chicago: University of Chicago Press, 1969.

______. *Computer-Aided Analysis of Amorite.* Assyriological Studies, no. 21. Chicago: Oriental Institute of the University of Chicago, 1980.

______. *Thoughts About Ibla: A Preliminary Evaluation, March 1977.* Syro-Mesopotamian Studies, vol. 1/1. Malibu: Undena Publications, 1980.

______. "Ebla and the Kish Civilization." In *La lingua di Ebla: Atti del Convegno internationale (Napoli, 22-23 aprile 1980)*, pp. 9-73. Istituto universitario orientale. Seminario di studi asiatici, Series Minor, vol. 14. Edited by Luigi Cagni. Napoli, 1981.

Gelb, I. J., Purves, P. M., and MacRae, A. A. *Nuzi Personal Names.* The University of Chicago Oriental Publications, Vol. 57. Chicago: University of Chicago Press, 1943.

Gelb, I. J. et al., eds. *The Assyrian Dictionary of the Oriental Institute of the University of Chicago.* Chicago: Oriental Institute; Glückstadt: J. J. Augustin, 1956-.

Gemser, Berend. *De beteekenis der persoonsnamen voor onze kennis van het leven en denken der oude Bayloniërs en Äsyriërs.* Wageningen: H. Veenman & Zonen, 1924.

Gesenius, Wilhelm. *Thesaurus philologicus criticus linguae Hebraeae et Chaldaeae Veteris Testamenti.* 2 vols. Leipzig, 1835-40.

______. *Gesenius' Hebrew Grammar.* Edited by E. Kautzsch and A. E. Cowley. 28th ed. Oxford: Oxford University Press, 1910.

Gevirtz, Stanley. "Jericho and Shechem: A Religio-Literary Aspect of City Destruction." *Vetus Testamentum* 13 (1963) 52-62.

Giacumakis, George. *The Akkadian of Alalaḫ.* Janua Linguarum. Series Practica, no. 59. The Hague: Mouton, 1970.

Gibson, John C. L. "Observations on Some Important Ethnic Terms in the Pentateuch." *Journal of Near Eastern Studies* 20 (1961) 217-38.

Giesebrecht, F. *Die alttestamentliche Schätzung des Gottesnamens und ihre religionsgeschichtliche Grundlage.* Königsberg: Thomas & Oppermann, 1901.

Ginsberg, H. L. "The Northwest Semitic Languages." In *The World History of Jewish People, Vol II: Patriarchs*, pp. 102-24. Edited by Benjamin Mazar. Tel Aviv: Jewish History Publications, 1967; Rutgers University, 1970.

Ginsburger, M. "Les explications des noms de personnes dans l'Ancien Testament." *Revue de l'histoire des religions* 92 (1925) 1-7.

Giveon, R., and Lemaire, A. "Sceau phénicien inscrit d'Akko avec scène religieuse." *Semitica* 35 (1985) 27-32, Plate V, b.

Glock, Albert E. "A New Taʿannek Tablet." *Bulletin of the American Schools of Oriental Research* 204 (1971) 17-31.

______. "Texts and Archaeology at Tell Taʿannek." *Berytus* 31 (1983) 57-66.

Goetze, Albrecht. "The Akkadian Masculine Plural in *-ānū/ī* and Its Semitic Background." *Language* 22 (1946) 121-30.

______. "Amurrite Names in Ur III and Early Isin Texts." *Journal of Semitic Studies* 4 (1959) 193-203.

Gogel, Sandra L. "A Grammar of Old Hebrew." 2 vols. Ph.D. dissertation, University of Chicago, 1985.

Goldberg, Ariella D. "Northern-Type-Names in the Post-Exilic Jewish Onomasticon." Ph.D. dissertation, Brandeis University, 1972.

Good, Robert M. "Hebrew and Ugaritic *NḤT*." *Ugarit-Forschungen* 17 (1985) 153-56.

Gordis, Robert. *The Biblical Text in the Making: A Study of the Kethib-Qere*. aug. ed. N.p.: KTAV, 1971.

______. "ʾmy wʾḥwty' wʿʾḥʾb'." In *The Word and the Book: Studies in Biblical Language and Literature*, pp. 45-46 (Hebrew section). New York: KTAV Publishing House, 1976.

Gordon, Cyrus H. *Ugaritic Textbook*. Analecta Orientalia, no. 38. Rome: Biblical Pontifical Institute, 1965.

______. "Notes on Proper Names in the Ebla Tablets." In *Eblaite Personal Names and Semitic Name-Giving*, pp. 153-58. Archivi reali di Ebla, Studi 1. Edited by Alfonso Archi. Rome: Missione archeologica italiana in Siria, 1988.

Görg, Manfred. "Mirjam -- ein weiterer Versuch." *Biblische Zeitschrift*, n.f. 23 (1979) 285-89.

______. "Ein Keilschriftfragment des Berichtes vom dritten Feldzug des Sanherib mit dem Namen des Hiskija." *Biblische Notizen* 24 (1984) 247-48, Plate 1.

______. "Marginalien zur Basis *NḤT*." *Biblische Notizen* 32 (1986) 20-21.

______. "Goliat aus Gat." *Biblische Notizen* 34 (1986) 17-21.

______. "Die Begleitung des Abimelech von Gerar (Gen 26,26)." *Biblische Notizen* 35 (1986) 21-25.

______. "Zum jüdischen Personennamen *MY'MN*." *Biblische Notizen* 38/39 (1987) 33-35.

Graham, M. Patrick. "A Connection Proposed Between II Chr 24,26 and Ezra 9-10." *Zeitschrift für die alttestamentliche Wissenschaft* 97 (1985) 256-58.

Gray, G. Buchanan. *Studies in Hebrew Proper Names.* London: Adam & Charles Black, 1896.

Greenfield, Jonas C. "Amurrite, Ugaritic and Canaanite." In *Proceedings of the International Conference on Semitic Studies, held in Jerusalem, 19-23 July 1965.* pp. 92-101. Jerusalem: Israel Academy of Sciences and Humanities, 1969.

Greßmann, Hugo. Review of *Die Ostkanaanäer*, by Theo Bauer. *Zeitschrift für die alttestamentliche Wissenschaft* 44 (1926) 301-2.

Grimme, Hubert. "Der Name Mirjam." *Biblische Zeitschrift* 7 (1909) 245-51.

Gröndahl, Frauke. Review of *Amorite Personal Names in the Mari Texts: A Structural and Lexical Study*, by Herbert B. Huffmon. *Orientalia* 35 (1966) 449-56.

______. *Die Personennamen der Texte aus Ugarit.* Studia Pohl, no. 1. Rome: Pontificium Institutum Biblicum, 1967.

Gustavs, A. "Die Personennamen in den Tontafeln von Tell Taʿannek." *Zeitschrift des deutschen Palästinas-Vereins* 50 (1927) 1-18.

______. "Die Personennamen in den Tontafeln von Tell Taʿannek." *Zeitschrift des deutschen Palästinas-Vereins* 51 (1928) 169-218.

Hallo, William W. "A Letter Fragment from Tel Aphek." *Tel Aviv* 8 (1981) 18-24.

Hallo, William W., and Tadmor, Hayim. "A Lawsuit from Hazor." *Israel Exploration Journal* 27 (1977) 1-11.

Halpern, Baruch. "Yaua, Son of Omri, Yet Again." *Bulletin of the American Schools of Oriental Research* 265 (1987) 81-85.

Hammond, Philip C. "An Ammonite Stamp Seal from ʿAmman." *Bulletin of the American Schools of Oriental Research* 160 (1960) 38-41.

Harding, G. Lankester. *An Index and Concordance of Pre-Islamic Arabian Names and Inscriptions.* Near and Middle East Studies, no. 8. Toronto: University of Toronto Press, 1971.

Harris, Zellig S. *A Grammar of the Phoenician Language.* American Oriental Series, vol. 8. New Haven: American Oriental Society, 1936.

______. *Development of the Canaanite Dialects: An Investigation in Linguistic History.* American Oriental Series, vol. 16. New Haven: American Oriental Society, 1939.

Hayes, William C. *A Papyrus of the Late Middle Kingdom in the Brooklyn Museum (Papyrus Brooklyn 35.1446).* N.p.: The Brooklyn Museum, 1955.

Hecker, Karl. *Grammatik der Kültepe Texts.* Analecta Orientalia, no. 44. Rome: Pontificium Institutum Biblicum, 1968.

Hehn, Johannes. "Zur Bedeutung der Siebenzahl." In *Vom Alten Testament: Karl Marti zum siebzigsten Geburtstage,* pp. 128-36. Beiheft zur die Zeitschrift für die alttestamentliche Wissenschaft, Band 41. Edited by Karl Budde. Giessen: Alfred Töpelmann, 1925.

Heider, George C. *The Cult of Molek: A Reassessment.* Journal for the Study of the Old Testament Supplement Series, no. 43. Sheffield: JSOT Press, 1985.

Helck, Wolfgang. *Die Beziehungen Ägyptens zu Vorderasien im 3. und 2. Jahrtausend v. Chr.* 2d rev. ed. Wiesbaden: Otto Harrassowitz, 1971.

Heller, J. "Noch zu Ophra, Ephron und Ephraim." *Vetus Testamentum* 12 (1962) 339-41.

Heltzer, M. "Eighth Century B.C. Inscriptions From Kalakh (Nimrud)." *Palestine Exploration Quarterly* 110 (1978) 3-9.

Herdner, A. "Nouveaux textes alphabetiques de Ras Shamra--XXIVe campagne, 1961." In *Ugaritica VII,* pp. 1-74. Mission de Ras Shamra, vol. 18. Paris: Geuthner; Leiden: E. J. Brill, 1978.

Herr, Larry G. *The Scripts of Ancient Northwest Semitic Seals.* Harvard Semitic Monographs, no. 18. Missoula: Scholars Press, 1978.

Hess, Richard S. "Amarna Proper Names." Ph.D. dissertation, Hebrew Union College-Jewish Institute of Religion (Cincinnati),

Hestrin, Ruth, and Dayagi-Mendels, Michal. *Inscribed Seals: First Temple Period.* Jerusalem: Israel Museum, 1979.

Hillers, D. R. "An Alphabetic Cuneiform Tablet from Taanach (TT 433)." *Bulletin of the American Schools of Oriental Research* 173 (1964) 45-50.

Hofner, Maria. "Südarabien." In *Wörterbuch der Mythologie. Vol. 1: Götter und Mythen im vorderen Orient,* pp. 483-552. Edited by Hans W. Haussig. Stuttgart: Ernst Klett, 1965.

Hommel, Fritz. "*ʾăšer,* ursprüngliche Substantiv zu trennen von *še-* (*ša*), ursprünglichem Pronominalstamm." *Zeitschrift der deutschen morgenländischen Gesellschaft* 32 (1878) 708-15.

______. *Zwei Jagdinschriften Asurbanibal's.* Leipzig: J. C. Hinrichs, 1879.

______. *Aufsätze und Abhandlungen arabistisch-semitologischen Inhalts.* Munich: G. Franz, 1892.

______. *Die altisraelitische Überlieferung in inschriftlicher Beleuchtung.* Munich: G. Franz, 1897.

Huehnergard, John. "Akkadian Evidence for Case-Vowels on Ugaritic Bound Forms." *Journal of Cuneiform Studies* 33 (1981) 199-205.

_______. "Five Tablets from the Vicinity of Emar." *Revue d'assyriologie et d'archéologie orientale* 77 (1983) 11-43.

_______. "Asseverative **la* and Hypothetical **lu/law* in Semitic." *Journal of the American Oriental Society* 103 (1983) 569-93.

_______. "Notes on Akkadian Morphology." In *"Working With No Data": Semitic and Egyptian Studies Presented to Thomas O. Lambdin*, pp. 181-93. Edited by David M. Golomb. Winona Lake: Eisenbrauns, 1987.

_______. *Ugaritic Vocabulary in Syllabic Transcription.* Harvard Semitic Studies, no. 32. Atlanta: Scholars Press, 1987.

_______. "Northwest Semitic Vocabulary in Akkadian Texts." *Journal of the American Oriental Society* 107 (1987) 713-25.

_______. *The Akkadian of Ugarit.* Harvard Semitic Studies, no. 34. Atlanta: Scholars Press, 1989.

Huffmon, Herbert B. *Amorite Personal Names in the Mari Texts: A Structural and Lexical Study.* Baltimore: Johns Hopkins Press, 1965.

Humbert, Paul. Review of *Lexicon in Veteris Testamenti libros*, by Ludwig Koehler and Walter Baumgartner. *Theologische Zeitschrift* 6 (1950) 58-63.

Hummel, Horace D. "Enclitic *mem* in Early Northwest Semitic, especially Hebrew." *Journal of Biblical Literature* 76 (1957) 85-107.

Hunsberger, David R. "Theophoric Names in the Old Testament and Their Theological Significance." Ph.D. dissertation, Temple University, 1969.

Hurwitz, Avi. "Originals and Imitations in Biblical Poetry: A Comparative Examination of 1 Sam 2:1-10 and Ps 113:5-9." In *Biblical and Related Studies Presented to Samuel Iwry*, pp. 115-21. Edited by Ann Kort and Scott Morschauser. Winona Lake: Eisenbrauns, 1985.

Ikeda, Y. S.v. "tōʿû, tōʿî." In *Enṣîqlôpedyâ Miqrāʾît*, 8:871-72.

Ingholt, Harald; Seyrig, Henri; Starcky, Jean; and Caquot, André. *Recueil des tesséres de Palmyre.* Paris: Imprimerie nationale and Librairie orientaliste Paul Geuthner, 1955.

Iordan, Iorgu. "Les rapports entre la toponymie et l'anthroponymie." *Onoma* 14 (1969) 14-22.

Ishida, Tomoo. "The Structure and Historical Implications of the Lists of Pre-Israelite Nations." *Biblica* 60 (1979) 461-90.

Israel, Felice. "The Language of the Ammonites." *Orientalia lovaniensia periodica* 10 (1979) 143-59.

_______. "Miscellanea Idumea." *Rivista biblica* 27 (1979) 171-203.

______. "Geographic Linguistics and Canaanite Dialects." In *Current Progress in Afro-Asiatic Linguistics: Papers of the Third International Hamito-Semitic Congress*, pp. 363-87. Amsterdam Studies in the Theory and History of Linguistic Science. Series IV, Current Issues in Linguistic Theory, vol. 28. Edited by James Bynon. Amsterdam: John Benjamins, 1984.

______. "Supplementum idumeum I." *Rivista biblica* 35 (1987) 337-56.

______. "Studi Moabiti I: Rassegna di epigrafia moabiti e i sigilli moabiti." In *Atti della 4ª Giornata di Studi Camito-Semitici e Indoeuropei (Bergamo, Istituto Universitario, 29 novembre 1985)*, pp. 101-38. Edited by G. Bernini and V. Brugnatelli. Milano, 1987.

______. "Les sceaux ammonites." *Syria* 64 (1987) 141-46.

Jackson, Kent P. *The Ammonite Language of the Iron Age*. Harvard Semitic Monographs, no. 27. Chico: Scholars Press, 1983.

______. "Ammonite Personal Names in the Context of the West Semitic Onomasticon." In *The Word of the Lord Shall Go Forth: Essays in Honor of David Noel Freedman in Celebration of His Sixtieth Birthday*, pp. 507-21. Edited by Carol L. Meyers and M. O'Connor. Winona Lake: Eisenbrauns, 1983.

Jastrow, Marcus. A *Dictionary of the Targumim, the Talmud Babli and Yerushalmi, and the Midrashic Literature*. Brooklyn: P. Shalom, 1967.

Jastrow, Morris, Jr. "The Element *bšt* in Hebrew Proper Names." *Journal of Biblical Literature* 13 (1894) 19-30.

______. "The Name of Samuel and the Stem *šʾl*." *Journal of Biblical Literature* 19 (1900) 82-105.

Jean, Charles-F. "Les noms propres de personnes dans les lettres de Mari." In *Studia Mariana*, pp. 63-97. Edited by André Parrot. Leiden: E. J. Brill, 1950.

Jirku, Anton. "Zur Götterwelt Palästinas und Syriens." In *Sellin Festschrift: Beiträge zur Religionsgeschichte und Archäologie Palästinas, Ernst Sellin zum 60. Geburtstage dargebracht*, pp. 83-86. Leipzig: D. Werner Scholl, 1927.

______. "Die Keilschrifttexte von Ras Šamra und das Alte Testament." *Zeitschrift der deutschen morgenländischen Gesellschaft* 89 (1935) 372-86.

______. "Die Mimation in den nordsemitischen Sprachen und einige Bezeichnungen der altisraelitischen Mantik." *Biblica* 34 (1953) 78-80. Reprinted in *Von Jerusalem nach Ugarit: Gesammelte Schriften*, pp. 371-73. Graz: Akademische Druck- u. Verlagsanstalt, 1966.

______. "Das n. pr. Lemuʾel (Prov. 31:1) und der Gott Lim." *Zeitschrift für die alttestamentliche Wissenschaft* 66 (1954) 151.

_______. "Zu einigen Orts- und Eigennamen Palästinas-Syriens." *Zeitschrift für die alttestamentliche Wissenschaft* 75 (1963) 86-88.

_______. "Ugaritische Eigennamen als Quelle des ugaritischen Lexikons." *Archiv orientální* 37 (1969) 8-11.

Jongeling, Karel. *Names in Neo-Punic Inscriptions.* Groningen, 1984.

Joüon, P. Paul. *Grammaire de l'hébreu biblique.* Rome: Institut Biblique Pontifical, 1923.

Kahle, Paul. *Der masoretische Text des Alten Testaments nach der Überlieferung der babylonischen Juden.* Leipzig: J. C. Hinrichs, 1902.

Kaila, Lauri G. G. *Zur Syntax des in verbaler Abhängigkeit stehenden Nomens im alttestamentlichen Hebräisch.* Helsinki, 1906.

Kampffmeyer, Georg. "Südarabisches: Beiträge zur Dialektologie des Arabischen, III." *Zeitschrift des deutschen morgenländischen Gesellschaft* 54 (1900) 621-60.

Kaufman, I. Tracy. "The Samaria Ostraca, A Study in Ancient Hebrew Palaeography." Ph.D. dissertation, Harvard University, 1966.

Kaufman, Stephen A. "The Enigmatic Adad-Milki." *Journal of Near Eastern Studies* 37 (1978) 101-9.

_______. "Reflections on the Assyrian-Aramaic Bilingual from Tell Fakhariyeh." *Maarav* 3 (1982) 137-75.

Kedar-Kopfstein, Benjamin. "The Interpretative Element in Transliteration." *Textus* 8 (1973) 55-77.

Kitchen, Kenneth A. Review of *Die Ortsnamenlisten aus dem Totentempel Amenophis III,* by Elmar Edel. *Bibliotheca orientalis* 26 (1969) 198-202.

Klein, Ralph W. *1 Samuel.* Word Biblical Commentary, vol. 10. Waco: Word Books, 1983.

Knauf, Ernst A. "Alter und Herkunft der edomitischen Königsliste Gen 36,31-39." *Zeitschrift für die alttestamentliche Wissenschaft* 97 (1985) 245-53.

Knudsen, Ebbe E. "An Analysis of Amorite." *Journal of Cuneiform Studies* 34 (1982) 1-18.

_______. "The Mari Akkadian Shift *ia* > *ê* and the Treatment of *I"h* Formations in Biblical Hebrew." *Journal of Near Eastern Studies* 41 (1982) 35-43.

Knudtzon, J. A. *Die El-Amarna-Tafeln.* 2 vols. Leipzig, 1915; reprint ed., Aalen, 1964.

Köhler, Ludwig. "Septuaginta-Eigennamen und ihre Entartung." In *Festgabe Adolf Kaegi von Schülern und Freunden, dargebracht zum 30. September 1919,* pp. 182-88. Frauenfeld, 1919.

_______. "Hebräische Vokakeln II." *Zeitschrift für die alttestamentliche Wissenschaft* 55 (1937) 161-74.

______. *Hebrew Man.* Translated by Peter R. Ackroyd. London: SCM Press, 1956.

Koehler, Ludwig, and Baumgartner, Walter. *Lexicon in Veteris Testamenti Libros.* With supplement. Leiden: E. J. Brill, 1958.

Koehler, Ludwig, and Baumgartner, Walter. *Hebräisches und aramäisches Lexikon zum Alten Testament.* 3 vols. 3d ed. Edited by Walter Baumgartner et al. Leiden: E. J. Brill, 1967-.

König, Eduard. *Historische-kritisches Lehrgebäude der hebräischen Sprache.* 2 vols. Leipzig: J. C. Hinrichs, 1881-97.

______. "Elisabeth." *Expository Times* 20 (1908-9) 185-86.

______. "Woher stammt der Name 'Maria'?" *Zeitschrift für die neutestamentliche Wissenschaft* 17 (1916) 257-63.

Könnecke, Clemens. *Die Behandlung der hebräischen Namen in der Septuaginta.* Programm des koeniglichen und groening'schen Gymnasiums zu Stargard in Pommern, no. 124. Stargard, 1885.

Kopf, L. "Arabische Etymologien und Parallelen zum Bibelwörterbuch." *Vetus Testamentum* 8 (1958) 161-215.

Kornfeld, Walter. "Onomastica aramaica und das Alte Testament." *Zeitschrift für die alttestamentliche Wissenschaft* 88 (1976) 105-12.

______. *Onomastica Aramaica aus Ägypten.* Österreichische Akademie der Wissenschaften, Philosophisch-historische Klasse Sitzungsberichte, Band 333. Vienna: Österreichische Akademie der Wissenschaften, 1978.

______. "Zur althebräischen Anthroponomastik ausserhalb der Bible." *Wiener Zeitschrift für die Kunde des Morgenlandes* 71 (1979) 39-48.

Kornfeld, Walter. "Beiträge zur alttestamentlichen Namensforschung." In *Mélanges bibliques et orientaux en l'honneur de M. Henri Cazelles,* pp. 213-18. Alter Orient und Altes Testament, Band 212. Edited by A. Caquot and M. Delcor. Kevelaer: Butzon & Bercker; Neukirchen-Vluyn: Neukirchener, 1981.

______. "Die Edomiterlisten (Gn 36; 1 C 1) im Lichte des altarabischen Namensmateriales." In *Mélanges bibliques et orientaux en l'honneur der M. Mathias Delcor,* pp. 231-36. Alter Orient und Altes Testament, Band 215. Edited by A. Caquot, S. Legasse & M. Tardieu. Kevelaer: Butzon & Bercker; Neukirchen-Vluyn: Neukirchener, 1985.

Kraeling, Emil G. "Metušelach." *Zeitschrift für die alttestamentliche Wissenschaft* 40 (1922) 154-55.

______. *The Brooklyn Museum Aramaic Papyri: New Documents of the Fifth Century B.C. from the Jewish Colony at Elephantine.* New Haven: Yale University Press, 1953; reprint ed., n.p.: Arno Press, 1969.

Krahmalkov, Charles. "Observations on the Affixing of Possessive Pronouns in Punic." *Rivista degli studi orientali* 44 (1969) 181-86.

_______. "Studies in Phoenician and Punic Grammar." *Journal of Semitic Studies* 15 (1970) 181-88.

_______. "Comments on the Vocalization of the Suffix Pronoun on the Third Feminine Singular in Phoenician and Punic." *Journal of Semitic Studies* 17 (1972) 68-75.

Krauss, Samuel. "Textkritik auf Grund des Wechsels von *h* und *m*." *Zeitschrift für die alttestamentliche Wissenschaft* 48 (1930) 321-24.

Krebernik, Manfred. *Die Personennamen der Eblatexte: Eine Zwischenbilanz.* Berliner Beiträge zum Vorderen Orient, Band 7 (Berlin: Dietrich Reimer, 1987).

Krenkel, M. "Das Verwandtschaftswort *ʿam*." *Zeitschrift für die alttestamentliche Wissenschaft* 8 (1888) 280-84.

Kurylowicz, Jerzy. "La position linguistique du nom propre." *Onomastica* (Wroclaw) 2 (1956) 1-14. Reprinted in *Esquisses linguistiques*, 16/1:182-95. International Library of General Linguistics, vols. 16/1 & 37. Edited by Eugenio Coseriu. Munich: Wilhelm Fink, 1973.

Kutler, Laurence. "A 'Strong' Case for Hebrew MAR." *Ugarit-Forschungen* 16 (1984) 111-18.

Kutscher, Eduard Y. "lšny ḥwtmwt ʿbryym." In *Kedem: Studies in Jewish Archaeology*, vol. 1, pp. 44-45. Edited by E. L. Sukenik. Jerusalem, 1942.

_______. *The Language and Linguistic Background of the Isaiah Scroll (1 Q Isa[a]).* Studies on the Texts of the Desert of Judah, vol. 6. Leiden: E. J. Brill, 1974.

_______. *Studies in Galilean Aramaic.* Ramat Gan: Bar-Ilan University, 1976.

_______. "The Language of the Genesis Apocryphon." *Scripta Hierosolymitana* 4 (1957) 1-35. Reprinted in *Hebrew and Aramaic Studies*, pp. 3-36. Edited by Zeev Ben-Ḥayyim, Aharon Dotan, and Gad Sarfatti. Jerusalem: Magnes Press, 1977.

_______. "Mittelhebräische und Jüdisch-Aramaisch im neuen Köhler-Baumgartner." Vetus Testamentum, Supplement 16 (1967) 158-67. Reprinted in *Hebrew and Aramaic Studies*, pp. 156-73. Edited by Zeev Ben-Ḥayyim, Aharon Dotan, and Gad Sarfatti. Jerusalem: Magnes Press, 1977.

_______. *A History of the Hebrew Language.* Jerusalem: Magnes Press; Leiden: E. J. Brill, 1982.

Lagarde, Paul de. *Orientalia.* 2 vols. Göttingen: Dieterich, 1880.

Largement, René. "Les oracles de Bileʿam et la mantique suméro-akkadienne." In *Mémorial du cinquantenaire 1914-64*, pp. 37-50.

Travaux de l'institut catholique de Paris, no. 10. Paris: Bloud & Gay, n.d.

Laroche, E. "Le dieu Sarrumma." *Syria* 40 (1963) 277-302.

La toponymie antique. Actes du Colloque de Strasbourg (12-14 juin 1975). Leiden: E. J. Brill, 1977.

Lawton, Robert. "Israelite Personal Names on Pre-Exilic Hebrew Inscriptions." *Biblica* 65 (1984) 330-46.

Layton, Scott C. "A New Interpretation of an Edomite Seal-Impression." *Journal of Near Eastern Studies* (forthcoming).

______. "The Semitic Root **Ǵlm* and the Hebrew Name ʿAlemet." *Zeitschrift für die alttestamentliche Wissenschaft* (forthcoming).

______. Review of *Theophoric Personal Names in Ancient Hebrew: A Comparative Study,* by Jeaneane D. Fowler. *Journal of Near Eastern Studies* (forthcoming).

Lemaire, André. *Inscriptions hébraïques. Tome 1: Les ostraca.* Littératures anciennes du Proche-Orient, vol. 9. Paris: Éditions du Cerf, 1977.

______. "Nouveaux sceaux nord-ouest sémitique." *Semitica* 33 (1983) 17-31.

______. "Nouveaux sceaux nord-ouest sémitiques." *Syria* 63 (1986) 305-25.

______. "Divinités égyptiennes dans l'onomastique phénicienne." In *Studia Phoenicia IV: Religio Phoenicia,* pp. 87-98. Edited by C. Bonnet, E. Lipiński, and P. Marchetti. Namur: Société des études classiques, 1986.

Lenormant, François. *Les origines de l'histoire d'après la Bible et les traditions des peuples orientaux..* 2 vols. Paris: Maisonneuve, 1880-84.

Leslau, Wolf. *Comparative Dictionary of Geʿez.* Wiesbaden: Otto Harrassowitz, 1987.

Levin, Saul. "Jocasta and Moses' Mother Jochebed." *Teiresias* 2, Supplement (1979) 49-61.

Levine, Baruch A. "Assyriology and Hebrew Philology: A Methodological Re-examination." In *Mesopotamien und seine Nachbarn: Politische und kulturelle Wechselbeziehungen im Alten Vorderasien vom 4. bis 1. Jahrtausen v. Chr.,* pp. 521-30. XXV. Rencontre Assyriologique Internationale, Berlin, 3. bis 7. Juli 1978, Teil 1. Edited by Hans-Jörg Nissen and Johannes Renger. Berlin: Dietrich Reimer, 1982.

Lewy, Julius. *Forschungen zur alten Geschichte Vorderasiens.* Mitteilungen der Vorderasiatisch-Aegyptischen Gesellschaft, vol. 2. Leipzig: J. C. Hinrichs, 1925.

______. "Les texts paléo-assyriens et l'Ancien Testament." *Revue de l'histoire des religions* 110 (1934) 29-65.

______. "The Origin of the Week and the Oldest West Asiatic Calendar." *Hebrew Union College Annual* 17 (1942-43) 1-152.

______. "The Old West Semitic Sun-God Ḥammu." *Hebrew Union College Annual* 18 (1944) 429-84.

______. "The Late Assyro-Babylonian Cult of the Moon and its Culmination at the Time of Nabonidus." *Hebrew Union College Annual* 19 (1945-46)405-89.

______. "Studies in Akkadian Grammar and Onomatology." *Orientalia* 15 (1946) 361-415.

Leys, O. "Der Eigenname in seinem formalen Verhältnis zum Appellativ." *Beiträge zur Namenforschung*, n.s., 1 (1966) 113-23.

Lidzbarski, Mark. "Semitische Kosenamen." In *Ephemeris für semitische Epigraphik*, 2:1-23. 3 vols. Giessen: Alfred Töpelmann, 1900-12.

______. "Phönizische und aramäische Krugaufschriften aus Elephantine." In *Abhandlungen der königlich preussischen Akademie der Wissenschaften*, Philosophisch-historische Klasse, pp. 1-20, Plates I-VI. Berlin: Königlichen Akademie der Wissenschaften, 1912.

Lipiński, E. "Le dieu Lim." In *La Civilisation de Mari*, pp. 151-60. XVe Rencontre Assyriologique Internationale. Edited by J.-R. Kupper. N.p.: Université de Liége, 1967.

______. Review of *Personal Names in the Phoenician and Punic Inscriptions*, by Frank L. Benz. *Bibliotheca orientalis* 32 (1975) 77-80.

______. *Studies on Aramaic Inscriptions 1.* Orientalia Lovaniensia Analecta, no. 1. Louvain: University Press, 1975.

______. "Apladad." *Orientalia* 46 (1976) 53-74.

______. "Études d'onomastique ouest-sémitique." *Bibliotheca orientalis* 37 (1980) 3-12.

______. "Formes verbales dans les noms propres d'Ebla et système verbal sémitique." In *La lingua di Ebla: Atti del Convegno internazionale (Napoli, 22-23 aprile 1980)*, pp. 191-210. Istituto universitario orientale. Seminario studi asiatici, Series Minor, vol. 14. Edited by Luigi Cagni. Napoli, 1981.

Lippi, Donatella. "New Considerations about 'Egyptian Syllabic Orthography'." *Oriens antiquus* 23 (1984) 93-95.

Lisowsky, G. "Die Transkription der hebraeischen Eigennamen des Pentateuch in der Septuaginta." Inaugural-Dissertation, Basel, 1940.

Little, Greta D. "Internal Grammar in Amharic Place-Names." *Names* 26 (1978) 3-8.

Liverani, Mario. "Antecedenti dell'onomastica aramaica antica." *Rivista degli studi orientali* 37 (1962) 65-76.

______. "Antecedenti del diptotismo arabo nei testi accadici di Ugarit." *Rivista degli studi orientali* 38 (1963) 131-60.

______. "Elementi innovativi nell'ugaritico non letterario." *Rendiconti della classe di scienze morali, storiche e filologiche della Accademia Nazionale dei Lincei* 19 (1964) 173-91.

______. Review of *Die Personennamen der Texte aus Ugarit*, by Frauke Gröndahl. *Oriens antiquus* 7 (1968) 290-92.

Locher, C. S.v. "ṭap." In *Theological Dictionary of the Old Testament*, 6 vols., 5:347-50. Edited by G. Johannes Botterweck and Helmer Ringgren. Grand Rapids: William B. Eerdmans, 1974-.

Loewenstamm, Samuel E. S.v. "bĕnînû." In *Enṣîqlôpedyâ Miqrāʾît*, 2:281.

______. S.v. "gînat." In *Enṣîqlôpedyâ Miqrāʾît*, 2:483-84.

______. S.v. "gešem, gašmû." In *Enṣîqlôpedyâ Miqrāʾît*, 2:568-69.

______. S.v. "dĕʿûʾēl." In *Enṣîqlôpedyâ Miqrāʾît*, 2:697.

______. S.v. "hōrām." In *Enṣîqlôpedyâ Miqrāʾît*, 2:855.

______. S.v. "zabdîʾēl." In *Enṣîqlôpedyâ Miqrāʾît*, 2:892.

______. S.v. "yatnîʾēl." In *Enṣîqlôpedyâ Miqrāʾît*, 3:953.

Löhr, Max. *Die Stellung des Weibes zu Jahwe-Religion und -Kult.* Leipzig: J. C. Hinrichs, 1908.

Long, Ralph B. "The Grammar of English Proper Names." *Names* 17 (1969) 107-26.

Loretz, Oswald. "Der Gott *ŠLḤ*, He. *ŠLḤ* I und *ŠLḤ* II." *Ugarit-Forschungen* 7 (1975) 584-85.

______. "Vom Baal-epitheton *ADN* zu Adonis und Adonaj." *Ugarit-Forschungen* 12 (1980) 287-92.

Lubetski, Meir. "*ŠM* as a Deity." *Religion* 17 (1987) 1-14.

Malamat, A. "Aspects of the Foreign Policies of David and Solomon." *Journal of Near Eastern Studies* 22 (1963) 1-17.

Mańczak, Witold. "Une tendance générale dans le développement de la flexion des noms de personnes." *Revue internationale d'onomastique* 12 (1960) 125-36.

Maraqten, Mohammed. *Die semitischen Personennamen in den alt- und reicharamäischen Inschriften aus Vorderasien.* Texte und Studien zur Orientalistik, Band 5. Hildesheim: Georg Olms, 1988.

Marchell, W. *Abba, Père! La prière du Christ et des chretiens.* Analecta Biblica, no. 19. Rome: Pontifical Biblical Institute, 1963.

Margalioth, M. "The Meaning of the Names Maḥlon and Kilion in the Book of Ruth." In *Studies in Bible and Exegesis: Arie Toeg in Memoriam*, pp. 119-21. Edited by U. Simon and M. Goshen-Gottstein. Ramat-Gan: Bar-Ilan University Press, 1980.

Margalit, Baruch. "Restorations and Reconstructions in the Epic of Aqht." *Journal of Northwest Semitic Languages* 9 (1981) 75-117.

______. "Lexicographical Notes on the *Aqht* Epic (Part 1: KTU 1.17-18)." *Ugarit-Forschungen* 15 (1983) 65-103.

______. "Ugaritic Lexicography IV: The Name AQHT." *Revue biblique* 95 (1988) 211-14.

Margoliouth, D. S. *The Relations between Arabs and Israelites prior to the Rise of Islam.* The Schweich Lectures, 1921. London: Oxford University Press, 1924.

Margueron, Jean, and Teixidor, Javier. "Un object à légende araméenne provenant de Meskéné-Emar." *Revue d'assyriologie et d'archéologie orientale* 77 (1983) 75-80.

Markey, T. L. "Crisis and Cognition in Onomastics." *Names* 30 (1982) 129-42.

Marquart, J. *Fundamente israelitischer und jüdischer Geschichte.* Göttingen: Dieterich, 1896.

Mazar (Maisler), B. "lwḥwt tʿnk." In *Sēper Qĕlôzner: mʾsp lmdʿ wlsprwt yph mwgš lprwpswr ywsp qlwznr lywbl hššym,* pp. 44-66. Edited by N. H. Torczyner (Tur-Sinai). Tel Aviv, 1937.

______. "Palestine at the Time of the Middle Kingdom in Egypt." *Revue de l'histoire juive en Egypte* 1 (1947) 33-68.

______. "lmḥqr hšmwt hprṭyym šbmqrʾ." *Lešonénu* 15 (1947) 37-44.

______. "The Military Élite of King David." *Vetus Testamentum* 13 (1963) 310-20.

______. "King David's Scribe and the High Officialdom of the United Monarchy of Israel." In *The Early Biblical Period: Historical Essays,* pp. 126-38. Edited by Shmuel Aḥituv and Baruch A. Levine. Jerusalem: Israel Exploration Society, 1986.

Mazor, Lea. "The Origin of the Curse upon the Rebuilder of Jericho--A Contribution of Textual Criticism to Biblical Historiography." *Textus* 14 (1988) 1-26.

McCarter, P. Kyle, Jr. *1 Samuel: A New Translation with Introduction, Notes & Commentary.* Anchor Bible, vol. 8. Garden City: Doubleday & Co., 1980.

______. *2 Samuel: A New Translation with Introduction, Notes & Commentary.* Anchor Bible, vol. 9. Garden City: Doubleday & Co., 1984.

Meshel, Z. "Kuntilat ʿAjrud--An Israelite Site in the Sinai Border." *Qadmoniot* 9/4 (1976) 119-24.

Meyer, Rudolf. "Probleme der hebräischen Grammatik." *Zeitschrift für die alttestamentliche Wissenschaft* 63 (1951) 221-35.

______. *Hebräische Grammatik.* 3d ed. 4 vols. Berlin: Walter de Gruyter, 1966-72.

Milano, Lucio. "Due rendiconti di metalli da Ebla." *Studi Eblaiti* 3/1-2 (1980) 1-21.

Milik, J. T. "An Unpublished Arrow-head with Phoenician Inscription of the 11th-10th Century B.C." *Bulletin of the American Schools of Oriental Research* 143 (1956) 3-6.

______. "Giobbe 38,28 in siro-palestinese e la dea ugaritica *Pdry bt ar*." *Rivista biblica* 3 (1958) 252-54.

______. "Les papyrus araméens d'Hermoupolis et les cultes syro-phéniciens en Égypte perse." *Biblica* 48 (1967) 546-622.

Montgomery, James A. *Arabia and the Bible*. Philadelphia: University of Pennsylvania Press, 1934.

______. "Arabic Names in I. and II. Kings." *The Moslem World* 31 (1941) 266-67.

______. *A Critical and Exegetical Commentary on the Books of Kings*. Edited by Henry S. Gehman. The International Critical Commentary. Edinburgh: T. & T. Clark, 1951.

Morag, Shelomo. "mêšaʿ: ʿywnym btkwnwt lšwn šl lhgym ʿbryym qdwmym." *Eretz-Israel* 5 (1958) 138-44.

Moran, William L. "The Use of the Canaanite Infinitive Absolute as a Finite Verb in the Amarna Letters from Byblos." *Journal of Cuneiform Studies* 4 (1950) 169-72.

______. "Mari Notes on the Execration Texts." *Orientalia* 26 (1957) 339-45.

______. "The Hebrew Language in Its Northwest Semitic Background." In *The Bible and the Ancient Near East: Essays in honor of William Foxwell Albright*, pp. 54-72. Edited by G. Ernest Wright. The Biblical Colloquium, 1961; reprint ed., Winona Lake: Eisenbrauns, 1979.

Moritz, Bernhard. "Edomitische Genealogien. I." *Zeitschrift für die alttestamentliche Wissenschaft* 44 (1926) 81-93.

______. "Die Könige von Edôm." *Le Muséon* 50 (1937) 101-22.

Moscati, Sabatino. *L'epigrafia ebraica antica*. Rome: Pontifico Instituto Biblico, 1951.

______. "Israel's Predecessors: A Re-Examination of Certain Current Theories." *Journal of Bible and Religion* 24 (1956) 245-56.

______. "On Semitic Case-Endings." *Journal of Near Eastern Studies* 17 (1958) 142-44.

______. *The Semites in Ancient History*. Cardiff: University of Wales Press, 1959.

______, ed. *An Introduction to the Comparative Grammar of the Semitic Languages*. Porta Linguarum Orientalium, New Series, vol. 6. Wiesbaden: Otto Harrassowitz, 1969.

Muilenburg, James. "A Qoheleth Scroll from Qumran." *Bulletin of the American Schools of Oriental Research* 135 (1954) 20-28.

Müller, Hans-Peter. "Das eblaitische Verbalsystem nach den bisher veröffentlichten Personennamen." In *La lingua di Ebla: Atti del Convegno interna-zionale (Napoli, 22-23 aprile 1980)*, pp. 211-33. Istituto universitario orientale. Seminario di studi asiatici, Series Minor, vol. 14. Edited by Luigi Cagni. Napoli, 1981.

______. "Zum eblaitischen Konjugationssystem." Vetus Testamentum, Supplement 36 (1985) 208-17.

Müller, Walter W. "Altsüdarabische Beiträge zum hebräischen Lexikon." *Zeitschrift für die alttestamentliche Wissenschaft* 63 (1975) 304-16.

Murtonen, A. *Hebrew in Its West Semitic Setting, Part One: Comparative Lexicon; Section A: Proper Names.* Studies in Semitic Languages and Linguistics, Vol. XIII. Leiden: E. J. Brill, 1986.

Naveh, Joseph. "The Scripts in Palestine and Transjordan in the Iron Age." In *Essays in Honor of Nelson Glueck: Near Eastern Archaeology in the Twentieth Century*, pp. 277-83. Edited by James A. Sanders. Garden City: Doubleday & Co., 1970.

______. "The Aramaic Ostracon from Tel Beer-sheba (Seasons 1971-76)." *Tel Aviv* 6 (1979) 182-98.

______. "The Ostracon from Nimrud: An Ammonite Name-List." *Maarav* 2 (1980) 163-71.

______. "Writing and Scripts in Seventh Century B.C.E. Philistia: The New Evidence from Tell Jemmeh." *Israel Exploration Journal* 35 (1985)8-21.

Nestle, Eberhard. *Die israelitischen Eigennamen nach ihrer religionsgeschichtlichen Bedeutung.* Haarlem: De Erven F. Bohn, 1876.

______. "Some Contributions to Hebrew Onomatology." *American Journal of Semitic Languages and Literatures* 13 (1896-97) 169-76.

Nöldeke, Theodor. "Bemerkungen über hebräische und arabische Eigennamen." *Zeitschrift der deutschen morgenländischen Gesellschaft* 15 (1861) 806-10.

______. Review of *Kinship and Marriage in early Arabia*, by W. Robertson Smith. *Zeitschrift des deutschen morgenländischen Gesellschaft* 40 (1886) 148-87.

______. "Kleinigkeiten zur semitischen Onomatologie." *Wiener Zeitschrift für die Kunde des Morgenlandes* 6 (1892) 307-16.

______. *Compendious Syriac Grammar.* 2d ed., rev. Translated by James A. Crichton. London: Williams & Norgate, 1904.

______. "Einige Gruppen semitischer Personennamen." In *Beiträge zur semitischen Sprachwissenschaft*, pp. 73-106. Strassburg: Karl J. Trübner, 1904.

______. "Zweiradikalige Substantive." In *Neue Beiträge zur semitischen Sprachwissenschaft*, pp. 109-78. Strassburg: Karl J. Trübner, 1910.

______. "Wechsel von anlautendem *n* und *w* oder Hamza." In *Neue Beiträge zur semitischen Sprachwissenschaft*, pp. 179-201. Strassburg: Karl J. Trübner, 1910.

______. "Glossen zu H. Bauer's Semitischen Sprachproblemen." *Zeitschrift für Assyriologie* 30 (1915-16) 163-70.

______. S.v. "Names. A. Personal Names." In *Encyclopaedia Biblica*, 4 vols., 3:3271-3307. Edited by T. K. Cheyne and J. S. Black. New York: Macmillan & Co., 1902.

North, Robert. "The Hivites." *Biblica* 54 (1973) 43-62.

Noth, Martin. "Gemeinsemitische Erscheinungen in der israelitischen Namengebung." *Zeitschrift des deutschen morgenländischen Gesellschaft* 81 (1927) 1-45.

______. *Die israelitischen Personennamen im Rahmen der gemeinsemitischen Namengebung.* Stuttgart: W. Kohlhammer, 1928; reprint ed., Hildesheim: Georg Olms, 1980.

______. "Die syrisch-palästinische Bevölkerung des zweiten Jahrtausends v. Chr. im Lichte neuer Quellen." *Zeitschrift des deutschen Palästina-Vereins* 65 (1942) 9-67.

______. "Mari und Israel: Eine Personennamenstudie." In *Geschichte und Altes Testament, Albrecht Alt zum 70. Geburtstag dargebracht*, pp. 127-52. Beiträge zur historischen Theologie, Band 16. Tübingen, 1953. Reprinted in *Aufsätze zur biblischen Landes- und Altertumskunde, Band 2: Beiträge altorientalischer Texte zur Geschichte Israel*, pp. 213-33. Edited by Hans W. Wolff. Neukirchener-Vluyn: Neukirchener, 1971.

______. *The History of Israel.* 2d. ed. New York: Harper & Row, 1960.

Noth, Martin. *Numbers: A Commentary.* The Old Testament Library. Philadelphia: Westminster Press, 1968.

Nötscher, F. "Bar Kochba, Ben Kosba: Der Sternsohn, der Prächtige." *Vetus Testamentum* 11 (1961) 449-51.

Nougayrol, Jean. *Le palais royal d'Ugarit III.* 2 vols. Mission de Ras Shamra, vol. 6. Paris: Imprimerie Nationale et C. Klincksieck, 1955.

______. *Le palais royal d'Ugarit IV.* 2 vols. Mission de Ras Shamra, vol. 9. Paris: Imprimerie Nationale et C. Klincksieck, 1956.

______. *Le palais royal d'Ugarit VI.* 2 vols. Mission de Ras Shamra, vol. 12. Paris: Imprimerie Nationale et C. Klincksieck, 1970.

Nougayrol, Jean; Laroche, Emanuel; Virolleaud, Charles; and Schaeffer, Claude F. A. *Ugaritica V.* Mission de Ras Shamra, vol. 16. Imprimerie Nationale et Paul Geuthner, 1968.

Nowack, W. *Richter, Ruth u. Bücher Samuelis.* Handkommentar zum Alten Testament. Göttingen: Vandenhoeck & Ruprecht, 1902.

O'Callaghan, Roger T. "Echoes of Canaanite Literature in the Psalms." *Vetus Testamentum* 4 (1954) 164-76.

Olshausen, Justus. *Lehrbuch der hebräischen Sprache.* Braunschweig: Friedrich Vieweg & Sohn, 1861.

Oren, Eliezer D., and Rappaport, Uriel. "The Necropolis of Maresha-Beth Govrin." *Israel Exploration Journal* 34 (1984) 114-53.

Owen, David I. "An Akkadian Letter from Ugarit at Tel Aphek." *Tel Aviv* 8 (1981) 1-17.

Pardee, Dennis. "Letters from Tell Arad." *Ugarit-Forschungen* 10 (1978) 289-336.

Parpola, Simo. *Neo-Assyrian Toponyms.* Alter Orient und Altes Testament, Band 6. Kevelaer: Butzon & Bercker; Neukirchen-Vluyn: Neukirchener, 1970.

Penzl, Herbert. "Personal Names and German Noun Inflection." *Names* 30 (1982) 69-75.

Peshiṭta Institute, ed. *The Old Testament in Syriac According to the Peshiṭta Version.* Leiden: E. J. Brill, 1972-.

Pettinato, Giovanni. "Testi cuneiformi del 3. millennio in paleo-cananeo rinvenuti nella campagna 1974 a Tell Mardīkh = Ebla." *Orientalia* 44 (1975) 361-74.

Plöger, Otto. *Sprüche Salomos (Proverbia).* Biblischer Kommentar Altes Testament, Band XVII. Neukirchen-Vluyn: Neukirchener, 1984.

Pope, Marvin H. "Ugaritic Enclitic *-m*." *Journal of Cuneiform Studies* 5 (1951) 123-28.

______. *Job: A New Translation with Introduction and Commentary.* Anchor Bible, vol. 15. Garden City: Doubleday & Co., 1965.

______. "Notes on the Ugaritic Rephaim Texts." In *Essays on the Ancient Near East in Memory of Jacob Joel Finkelstein*, pp. 163-82. Memoirs of the Conneticut Academy of Arts & Sciences, vol. 19. Edited by Maria de Jong Ellis. Hamben, CT: Archon Books for the Academy, 1977.

Porten, Bezalel. *Archives from Elephantine: The Life of an Ancient Jewish Military Colony.* Berkeley: University of California Press, 1968.

______. "'Domla'el' and Related Names." *Israel Exploration Journal* 21 (1971) 47-49.

Posener, G. *Princes et pays d'Asie et de Nubie. Textes hiératiques sur des figurines d'envoûtement du moyen empire.* Bruxelles: Fondation égyptologique reine élisabeth, 1940.

Praetorius, Franz. "*Fuʿail* im Hebräischen und Syrischen." *Zeitschrift der deutschen morgenländischen Gesellschaft* 57 (1903) 524-29.

______. "Über einige weibliche Caritativnamen im Hebräischen." *Zeitschrift der deutschen morgenländischen Gesellschaft* 57 (1903) 530-34.

______. "Über einige Arten hebräischer Eigennamen." *Zeitschrift der deutschen morgenländischen Gesellschaft* 57 (1903) 773-82.

Prignaud, J. "Scribes et graveurs à Jerusalem vers 700 AV. J.-C." In *Archaeology in the Levant: Essays for Kathleen Kenyon*, pp. 136-48. Edited by R. Moorey and P. Parr. Warminster: Aris & Phillips, 1978.

Procksch, Otto. *Die Genesis, übersetzt und erklärt.* Leipzig: A. Deichert, 1913.

Puech, Émile. "Inscriptions funéraires palestiniennes: tombeau de Jason et ossuaries (Planches V-VII)." *Revue biblique* 90 (1983) 481-533.

Pulgram, Ernst. "Theory of Names." *Beiträge zur Namenforschung* 5 (1964) 149-96.

Rabin, C. "Archaic Vocalisation in Some Biblical Hebrew Names." *Journal of Jewish Studies* 1 (1948-49) 22-26.

______. "The Diptote Declension." In *Arabic and Islamic Studies in Honor of Hamilton A. R. Gibb*, pp. 547-62. Edited by George Makdisi. Leiden: E. J. Brill, 1965.

______. "The Structure of the Semitic System of Case Endings." In *Proceedings of the International Conference on Semitic Studies, held in Jerusalem, 19-23 July 1965*, pp. 190-204. Jerusalem: Israel Academy of Sciences and Humanities, 1969.

Rabinowitz, Isaac. "Aramaic Inscriptions of the Fifth Century B.C.E. from a North-Arab Shrine in Egypt." *Journal of Near Eastern Studies* 15 (1965) 1-9.

Rainey, Anson F. "Family Relationships in Ugarit." *Orientalia* 34 (1965) 10-22.

______. "Notes on the Syllabic Ugaritic Vocabularies." *Israel Exploration Journal* 19 (1969) 107-9.

______. "Gleanings from Ugarit." *Israel Oriental Studies* 3 (1973) 34-62.

______. "Two Cuneiform Fragments from Tel Aphek." *Tel Aviv* 2 (1975) 125-29.

______. "Morphology and Prefix-Tenses of West Semitized El ʿAmarna Tablets." *Ugarit-Forschungen* 7 (1975) 395-426.

______. "A Tri-Lingual Cuneiform Fragment from Tel Aphek." *Tel Aviv* 3 (1976) 137-40.

______. "The Toponymics of Eretz-Israel." *Bulletin of the American Schools of Oriental Research* 231 (1978) 1-17.

______. *El Amarna Tablets 359-79, Supplement to J. A. Knudtzon Die El-Amarna-Tafeln.* 2d rev. ed. Alter Orient und Altes Testament, Band 8. Kevelaer: Butzon & Bercker; Neukirchen-Vluyn: Neukirchener, 1978.

Ranke, Hermann. *Early Babylonian Personal Names.* Philadelphia, 1905.

______. *Die ägyptischen Personennamen.* 3 vols. Glückstadt: J. J. Augustin, 1935-77.

Rapaport, I. *The Hebrew Word* Shem *and Its Original Meaning: The Bearing of Akkadian Philology on Biblical Interpretation.* Melbourne: Hawthorne Press, 1976.

Rasmussen, Carl G. "A Study of Akkadian Personal Names from Mari." Ph.D. dissertation, The Dropsie University, 1981.

Reisner, G. A.; Fischer, C. S.; and Lyon, D. G. *Harvard Excavations at Samaria.* 2 vols. Cambridge: Harvard University Press, 1924.

Rendsburg, Gary A. "Evidence for a Spoken Hebrew in Biblical Times." Ph.D. dissertation, New York University, 1980.

______. "Diglossia in Ancient Hebrew as Revealed Through Compound Verbs." In *Bono Homini Donum: Essays in Historical Linguistics in Memory of J. Alexander Kerns,* 2 vols, 2:665-77. Edited by Yoël Arbeitman & Allan R. Bomhard. Amsterdam: John Benjamins, 1981.

______. "The Ammonite Phoneme /Ṯ/." *Bulletin of the American Schools of Oriental Research* 269 (1988) 73-79.

Renouf, P. le Page. "The Ḳenbetu and the Semitic South." *Proceedings of the Society of Biblical Archaeology* 10 (1887-88) 373-76.

Ribichini, S., and Xella, P. "Il dio PDR." *Ugarit-Forschungen* 16 (1984) 267-72.

Richardson, M. E. J. "Ugaritic Place Names with Final *-y*." *Journal of Semitic Studies* 23 (1978) 298-315.

Rin, Svi. "Ugaritic-Old Testament Affinities." *Biblische Zeitschrift,* n.f., 7 (1963) 22-33.

Rin, Svi, and Rin, Shifra. "Ugaritic-Old Testament Affinities." *Biblische Zeitschrift,* n.f., 11 (1967) 174-92.

Robertson, David A. Review of *Psalms I, 1-50,* by Mitchell Dahood. *Journal of Biblical Literature* 85 (1966) 484-86.

______. "The Morphemes -y(-ī) and -w(-ō) in Biblical Hebrew." *Vetus Testamentum* 19 (1969) 211-23.

______. *Linguistic Evidence in Dating Early Hebrew Poetry.* Society of Biblical Literature Dissertation Series, no. 3. Missoula: Society of Biblical Literature, 1972.

Röllig, W. "El als Gottesbezeichnung im Phönizischen." In *Festschrift Johannes Friedrich zum 65. Geburtstag am 27. August 1958 gewidmet*, pp. 403-16. Edited by R. von Kienle, A. Moortgat et al. Heidelberg: Carl Winter, 1959.

Rosenbaum, Jonathan, and Seger, Joe D. "Three Unpublished Ostraca from Gezer." *Bulletin of the American Schools of Oriental Research* 264 (1986) 51-60.

Rosenberg, Roy A. "The God Ṣedeq." *Hebrew Union College Annual* 36 (1965) 161-77.

______. "Yahweh Becomes King." *Journal of Biblical Literature* 85 (1966) 297-307.

Roth, C. et al., eds. *Encyclopaedia Judaica.* 16 vols. Jerusalem: Keter, 1972.

Rothstein, J. W., and Hänel, Johannes. *Das erste Buch der Chronik.* Leipzig: A. Deichertsche, 1927.

Rudolph. Wilhelm. *Esra und Nehemia, samt 3. Esra.* Handbuch zum Alten Testament, erste Reihe, Band 20. Tübingen: J. C. B. Mohr (Paul Siebeck), 1949.

______. *Chronikbücher.* Handbuch zum Alten Testament, erste Reihe, Band 21. Tübingen: J. C. B. Mohr (Paul Siebeck), 1955.

Ryckmans, G. *Les noms propres sud-sémitiques.* 3 vols. Bibliothèque du Muséon, no. 2. Louvain, 1934-35.

Safran, Jonathan. "Ahuzzath and the Pact of Beer-Sheba." *Zeitschrift für die alttestamentliche Wissenschaft* 101 (1987) 184-98.

Sarfatti, Gad B. "Hebrew Inscriptions of the First Temple Period--A Survey and Some Linguistic Comments." *Maarav* 3 (1982) 55-83.

Sarna, Nahum M. "*ʾytnym*, Job 12:19." *Journal of Biblical Literature* 74 (1955) 272-73.

Scerbo, F. *Lessico dei nomi propri ebraici del vecchio testamento.* Firenze: Libreria editrice fiorentina, 1913.

Schalit, Abraham. *Namenwörterbuch zu Flavius Josephus.* Leiden: E. J. Brill, 1968.

Schneider, Th. "Die semitischen and ägyptischen Namen der syrischen Sklaven des Papyrus Brooklyn 35.1446 verso." *Ugarit-Forschungen* 19 (1987) 255-82.

Schrader, Eberhard. *Die Keilinschriften und das Alte Testament.* 3d ed. Berlin: Ruether & Beichard, 1903.

Schulthess, Friedrich. "Zwei etymologische Versuche." *Zeitschrift für die alttestamentliche Wissenschaft* 30 (1910) 61-63.

Segert, Stanislav. *A Grammar of Phoenician and Punic.* Munich: C. H. Beck, 1976.

_______. *A Basic Grammar of the Ugaritic Language, with Selected Texts and Glossary.* Berkeley and Los Angeles: University of California Press, 1984.

_______. "Diptotic Geographical Feminine Names in the Hebrew Bible." *Zeitschrift für Althebraistik* 1 (1988) 99-102.

Sellin, Ernst. *Tell Ta'annek.* Denkschriften der kaislerlichen Akademie der Wissenschaften in Wien, Philosophisch-historische Klasse, vol. 50. Vienna, 1904.

_______. *Eine Nachlese auf dem Tell Ta'annek in Palästina.* Denkschriften der kaislerlichen Akademie der Wissenschaften in Wien, Philosophisch-historische Klasse, vol. 52/3. Vienna, 1905.

Sethe, Kurt. *Die Ächtung feindlicher Fürsten, Völker und Dinge auf altägyptischen tongefäßscherben des mittleren Reiches.* Abhandlungen der preussischen Akademie der Wissenschaften, Philosophisch-historische Klasse, no. 5. Berlin: Akademie der Wissenschaften, 1926.

Shiloh, Y. "qbwṣt bwlwt ʿbrywt mʿyr dwd." *Eretz-Israel* 18 (1985) 73-87, Plates 16-18.

_______. "A Group of Hebrew Bullae from the City of David." *Israel Exploration Journal* 36 (1986) 16-38, Plates 6-7.

Silverman, Michael H. "Jewish Personal Names in the Elephantine Documents: A Study in Onomastic Development." Ph.D. dissertation, Brandeis University, 1967.

_______. "Aramean Name-Types in the Elephantine Documents." *Journal of the American Oriental Society* 89 (1969) 691-709.

_______. "Hebrew Name-Types in the Elephantine Documents." *Orientalia* 39 (1970) 465-90.

_______. *Religious Values in the Jewish Proper Names at Elephantine.* Alter Orient und Altes Testament, Band 217. Kevelaer: Butzon & Bercker; Neukirchen-Vluyn: Neukirchener, 1985.

Singer, Abraham D. "h'm' hswpyt' (=mā?) bšpt lwḥwt ʾwgryt." *Bulletin of the Jewish Palestine Exploration Society* 10 (1943) 54-62.

Sivan, Daniel. *Grammatical Analysis and Glossary of the Northwest Semitic Vocables in Akkadian Texts of the 15th-13th C.B.C. from Canaan and Syria.* Alter Orient und Altes Testament, Band 214. Kevelaer: Butzon & Bercker; Neukirchen-Vluyn: Neukirchener, 1984.

Skinner, John. *A Critical and Exegetical Commentary on Genesis.* 2d ed. The International Critical Commentary. Edinburgh: T. & T. Clark, 1930.

Skipworth, G. H. "Hebrew Tribal Names and the Primitive Traditions of Israel." *JQR*, o.s., 11 (1898-99) 239-65.

Smith, Elsdon C. "The Significance of Name Study." In *Proceedings of the Eighth International Congress of Onomastic Sciences*, pp. 492-99. Janua Linguarum, Studia memoriae Nicolai van Wijk dedicata. Series Maior, vol. 17. Edited by D. P. Block. Paris: Mouton & Co., 1966.

Smith, Henry P. *A Critical and Exegetical Commentary on the Books of Samuel.* The International Critical Commentary. Edinburgh: T. & T. Clark, 1899.

Smith, W. Robertson. "Animal Worship and Animal Tribes among the Arabs and in the Old Testament." *The Journal of Philology* 9 (1880) 75-100.

Soggin, J. Alberto. *Judges: A Commentary.* Translated by John Bowden. The Old Testament Library. Philadelphia: Westminster Press, 1981.

Sollberger, Edmond. *Administrative Texts Chiefly Concerning Textiles (L. 2752).* Archivi reali di Ebla, vol. VIII. Rome: Missione archeologica italiana in Siria, 1986.

Sommerfeld, Walter. "Untersuchungen zur Geschichte von Kisurra." *Zeitschrift für Assyriologie* 73 (1983) 204-31.

Speiser, E. A. "The name Bildad." *Archiv für Orientforschung* 6 (1930-31) 23.

______. "Studies in Semitic Afformatives." *Journal of the American Oriental Society* 56 (1936) 22-46. Reprinted in *Oriental and Biblical Studies: Collected Writings of E. A. Speiser*, pp. 403-32. Edited by J. J. Finkelstein and Moshe Greenberg. Philadelphia: University of Pennsylvania Press, 1967.

______. *Genesis: Introduction, Translation, and Notes.* Anchor Bible, vol. 1. Garden City: Doubleday & Co., 1964.

Stade, Bernhard. *Lehrbuch der hebräischen Grammatik.* Leipzig: F. C. W. Vogel, 1879.

Stamm, Johann J. *Die akkadische Namengebung.* Darmstadt: Wissenschaftliche Buchgesellschaft, 1968.

______. *Beiträge zur hebräischen und altorientalischen Namenkunde.* Orbis biblicus et orientalis, vol. 30. Freiburg: Universitätsverlag; Göttingen: Vandenhoeck & Ruprecht, 1980.

______. "Der Name Zedekia." In *De la Tôrah au Messie. Études d'exégèse et d'herméneutique bibliques offertes à Henri Cazelles pour ses 25 années d'enseignement à l'Institute Catholique de Paris (Octobre 1979)*, pp. 227-35. Edited by Maurice Carrez, Joseph Doré, and Pierre Grelot. Paris: Desclée, 1981.

______. S.v. "Names. In the Bible." In *Encyclopaedia Judaica*, 12:803-6.

Stark, Jürgen K. *Personal Names in Palmyrene Inscriptions.* Oxford: Clarendon Press, 1971.

Stolper, Matthew W. "Management and Politics in Later Achaemenid Babylonia: New Texts from the Murašû Archive." 2 vols. Ph.D. dissertation, University of Michigan, 1974.

______. "A Note on Yahwistic Personal Names in the Murašû Texts." *Bulletin of the American Schools of Oriental Research* 222 (1976) 25-28.

Sukenik, E. L. et als., eds. *Enṣîqlôpedyâ Miqrāʾît.* 8 vols. Jerusalem: Bialik Institute, 1950-82.

Swiggers, Pierre. "A Syncretistic Anthroponym in the Aramaic Documents from Egypt." *Beiträge zur Namenforschung*, n.s., 16 (1981) 348-50.

______. Review of *West Semitic Personal Names in the Murašû Documents*, by Michael D. Coogan. *Journal of Near Eastern Studies* 42 (1983) 75-77.

______. "Proper names, Languages and Scripts." *Beiträge zur Namenforschung*, n.s., 19 (1984) 381-84.

Tallqvist, Knut L. *Assyrian Personal Names.* Acta Societatis Scientiarum Fennicae, vol. 48/1. Helsinki, 1914.

______. *Akkadische Götterepitheta.* Studia Orientalia, no. 7. Helsinki: Societas Orientalis Fennicae, 1938.

Talmon, Shemaryahu. "The Ancient Hebrew Alphabet and Biblical Text Criticism." In *Mélanges Dominique Barthélemy: Études bibliques offertes à l'occasion de son 60e anniversaire*, pp. 498-530. Orbis biblicus et orientalis, vol. 38. Edited by Pierre Casetti, Othmar Keel et Adrian Schenker. Fribourg: Éditions Universitaires; Göttingen: Vandenhoeck & Ruprecht, 1981.

Teixidor, Javier. "Un nouveau papyrus araméen du règne de Darius II." *Syria* 41 (1964) 285-90.

Thompson, J. A. "On Some Stamps and a Seal from Lachish." *Bulletin of the American Schools for Oriental Research* 86 (1942) 24-27.

Thompson, Thomas L. *The Historicity of the Patriarchal Narratives: The Quest for the Historical Abraham.* Beiheft zur Zeitschrift für die alttestamentliche Wissenschaft, Band 133. Berlin: Walter de Gruyter, 1974.

Thureau-Dangin, F. "Un comptoir de laine pourpre à Ugarit d'après une tablette de Ras-Shamra." *Syria* 15 (1934) 137-46.

Tigay, Jeffrey H. *You Shall Have No Other Gods: Israelite Religion in the Light of Hebrew Inscriptions.* Harvard Semitic Studies, no. 31. Atlanta: Scholars Press, 1986.

Tomasson, Richard F. "The Continuity of Icelandic Names and Naming Patterns." *Names* 23 (1975) 281-89.

Tonneau, Raphael. "II. -- Épigraphie grecque du Négeb." *Revue biblique* 36 (1927) 93-98.

Torczyner, Harry. *Lachish I: The Lachish Letters.* London: Oxford University Press, 1938.

Tsevat, Matitiahu. "The Canaanite God Šälaḥ." *Vetus Testamentum* 4 (1954) 41-49.

______. "Additional Remarks to 'The Canaanite God Šälaḥ'." *Vetus Testamentum* 4 (1954) 322.

______. S.v. "šĕmûʾēl." In *Enṣîqlôpedyâ Miqrāʾît,* 8:70-71.

______. "Die Namengebung Samuels und die Substitutionstheorie." *Zeitschrift für die alttestamentliche Wissenschaft* 99 (1987) 250-54.

Tuland, C. G. "Hanani--Hananiah." *Journal of Biblical Literature* 77 (1958) 157-61.

Tuttle, Gary A. "Case Vowels on Masculine Singular Nouns in Construct in Ugaritic." In *Biblical and Near Eastern Studies: Essays in Honor of William Sanford LaSor,* pp. 253-68. Edited by Gary A. Tuttle. Grand Rapids: William B. Eerdmans, 1978.

Ullendorff, Edward. "Is Biblical Hebrew a Language?" *Bulletin of the Schools of Oriental and African Studies* 34 (1971) 241-55. Reprinted in *Is Biblical Hebrew a Language?,* pp. 3-17. Wiesbaden: Otto Harrassowitz, 1977.

Ulmer, Friedrich. *Die semitischen Eigennamen im Alten Testament.* Leipzig: W. Drugulin, 1901.

Ungnad, Arthur. *Grammatik des Akkadischen.* rev. ed. Munich: C. H. Beck, 1969.

Utley, Francis L. "The Linguistic Component of Onomastics." *Names* 11 (1963) 145-76.

Van Selms, Adrianus. "Judge Shamgar." *Vetus Testamentum* 14 (1964) 294-309.

______. "A Forgotten God: *Laḥ.*" In *Studia biblica et semitica: Theodoro Christiano Vriezen qui munere professoris theologiae per xxv annos functus est, ab amicis, collegis, discipulis dedicata,* pp. 318-26. Wageningen: H. Veenman & Zonen, 1966.

______. "Some Reflections on the Formation of the Feminine in Semitic Languages." In *Near Eastern Studies in Honor of William Foxwell Albright,* pp. 421-31. Edited by Hans Goedicke. Baltimore: Johns Hopkins Press, 1971.

Van Seters, John. "The Terms 'Amorite' and 'Hittite' in the Old Testament." *Vetus Testamentum* 22 (1971) 64-81.

Van Zyl, A. H. "The Meaning of the Name Samuel." *Proceedings of the Twelfth Meeting of Die ou-testamentiese werkgemeenskap in Suid-Afrika* (1969) 122-29.

Vattioni, Francesco. "I sigilli ebraici." *Biblica* 50 (1969) 357-88.

______. "I sigilli, le monete e gli avori aramaici." *Augustinianum* 11 (1971) 47-87.

______. "I sigilli ebraici II." *Augustinianum* 11 (1971) 447-54.

______. "Sigilli ebraici III." *Annali dell'istituto orientali Napoli* 38 (1978) 227-54.

______. "Antroponimi fenicio-punici nell'epigrafia Greca e Latina del Nordafrica." *Annali de Seminario di studi del mondo classico. Istituto Universitario Orientale. Sezione di archeologia e storia antica* 1 (1979) 153-90.

______. "I sigilli fenici." *Annali dell'istituto orientali Napoli* 41 (1981) 177-93.

______. *Le iscrizioni di Ḥatra. Annali dell'istituto orientali Napoli*. Supplement, no. 28. Napoli, 1981.

Völter, D. "Mirjam." *Zeitschrift für die alttestamentliche Wissenschaft* 38 (1919-20) 111-12.

von Soden, Wolfram. "Der hymnisch-epische Dialekt des Akkadischen." *Zeitschrift für Assyriologie* 41 (1933) 90-183.

______. "Aramäische Wörter in neuassyrischen und neu- und spätbabylonischen Texten. Ein Vorbericht. I (*agâ* - **mūš*)." *Orientalia* 35 (1966) 1-20.

______. *Grundriss der akkadischen Grammatik*. Analecta Orientalia, vols. 33/47. Rome: Pontifical Biblical Institute, 1969.

______. "*Mirjām* -- Maria '(Gottes-)Geschenk'." *Ugarit-Forschungen* 2 (1977) 269-72. Reprinted in *Bibel und Alter Orient: Altorientalische Beiträge zum Alten Testament von Wolfram von Soden*, pp. 129-33. Beiheft zur Zeitschrift für die alttestamentliche Wissenschaft, Band 162. Edited by Hans-Peter Müller. Berlin: Walter de Gruyter, 1985.

Wagner, Max. *Die lexikalischen und grammatikalischen Aramaismen im alttestamentlichen Hebräischen*. Beiheft zur Zeitschrift für die alttestamentliche Wissenschaft, Band 96. Berlin: Alfred Töpelmann, 1966.

Walker, Norman. "Elohim and Eloah." *Vetus Testamentum* 6 (1956) 214-15.

______. "Do Plural nouns of majesty exist in Hebrew?" *Vetus Testamentum* 7 (1957) 208.

Weber, R., ed. *Biblia sacra iuxta Vulgatam versionem*. 3d, rev. ed. 2 vols. Stuttgart: Deutsche Bibelgesellschaft, 1983.

Wehr, Hans. *A Dictionary of Modern Written Arabic (Arabic-English).* 4th ed. Edited by J. Milton Cowan. Wiesbaden: Otto Harrassowitz, 1979.

Weinreich, Uriel; Labov, William; and Herzog, Marvin I. "Empirical Foundations for a Theory of Language Change." In *Directions for Historical Linguistics: A Symposium*, pp. 97-188. Edited by W. P. Lehmann and Yakob Malkiel. Austin: University of Texas Press, 1968.

Weippert, Helga, and Weippert, Manfred. "Die 'Bileam'-Inschrift von *Tell Dēr ʿAllā*." *Zeitschrift des deutschen Palästina-Vereins* 98 (1982)77-103.

Weippert, Manfred. "Jau(a) mār ḫumrî--Joram oder Jehu von Israel?" *Vetus Testamentum* 28 (1978) 113-18.

Westermann, Claus. *Genesis 1-11: A Commentary.* Translated by John J. Scullion. Minneapolis: Ausburg Publishing House, 1984.

______. *Genesis 12-36.* Translated by John J. Scullion. Minneapolis: Augsburg Publishing House, 1985.

Widmer, Gottfried. "Hebräische Wechselname." In *Vom Alten Testament: Karl Marti zum siebzigsten Geburtstage*, pp. 297-304. Beiheft zur Zeitschrift für die alttestamentliche Wissenschaft, Band 41. Edited by Karl Budde. Giessen: Alfred Töpelmann, 1925.

Winnett, Fred V. "The Arabian Genealogies in the Book of Genesis." In *Translating and Understanding the Old Testament: Essays in Honor of Herbert Gordon May*, pp. 171-96. Edited by Harry T. Frank and William L. Reed. Nashville: Abingdon, 1970.

Winnett, F. V., and Reed, W. L. *Ancient Records from North Arabia.* Near and Middle East Series, vol. 6. Toronto: University of Toronto Press, 1970.

Wiseman, D. J. *The Alalakh Tablets.* Occasional Publications of the British Institute of Archaeology at Ankara, no. 2. London: British Institute of Archaeology, 1953.

______. "Supplementary Copies of the Alalakh Tablets." *Journal of Cuneiform Studies* 8 (1954) 1-30.

______. "Abban and Alalaḫ." *Journal of Cuneiform Studies* 12 (1958) 124-29.

______. "Ration Lists from Alalakh VII." *Journal of Cuneiform Studies* 13 (1959) 19-32.

______. "Ration Lists from Alalakh IV." *Journal of Cuneiform Studies* 13 (1959) 50-62.

Wood, W. Carleton. "The Religion of Canaan: The Canaanite Period (1800-1200 B.C.)." *Journal of Biblical Literature* 35 (1916) 163-279.

Wright, W. *A Grammar of the Arabic Language.* 3d ed. 2 vols. Cambridge: Cambridge University, 1971.

Wuthnow, Heinz. *Die semitischen Menschennamen in griechischen Inschriften und Papyri des vorderen Orients.* Studien zur Epigraphik und Papyruskunde, Band I/4. Leipzig: Dieterich, 1930.

Yadin, Yigael. "ḥwtm ʿbry mtl-g'mh." *Eretz-Israel* 6 (1960) 53-55.

Young, D. W. "Notes on the Root *ntn* in Biblical Hebrew." *Vetus Testamentum* 10 (1960) 457-59.

Young, Edward J. *The Prophecy of Daniel: A Commentary.* Grand Rapids: William B. Eerdmans, 1949.

______. "Adverbial *-u* in Semitic." *Westminster Theological Journal* 13 (1951) 151-54.

Youngblood, Ronald. "Amorite Influence in a Canaanite Amarna Letter (*EA* 96)." *Bulletin of the American Schools of Oriental Research* 168 (1962) 24-27.

Zaborski, Andrzej. "Biconsonantal Verbal Roots in Semitic." *Prace Jezykoznawcze* 35 (1971) 51-98.

Zadok, Ran. "Geographical and Onomastic Notes." *Journal of the Ancient Near Eastern Society* 8 (1976) 113-26.

______. Review of *Studies in Aramaic Inscriptions and Onomastics I,* by E. Lipiński." *Bibliotheca orientalis* 33 (1976) 227-31.

______. *On West Semites in Babylonia During the Chaldean and Achaemenian Periods: An Onomastic Study.* Jerusalem: H. J. & Z. Wanaarta and Tel-Aviv University, 1977.

______. "Historical and Onomastic Notes." *Die Welt des Orients* 9 (1977-78) 35-56.

______. "On Some Egyptians in First-Millennium Mesopotamia." *Göttinger Miszellen* 26 (1977) 63-68.

______. "Phoenicians, Philistines, and Moabites in Mesopotamia." *Bulletin of the American Schools of Oriental Research* 230 (1978) 57-65.

______. Review of *West Semitic Personal Names in the Murašû Archives,* by Michael D. Coogan. *Israel Exploration Journal* 28 (1978) 290-92.

______. "West Semitic Toponyms in Assyrian and Babylonian Sources." In *Studies in Bible and the Ancient Near East, Presented to Samuel E. Loewenstamm on His Seventieth Birthday,* 1:163-79. 2 vols. Edited by Yitschak Avishur and Joshua Blau. Jerusalem: E. Rubinstein, 1978.

______. *The Jews in Babylonia During the Chaldean and Achaemenian Periods according to the Babylonian Sources.* Studies in the History of the Jewish People and the Land of Israel, Monograph Series, vol. 3. N.p.: University of Haifa, 1979.

Zadok, Ran. *Sources for the History of the Jews in Babylonia During the Chaldean and Achaemenian Periods. With an Appendix on*

West Semitic Names in 1st-Millennium Mesopotamia. Jerusalem, 1980.

———. "Notes on the Biblical and Extra-Biblical Onomasticon." *Jewish Quarterly Review*, n.s., 71 (1980/81) 107-17.

———. "Arabians in Mesopotamia during the Late-Assyrian, Chaldean, Achaemenian and Hellenistic Periods Chiefly According to the Cuneiform Sources." *Zeitschrift der deutschen morgenländischen Gesellschaft* 131 (1981) 42-84.

———. Review of *The Extra-biblical Tradition of Hebrew Personal Names from the First Temple Period to the End of the Talmudic Period*, by M. Ohana and M. Heltzer. *Die Welt des Orients* 13 (1982) 168-72.

———. "Remarks on the Inscription of *HDYSʿY* From Tall Fakhariya." *Tel Aviv* 9 (1982) 117-29.

———. "Notes on the Early History of the Israelites and Judeans in Mesopotamia." *Orientalia* 51 (1982) 391-93.

———. "On the Historical Background of the Sefîre Treaty." *Annali dell'istituto orientali di Napoli* 44 (1984) 529-38.

———. "Assyro-Babylonian Lexical and Onomastic Notes." *Bibliotheca orientalis* 41 (1984) 33-46.

———. "Die nichthebräischen Namen der Israeliten vor dem hellenistischen Zeitalter." *Ugarit-Forschungen* 17 (1985) 387-98.

———. "Notes on the Prosopography of the Old Testament." *Biblische Notizen* 42 (1988) 44-48.

———. "Zur Struktur der nachbiblischen jüdischen Personennamen semitischen Ursprung." In *Trumah, 1. Hochschule für jüdischen Studien, Heidelberg*, pp. 243-343. Wiesbaden: Ludwig Reichert, 1988.

———. S.v. "śārâ, śāray." In *Enṣîqlôpedyâ Miqrāʾît*, 8:390-91.

———. S.v. "šm, šmwt ʿṣm prṭyym byśrʾl, [g] mwrpwlwgyh." In *Enṣîqlôpedyâ Miqrāʾît*, 8:51-65.

Zevit, Ziony. "The Question of Case Endings on Ugaritic Nouns in Status Constructus." *Journal of Semitic Studies* 28 (1983) 225-32.

Ziffer, I. "A Hebrew Inscription on a Bronze Bowl in the Haaretz Museum Collection." In *Israel - People and Land*, Eretz Israel Museum Yearbook, Vol. 4, pp. 79-81. Edited by R. Zeevy. Tel Aviv: Eretz Israel Museum, 1986-87.

Zorell, Franciscus. "Was bedeutet der Name Maria?" *Zeitschrift für katholische Theologie* 30 (1906) 356-60.

———. *Lexicon Hebraicum Veteris Testamenti.* Rome: Biblical Institute Press, 1940-84.

Indices

1. Names

a. *Main entries*

Canaanite

ʾăbûgayil 87-88
ʾûlām 168
ʾônām 169
ʾăḥuzzām 170
ʾăḥuzzat 205
ʾĕlîšebaʿ 213-15
ʾeprāt 223-24
bĕkôrat 206
bōkĕrû 94-95
bilʿām 170-72
bĕnînû 95-96
bāśĕmat 206-7
bĕtûʾēl 55-57
gĕʾûʾēl 88-89
gabrîʾēl 131-34
gînat 207-209
golyāt 224-25
gĕnūbat 209-10
gaʿtām 172-73
gēršōm 181
dānîyē(ʾ)l 129-30
dĕʿûʾēl 89
hădôrām 57-59
hôhām 182
hêmām 182
hōrām 173
zētām 173-74
ḥûpām 174-75
ḥûrām 59-60
ḥûšām 175
ḥizqî 125-26
ḥizqîyāh 122-25
ḥămûṭal 60-62
ḥammûʾēl 62-63
ḥannîʾēl 134-37
ṭāpat 210-11
yĕhôšabʿat 211-13
yĕmûʾēl 63-66
yaʿlām 183
yĕqûtîʾēl 137-38
yĕśîmīʾēl 138-39
yatnîʾēl 126-29
yitrô 98-99
kimhām 175-76
māḥălat 215-17
mānaḥat 225
mĕlîkû 96
malkî-ṣedeq 139-40
malkām 176
miryām 183-86
mišʿām 176-78
mĕtûšāʾēl 66-72
mĕtûšelaḥ 73-74
naḥat 225-27
nĕmûʾēl 89
sallû 96
ʿabdî 130-31
ʿabdîʾēl 122
ʿîrû 96-97
ʿîrām 178-79
ʿamrām 186-88
(ben)-ʿănāt 217-18
ʿašwāt 227-28
pĕnûʾēl 74-76
pirʾām 179
pĕtûʾēl 90
ṣidqîyah 140-42
qĕmûʾēl 76-78
rîpat 228
rĕʿû 97
rĕʿûʾēl 91-94
śāray 246-48
šûḥām 179-80
šimʾām 188-89
šĕmûʾēl 78-87
šimʿāt 218-20
šimrāt 221-22
šĕpûpām 180-81
tôqhat 222-23
tōḥû 97-98
tōʿû 98

Aramaic

ʾăḥûmay 100-101
zabdî 145
zabdîʾēl 142-45

Arabian

ʾăbîmāʾēl 190
ʾalmôdād 192-93
lĕmôʾēl 190-92

b. *Other Names Discussed*

Akkadian

bil-^{d}adad 171 n90
^{f}muti-bāšti 68 n136

Eblaite

a-ʾà-lu 156
a-ʾà-lum 156
a-ba$_4$-me 156
a-ḫu-kam$_4$ 60, 101 n298
a-ḫu-lu 101 n298
wa-ti-nu 128

Amorite

a-a-a-bu-ú 84
a-ḫi-ì-lí 114-15 n37
a-ḫu-ka-a-bi 148 n185
a-ḫu-um 101 n298
a-ḫu-um-la-a-bi 148 n185
a-ḫu-um-ma-ilu 101 n298
a-ma-at-^{d}ba-a-la 110
am-ti-aš-ta-ra 110
ba-lum-qa-mu-um 77-78
bi-it-ta-mal-ki 110
bi-it-ti-^{d}da-gan 110
DUMU-ḫa-nu-ta 7 n27
ḫa-ab-du-a-mi-im 39
ḫu-ra-za-a-ia 243
ḫu-ra-za-tum 243
ia-am-mu-ú 66
ia-qar-tum 200
i-la-a-bi 157
ila-ma-a-bi 157
ì-lí-su-ú-mu 87
ì-lí-zi-id-qi 142
mi-il-ki-ilu 157
mi-il-ku-ma-ilu 157
mu-tu-i-la 69
mu-ut-ḫu-bur 72 n155
qa-mu-ma-ìl 77 n175
qa-mu-ma-ilu 78
qí-iš-ti-ad-mu 110
qí-iš-ti-li-lim 110
qí-iš-ti-^{d}ma-am-ma 110
qí-iš-ti-^{d}ma-ma 110
qí-iš-ti-^{d}nu-nu 110
sa-ma-ri-a-du 221 n113
sa-ma-ri-ilu 221 n113
^{d}su-mu-a-bu 86
su-mu-a-mi 84
su-mu-ḫa-mu 84
^{d}su-mu-ilu 86
su-mu-la-li-a 87 n236
ši-im-ra-al-la 221
šu-ba-ila 51 n56
šu-ba-ḫa-li 51 n56
šu-ba-ni-ilu 51 n56
zi-im-ri-ia 121
zi-im-ri-ilu 121, 163
zi-im-ri-i-lu-ma 163 n147
zi-im-ri-ilu-ma 163
zu-ú-ša-a-bi 71 n151

Ugarit

ʾaqht 222-23 n121
ʾilym 52 n65
ʾilštmʿ (GN) 12
ʾulm 168
ʾdnnʿm 43
ʾdnṣdq 140
bn gntn 208 n48
bn mṯ 177
bʿlmʿḏr 165
bʿlmṯpṭ 165
gʿyn 173
ṭly 244
ymʾil 52 n65, 65-66
yqr 165
yrgbbʿl 43
yrgblʾim 192
krmn 209 n53
mṯpṭ 165 n56
ʿbdʾilm 163
ʿbdrpʾu 43
ʿbdṯrm 165 n55
pdry 244
rʿy 94 n261
šlmym 66 n130
šmmlk 43
špšm 164

a-bi-ra-mu 77
abdi-ili-mu 163
abdi-ir-ši 114
abdi-ḫa-ma-ni 114
abdi-yammi 66
abdi-šarru-ma 165
^{f}a-ḫa-ti-milki 44, 113
^{f}a-ḫa-tum-milki 44, 113
a-ḫi-milki 114
[bin]-ili-ma-ra-kub 163
gi-na-ta-na 208 n48
^{f}ṭá-la-ia 244
ia-qa-ri 165
ia-qa-rum 164
^{f}i-nu-uʾ-mi 66 n130
^{URU}ilu-iš-tam-i 12
kar-mu-nu 209 n53
nu-ú-ma-ia 245
nu-ú-ma-ia-nu 245
^{f}pí-id-da 248 n33
^{f}pí-id-da-ia 248 n33
^{d}pi-id-ra-i 244
^{f}pí-zi-ib/bi-li 42 n 19
ṣi-id-qa-nu 142 n161
šu-baʿlu 9 n36

Alalakh

ia-am-mu 66
nu-ri-i-el-mu 163
u-ri-el-mu 163

Taanach

abdi-šar-ru-ma 165n55
abdi-ša-ru-ma 165 n55
aḫi-ia-mi 64 n22
e-lu-ra-ma 42, 77
e-lu-ra-ḫé-ba 42
e-lu-ra-p[í?-í?] 42
zi-bi-lu 42

Hazor

gi-la-di-ma (GN) 161 n40
^{f}su-mu-la-ilu 84

El Amarna

a-na-ti 218 n101
bá-a-lu-ú-ma 161-62
ba-lu-mé-er 42
ba-lum-me-e 161-62
be-el-[š]a-a[m-ma] 171 n87
bi-en-e-lí-ma 161-64, 167 n70
mu-ut-balu-me 162
rabi-ṣí-id-qí 142 n161
ši-ip-ṭì-baʿlu 130 n112
šu-mu-ḫa-d[i] 42

WS PNN in execration texts

ʾab-i-ja-m-m-u 159
já-m-i-l-u 65-66
m()-l-k-r-m 191-92 n184

WS PNN in NA & N/LB

NA ab-di-li-mu 163 n48
N/LB a-bu-ga-á 102
NB ^{d}AD.gi-ši-ri-zab-du 144 n173
NB aḫ-a-bu-ú (WS?) 102
NA a-ḫi-mil-ki 150 n194
N/LB a-ḫu-ia-a-li-e 102
NB aḫu-im-mi-e 101
NB aḫu-ú-na-a (WS?) 102
NA a-me-ra-ma 188
NA am-mu-la-di-in 102
N/LB am-ri-im-me 188
NA apladu-sa-⌜bi⌝-ʾ 213 n75
NA ^{URU}ap-pa-ru 223 n122
N/LB ^{f}a-qu-ba-tu$_{4}$ 230
N/LB ^{f}a-qu-ba-ʾ 230
NB ⌜ba⌝-li-ia-a-ma 171 n88
N/LB Bēl-am-ma/mu 171
N/LB Bēl-am-mu 171
NA ga-ba-ri 134
N/LB ga-ba-ri-e (appellative) 134
N/LB ga-ba-ri-adad 133-34
N/LB gab-ri-il-lu 134
NA gab-ri-ilu 134
N/LB gab-ru-ú 133 n127
NA ga-zi-lu 210
NA gi-ri-da-di 151, 193 n193
N/LB gi-ru-adad 151
N/LB ha-lu-ú-mil-ki 102
N/LB ḫi-in-ni-ilu 137
N/LB ^{d}ḫu-ú-na-tan-na 7 n27
NA ia-ta-na-e-li 127
NB id-di-ri-ia-il 125 n 86
N/LB ilu-ga-bar 134
N/LB ilu-ga-ba-ri 134
NA ilu-gab-bi-ri 132 n117
NA ilu-gab-ri 132
N/LB ilu-gab-ri 132
NA ilu-ḫi-ni 137
NB ma-at-tan-ia-a-ma 151
NB ma-at-ta-ni-ia-a-ma 151
NB ma-at-tan-ni-ʾ-ia-a-ma 151-52
NA ^{f}nin-qa-a-a 248
NA pa-du-ú-ili 102
NA pu-du-ili 102
NA qa-am-ba-na 77
NA ra-ʾ-u/ú 97
NA sa-la-ma-me 194
NA sa-lam-me 194
NA ^{f}sa-ra-a-a (Akk.?) 246, 248
NA se-eb-i-tú 212 n69
NA ṣi-id-qa-a 142 n161
NA ṣi-id-qí-ilu 142
N/LB šá-la-am-mu 194
N/LB ^{f}šar-ra-a (Akk.?) 246
NB za-ab-di-ia/iá 144
NB zab-di-ia/iá 144
N/LB zab-di-ilu 144
NB za-bid-da-a 144 n174
N/LB zi-id-qí 142 n161

Hebrew Bible

Canaanite

ʾăbîʾēl 146
ʾăbîyām 189 n174
ʾabrām 22-23
ʾădāmî hanneqeb (GN) 117
ʾădōnî(-)bezeq (title) 117-18
ʾădōnîyāhû 119
ʾădōnî-ṣedeq 140
ʾădōnîrām 58
ʾădōrām 58
ʾônān 169
ʾaḥʾāb 148
ʾăḥîyāhû 149 n193
ʾăḥîraʿ 93-94&n261
ʾiyyôb 101 n296
ʾappayim 167
ʾeldāʿâ 91
ʾēlîyāh 119
ʾelʿûzay 59 n98, 119 n 57
ʾeprayim 167, 223 n122
ʾeštĕmōh (GN) 12
ʾeštĕmōaʿ (GN) 12
bildad 171 n90
ben-hădad 19
baʿălîs 7 n27
baqbuqyāh 120

gat rimmôn (GN) 115
dannâ (GN) 129 n108
diblayim 167
hārûm 189
hôšāmā' 7 n27
zimrî 121
zattû' (Iranian) 174
ḥûrām 175
ḥû/ūšîm 167
ḥîrô/ām 189
ḥel'â 216
ḥāmûl 63
ḥănānî 120
ḥănanyāh 120
ḥeṣrô 99
yiblĕʿām (GN)171-72
yĕhûdî 119
yĕhôṣādāq 141&n160
yôrām 57-58
yôṣādāq 141&n160
yôtām 136 n139
yāʿēl 183 n148
yaʿlâ/yaʿălā' 183 n148
yitnān (GN) 127 n93
yitrān 99
kilyôn 216
karmî 209 n53
kûšî 119
layiš/lešem (GN) 166 n63
mû/ūšî 178 n123
maḥlâ 216-17
maḥlôn 216
mêšā' 177 n118, 178 n127
mĕpîbōšet 20 n73, 59 n98
naḥălî'ēl (GN) 117
ʿabdĕ'ēl 122
ʿănātôt 167 n70
ʿuzzîyāhû 123
ṣûrî'ēl 121, 148
ṣûrîšadday 121 n69
ṣĕrû/ūyâ 207
ṣārĕpat (GN) 202 n13
qeren happûk 207
rēʿî 94
rešep 218 n101
śĕʿōrîm 167
šabbĕtay 215
šûbā'ēl 51
šaḥărayim 167
šîlô/ō(h) (GN) 99
šallûn! 169 n80
šelaḥ 73 n163, 218 n101
šilḥî 73 n163
šĕmîdāʿ (GN) 85
šemer 221
šimʿâ 219
šimrî 221

Aramaic

hădadʿezer 19
yĕdîăʿēl 54 n75

Arabian

'āgûr 191&n181
gašmû/gešem 94
yāqeh 191&nn180-81
ʿomrî 187-88

Epigraphic Hebrew

'ḥm' 100
'nyhw 169
bʿlmʿny 119
ddymš 177-78
hryhw 173
zt' (Iranian) 174
ḥym (WS) 64 n122
ḥn' 137 n146
ḥnh 203
ṭbšln! 169 n80
ywkn 7 n27
yntn 7 n27
krmy 209 n53
mʿdnh 203
nby 119
ngby 119
ʿnmš 177-78
ʿšy 228
šbʿt 212, 229

Ammonite

'dnnr 43 n23
gn' (WS) 208-9 n50
hwšʿl 54 n76
mkm'l 194
mr'l 184 n152
ʿbdhbʿl 152
ʿlyh 203-4
plṭw 103
šmʿl 54 n76

Moabite

kmš 218 n101
kmšm'š 177 n119

Phoenician-Punic

'b(y)bʿl 43 n23
'bšlḥ 73-74 n163
'ḥtmlk 149
'lwʿz' (?) 102-3
'šršlḥ 73-74 n163
bʿl'šrt 204 n30
bʿlḥn' 137 n144
bʿlntn 128
hrbʿl 173
ḥn' 137 n146
ḥnbʿl 135, 137
ḥnw'l 102
ytnt 127 n93
mšlḥ 73-74 n163
mtny 152
mtnybʿl 152
mtršbd' 71 n151
nmlm 179
ntn 128
ntnbʿl 128
ʿbd'lm 163
ʿbdrʿ 93 n256, 97
ʿzybʿl 152
ʿkbrm 179
ṣdqmlk 140
šlḥ 73-74 n163

Old Aramaic

brg'yh 89&n242
hdd gbr (DN + title) 133 n124
hdysʿy 119
hdrqy 93 n258

Imperial Aramaic

ʾḥ(y)ʾb 148 n185
ʾtrly 17 n62
gnt 208, 229
ddy 193 n193
ḥmʾ 61 n109
ḥnʾ 137 n146
yhwḥn 137 nn145-46
yhwḥnn 137 n146
yhwṭl 61 n108
yrḥw 103
ytnʾ 128
mḥlm 195 n201
mnḥn! 169 n80
mšlk 177-78
ʿbdṣdq 140 n157
ʿnny 120
ʿnnyh 120
plṭw 103
šbʿm 195
šlwmm 194-95
šlmm 194-95

Jewish Aramaic

gĕnîbāh/ʾ 210&n62

Palmyrene

ḥlyʾ/w 217
ḥnʾ 137 n146
ʿšy 227-28

Hatran

ʿšy 227-28

Arabian

Saf. ḥly 215
Liḥ. ḥmrm 179, 195
Liḥ. yʿl 183 n148
Sab. yʿl 183 n148
Saf. yʿl 183 n148

2. Selected Topics

Akkadian
  case endings 37
  construct state 108-9
  mimation 155-56
ʾaleph
  elision of initial 60
  elision of medial 54&n76, 55 n78, 101
Amorite
  case endings 38-39
  construct state 110-12
  feminine -aya 241-43
  feminine morphemes 199-200
  mimation 156-57
  particle la 83-84 n212, 87
  spelling *Cu-ú 81-83&n210
  *ʿabd- type names 39, 110-12
Aramaic PNN 15 n55, 62 n110
  with feminine -at 229-30
  with feminine *-â 229-30
Barth-Ginsburg law 11
Canaanite shift 77 n171, 99, 126 n87, 195, 207
case endings
  on DNN 59, 66, 77 n173
  genitive 39, 43-44, 45, 47, 113, 146 n179
  on kinship terms 49, 60, 101-2, 116, 146 n179
  loss of 44-46, 49
  reanalysis of 46-47, 109
  retention in construct state 44 n25, 48, 109 n10, 112
declension
  diptotic 37, 38 n6, 42
  triptotic 37, 42
DNN
  Haddu 59, 193 n193
  Lim 191-92
  ʿAnu 178&n123, 217 n99
  as shortened PNN 73 n163, 96 218 n101
  case endings on 59, 66, 77 n173
dual -ayim 167
Egyptian execration texts 31
  case endings 39-42
  feminine morphemes 200-201
  mimation 157-59
gemination
  lack of 56, 59&n98, 65 n127, 101, 211
  secondary 62-63, 174-75, 180 n136
gentilic adjective 119
Gt stem 12
GNN 4-6, 11-12
  *gintu- type 115
kinship terms
  in PNN 145-50
letters
  graphic confusion of
    ʾ/t 55 n78

d/r 91, 228 n141
y/w 88, 96
y/n 65 n126
h/m 189
m > n 169 n80
matres lectionis 13, 18, 38, 76 n168, 101, 112 n23, 115, 202
see also phonology
matronyms 209, 220&n112
Nabatean PNN
ending with -w 103
nominalization 39, 43
nota accusativi 46, 48-49
nun
(non-)assimilation of 43 n22
loss of final -n 99
poetry
archaisms in 8
phonology
a > i 124 n80
â < *at 202-4
î < *ĭ 112 n23
ô < *ā 99
ô < *u 47-48, 58
ō < *u 58
û < w 89, 94
û < *u 57 n86
û < *ū 60, 76 n168
plural
*-ūma/-īma 161-64, 167
of majesty 161-62
PNN
classification of 15-18
*C_1ĕC_2ûʾēl type 50-55, 56, 65 n127, 104, 235
imperative type 92
preposition l in 192
servant + X type 25&n92, 39, 110-12
quiescence of
ʾaleph 130 n110
see also ʾaleph, elision of
heh 191 n180
reanalysis 47, 109, 125, 174, 218
roots
*ʾwl II 168
*ʾwn 169
*ʾḫḏ 170, 205
*blʿ 172
*gʾh 89
*gyn 208
*gnn 207 n42, 208
*gʿh 173
*grš 181
*dnn 129 n108
*dʿh 91
*hmm 182
*zbd 142 n164
*znq 160 n34
*ḫwš I & II 175
*ḫzq 125
*ḫlh I & II 215-17
*ḫnn 136
*ḫml 63
*ṭll 61
*ṭpp I 211
*ẓll 61
*ydʿ 92
*yqh 191 n181, 222
*yqy 138
*yṯʿ 178
*ytn I & II 127-28
*mut(v) 68-69, 113 n30
*mwš 178
*nḫt I & II 225-27
*ntn 127-28
*ʿlm III 183
*ʿmr 187-88
*ʿśh 228
*pth I 90
*rw/ym 186, 188
*rʿh I & II 93-94
*śrh 247
*šbʿ 212-13
*šlḫ 73-74 n163
*švm 78 n177
*šmʿ 220
*šmr 222
scripts
alphabetic 26
syllabic cuneiform 26-27
hieroglyphic 27-28
suffixes
1st c.s. pronominal 43, 118-119, 125 n86, 137 n144, 146-48
3rd m.s. pronominal 48 n42, 81, 82, 84 n218, 99 n283, 137 n144
3rd m.pl. pronominal 167-68, 169, 176
hypocoristic -î < *-iya 119-20
hypocoristic -vya 241-42
nominal *-ānu 42 n16, 99, 156, 181, 208 n48, 216 n90, 243

n10
-î (in poetry) 115-16
-ô (in poetry) 47-48
-ô < *-ôn 99
Ugaritic
case endings 42-44
construct state 112-13
deity list (Ug VII:1-3) 162
feminine -aya 243-45
feminine morphemes 201
mimation 164-65
polyglot vocabularies 161-62
*ʿbd- type PNN 113-14

3. Biblical verses

Gen

4:17-24 67
30:20 143
49:11 117

Exod

6:23 214

Num

21:19 117

Deut

33:16 117

Josh

19:33 117

Judg

1:5-7 117
1:27 172 n95
3:31 208&n47

2 Kgs

15:10 208

Isa

9:5-6 133 n124

Hos

2:18 125 n86

Ps

18:1-2 123
27:1 125 n86

Job

33:18 74
36:12 74
36:16 227

Prov

31:1 191

1 Chr

2:42 178 n126
4:17 185 n157
8:8-12 178 n127
8:38 94-95
9:44 94-95

2 Chr

24:26 220

www.ingramcontent.com/pod-product-compliance
Lightning Source LLC
Chambersburg PA
CBHW021119300426
44113CB00006B/209
* 9 7 8 1 5 5 5 4 0 5 1 3 7 *